Y0-BDQ-720

J. M. HODGES LEARNING CENTER
WHARTON COUNTY JUNIOR COLLEGE
WHARTON, TEXAS 77488

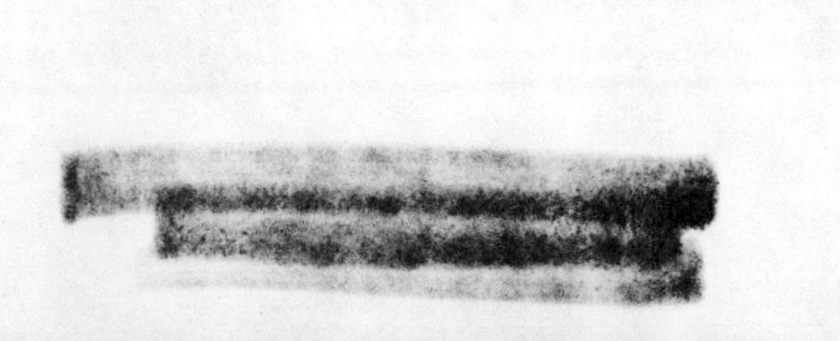

DEANS' LIST OF RECOMMENDED READING FOR PRELAW AND LAW STUDENTS

DEANS' LIST OF RECOMMENDED READING FOR PRELAW AND LAW STUDENTS

Selected by the Deans and Faculties of American Law Schools

Compiled and Edited with Annotations by

JULIUS J. MARKE

Professor of Law and
Law Librarian Designate St. John's University
and
Former Law Librarian New York University
School of Law

EDWARD J. BANDER

Suffolk University Law School

SECOND EDITION

OCEANA PUBLICATIONS, INC.
New York . London . Rome

Library of Congress Cataloging in Publication Data

Marke, Julius J.
Dean's list of recommended reading for prelaw and law-students.

Includes index.
1. Law—United States—Bibliography. 2. Social sciences—Bibliography. I. Bander, Edward J. II. Title.
KF1.Mc 1983 016.34 84-3535
ISBN 0-379-20170-4

Manufactured in the United States of America

TO
PHILIP F. COHEN
THE PARAGON OF PUBLISHERS

TABLE OF CONTENTS

NOTE: A plus sign (+) indicates the selection was in the first edition. An asterisk (*) indicates that the item was considered suitable for pre-law students in the first edition.

ACKNOWLEDGMENTS

To Bob, Ellen, Eric, Gail, Helen, Irene, Janet, Julia, Lisa, Nancy, Pamela, Pat, Paula, Susans - thank you for your help and cooperation.

To the law students who work for the library - I am ever grateful to all of you.

To the work study students - Right on!

To the reference librarians at B.C., Brandeis, Concord Public, Harvard, etc. who lent a helping hand - you are the salt of the earth.

To my Digital WT/78 - you did it all (with Alfred's help).

To OCLC - the time you saved me.

And to Joseph who made me think about acknowledgments (See PW 12/16/83).

Edward J. Bander
12/28/83

PREFACE TO THE SECOND EDITION

If a Hall of Fame for the legal profession is ever established, the DEANS' LIST OF RECOMMENDED READING FOR PRELAW AND LAW STUDENTS will be a prime source for candidates. Here are all the hallowed names of men and women who have contributed to law as known in our Western civilization. From thinkers as early as Plato to those as contemporary as Grant Gilmore, the list of names that appears in the DEANS' LIST includes all the immortals.

As one reads from Aristotle to Peter Zenger, one is also aware that the DEANS' LIST is not limited to lawyer-authors. There is a galaxy of names connected with other disciplines - Charles Dickens with literature, John Stuart Mill with political theory, E. Adamson Hoebel with anthropology, and so on.

For good reason, all the titles and annotations in the First Edition are included in the Second, although with some editing. The First Edition has become a classic, and this edition is built on that strong foundation. The editors have taken the liberty of adding many more titles in the annotations to provide balance and perspective.

We hope that those who browse through this book will be inspired to read the masters. We believe that as they peruse the ideas and ideals of our antecedents they will understand why the law is a great calling, and that those who decide to pursue a career in the law will hear the call.

Julius J. Marke
Edward J. Bander

INTRODUCTION

> "A lawyer without history or literature is a mechanic, a mere working mason. If he possesses some knowledge of these, he may venture to call himself an architect."
>
> Sir Walter Scott

The above quotation may be overworked, but the message is clear. The education of a law student and lawyer is never complete.

That is why it is particularly gratifying for me to welcome this new edition of the Deans' List of Recommended Reading. Not only is it a vital compilation of books with which people involved in the legal profession should be familiar, but, in addition, the annotations supplied by the compilers are both erudite and enlightening.

I am particularly proud that a good share of the work on this book was conducted at Suffolk University where we have endeavored to foster a collection that would assist our law faculty to train law students in the grand manner.

The legal profession owes a debt to Julius J. Marke, whose illustrious accomplishments are well known to all, and to our librarian, Ed Bander, who has served us at Suffolk University with distinction.

Dean David J. Sargent
Suffolk University Law School

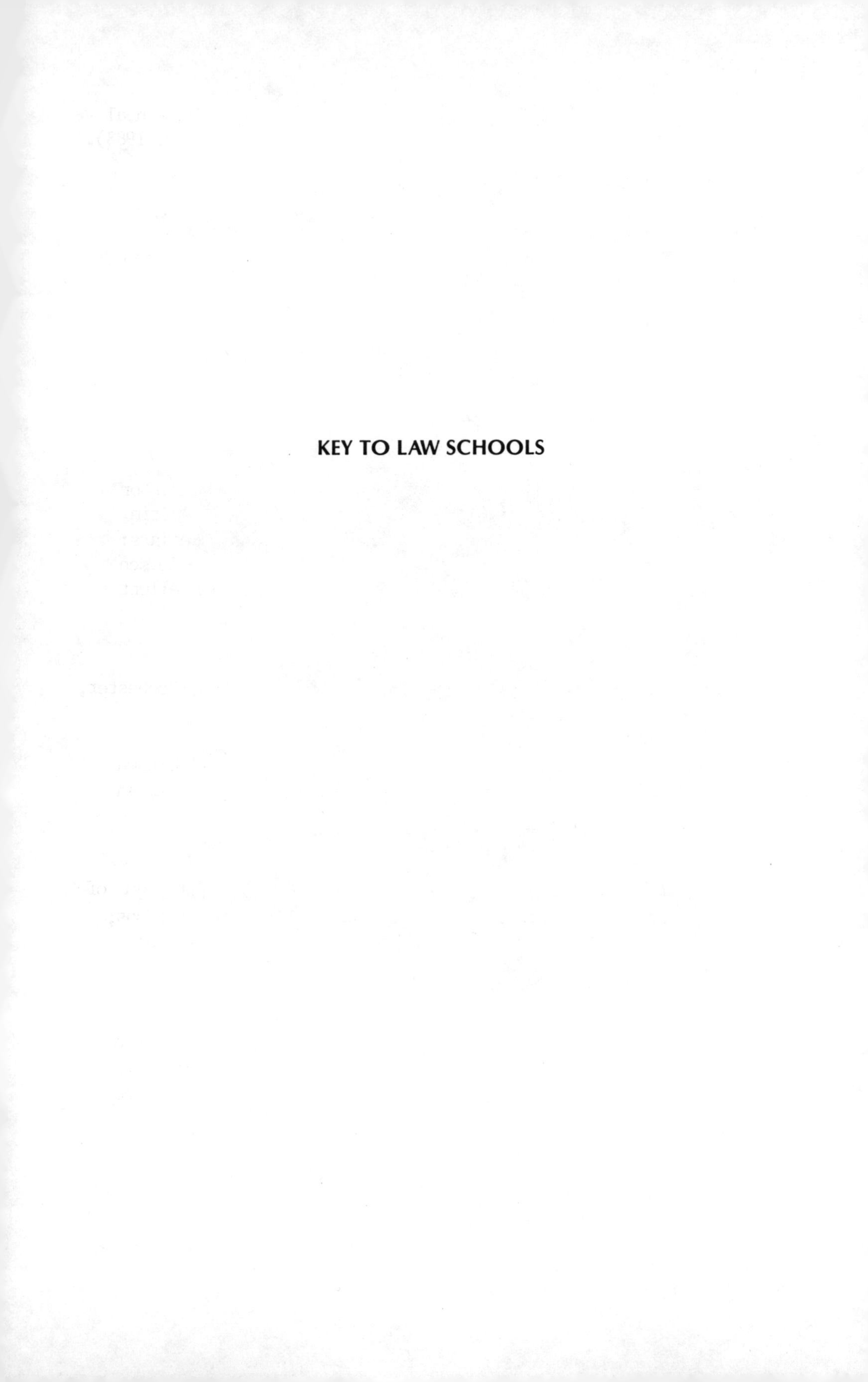

KEY TO LAW SCHOOLS

KEY TO LAW SCHOOLS

NOTE: This is a combined list of the first and second editions.

Abbrevi-
ation

A1 Albany Law School, Union Univ. Dean Clements. Reply from Prof. Joan Zweifel, Librarian

A2 Boston Univ. School of Law. Dean Elwood H. Hettrick

A2.5 Boston College. Dean Huber. Sharon Hamby, Law Librarian

A3 Brooklyn Law School. Dean Jerome Prince

A4 Catholic Univ. of America. School of Law, Dean Vernon X. Miller. Reply from Prof. Arthur J. Keeffe

A5 College of William and Mary, Marshall-Wythe School of Law Dean D.W.Woodbridge

A6 Columbia Univ. School of Law. Dean William C. Warren. Reply from Assistant Dean Ellis L. Phillips, Jr.

A6.5 Delaware Law School

A7 Emory Univ., Lamar School of Law. Dean William M. Hepburn

A8 Florida Agri. and Mech. Univ. College of Law Dean Thomas M. Jenkins. Reply from President George W. Gore, Jr.

A9 Fordham Univ. School of Law. Dean William Hughes Mulligan

A10 Franklin Univ. Law School. Dean Stanley A. Samad

A11 George Washington Univ. Law School. Acting Dean Oswald S. Colclough. Reply from C.D. Benson, Assistant Dean

A11.5 Gonzaga Univ. School of Law

A12 Harvard Univ. Law School. Dean Erwin N. Griswold

A13 Howard Univ. School of Law. Dean George M.Johnson. Reply from Cynthia Straker, Law Librarian

A14 Indiana Univ. School of Law. Dean Leon H. Wallace

A15 The Judge Advocate General's School- Reply from Col. George E. Mickel, JAGC Acting Commandant (in the absence of Col. Rieger)

A16 Louisiana State Univ. Law School. Dean Paul M. Hebert

A17 Mercer Univ. Law School. Acting Dean James C. Quarles

A18 New York Law School. Dean Alison Reppy

A19 New York Univ. School of Law. Dean Russell D. Niles

A20 North Carolina College of Durham Law School Dean Albert L. Turner

A20.5 Northeastern Univ. Law School

A21 Northwestern Univ. School of Law. Dean Harold C. Havighurst

A22 Notre Dame Law School. Dean Joseph O'Meara

A23 Ohio State Univ. College of Law. Dean Frank R. Strong. Reply from Associate Dean Robert J. Nordstrom

A24 Rutgers Univ. School of Law. Dean Lehan K. Tunks
A24.5 St. John's University School of Law. Dean Patrick J. Rohan
A25 St.Louis Univ. School of Law. Dean McDonough. Reply from Eileen H. Searls, Law Librarian
A25.5 St. Mary's Univ. of San Antonio School of Law
A26 South Carolina State Col.,School of Law. Dean T. Robert Gay
A27 Southern Methodist Univ.School of Law. Dean Storey. Reply from J.W. Riehm, Academic Assistant
A27.5 Southwestern Univ. School of Law
A28 Stanford Univ. Law School. Dean Spaeth. Reply from Prof. John Henry Merryman
A29 Stetson Univ. College of Law. Dean Harold L. Sebring
A29.5 Suffolk Univ. Law School. Edward J. Bander, Law Librarian
A30 Syracuse Univ. College of Law. Dean Ralph E. Kharas
A31 Temple Univ. School of Law. Dean Benjamin F. Boyer
A31.5 Texas Christian School of Law
A31.7 Touro Law School
A32 Tulane Univ. School of Law. Dean Forrester (absent for 56-57 school year). Reply from Eugene A. Nabors, acting for Dean
A33 Univ. of Alabama School of Law. Dean M. Leigh Harrison
A34 Univ. of Arizona College of Law. Dean John D. Lyons
A35 Univ. of Arkansas School of Law. Dean Covington. Reply from Dean Covington and Prof. Robert A. Leflar
A35.5 Univ. of Bridgeport School of Law
A36 Univ. of Buffalo School of Law. Dean J.D. Hyman
A37 Univ. of California. The Hastings College of Law. Dean David E. Snodgrass
A38 Univ. of California School of Law (Los Angeles).Dean Albert J. Harno. Reply from Prof. Louis Piacenza, Law Librarian
A38.5 Univ. of Conn. School of Law. Dean Philip I. Blumberg; Librarian Shirley R. Bysiewicz
A39 Univ. of Cincinnati College of Law. Dean Roscoe L. Barrow
A40 Univ. of Colorado School of Law. Dean Edward King and Prof. Don Sears
A41 Univ. of Denver College of Law. Dean Gordon Johnston
A42 Univ. of Florida College of Law. Dean Henry A. Fenn
A43 Univ. of Georgia School of Law. Dean J. Alton Hosch. Reply from Helen Gray Gillam, Law Librarian
A43.5 Univ. of Hawaii School of Law. Jerry Dupont, Law Librarian
A44 Univ. of Houston College of Law. Dean Newell H. Blakely (Acting)
A45 Univ. of Idaho College of Law. Dean Edward S. Stimson
A46 Univ. of Illinois College of Law. Dean Albert J. Harno
Univ. of Iowa. See A73
A47 Univ. of Kansas City School of Law. Dean Marlin M. Volz. List prepared by Prof. Clarke and her committee

A48 Univ. of Kentucky College of Law. Dean Matthews. Reply from Dorothy Salman, Law Librarian
A48.5 Univ. of Maine School of Lawf
A49 Univ. of Maryland School of Law. Dean Howell. Reply from Margaret E. Coonan, Law Librarian
A50 Univ. of Miami School of Law. Dean Russell A. Rasco
A51 Univ. of Minnesota Law School. Dean William B. Lockhart. Reply from Robert C. McClure, Prof. of Law
A52 Univ. of Mississippi School of Law. Dean Robert J. Farley. Reply from William P. Murphy, Professor of Law
A53 Univ. of Nebraska College of Law. Dean Edmund O. Belshelm
A54 Univ. of New Mexico College of Law. Dean A. L. Gausewitz
A55 Univ. of North Dakota School of Law. Dean O. H. Thormodsgard
A56 Univ. of Oklahoma College of Law. Dean Earl Sneed, Jr.
A57 Univ. of Pennsylvania Law School. Dean Jefferson B. Fordham
A57.1 Prelaw Handbook, 1982
A57.6 Univ. of Richmond School of Law
A57.7 Univ. of Santa Clara School of Law
A58 Univ. of South Carolina School of Law. Dean Samuel L. Prince.
A58.5 St. Mary's Univ. School of Law
A59 Univ. of Texas School of Law. Dean Page Keeton
A60 Univ. of Toledo College of Law. Dean Charles W. Fornoff
A61 Univ. of Utah College of Law. Dean Daniel J. Dykstra
A62 Univ. of Virginia Law School. Dean F.D.G. Ribble
A63 Univ. of Washington School of Law. Dean George N. Stevens. Reply from Arval Morris, Assistant to the Dean
A64 Univ. of Wisconsin Law School. Dean John Ritchie
A65 Univ. of Wyoming, College of Law. Dean Hamilton (out of town). Reply from Prof. George Trowsdale, Law Librarian
A66 Valparaiso Univ. School of Law. Dean K.D. Stalland
A67 Vanderbilt Univ. School of Law. Dean John W. Wade
A68 Villanova Univ. School of Law. Dean Harold Gill Reuschlein
A69 Wake Forest College School of Law. Dean Weathers. Reply from Jeanne Tillman, Law Librarian
A70 Washburn Univ. School of Law. Dean Schuyler W. Jackson
A71 Washington Univ. School of Law. Dean Green. Reply from Prof. Jean Ashman, Law Librarian
A71.5 Wayne State Univ. School of Law
A71.8 Western New England Law School. Dean Howard I. Kalodner, Donald J. Dunn, Law Librarian
A72 Western Reserve Univ., Franklin T. Backus Law School. Dean Fletcher R. Andrews
A72.5 William Mitchell School of Law
A73 Univ. of Iowa. Dean Mason Ladd
A74 Williams, Glanville, Learning the Law, 1982

DEANS' LIST OF RECOMMENDED READING FOR PRELAW AND LAW STUDENTS

ACCOUNTING

The importance of accounting to lawyers is generally recognized by the legal profession. Its functions and principles must be known by the lawyer whether in private practice or government service.

1

FIFLIS, TED J. and HOMER KRIPKE. Accounting for business lawyers - teaching materials. 2d ed. St.Paul, West, 1977. 684p.
A24.5

"Drawing both from accounting and legal literature, Fiflis and Kripke emphasized the importance of taking accounting concepts into consideration in negotiating and drafting shareholder agreements, deferred compensation arrangements and other financially oriented contracts....a first-rate collection of teaching materials for law students, but also an extremely useful tool for all lawyers engaged in a business practice.- Bruce Allen Mann, University of Colorado Law Rev. 49:263 (1978). See also Mark Stevens, The big eight (1981) reviewed by Abraham J. Briloff, Texas Law Rev. 61:1357 (1983).

2

KATZ, WILBER G. Introduction to accounting. Chicago, Callaghan, [1954] 236p. +
A28

Dean Katz was one of the first to teach lawyers the necessity of learning accounting principles. His books are always helpful.

3

SELLIN, HENRY, ed. Attorney's handbook of accounting. 3d ed. New York, Matthew Bender, 1982. loose-leaf.
A31.7

A collection of papers by authorities on financial statements; balance sheets: assets; balance sheet: liabilities; balance sheet: owners' equity; income statement; books of account, accountant's working papers; inventory methods and techniques; reserve accounts;

partnership accounting; corporation accounting; accounting for professional corporations; accounting for nonprofit organizations, estate accounting and taxation; pension and profit-sharing plan accounting; accounting for regulatory agencies; accounting for a merchandising business; accounting for a manufacturing business; accounting for stockbrokers and stockdealers; accounting for real estate business; accounting for oil and gas; forensic role of the accountant in tax cases.

ADMINISTRATION OF JUSTICE

See also CRIMINAL LAW AND PROCEDURE

6

ABEL-SMITH, BRIAN AND ROBERT STEVENS. In search of justice: society and the legal system. London, Penguin Press, 1968. 384p. A31.7

"This book is for those greatly interested in the administration of justice and its improvement, and to them it will give much information and food for thought and discussion." Katherine Parkes, Georgetown Law Jl 59:462 (1970). See also the authors' Lawyers and the Courts (1967). [A74] See also Modern Law Rev. 32:336 (1969) for a critical review.

7

AMERICAN ACADEMY OF POLITICAL AND SOCIAL SCIENCE, PHILADELPHIA. Judicial administration and the common man, edited by Benjamin Kaplan [and] Livingston Hall. Philadelphia, 1953. 243p. [Its Annals, v. 287] +
A11

A symposium in which important aspects of judicial administration are considered. An impressive group of contributors discuss the attitudes past and present of the common man toward the legal system, and how law impinges on him as litigant and witness in various familiar settings ranging from the traffic court to the probate court. The jury as a working institution, the cost of justice, and judicial reform are also carefully considered.

8

BERMAN, HAROLD J. Justice in Russia; an interpretation of Soviet Law. Cambridge, Harvard Univ. Press, 1950. 322p. +
A15

Professor Hazard recommends this book for the legal and political theorist for use in classes devoted to subjects such as jurisprudence, law and society, and comparative law. The book is well written and non-technical. Berman believes that law has become a part of the Soviet system out of necessity. See Columbia Law Rev. 51:139. Professor Berman is also the author of Law and revolution, the formation of the Western legal tradition (1983).

9

BORCHARD, EDWIN M. Convicting the innocent; errors of criminal justice, [with] the collaboration of E. Russell Lutz...New Haven, Yale Univ. Press, 1932. 421p. *+
A8, A30, A39, A43

A thoughtful collection of 65 cases involving miscarriage of criminal justice together with suggestions for possible remedies by a late Professor of Law at Yale. The causes of error were due in the main to mistaken identity, circumstantial evidence, perjury, or some combination of these. [A39, A43]. Read this with Judge Jerome Frank's posthumous book Not Guilty (1957), which in a way brings Borchard up-to-date, and makes pertinent comments on the legal system which allows the innocent to suffer. [See No. 703]

10

COUDERT, FREDERIC R. Certainty and justice; studies of the conflict between precedent and progress in the development of the law. N.Y., Appleton, 1914. 319p. *+
A7

The importance of certainty in the administration of justice is considered in light of some difficult cases experienced by the author as a practitioner as well as his understanding of continental legal procedure.

11

DENNING, SIR ALFRED T. The road to justice. London, Stevens, 1955. 118p. +
A29.5

Addressed to neophytes in the law, this book sets forth "the principles which must be observed in any country if justice is to be done therein." The Lord Justice of the English Court of Appeal considers the "indispensables of our law, the just judge and the honest lawyer." He treats both the good and the bad to be found in both. See Law Q. Rev. 72:282 (1956). See also Lord Denning's The Family Story (1981) [A74]

12

FRANK, JEROME. Courts on trial; myth and reality in American justice. Princeton, Princeton University Press, 1949. 441p. *+
A20, A24, A27.5, A28, A38.5, A40, A42, A43.5, A53, A64, A71.5

An important volume on the problem of "fact uncertainty" in the administration of justice by a late leading American jurist. See Harvard Law Rev. 63:1466 (1950).

13

FRANK, JOHN P. American law: the case for radical reform. New York, Macmillan Co., 1969. 216p.
A29.5

The author is a lawyer, law teacher, and former law clerk to Justice Hugo Black. Mr. Frank complains about the law's delays...about the complexity of the law under Rule 23 of the Federal Rules of Civil Procedure relating to class actions...that our divorce laws are antiquated ... about summary judgment procedure ... of dilatory lawyers ... Anyone who wants proposals to espouse for the improvement of the administration of justice in this country will find them in Mr. Frank's book." O.John Rogge, Georgetown Law Journal 58:658 (1970).

14

GLUECK, SHELDON. Crime and justice....Boston, Little, Brown, 1936. 349p. *+
A28, A35, A45, A61

Professor Glueck of Harvard University School of Law, stresses "the ills of criminal justice in the belief that by studying the diseased organ we may be able to obtain some light on the destructive forces at work and perhaps some hints as to the therapeutic and prophylactic measures that are indicated."

15

HUTCHESON, JOSEPH C. Judgment intuitive. Chicago, Foundation Press, 1938. 227p. +
A45

Judge Jerome Frank once designated 18 persons as "a minority group of brilliant critics of our legal system." In this group he placed Judge Hutcheson. The title of this volume is taken from an address "The Judgment Intuitive: The Function of the Judicial Hunch." See Cornell Law Q. 25:326 (1940).

16

JACKSON, RICHARD M. The machinery of justice in England. 2d ed. Cambridge [Eng.] Univ. Press, 1953. 371p. +
A28, A41

One of the best books on the subject. Highly readable, scholarly and "fascinating" analysis of the English legal system and the work of its court. Good, brief, historical background prepares reader for independent evaluation. Jackson perceives the strength and weakness of the system and his judgment is always sound. The latest edition was published in 1977.

17

KEETON, ROBERT E. Venturing to do justice. Cambridge, Harvard Univ. Press, 1969. 183p.
A24.5

What Professor Keeton has done is to write about the situations in which courts have been overruling cases from 1958 to 1968. In his words, the list of cases 'covers more than ninety overruling decisions on at least thirty-five topics, even if immunities and strict products liability are each counted as only one topic.′ Washington University Law Q. 1969:471.

17a

MAYERS, LEWIS. The American legal system; administration of justice in the United States by judicial, administrative, military, and arbitral tribunals. N.Y., Harper, [1955]. 589p. *+
A6, A19, A43, A47, A49, A56

A systemic account of American legal institutions - as distinguished from American law - in all their varied aspects. [A56].

18

MORELAND, CARROLL C. Equal justice under law. N.Y., Oceana, 1957. 128p. *+
A24, A57

A clear, concise, non-technical and well written account of American administration of justice. Moreland succinctly sets forth the background of our legal system, our constitutional guaranties, the state courts′ jurisdiction and organization as well as the federal courts′ and a quick survey of the legal education system, the appointment or election of judges and the role of the organized bar.

19

ORFIELD, LESTER B. Criminal procedure from arrest to appeal. N.Y, N.Y.U. Press, 1947. 614p. +
A56

A complete discussion of the procedure for the prosecution of crimes in America. [A56] Neither a texbook on criminal procedure nor a practical guide but interesting and instructive. See Columbia Law Rev. 48:1265 (1948).

20

POUND, ROSCOE. Criminal justice in America. N.Y., Henry Holt, [c1930]. 226p. *+
A35, A45, A61

Why is criminal justice administered inefficiently in America? Dean Pound considers this and also brings out "the causes of this perplexing problem from the pioneer spirit to the inadequacy of the present administrative machinery of criminal justice." He also "suggests some constructive proposals for improving our criminal judicial machinery." See Illinois Law Rev. 26:478 (1931)

21

PUTTKAMMER, ERNST W. Administration of criminal law. Chicago, Univ. of Chicago Press, [1953]. 249p. +
A28, A56

Description of how criminal law functions and how lawyers look at its problems. [A56].

22

ROBINSON, WILLIAM M. Justice in grey; a history of the judicial system of the Confederate States of America. Cambridge, Harvard Univ. Press, 1941. 713p. +
A7

A detailed account of administration of justice in the Confederacy. The whole court system is explained as well as administration of martial law and the functioning of the Department of Justice. Based on primary source material, the book is well done. See Harvard Law Rev. 55:172 (1941).

23

RODELL, FRED. Woe unto you, lawyers! With an introduction by Jerome Frank. 2d ed. N.Y., Pageant Press, [c1957]. 84p. (reprinted by Oceana Publications). *+
A8, A39, A45

Published originally in 1939, its references and allusions are somewhat outdated. The book severely criticizes our legal system and legal methods. Rodell advocates codification and simplification of the law to the point where judges and lawyers will be unnecessary. Judge Frank in his introduction believes that Rodell has "overstated his adverse comments. His condemnations of lawyers and judges are...demonstrably excessive... His proposed reforms ...too glib... Nevertheless it will tend to provoke inquiry into our methods of administering justice...and, in a democracy, every branch of government should recurrently receive such an inquiry."

24

SEYMOUR, WHITNEY NORTH, Jr. Why justice fails. N.Y., William Morrow, 1973. 238p.
A57.1

"Mr. Seymour's thesis is that our system of justice to a large extent has failed in its dual purpose of rehabilitating the guilty and deterring the prospective criminal. [outline of what has caused the failure and recommendations for improving the system] Walter P. Armstrong, Jr., A.B.A.Jl 60:774 (1974).

25

SHARTEL, BURKE. Our legal system and how it operates; five lectures, delivered at the University of Michigan...Ann Arbor, University of Michigan Law School, 1951. 629p. *+
A19, A24, A28, A43, A48, A49, A56, A60 (Chap.)

These Cooley lectures were delivered in 1948. They give a description of the American legal system as it existed; useful as an introductory text for the first year law student. [A56].

26

SMITH, REGINALD H. Justice and the poor....N.Y., Scribner's, 1919. 271p. *+
A35

The subtitle indicates the purpose of this book: "A study of the present denial of justice to the poor and of the agencies making more equal their position before the law, with particular reference to legal aid work in the United States." Laski believes it offers a wealth of information upon the whole subject, and Hurst recommends it for "background reading." Dated but provocative.

27

STONE, HARLAN F. ...Law and its administration. N.Y., Columbia Univ. Press, 1915. 232p. +
A28, A36, A37

A reading of this book will give a better understanding of our legal system.

28

TAFT, HENRY W. Witnesses in court, with some criticisms of court procedure...; with a foreward by Frederick E. Crane....N.Y., Macmillan, 1934. 98p. +
A45

A refreshing simple and homely, although mature, book describing with sympathy and understanding the sad plight of the honest witness in court. He blames judges for many things most seriously criticized in administration of justice. See Harvard Law Rev. 47:1076 (1934).

29

TRAIN, ARTHUR C. Courts and criminals....N.Y., Scribner's, 1922. 304p. +
A28

Well written book by the author of the "Tutt" series (See FICTION), on some rather important subjects such as the presumption of innocence, preparing a criminal case for trial, sensationalism and jury trials, detectives who detect, women in the courts, and tricks of the trade.

30

——. From the district attorney's office; a popular account of criminal justice. N.Y., Scribner's, 1939. 431p. *+
A28, A35, A36

Although written entertainingly and with a light touch, the book "contains a well-organized and close-knit picture of metropolitan criminal justice, full of wise recommendations for change, in which theory and practice are interwoven as only Mr. Train can do." See Harvard Law Rev. 53:520 (1940).

31

——. On the trail of the bad men. N.Y., Scribner's, 1925. 427p. +
A28

A series of articles on crime in the early West and administration of criminal justice then. Interesting accounts.

32

VANDERBILT, ARTHUR T. The challenge of law reform. Princeton, Princeton Univ. Press, 1955. 194p. +
A6, A19, A46, A62, A64

Judge Phillips considers this book as "a thought provoking and stirring challenge to judges, lawyers, and laymen alike." Chief Justice Vanderbilt is well qualified to discuss this subject and he covers the need for reform, better judges and better jurors, simplified judicial structure and procedure, effective administration and less delay and modernizing the law through law centers. See N.Y.U.L.Rev. 31:860 (1956).

33

——. Men and measures in the law; five lectures delivered...at the Univ. of Michigan, April 1948; with an introd. by E. Blythe Stason. N.Y., Knopf, 1949. 156p. (William W. Cook Foundation Lectures, v. 4). +
A7,A24, A27, A43, A56

A readable perspective on the role of authority in the ordering, adjusting, or resolving of overlapping rights and values, interacting with the pody politic. [A24]. It deals with fundamental problems confronting the legal profession in America and offers recommendations for procedural reform.

34

——, ed. Minimum standards of judicial administration; a survey of the extent to which the standards of the American Bar Association for improving the administration of justice have been accepted throughout the country. [N.Y.] Published by The Law Center of N.Y.U. for The National Conference of Judicial Councils, 1949. 752p. +
A15

This report deals with "the minimum standards needed in a practical way to make our court procedure work in the twentieth century." The publication of the book was motivated by the desire to make clear to lawyers and laymen alike the extent to which each state is measuring up to minimum practical standards of judicial administration. See Jl.Am.Jud.Soc. 33:176 (1949).

35

WIGMORE, JOHN HENRY. A panorama of the world's legal systems...with five hundred illustrations....St.Paul, West [c1928], 3 v. *+
A7, A19, A28, A41, A45, A72

This is a handsome 3 volume work profusely illustrated in color. It has also been published in a one volume library edition with black and white illustrations. If you find you are not inclined to read the entire work,I recommend the 3d volume and particularly chapters 16 and 17, which cover the Anglo-American system and are therefore of more immediate interest. Dean Havighurst, Northwestern.

ADMINISTRATIVE LAW

36

ALLEN, SIR CARLETON KEMP. Law and orders. 2d ed. London, Stevens & Sons, 1956. 474p.
A24.5

"...trenchant work on delegated legislation....It is a service of great value to expose even the incidental weaknesses of our legislative and administrative machinery....The book, furthermore, has passages on public inquiries, natural justice...." H.W.R.Wade, Law Q. Rev. 73:411 (1957).

37

ANDERSON, STANLEY V. Ombudsman papers: American experience and proposals. Berkeley, Institute of Governmental Studies, 1969. 420p.
A31.7

The author is an unabashed advocate for the ombudsman concept....a scholarly presentation of both the concept's strengths and its weaknesses....possible uses of an ombudsman who might entertain complaints against arbitrary action by nongovermental entities....a rich resource source." Philip J. Hannon, Law and Society Rev. 5:299 (1970).

38

CARY, WILLIAM L. Politics and the regulatory agencies. N.Y., McGraw-Hill, 1967. 149p.
A24.5

"Professor Cary's book is a short, concise exposition of [the theme that government regulatory agencies are stepchildren whose custody is contested by both Congress and the Executive, but without very much affection from either one], relating his experiences as Chairman of the Securities and Exchange Commission, but also including related experiences and problems of the other regulatory agencies...[h]is recommendations...and his frank and honest exposition of his own experiences, provide a unique avenue for further understanding the function of a continuing, vital element of the present government structure." Fordham Law Rev. 35:571 (1967).

39

DAVIS, KENNETH CULP. Discretionary justice: a preliminary inquiry. Baton Rouge, Louisiana State Univ. Press, 1969. 233p.
A38.5

"Professor Davis has now offered a short book elaborating on [his] eighteen 'preliminary ideas' about ways to protect against arbitrary exercise of administrative discretion when hearing safeguards are inappropriate." The central theme is that nine-tenths of injustice in our legal system flows from discretion and one-tenth from rules. Alan V. Washburn, Boston Univ. Law Rev. 49:620 (1969).

40

FRANK, JEROME. If men were angels; some aspects of government in a democracy. N.Y., Harper [1942]. 380p. *+
A8, A49

Here Judge Frank shifts his emphasis from the position he took in Law and the Modern Mind (1930) [See No.1358]. Whereas in both books he argues against the possibility of "legal soothsaying," in the earlier he stressed the uncertainty of vagueness in legal rules but in this volume his emphasis is on the uncertainty as to facts. His present position admits the possibility of agreement on the rules but denies the possibility (as a generalization) of agreement on the facts. See Harvard Law Rev. 56:1020 (1943).

41

FREEDMAN, JAMES O. Crisis and legitimacy: the administrative process and American government. Cambridge, Eng., Cambridge Univ. Press, 1978. 324p.
A24.5

As the author "notes in his earnest defense of administrative process...virtually every American generation has felt 'a persisting sense of uneasiness and concern about the problematic place of administrative agencies in the machinery of government...' Although Freedman's richly documented work does not always convincingly impart its faith in administrative agencies as the panacea of contemporary society, it is a worthwhile statement of an important position in the ongoing debate over the size and role of the federal government." Harvard Law Rev. 92:1184 (1979).

42

FRIENDLY, HENRY J. The Federal administrative agencies. Cambridge, Harvard Univ. Press, 1962. 180p.
A29.5

"Judge Friendly confines himself to a basic problem, namely the capacity of our prime federal administrative tribunals to fashion articulate, workable and predictable standards for the determination of issues that they are called upon to resolve. ...[The author] considers this problem of the articulation of standards as it affects four commissions - the Interstate Commerce Commission, the National Labor Relations Board, the Federal Communications Commission and the Civil Aeronautics Board." James M. Landis, Univ. of Chicago Law Rev. 30:597 (1963).

43

GELLHORN, WALTER. When Americans complain; governmental grievance procedures. Cambridge, Harvard Univ. Press, 1966. 239p.
A31.7

"...in this book we find remarkably enlightening vignettes of congressional casework, of two prototype agencies' responses to that casework (Post Office and Labor Departments), and of the Office of Inspector General in the Department of Agriculture. Budget Bureau and GAO activities are summarized in a mere five paragraphs, but the summaries usefully point up the gains of interrelated work among critics. Gellhorn concludes that Washington needs more, better-designed, ombudsman-type critics, not a single ombudsman or ombudsman's office which the capital presumably would overwhelm." Frank C. Newman, Columbia Law Rev. 1967:784.

44

LANDIS, JAMES M. The administrative process. New Haven, Yale Univ. Press, 1938. 160p. *+
A6, A28, A35

A valuable work by a former Dean of the Harvard Law School on the administrative process brought out mainly by an analysis of the activities of the Securities and Exchange Commission.

45

PRETTYMAN, E. BARRETT. Trial by agency. Charlottesville, Virginia Law Review Association, 1959. 60p.
A31.7

"...three lectures on American administrative law. ...This is a practical lecture on handling complicated cases by an expert....Whether an agency should have judicial power to interpret and apply its own rules and law is a timely, interesting and provocative topic and to deal with the question clearly and concisely is quite a successful achievement. Stanley Reed, Georgetown Law Rev. 48:611 (1960).

46

ROBSON, WILLIAM A. Justice and administrative law; a study of the British constitution. 3d ed. London, Stevens, 1951. 674p. +
A28

In a clear and persuasive style Robson develops the theme that administrative regulation in England is good provided certain reforms he recommends are carried out. References to many important sources are used by the author.

47

VINING, JOSEPH. Legal identity; the coming of age of public law. New Haven, Yale Univ. Press, 1978. 256p.
A24.5

"...the developing law of standing in federal administrative litigation....the concept of legal identity and the role of litigants in personifying social values....One of the greatest attractions of this book is that it spins off intellectual sparks at a great rate....the history of standing as a legal term of art..." Michael Boudin, Michigan Law Rev. 77:503 (1979).

48

WADE, H.W.R. Towards administrative justice. Ann Arbor, Univ. of Michigan Press, 1963. 138p.
A24.5

"...undertakes to compare English and American efforts in 'tempering power with justice.'" Louis L. Jaffe, Stanford Law Rev. 16:485 (1964).

ADVOCACY

See also APPELLATE PRACTICE, PRACTICE OF LAW and THE LEGAL PROFESSION; THE TRIAL and ITS PRELIMINARIES

55

FIELD, MOSES. Famous legal arguments. Buffalo, Hein, [c.1887]. 198p. +
A43.5

"Showing the art, skill, tact, genius and eloquence displayed by ... great advocates in ... celebrated trials ..." - subtitle.

56

PARRY, SIR EDWARD A. The seven lamps of advocacy. [London] Unwin, [1923] N.Y., Scribner's, 1924. 110p. *+
A35

Judge Parry ponders on what makes a successful advocate aside from a handsome income. He offers wise, practical, hints and a collection of good anecdotes. See Harvard Law Rev. 38:1003 (1925).

57

VEEDER, VAN VECHTEN, ed. Legal masterpieces; specimens of argumentation and exposition by eminent lawyers. Chicago, Callaghan, 1903. 1324p.
A29.5

Confining himself to the works of twenty lawyers, Veeder prefixes an interesting and instructive study of forensic argument to each selection presented. He also provides a short biography as well as a careful analysis of each jurist's life, work, and influence. Included in the collection are specimens from Daniel Webster, Jeremiah S. Black, David Dudley Field, William M. Evarts, and James C. Carter. See Harvard Law Rev. 17:214 (1904).

58

WELLMAN, FRANCIS L. Day in court; or the subtle arts of great advocates. ...N.Y., Macmillan, 1910. 257p. *+
A6, A12, A23, A29, A35, A41, A43, A49, A71

For first year students to be reread in 2nd and 3rd years. The acquisition of a law background will give greater insight in the book. [A12]. Not only highly entertaining but also helpful and suggestive to the neophyte in the law.

ANCIENT and PRIMITIVE LAW

See also LEGAL HISTORY; ROMAN LAW

62

HOEBEL, E. ADAMSON. The law of primitive man; a study in comparative legal dynamics. Cambridge, Harvard Univ. Press, 1954. 357p. *+
A64

In this important and stimulating book a Professor of Anthropology attempts to deduce certain generalizations as to the development of legal order in primitive societies from a case study of five carefully selected primitive "law ways." See N.Y.U.L.Rev. 31:248 (1956).

63

LLEWELLYN, KARL N. The Cheyenne way; conflict and case law in primitive jurisprudence [with] E. Adamson Hoebel, Norman, Univ. of Oklahoma Press, 1941. 360p. +
A7, A51 (1st year), A57.1

The authors apply to primitive material the case system in the legal significance of the term; and the problem they seek to illuminate is that of juristic method in Anglo-American law. Both are distinguished in their fields - law and anthropology. See Harvard Law Rev. 55:707 (1942).

64

MALINOWSKI, BRONISLAW. Crime and custom in savage society....N.Y., Humanities Press, 1951. 132p. *+
A36

Malinowski is considered a great authority in this field. This book is recommended by Dean Pound for the study of "legal institutions of primitive and uncivilized peoples."

ANECDOTES, FACETIAE, SATIRE, etc.

69

Glanville Williams also includes the following in his Studying Law: Maurice Healey's The Old Munster Circuit (1939), W.S. Gilbert [see No. 870], Complete Forensic Fables (1928, 1983) by "O" (Theo Matthew).

70

BANDER, EDWARD J., ed. Mr. Dooley on the Choice of Law. Charlottesville, Va., Michie, 1963. 231p.
A58.5

A selection of legal items from Finley Peter Dunne's essays that appeared in his books and newspapers at the turn of the century. Mr. Dooley's humerous dialogues, flavored with an Irish brogue, were enjoyed by Justice Holmes, Dean Acheson, and many other legal minds. Read Mr. Dooley on the Supreme Court, on Cross-examination, on Women's Rights and many other topics. See also the author's Mr. Dooley and Mr. Dunne (1982).

71

HERBERT, ALAN P. Codd's last case and other misleading cases...London, Methuen [1952] 152p. +
A28

[See numbers 73 and 74]

72

____. Holy deadlock....London, Methuen [1934] 311p. +
A28

An entertaining account of English divorce proceedings.

73

____. Misleading cases in the common law...[with] an introduction by Lord Hewart ...7th ed. [London, Methuen, 1932] 176p. N.Y., Putnam's, 1930. 236p. +
A6, A7

May be misleading, but they are certainly amusing. Read especially the Haddock case in which a cow bearing a stencilled check for 57 pounds is tendered in payment of income tax. Should it be endorsed on the abdomen? Was this a proper check? His definition of a reasonable man has been much quoted.

74

____. Uncommon law; being sixty-six misleading cases, revised and collected in one volume, including ten cases not published before...[with] an introduction by Lord Atkin. London, Methuen [1935] 494p. *+
A1, A3, A8, A14, A19, A27, A28, A35, A39, A42, A43, A43.5, A54, A56, A63, A64, A71.5, A74

Reports of fictitious cases reprinted from Punch, which provide amusement along with pointed criticism of some glaring defects in the legal system. [A54]. The author is an English satirist and lawyer. Other fictitious cases are compiled in the author's volumes: Misleading Cases in the Common Law, More Misleading Cases, and Still More Misleading Cases.

75

POLAK, ALFRED L. Legal fictions; a series of cases from the classics...London, Stevens, 1945. 127p. +
A28

Collection of stories of ancient mythology brought into court and dressed in garb of modern trial. [A28]. The author exhibits a happy combination of Aristophanic wit, ingenious burlesque and legal scholarship. See Law Q. Rev. 62:293 (1946).

76

PROSSER, WILLIAM L. The judicial humorist; a collection of judicial opinions and other frivolities. Boston, Little, Brown, 1952. 284p. +
A20, A27, A28, A64

In this anthology of judicial wit, the gilt-edged personality of Dean Prosser outcrops between lines spoken by famous characters of humor such as Serjeant Buzfuz, Mr. Pickwick, et al. The reader experiences a pleasant retreat from routine as he indulges in a delightful collection of both time-worn and recent anecdotes, poems and unusual opinions by courts endeavoring to find in the law light-heartedness and humor. See Texas Law Rev. 31:352 (1953).

APPELLATE PRACTICE
See also ADVOCACY

80

CARRINGTON, PAUL D, DANIEL J. MEADOR AND MAURICE ROSENBERG. Justice on appeal. St. Paul, West, 1976. 263p.
A24.5

"The focus of Justice on Appeal is on the improvement of the appellate process in the face of problems which necessarily arise in any system in which a suddenly accelerated pace of production has occurred, particularly in a system in which measured deliberation and acceptable reasoning are essential. The authors look at the problems objectively from a vantage-point outside the system, undaunted by the armor of opacity in which an appellate court often encases itself....It is time that the [legal] profession understand...the art of judging. Justice on Appeal resolutely faces the problems of modern appellate courts and deserves the careful consideration of appellate judges to the solutions it suggests." James D. Hopkins, Columbia Law Rev. 77:332 (1977)

81

CHARPENTIER, ARTHUR A., ed. Counsel on appeal. N.Y., McGraw-Hill, 1968. 223p.
A31.7

This book "puts together a series of lectures on appellate advocacy sponsored by the Association of the Bar of the City of New York...Each of [the lecturers] has been a truly brilliant appellate practitioner [including Harris Steinberg, Milton Pollack, Whitman Knapp, Samuel Gates, Thurgood Marshall, Simon Rifkind, and Judge Charles Breitel]." Charles S. Desmond, Buffalo Law Rev. 19:693 (1970).

82

DAVIS, JOHN W. The argument of an appeal. Philadelphia, Committee on Continuing Legal Education of the American Law Institute, 1952. 109p.
A29.5

"...the reader will derive almost as much pleasure and advantage from reading it as he would have gained had his been the privilege of a personal chat with the distinguished advocate himself....The ten commandments which [the author] proceeds to announce are both wise and witty." George Wharton Pepper, A.B.A.Jl. 39:53 (1953). An essay bearing this title can be found in the Harvard Law School Introduction to Advocacy (1981, p. 144-153). Also in this publication, the student can read with profit Walter V. Schaefer's "The Appellate Court" and "The Advocate as a Lawmaker in the Reviewing Courts"; and Frederick Bernays Wiener's "Oral Advocacy."

83

LEVY, HERBERT MONTE. How to handle an appeal. N.Y., Practicing Law Institute, 1968. 1629p.
A29.5

"...serves a useful function....in pointing to the lessons of experience along the appellate road. It is worth a study by the young lawyer or by the lawyer who has not done considerable appellate work but is preparing for an appeal. It may not prove to be enough by itself, particularly for appeals after a trial. The book is, nevertheless, a professional job and merits the attention of the profession." Sheldon H. Elsen, N.Y.U.Law Rev. 44:239 (1969).

ART AND THE LAW

86

ADAMS, LAURIE. Art on trial; from Whistler to Rothko. N.Y., Walker & Co., 1975. 236p.
A29.5

"...libel action...by Jimmy Whistler against John Ruskin;...whether Constantin Brancusi's bronze sculpture,

Bird in Space, was and is an 'original work of art' ...Hahn v. Duveen...Hans van Meegeren [forgery]...State v. Radich [flag desecration] and The Matter of Rothko ...A delight to read." Samuel Sonenfield and Gail M. Schaffer, Cleveland State Law Rev. 25:417 (1976). See also Robert E. Duffy, Art law, representing artists, dealers, and collectors (1977).

BENCH AND BAR

See also BIOGRAPHY

90

BURDICK, WILLIAM L. The bench and bar of other lands. Brooklyn, N.Y., Metropolitan Law Book Co. [c1939] 652p. *+
A72

Dean Burdick's purpose was not to write a technical book but rather "a narrative of things an American law teacher has seen and heard in the courts abroad." He treats these foreign judicial systems with understanding and accuracy.

91

DERRIMAN, JAMES. Pageantry of the law. London, Eyre & Spottisoode, 1955. 224p. +
A19

The pomp and circumstance of the law and its administration in England and Wales are described with fascinating detail. Derriman answers questions such as "Where and how is a new judge sworn in? What is the origin of the Lord Chancellor's gold-laced robes?" He also adds much information on the Inns of Court, legal study and practice of law.

92

MEGARRY, ROBERT E. Miscellany-at-law; a diversion for lawyers and others. London, Stevens [1955] 415p. +
A74

An extremely interesting anthology of judicial wit, curiosities of the law and lawyers, written with a light touch but sound scholarship. The legal wit collected is not of the "humerous" type but rather of "verbal felicity endemic in the law which lifts many a page of the law reports into the realm of literature."

93

____. A second miscellany-at-law; a further diversion for lawyers and others. London, Stevens, 1973. 420p.
A74

"This essentially nonfiction volume about the law, laws, courts, judges, lawyers, and selected others, is a deft work of humor and scholarship, each of which enhances the reader's appreciation of the other....Any American lawyer or layman with a sense either of humor or of legal history and doctrine, will be delighted with this book." Elmer M. Million, Oklahoma Law Rev. 27:574 (1974).

94

O'NEALL, JOHN B. Biographical sketches of the bench and bar of South Carolina...Charleston, Courtenay, 1859. 2 v. +
A58

Recommended as of particular local interest for South Carolina by Dean Prince, Univ. of South Carolina.

95

POUND, ROSCOE. The lawyer from antiquity to modern times, with particular reference to the development of bar associations in the U.S. ...St. Paul, West, 1953. 404p. *+
A6.5, A40, A43, A46, A49, A67, A72

With the purpose of delineating the significance of law as a profession, Dean Pound portrays the evolution of the lawyer's function in the judicial process from Ancient Greece to contemporary America. In appealing to the legal profession to maintain its time-honored independence and in discussing the historical development of the bar, he is always interesting and stimulating.

96

TAFT, HENRY W. A century and a half at the New York bar, being the annals of a law firm and sketches of its members, with brief references to collateral events of historical interest. N.Y., privately printed, 1938. 305p. *+
A6

Annals and sketches of a leading law firm in New York City: Cadwalader, Wickersham and Taft.

97

WARREN. CHARLES A. A history of the American bar....Boston, Little, Brown, 1911. 586p. +
A35, A48

A careful, fairly balanced detailed account of the bars of the different colonies. Each is distinct, yet the reader can readily follow the tendency toward unity, toward a real American bar. Also examined are the most significant features of our legal history from 1789 to 1860. Traced, too, are the origin and infancy of railroad law, corporation law, insurance law, personal injuries law, legal education and the writing of modern law books. See Harvard Law Rev. 25:675 (1912).

THE BIBLE

100

THE HOLY BIBLE. *+
____. Authorized or King James version. (1611).
____. Revised version (Oxford parallel Bible).
____. Revised Standard version. (Nelson 1952; Oxford Univ. Press 1965).
____. American Revised.
____. Douay Bible. Confraternity ed. (Catholic).
____. Old Testament (Jewish Publ. Society).
____. ____. Translation by James Moffatt (1925).
____. ____. American translation (1939).
____. Jerusalem Bible (1966).
____. New American Bible (1970).

An understanding of The Bible is implied in all reading lists - especially for lawyers - who must look to it for guidance in many activities with which they will be concerned. Judge Vanderbilt states in his report on prelegal education: "I have never known a judge or a practitioner or a law professor who deserved to be called great, who was not well versed in the best of English and American literature, especially the Bible and Shakespeare."

The Revised version (Oxford) is a good parallel text. The American version differs at times from the English version. The new Revised Standard version was prepared by a group of distinguished scholars. The Douay version is the authorized Catholic translation from the Latin Vulgate. The Moffatt translation is considered good. Consult Sheehy, Guide to reference books (1976 plus supplements) for additional texts and evaluations. Publishers Weekly has an annual issue on religious texts (For example the issue of Sept. 30, 1983).

BIBLIOGRAPHY AND REFERENCE

110

BURTON, WILLIAM C. Legal thesaurus. N.Y., Macmillan, 1980. 1058p.
A29.5

A unique tool for finding synonyms, associated legal concepts, and foreign phrases and translations.

111

GUIDE TO AMERICAN LAW. St. Paul, West, 1983- . Vol. 1-
A29.5

An enclopedic treatment of law by subject, person or special topic. For example: anarchy, John Austin, jurisprudence. Includes signed articles by noted scholars: Arthur Larson (affirmative action), Norman Dorsen (A.C.L.U.), and Robert B. McKay (apportionment). Excellent indexing and illustrations.

112

MCNAMARA, M. FRANCES. 2000 famous legal quotations. Rochester, Lawyers Cooperative Pub. Co., 1967. 718p.
A29.5

A scholarly and well-edited arrangement of well-known quotations arranged alphabetically by subject and with an index and author listing.

113

NEW YORK UNIVERSITY. SCHOOL OF LAW. LIBRARY. A catalogue of the law collection at New York Univ., with selected annotations; compiled and edited by Julius J. Marke....N.Y., Law Center of N.Y.U., 1953. 1372p. +
A19, A27, A28

This catalogue has been recommended by many authorities as a good starting point for ascertaining the right work for the subject involved. The annotations are helpful in that they describe the contents of the book and its value to the researcher.

114

RAISTRICK, DONALD and JOHN REES. Lawyers' law books, a practical index to American and English legal literature. London, Professional Books, 1977. 576p. Supplement 1982. 138p.
A29.5

A listing of books by subject with an author and short title index. For an excellent but dated practical book that deserves a new edition, see Sloane, Recommended Law Books (A.B.A. 1969) which made an excellent resource for law firm libraries.

115

REDDEN, KENNETH R. and E. L. VERON. Modern legal glossary. Charlottesville, Va., Michie, 1980. 576p.
A29.5

A dictionary of legal terms, phrases and concepts rather than words. Includes names of professional associations, government agencies, and international organizations; foreign phrases, famous trials, popular names of cases and statutes, biographical notes on legal personalities, etc. An entertaining book.

116

WALKER, DAVID M. The Oxford companion to law. Oxford, Oxford Univ. Press, 1980. 1366p.
A29.5

An alphabetical arrangement of terms, concepts, short biographies, famous cases and acts, etc. Most entries are short but UNITED STATES LAW, JUSTICE, ENGLISH LAW and other entries are given extended treatment. Includes bibliographical material.

BIOGRAPHY

"Actually, better than any of these [other books recommended] I would think, is a good biography of eminent American jurists such as Marshall, Cardozo, Brandeis, or American lawyers such as Abraham Lincoln. I think that if a student can become imbued with the spirit of some of the great men of the law, this might be more helpful in his own development than introductory materials which are more prosaic in nature." Dean Mulligan, Fordham University.

Individual Biographies and Autobiographies
(Collected biographies begin at No. 325)

130

ACHESON, DEAN. Morning and noon. N.Y., Houghton Mifflin, 1965. 614p.
A31.7

Mr. Acheson was a prominent Washington lawyer who played a significant political role during the Truman administration. "Stylistically, the witty and polished Acheson memoir is simply in a class by itself, although it too carries a few disappointments. For one thing, the author's fastidious demarcation between public and private has left much unwritten....Sketches of the author's boyhood ...picks up Mr. Justice Brandeis a few years after the confirmation controversy and presents some appealing glimpses of the judge from the subdued perspective of his law clerk..." Gerald T. Dunne, Saint Louis Univ. Law Jl. 10:589 (1966). Other Acheson books are: Among Friends (1980) and Present at the Creation (1969).

131

ADAMS, HENRY. The education of Henry Adams, an autobiography. N.Y., Modern Library, 1931. 517p. (first published in 1918). *+
A28, A35, A61

Henry Adams was famous as an historian and commentator on the human race. For many years he was involved in the "search for an education" or the "secret of social evolution, a science or philosophy of history." This book should be read with his Mont Saint Michel (1904). Adams is also known for his History of the U.S. (1889-91). Carl Becker considers the Education "undoubtedly one of the most remarkable autobiographies in the language." See Encyc. Soc. Sci. 1:431.

132

ADAMS, JOHN. John Adams and the American revolution, by Catherine D. Bowen. Boston, Little, Brown, 1950. 699p. +
A6, A28, A38.5

Covers the period from 1745 when John was ten to 1776, when he was forty. The atmosphere of 18th century New England is interwoven throughout the biography with fascinating effectiveness. The defense by John Adams of the defendants in the Boston Massacre Trial is also very well done.

133

____.The Adams papers; legal papers of John Adams. Cambridge, Harvard Univ. Press, 1965. 3 vols.
A29.5

"...supplement but do not supersede the material made available in the Diary and Autobiography first edited by Charles Francis Adams in the 1850s and recently re-edited as part of Series I of the The Adams Papers ...In selected cases from the "few hundred" documented, the editors utilized criteria such as whether a case illuminated a particular legal point, contained an interesting document, gave balance to the general picture of Adams' practice or possessed historical or social interest...The pleadings assembled by Adams as a form book...the detailed treatment of the vice admiralty court jurisdiction in Massachusetts Bay...[and] the Boston Massacre [are] valuable contribution[s] to American legal history...[A] substantial contribution to the history of American law during an important era of the colonial period." Joseph H. Smith, Columbia Law Rev. 1966:1385 (1966).

134

ARNOLD, THURMAN. Fair fights and foul; a dissenting lawyer's life. N.Y., Harcourt, Brace & World, 1965. 292p.
A43.5

"...he has written a somewhat impressionistic but splendidly illuminating account of the Yale Law School in the thirties....His shrewd observations far outnumber the inaccuracies and naivetes, which I, being a book reviewer, have unfairly emphasized....As legal autobiography goes, it is very hard to beat." Joseph W. Bishop, Jr., Villanova Law Rev. 12:211 (1967).

135

BACON, FRANCIS. Francis Bacon; the temper of a man by Catherine Drinker Bowen. Boston, Little Brown, 1963. 245p.
A24.5

Bacon's essays should not be neglected, particularly his "Of Judicature." [A74] Bacon was not only a philosopher and essayist, but a protagonist of Lord Coke. See also Edmond Cahn, Lawyer as scientist and scoundrel, reflections on Francis Bacon's quadricentennial, N.Y.U. Law Rev. 36:1 (1961).

136

BALLANTINE, WILLIAM. Some experiences of barrister's life...London, R. Bentley, 1883. 394p. *+
A28, A35, A71.5, A74

William Ballantine (1812-1887) was a successful serjeant-at-law, specializing in criminal cases, and noted for his ability in cross examination. He defended unsuccessfully the Tichborne claimant, who claimed that he was the long lost son of the wealthy but deceased Mr. Tichborne. See also Douglas Woodruffe, The Tichborne Claimant. [A74]

137

BEAN, ROY E. Vinegarron; the saga of judge Roy E. Bean, law west of the Pecos, by Ruel McDaniel. Kingsport, Tenn., Southern Pub., 1936. 143p. *+
A28

Good for local color.

138

BELLI, MELVIN with ROBERT BLAIR KAISER. Melvin Belli; My life on trial: an autobiography. N.Y., Morrow. 1976.; N.Y., Popular Library, 1977. 413p.
A43.5

A leading trial lawyer shares some of his trials and tribulations.

139

BENTHAM, JEREMY. His life and work, by Charles M. Atkinson. London, Methuen, 1905. 247p. +
A19, A43.5

Bentham was the great law reformer of the late 18th and ealy 19th centuries. This is a painstaking and brilliantly written account of his life. It can be read with interest even by those who do not care "a sixpence" for his philosophy. Bentham's character is fascinating. See also Mary L. Mack's Jeremy Bentham (1962). [A74]

140

BLACK, HUGO. The vision and the dream of Justice Hugo L. Black: an examination of a judicial philosophy by Howard Ball. Univ. of Alabama Press. 1975. 232p.
A43.5

141

____. Hugo Black and the judicial revolution by Gerald T. Dunne. N.Y., Simon and Schuster, 1977. 492p.
A48.5

"Since [Black] ordered the destruction of most of his papers, a thorough inquiry into the development of his thinking is bound to be handicapped. Fortunately, Gerald Dunne's own perseverance seems to have compensated for some of what has been irretrievably lost. [This book] stands as one of the major avenues of access to those seeking to confront both intellectually and personally this giant of American constitutional jurisprudence." D. Grier Stephenson, Jr., Virginia Law Rev. 1087 (1977).

142

____. Mr. Justice Black, the man and his opinions, [by John P. Frank] Introd. by Charles A. Beard. N.Y., Knopf, 1949 [c.1948] 357p. *+
A27, A43, A61, A71.5, A72

Mr. Justice Black, the first Franklin Roosevelt appointee to the Supreme Court, was a staunch defender of First Amendment rights. The author served as his law clerk, and offers all sides of his character - the good and the bad. He also analyzes with authority his more signifigant opinions. See also Hugo Black Jr., <u>My father, a remembrance</u> (1975). [A57.1]; also Daniel J. Meador, <u>Mr. Justice Black and his books</u> (1974). [A57.1]

143

____. Hugo L. Black; a study in the judicial process. [By Charlotte Williams] Baltimore, Johns Hopkins Press, 1950. 208p.*+
A27, A28

The author believes that "while a study of the work of a single justice...can but partially reflect movements in the mainstream of juristic thought, it is nevertheless true than an understanding of such movements demands a consideration of the opinions and philosophies of the individual members of the court."

144

BLACK, JEREMIAH S....A defender of the Constitution and the Ten Commandments, by William H. Brigance. Philadelphia, Univ. of Pennsylvania Press, 1934. 303p. +
A19

In addition to outlining the colorful career of Judge Black, the author has written an excellent historical study of the Buchanan Administration and the Reconstruction Period. Black became Chief Justice of Pennsylvania, a member of Buchanan's Cabinet and counsel in the Milligan and McArdle cases. Many amusing examples of his invective are given. See Harvard Law Rev. 48:718 (1935).

145

BLACKSTONE, SIR WILLIAM...By David A. Lockmiller. Chapel Hill, Univ. of North Carolina Press, 1938. 308p. *+
A28, A45, A72

Lockmiller writes simply and well. Blackstone's decisions are considered as well as some of his verses. This is a good evaluation of Blackstone, the man, his times and works. See also Julius Marke's Vignettes of legal history, second series (1977) for the significance of Blackstone's Commentaries on the Law of England.

146

BOTEIN, BERNARD. Trial judge; the candid, behind-the-bench story of Justice Bernard Botein. N.Y., Simon and Schuster, 1952. 337p. (also a 1963 ed.). *+
A43.5

Judge Botein has given us a fascinating story of "what makes a trial judge tick" under his impersonal judicial robes. It is a story that every trial judge might wish he had written, and while written especially for laymen, it is one that every judge and lawyer will wish to read. See Texas Law Rev. 31:348 (1953).

147

BOWEN, CHARLES S. C. BOWEN, baron. Lord Bowen, a biographical sketch with a selection from his verses. By Sir Henry Stewart Cunningham. [London and Beccles] Printed for private circulation [by W. Clowes & Sons] 1896. 256p. +
A8, A19, A11, A36, A40, A64

The legal biography is, as a rule, a tedious affair. One lawyer's life is much like another's. There have been three notable exceptions to the rule in recent times: The

Life of Lord Campbell by his daughter. The Recollections of Montague Williams and The Life of Lord Bowen by Sir Henry Cunningham were all eminently readable books. Lord Bowen was a great judge and a great wit.

148

BRANDEIS, LOUIS. Brandeis of Boston, by Allon Gal. Cambridge, Harvard Univ. Press, 1980. 271p.
A35

The emergence of Brandeis as attorney for the people.

149

____. The words of...edited by Solomon Goldman, with a foreword by William O. Douglas. N.Y., H. Schuman [1953] 200p.+
A28, A71.5

Brandeis was a distinguished Justice of the Supreme Court of the U.S. for 23 years and delivered around 600 judgments. He is noted as a dissenter and a great liberal. "He never failed to recognize the role of law as an instrument of social advancement...he initiated many changes in socio-legal thinking," wrote President Eisenhower.

150

____. Brandeis; the personal history of an American ideal, by Alfred Lief. N.Y., Stackpole, 1936. 508p. *+
A27, A28, A35, A44, A62

An able presentation of his early life and education, his corporate practice, his success as a business lawyer and his public life.

[151-152 saved]

153

____. The social and economic views of Mr. Justice Brandeis, the personal history of an American ideal by Alfred Lief. N.Y., Vanguard Press, 1930. 419p. N.Y., Stackpole Sons, 1936. 508p.
A43.5

154

____. Brandeis; a free man's life, by Alpheus T. Mason. N.Y., Viking Press, 1946. 713p. *+
A1, A2, A2.5, A8, A12, A14, A19, A21, A23, A27, A29, A30, A38.5, A39, A43, A43.5, A54, A56, A57, A59, A63, A64, A68, A71.5, A72

An interesting and well researched account of a great career at the bar and as a justice of our highest court. A reviewer has said that for law students, the book might well have been entitled: "A case history of a successful legal career." [A12] For a current appraisal of Brandeis, see Bruce Allen Murphy, The Brandeis/Frankfurter Connection; the secret political activities of the Supreme Court Justices (1982) reviewed by Russell Wheeler in Michigan Law Rev. 81:931 (1983). For a review essay by a former student of Justice Frankfurter and a law clerk to Justice Brandeis, see Nathaniel L. Nathanson, Northwestern Univ. Law Rev. 78:494 (1983). See also Lewis J. Paper, Brandeis (1983).

155

____. Brandeis and the modern state, by Alpheus T. Mason...foreword by Norman Hapgood. Wash., D.C., National Home Library, 1936. 263p. *+
A6, A35, A62

Treats chiefly the public welfare activities, the ideology and constitutional principles of Mr. Justice Brandeis. It is a thoughtful and systematic attempt to evaluate the living philosophy of a man. See Harvard Law Rev. 47:735 (1934).

156

____. The Brandeis reader; the life and contribution of Mr. Justice Louis D. Brandeis...Edited with commentary by Ervin H. Pollack. N.Y., Oceana, 1956. 256p. (Docket series, v. 7). +
A3, A6, A23, A38.5, A50, A55, A57.1, A71.5

Selection of original writings, opinions, speeches, written by and about Brandeis, linked by notes and commentary by the editor. Maintains a high standard and contains to a remarkable extent the quintessence of thinking and writing of Mr. Justice Brandeis. See Jurid. Rev. n.s. 2:107.

157

____. Letters of Louis D. Brandeis. Ed. by Melvin I. Urofsky and David W. Levy. Albany, State Univ. of New York Press, 1971-8. 5 vols.
A29.5

Justice Brandeis' papers are also available on microfilm and provide a revealing glimpse into his professional career, government work, and Zionist activities.

158

BROOKS, AUBREY L. A southern lawyer; fifty years at the bar. Chapel Hill, Univ. of N.C. Press [1950.] 214p. +
A59

Brooks writes well—witty and urbane. He also

exemplifies the very best traditions of both the South and the legal profession. He describes many of the trials in which he has participated. The play Coquette was later based on one of his trials, State v. Cole. See A.B.A.Jl. 37:217 (1951).

159

BRYCE, JAMES BRYCE, viscount. James Bryce, by H. A. L. Fisher....N.Y., Macmillan, 1927. 2v. +
A19

This has been described as "a truly fascinating study of a most interesting character." Bryce, of course, is noted for his American Commonwealth. He was also a British jurist, historian, and politician, who practiced law for several years until his appointment as Regius Professor of civil law at Oxford. He later became a cabinet member and British Ambassador at Washington.

160

BUSCH, FRANCIS X. In and out of court. Foreword by Russell Whitman...illustrated by J. Kelly Fitzpatrick. Chicago, De Paul Univ. Press, 1942. 306p. *+
A44, A54

The author has culled a rich variety of original anecdotes which capture the charm, wit, and pathos that make up the daily drama of life in the courts. [A54] Will delight old practitioners and is recommended for neophyte members of the legal profession. See Fordham L. Rev. 11:246 (1942).

161

CAMPBELL, JOHN CAMPBELL, BARON. Life of John, Lord Campbell, Lord High Chancellor of Great Britain; consisting of a selection from his autobiography, diary and letters; edited by his daughter, the Hon. Mrs. Hardcastle. 2d ed. London, J. Murray, 1881. 2v.
A19, A71.5 *+

[See No. 147] Lord Campbell is best known for his Lives of the Chief Justices. See also R.F.V. Heuston's Lives of the Lord Chancellors, 1885-1940 (1964). [A74].

162

CARDOZO, BENJAMIN N. American judge, by George S. Hellman. N.Y., Russell & Russell, 1969, c.1940. 339p. +
A71.5

Cardozo is ranked by Dean Pound as one of the ten judges first in American judicial history. This book is of value for his personal life.

163

___. Cardozo and frontiers of legal thinking, with selected opinions, by Beryl H. Levy. N.Y., Oxford Univ. Press, 1938. 315p. (also Kennikat 1969). *+
A43.5, A72

An excellent book containing many of Cardozo's opinions and legal thoughts.

164

___. Mr. Justice Cardozo; a liberal mind in action, by Joseph I. Pollard; with a foreword by Roscoe Pound. N.Y., Yorktown Press [c1935.] 327p. +
A27, A28, A43.5

Rather than a biography it is an account of Cardozo's legal thinking as exemplified in his judicial work.

165

CARSON, EDWARD H. CARSON, baron. Carson; the life of Sir Edward Carson, Lord Carson of Duncairn. London, Heinemann [1932,1953.] 515p. +
A10

Carson had an extraordinary career as a lawyer - especially as an advocate. He participated in the Oscar Wilde case, where possibly Wilde got the better of it—but Carson was always very effective in court. Recommended for law students and lawyers.

166

___. Carson, the advocate, by Edward Marjoribanks, with a preface by the Rt. Hon. Viscount Hailsham. N.Y., Macmillan, 1932. 455p. *+
A27, A28, A45, A72

Carson is considered here mainly as an advocate. Many of his cases are related here.

167

CECIL, HENRY. Just within the law, memories and reminiscences. London, Hutchinson, 1975. 220p.
A31.7

"Henry Cecil is...a two-career man, who has achieved excellence in law under his own name, Henry Leon [as a County Court Judge]; and in letters under the name of Henry Cecil....With wit and charm, combining entertainment and instruction, he writes of what he knows, and what he has seen and done, during his passage through life, with emphasis on his two careers...[The theme for this book is] the present state of the law and its betterment." Roy St. George Stubbs, Manitoba Law Jl 7:219 (1976-7). See also Cecil's works of fiction [Nos. 847-850].

168

CHOATE, JOSEPH H. Joseph H. Choate, New Englander, New Yorker, lawyer, ambassador, by Theron G. Strong. N.Y., Dodd, Mead, 1917. 390p. *+
A72

Joseph Choate was one of the greatest lawyers of his age (late 19th cent. and early 20th cent.). He was unsurpassed in cross-examination. This book contains some errors of fact but it explains the man and the lawyer.

169

CICERO, MARCUS TULLIUS. Eternal Lawyer, a legal biography of Cicero, by Robert N. Wilkin. N.Y., Macmillan, 1947. 264p. *+
A19, A28, A43.5, A54, A72

A delightful and instructive biography of Cicero as a lawyer - the greatest lawyer of the ancient world. See Am.Pol.Sci.Rev., Aug., 1947.

170

COKE, SIR EDWARD. The lion and the throne; the life and times of Sir Edward Coke (1552-1634), by Catherine D. Bowen. Boston, Little, Brown [1957.] 652p. *+
A2.5, A19, A35.5, A43.5, A47, A49, A67, A71.5, A74

"Of all the long line of judges who have rendered England famous among the nations for the excellence and impartiality of the administration of justice, the chief place has been unhesitatingly awarded to Coke. To him, in no small degree, may be attributed the victory of the common law over all the rival systems and influences which threatened it." Lord Birkenhead. This volume is a triumph of legal and judicial biography. It combines exhaustive legal and historical research with splendid artistic skill in the telling of a dramatic story of life in one of the most exciting eras of English history. See N.Y. Times Book Rev., March 10, 1957.

[171-172 saved]

173

____. Edward Coke, oracle of the law....by Hastings Lyon and Herman Block....Boston and N.Y., Houghton Mifflin, 1929. 385p.*+
A19, A72

Accuracy has not been sacrificed to vividness in this biography. Describes dramatically Coke's long rivalry with Bacon, Coke's stand against James I to maintain the supremacy of the common law, etc. See Harvard Law Rev. 43:684 (1930).

174

CRAVATH FIRM. The Cravath firm and its predecessors, 1819-1947, by Robert T. Swaine....N.Y., Priv. print. at Ad Press, Ltd., 1946-1948. 3 v. +
A6, A19

Mr. Swain's account of his famous law firm has already become a classic of its type. It is primarily a study in the evolution of a modern big-city, big-business, big-league law firm. It also presents the materials for a critical analysis of the changing role of the lawyer in relation to modern business and government; also gives background to many famous law suits. See Yale Law Jl 58:650 (1949).

175

DARROW, CLARENCE S. The story of my life, illustrated from photographs. N.Y., Scribner's, 1932. 495p. +
A43.5, A57.1, A59

Clarence Darrow died in 1938 at the age of 81. There was no doubt at the time that he was one of the leading advocates in America. As a trial lawyer he was unequalled. Much can be gained by becoming more familiar with Darrow the man and the lawyer.

176

____. Clarence Darrow for the defense, a biography by Irving Stone. Garden City, N.Y., Doubleday, Doran, 1941. 570p. *+
A19, A27, A41, A43.5, A54, A57.1, A61, A71.5

An excellent account of Darrow's turbulent career at the bar. Darrow participated in many violent law suits, involving racial prejudice, religious freedom, rights of labor, free speech and capital punishment. See Yale Law Jl 51:362 (1941).

177

____. Darrow, a biography, by Kevin Tierney. N.Y., Thomas Y. Crowell, 1979. 490p.
A30.5

"...Why of all the ingenious and industrious tribe of lawyers, is Darrow alone remembered? [discusses Lincoln, Webster, Wirt and why they are not as well known as lawyers]...fascinating portrait of Darrow, more complex as a man and more ambitious as a symbol than anything we have had before...Darrow's attitude toward the technicalities, tactics, and strategy of the practice of law is illuminating...he was a trial lawyer of tremendous power. ...[If we had a niche reserved for infidels] Darrow would be there. [The author] has provided all the material any reader could require for drawing his own conclusions..." H. C. Macgill, Conn. Law Rev. 12:410 (1980).

178

____. Attorney for the damned. Ed. by Arthur Weinberg. N.Y., Simon & Schuster, 1957. 552p.
A43.5

Darrow's closing arguments, debates, and addresses. It is interesting to compare Darrow's addresses to the jury with the fictionalized account in Norman Katkov, Blood and orchids (1983) of the Massie case.

179

DAVIS, JOHN W. Lawyer's lawyer; the life of John W. Davis by William H. Harbaugh. N.Y., Oxford Univ. Press, 1973. 648p.
A57.1

"While the unpopularity of the bar has been a recurrent theme in American legal history, the present climate suggests a need for re-examining the attorney's role in twentieth century American society. An excellent source for such a study is [this] fine biography. The author has produced a readable account that skillfully probes Davis's long career as a talented lawyer." James W. Ely, Michigan Law Rev. 72:1495 (1974).

180

DOE, CHARLES. Chief Justice: the judicial world of Charles Doe by John Phillip Reid. Cambridge, Harvard Univ. Press, 1967. 489p.
A30.5

The author "plainly likes the unpretentious,

stubbornly individualistic Yankee judge whom he has studied so long and closely. But he has also kept a scholar's detachment. Reid concludes that, despite his bold willingness to innovate, Doe had little influence on the development of the law outside New Hampshire. ...Professor Reid has put the reader in possession of material from which he can make his own over-all judgment." Willard Hurst, Univ. of Pennsylvania Law Rev. 115:1020 (1967).

181

DOUGLAS, WILLIAM O. The Court years, 1939-75. N.Y., Random, 1980. 434p.
A35.5

Reviewed in Michigan Law Rev. 80:781 (1982). See also Vern Countryman, The Judicial Record of Justice William O. Douglas (1974). [A57.1]

182

____. Go east, young man: the early years. N.Y., Random House, 1974. 493p.
A35.5, A57.1

Another of Justice Douglas' autobiographical volumes.

183

____. Independent journey; the life of William O. Douglas by James F. Simon. N.Y., Harper & Row, 1980. 503p.
A1

Justice Douglas was one of the leading liberal Supreme Court Justices during a period of constitutional activism.

184

ERSKINE, HENRY, Lord. For the defense: Thomas Erskine, the most enlightened liberal of his times, 1750-1823. [By Lloyd P. Stryker.] Garden City, N.Y., Doubleday, 1947. 624p. *+
A11, A19, A21, A22, A27, A28, A47, A62, A72

Erskine had an outstanding legal career as an advocate, prosecutor, judge and legislator. He made his greatest impression as an advocate. He defended Tom Paine and his Rights of Man and other popular causes. Many interesting courtroom scenes are depicted. See Columbia Law Rev. 47:1091 (1947).

185

ERVIN, SAM. Just a country lawyer; a biography of Senator Sam Ervin, by Paul R. Clancy. Bloomington, Indiana Univ. Press, 1974. 310p.
A57.1

Senator Ervin played a prominent role in the Watergate proceedings and is a spokesman for conservative approaches to constitutional problems.

186

EVARTS, WILLIAM M....Lawyer, diplomat, statesman, by Chester L. Barrows. Chapel Hill, Univ. of N.C. Press, 1941. 587p. *+
A44

Barrows brings out the qualities that made Evarts one of the outstanding lawyers of his era.

187

FALLON, WILLIAM J. The great mouthpiece by Gene Fowler. N.Y., Blue Ribbon Books, 1931. 403p. Bantam, 1962. 403p.
A57.1

Biography of a famous New York criminal lawyer.

188

FENTON, D.X. Ms. Attorney. Phila., Westminister Press, 1974. 160p.
A65

Although there is some stress on prejudice against women in law school and the legal profession, this book is basically a journalistic account of how to get into law school, what to study, and what law practice is about.

189

FIELD, STEPHEN J. Personal reminiscences of early days in California, with other sketches....To which is added the story of his attempted assassination by a former associate on the Supreme bench of the state, by Hon. George G. Gorham. Printed for a few friends. Not published. [Wash., D.C., 1893.] 406p. +
A28

Stephen was the younger brother of David Dudley Field, noted for his advocacy of codifications. He emigrated to California in 1849 and drafted the 1851 California Practice Act which was largely based upon the elder brother's work in civil procedure in N.Y. He later became Associate Justice of the Supreme Court of the U.S. This book has been described by J. N. Pomeroy, Jr. as "that most delightful book of autobiographical sketches."

190

___. Stephen J. Field, craftsman of the law, by Carl B. Swisher ... Wash., Brookings Institution, 1930. 473p. * +
A27, A28, A43.5, A61, A71

This is a competent account.

[Nos. 191, 192 saved]

193

FRANKFURTER, FELIX. From the diaries of Felix Frankfurter with a biographical essay and notes, edited by Joseph P. Lash. N.Y., Norton, 1975. 366p.
A35.5, A57.1

"These diaries make apparent why Frankfurter was not the dominant figure on the court predicated on his past career. The liberal become conservative, the activist a passivist. Time will only tell if his insistence on the court not invading the political thicket was the best route to a fuller democracy." See Leonard B. Boudin, Harvard Law Rev. 89:282 (1978).

194

___. Felix Frankfurter reminisces. Recorded in talks with Harlan B. Phillips. N.Y., Reynal & Co., 1960. 310p. Also Greenwood Press, 1978.
A43.5, A71.5

"...not only an engaging book, it is an important one - important as an illustration of the legal mind, and as a source of candid critical comment on numerous significant personages, but important too because it represents an intimate conversation between Frankfurter and one [Dr. Phillips] who knew enough about the period of his life to stimulate his memory with those questions which would release the controls and display the conciseness of thought, the breadth of understanding, the humor and wit, and the sober, even dedicated personality who was the subject of this enterprise." Francis Perkins, Cornell Law Q. 46:380 (1961). See also H.N. Hirsch, The enigma of Felix Frankfurter (1981) and the Murphy book [No. 154].

195

____. Roosevelt and Frankfurter; their correspondence, 1928-1945. ... annotated by Max Freedman. Boston, Little, Brown, 1968. 772p.
A71.5

A few glimpses into areas of significance to law such as the Supreme Court packing attempt, Learned Hand's non appointment to the Supreme Court, Frankfurter's "hot dogs." See Robert T. Basseches, Duquesne Law Rev. 7:193 (1968).

196

____. Felix Frankfurter, scholar on the bench by Helen Shirley Thomas. Johns Hopkins, 1960. 381p.
A43.5

"...a rather repetitious running comment upon Mr. Justice Frankfurter's judicial decisions, classified as to subject matter, with correlative references to his prejudicial writing or action upon like problems." Maurice H. Merrill, Oklahoma Law Rev. 13:476 (1960).

197

FRANKLIN, BENJAMIN. The autobiography of Benjamin Franklin ...(In his complete works, edited by John Bigelow. N.Y., Putman's 1887-1888. 10 v.). +
A47

Franklin's autobiography "unquestionably ranks among the few great autobiographies ever written." Encyc. Brit. 11th ed. The faculty committee of the Univ. of Kansas City recommends that lawyers should be acquainted with it in furtherance of the goal that "first of all a lawyer ought to be an educated man."

198

FULLER, MELVILLE W. Chief Justice of the U.S., 1888-1910, by Willard L. King. N.Y., Macmillan, 1950. 394p. Chicago, Univ. of Chicago Press, 1967. 337p. *+
A21, A27, A28, A49, A54

This book painstakingly and engagingly written tells the story of the best presiding judge "the Supreme Court ever had, the story of a jurist who ranks in eminence with Marshall and Taney." [A54]

199

GARRY, CHARLES & ART GOLDBERG. Streetfighter in the courtroom; the people's advocate. N.Y., Dutton, 1977. 268p.
A43.5

The courtroom battles for civil rights are recounted in this biography of Mr. Garry.

200

GOMPERS, SAMUEL ...Champion of the toiling masses, by Rowland H. Harvey. Stanford, Cal., Univ. Press, 1935. 376p. *+
A35, A59, A61

The story of a pioneer labor leader who greatly influenced the development of labor law and labor relations in this country.

201

HALDANE, RICHARD B. HALDANE, 1st viscount....An autobiography. Garden City, N.Y., Doubleday, Doran, 1929. 391p. *+
A19, A27, A35, A59, A62

One of the great books of our time. A lawyer and statesman who had worked out a philosophy of life. Especially valuable to lawyers for the account of his methods of arguing before an Appellate Court. See Harvard Law Rev. 58:600 (1945).

202

HALL, SIR EDWARD M. For the defence; the life of Sir Edward Marshall Hall, by Edward Marjoribanks, M.P., with an introduction by the Rt. Honourable The Earl of Birkenhead....N.Y., Macmillan, 1929. 471p. *+
A27, A28, A35, A41, A43.5, A58, A71, A72, A74

Hall was a great English criminal lawyer. He was "for the defense" in many trials and always was impressive with his great technical skill and brilliant oratory. A reviewer is of the opinion that the book reveals to what extent the legal profession in Great Britain have outstripped us here in America in the matter of their procedure in criminal trials. See Harvard Law Rev. 43:1323 (1930).

203

HAMILTON, ALEXANDER. The Young Hamilton by James Thomas Flexner. Boston, Little, Brown, 1978. 497p.
A25.5

A psychological biography that concentrates on Hamilton's first 26 years and attempts to account for both his genius and aberrations. [See also No. 1145].

204

_____. The Alexander Hamilton Reader, by Margaret E. Hall. N.Y., Oceana, 1957. 257p. (Docket Series No. 9.). *+
A3, A35, A41, A50, A55, A73

In addition to the important role he played in public adminstration, Hamilton was also a successful advocate.

The production of these books [Hamilton Reader and Maitland Reader] by Oceana Publications, has been a most noteworthy undertaking and brings to the public in an interesting style some of the best public writing on and by great men of the law. I have recommended the reading of these books to law students and also to pre-law students who are interested in some collateral reading before entering the law school....I am surely glad that a publisher has seen fit to publish materials of this kind in popular editions that every one can afford to buy. Dean Mason Ladd, Iowa.

[205 saved]

206

HARLAN, JOHN MARSHALL. The Great Dissenter, John Marshall Harlan by Frank B. Latham. N.Y., Cowles Book Co., 1970. 175p.
A31.7

"...a very dynamic treatise on the political and constitutional history of the United States. ...Mr. Justice Harlan was the first of the modern liberal judges and truly the 'Great Dissenter.' To the year of his death in 1911 he wrote dissenting opinions, a total of 380. Whether your purposes be pedagogical, literary, or otherwise, Mr. Latham's book is a must. To the latter I am certain Mr. Justice Harlan would write no dissent." Johnny J. Butler, Howard Law Jl 16:183 (1970).

207

HARRIMAN, E.H. ...A biography, by George Kennan. Boston and N.Y., Houghton, Mifflin & Co., 1922. 2 v. *+
A35, A59

Harriman was an American railroad magnate and finacier (1848-1909). He played an important role in the consolidation of the American railroad system. His financial manipulations influenced the government to grant authority to the Interstate Commerce Commission to regulate railroads more comprehensively.

208

HAYS, ARTHUR G. City lawyer; the autobiography of a law practice. N.Y., Simon and Schuster, 1942. 482p. *+
A27, A28, A35, A36, A44.

Loosely written, but highly entertaining. Hays participated in some rather important litigation such as the Scopes Trial, the Wendel Will case and the Reichstag Fire Trial. He also considers the civic responsibility of lawyers. This has been recommended for all candidates for the Bar. See Harvard Law Rev. 56:333 (1942).

209

HINE, REGINALD L. Confessions of an un-common attorney. N.Y., Macmillan, 1947 [c1945.] 268p. +
A20, A27, A28, A74

Hine was a most successful English country lawyer, who was also an antiquary and local historian. He had many peculiar clients and he also considers the influence on his career of laymen such as writers, doctors, clergymen and teachers. The lawyer's approach to religion is also interestingly considered.

210

HOGAN, FRANK. Mr. District Attorney by Barry Cunningham and Mike Pearl. N.Y., Mason Charter Pub'rs, 1970. 290p.
A24.5

"...a eulogy of Frank Hogan [former New York City District Attorney], a biography of Hogan, a chronicle of New York City politics, and a story book of some of the exciting cases and personalities associated with the Manhattan district attorney's office over the thirty years Hogan was there...required reading for those interested in New York City politics." Cases considered include the basketball point-shaving scandal of the 1950s, the fall of renowned gangsters like Dutch Schultz and Lepke Buchalter, the Clifford Irving Scandal, the two trials of Jimmy Hines, etc. Henry Rothblatt, New York Law School Law Rev. 23:364 (1977).

[Nos. 211 and 212 saved]

213

HOLMES, OLIVER WENDELL, JR. Collected legal papers. N.Y., Harcourt, Brace & Howe, 1920. 316p. +
A6, A28, A49, A62, A64, A71.5

This compilation includes The Path of the Law, Montesquieu, and his celebrated essay on John Marshall. Excellent examples of the majestic cadence of Holmes' prose. [See, also, annotation for No. 225].

214

____. Speeches. Boston, Little, Brown, 1913. 103 p. +
A62

First published in 1891. Includes "The profession of the law," "The use of law schools," "The soldier's faith," "John Marshall," "Law and the courts," and testimonials to local bar luminaries.

215

____. Holmes-Laski letters; the correspondence of Mr. Justice Holmes and Harold J. Laski, 1916-1935, edited by Mark de Wolfe Howe, with a foreword by Felix Frankfurter. Cambridge, Harvard Univ. Press, 1953. 2v. +
A27, A28, A39, A43.5, A47, A64

Laski was an English professor and political scientist, well known for his writings. His friendship with Holmes resulted in a wonderful collection of letters written to each other reflecting humor, literary style and their deep thoughts.

216

____. Holmes-Pollock letters, the correspondence of Mr. Justice Holmes and Sir Frederick Pollock, 1874-1932, edited by Mark de Wolfe Howe...with an introduction by John Gorham Palfrey....Cambridge, Mass., Harvard Univ. Press, 1941. 2 v. *+
A7, A21, A27, A28, A39, A43.5, A62, A64, A74

These letters are extremely good reading and of absorbing interest to students of the law in England and America. They are highly literary, casual but with a finished casualness. The fire that burns in them is a gentle literary fire. They have superbly the qualities of good conversation, carried on over the difficult conditions of distance and delay but for that very reason even better suited to their purpose....They talk freely about shop, and shop for them is an absorption not with the practice of the law but with law as history and law as civilization. See Harvard Law Rev. 58:1069 (1942).

217

____. Justice Holmes to Doctor Wu; an intimate correspondence, 1921-1932. N.Y., Central Book Co. [1947?] 58p. +
A27, A28

His letters to Wu contain much of his philosophy of life and attitude toward his work, of his feeling toward his fellow Justices, of his theory of style and his criticisms of books read. See A.B.A.Jl 34:37 (1948).

218

____. Justice Oliver Wendell Holmes; a biography by Silas Bent. N.Y., Vanguard Press, 1932. 386p. +
A27, A45

Oliver Wendell Holmes, Jr., had been a judge for 50 years when he retired as Associate justice of the Supreme Court. Dean Pound lists him as one of the ten judges ranked first in American judicial history. He was also a leading legal historian and a philosopher of penetrating, analytic force. His literary style is scintillating, picturesque and epigrammatic. This is a shrewd and suggestive biography, although rambling and occasionally incorrect, says Max Lerner.

219

____. Mr. Justice Holmes, by Francis B. Biddle. N.Y., Scribner's, 1942. 214p. *+
A8, A21, A39, A43.5, A48.5

A warm, personalized "profile" of the late Justice, written by a distinguished lawyer who served as Holmes' clerk in 1912 and who is best known as U.S. Attorney-General from 1941-45. [A39]

220

____. Yankee from Olympus; Justice Holmes and his family, by Catherine D. Bowen. Boston, Little, Brown, 1944. 475p. *+
A6, A11, A15, A19, A20, A27, A28, A30, A35, A36, A38.5, A39, A40, A41, A43, A43.5, A44, A47, A49, A54, A59, A61, A67, A71, A71.5, A72

This warmly human biography is a work of art which takes for its theme an American epic of dissent as being characteristic of the American mind at its strongest and best. [A43] The author traces the history of Holmes and his family for 135 years, thereby presenting a sequence of three professions—the ministry, medicine and law in crescendo, each son rising higher than his father. [A54]

221

____. Mr. Justice Holmes and the Supreme Court, by Felix Frankfurter. Cambridge, Harvard Univ. Press, 1938. 139p. +
A20, A41, A45, A71.5

A slender but important volume, these lectures reveal in action a mind as keen and liberal as the judge's own. J. P. Pollard, N.Y. Times, October 30, 1938.

222

___. Justice Oliver Wendell Holmes, by Mark de Wolfe Howe. Cambridge, Harvard Univ. Press, 1957. v. 1. The shaping years, 1841-1870. 330p. +

A12, A19

This would have been the definitive "official" biography except for the untimely death of Professor Howe. Professor Howe's style is scholarly - yet extremely interesting. He is also concerned about the "ideas" and thinking of Holmes and his contemporaries. The result is a fascinating book.

223

___. Justice Oliver Wendell Holmes, by Mark de Wolfe Howe. Cambridge, Harvard Univ. Press, 1963. v. 2. The proving years, 1870-1882. 295p.

A35.5, A43.5, A74

"...takes Holmes at age 29(1870), just launched on editing the twelfth edition of Kent's Commentaries, and ends with his appointment in December 1882 to the Massachusetts Supreme Judicial Court, as he nears age 42. In these 12 years he is married, engages in somewhat desultory practice with his brother, is coeditor of the American Law Review and lectures part time at Harvard College, and finally enters full practice of the law in partnership with Shattuck and Munroe in 1873." Willard Hurst, Harvard Law Rev. 77:382 (1963).

224

___. The legacy of Holmes and Brandeis; a study in the influence of ideas, by Samuel J. Konefsky. N.Y., Macmillian, 1956. 316p. +

A19, A57.1

Konefsky's book is primarily an analytical examination of the contribution of each man to certain areas of constitutional problems. His summaries of the issues are lucid, his quotations from the judgments are shrewdly chosen, and his estimate of the legal influence of these particular ideas is cogent. He has not, of course, written a hornbook. The book contains sound scholarship, wit and perception, even though one might cite a few contradictions in his opinions. See Univ. Fla. Law Rev. 10:112 (1957).

225

____. The mind and faith of Justice Holmes; his speeches, essays, letters, and judicial opinions. Selected and edited with introd. and commentary by Max Lerner. N.Y., Modern Library [1954, c1943.] 474p. *+
A1, A8, A14, A19, A21, A27, A28, A30, A35, A39, A43.5,A54, A56, A59, A63, A64, A71, A71.5, A72

This includes much that is in Holmes' Collected Legal Papers and also many of his opinions. If you can't read all of this book at least read The Path of the Law, one of Holmes' best known lectures. Dean Havighurst, Northwestern.

226

____. The Holmes Reader; the life, writings, speeches, constitutional decisions, etc., of the late Oliver Wendell Holmes, as well as an evaluation of his work and achievements by eminent authorities, selected and edited by Julius J. Marke. N.Y., Oceana, 1955. 282p. (Oceana's Docket series, No. 1). *+
A3, A6, A18, A19, A35, A41, A50, A55, A57.1

The editor has made a very judicious and satisfying selection of the very considerable amount of matter by and about Holmes. He also deserves credit for the eight page anthology in the appendix of some of Holmes' most brilliant epigrams, phrases and purple passages. It is an excellent book and contains a very well-balanced selection of material which gives a rounded picture of the man and presents the pith and marrow of his thought. See Jur. Rev. 1957, Pt. I:105.

227

HOLTZMANN, FANNY. The lady and the law; the remarkable life of Fanny Holtzmann by Ted Berkman. Boston, Little Brown, 1976. 403p.
A43.5, A57.1

Ms. Holtzmann's role in the creation of Israel and her libel suit involving Rasputin and MGM are among the biographical items covered in this book.

228

HOWE, WILLIAM F. Howe and Hummel, their true and scandalous history by Richard H. Rovere; illus. by Reginald Marsh....N.Y., Farrar, Straus, 1947. 190p. *+
A27, A64, A71.5

This pleasantly written and illustrated account of the life of two deplorable New York lawyers who flourished in the second half of the 19th century offers some welcome material for that mythical institution, the lawyer's leisure hour. See Law Q. Rev. 64:567 (1948).

229

HUGHES, CHARLES E. Charles Evans Hughes and American democratic statemanship, by Dexter Perkins. Boston, Little, Brown [1956] 200p. +
A19

A readable, scholarly account of a former Governor of N.Y., Republican nominee for President, leader of the bar and U.S. Supreme Court Justice.

230

___. Charles Evans Hughes, by Merlo J. Pusey. N.Y., Macmillan, 1951. 2 v. *+
A6, A7, A8, A12, A19, A21, A23, A27, A28, A29, A36, A41, A43.5, A44, A49, A57, A59, A61, A62, A68, A72

A definitive and interesting account of a famous recent leader of the legal profession. [A12] First year law students should read this and then re-read in 2nd and 3rd years. They will get more out of it based on their wider legal background.

[No. 231 is saved]

232

HUMPHREYS, SIR TRAVERS. His career and cases, by Bechhofer Roberts. London, The Bodley Head, 1936. 336p. +
A23

An entertaining account of the more interesting cases with which Sir Travers was connected, first as counsel, then as a judge. All types of cases are related with the majority involving murder. Many are better stories than the very best detective stories. Sir Travers "matched steel" with the most brilliant and resourceful members of the English bar. See Canadian Bar Rev. 15:211 (1937). See also Sir Humphreys' Criminal Days (1946). [A74]

233

JAY, JOHN. John Jay, defender of liberty against kings and peoples, by Frank Monaghan. N.Y., Bobbs, Merril, 1935. 497p. +
A19

Jay was the first Chief Justice of the U.S., appointed by Washington who was noted for his careful and judicious appointments. He also contributed to the Federalist Papers and is noted for his opinion in Chrisholm v. Georgia. This is a scholarly book, yet written with style.

234

JEFFERSON, THOMAS, Pres., U.S. Jefferson and Hamilton; the struggle for democracy in America, by Claude G. Bowers. Boston and N.Y., Houghton Mifflin Co. [1926.] 531p. +
A59

W. E. Dodd reviewing this book in the N.Y. Tribune, Dec. 6, 1925, considered it to be "the most interesting book that has ever been written about the two great antagonists this country has produced, and the truest story of Jefferson and Hamilton."

235

____. Thomas Jefferson, an intimate history by Fawn McKay Brodie. N.Y., Norton, 1974. 591p.
A25.5

The paradoxes of Jefferson's life, particularly his alleged love affair with a black slave, Sally Hemmings.

236

____. Thomas Jefferson, the Apostle of Americanism, by Gilbert Chinard. Boston, Little, Brown, 1929. 548p. *+
A28, A35, A59, A61

This is the anti-Federalist viewpoint.

237

JEFFREYS, GEORGE JEFFREYS, 1st baron. Judge Jeffreys, by H. Montgomery Hyde. London [etc.] G. G. Harrap. [1940.] 328p. +
A19, A28

Authoritative biography of "Bloody Jeffreys" - the "hanging judge" of 17th century England. A book of absorbing interest and high literary craftsmanship. Jeffreys was an extraordinary lawyer and judge. See A.B.A.Jl. 35:124. See also Mr. Hyde's Norman Birkett (1964).

238

____.Jeffreys by P.J. Helm. N.Y., Thomas Y. Crowell, 1966. 201p.
A43.5

"Sir George Jeffreys clawed his way to the top in the roiling Restoration to become at age thirty-eight the youngest Lord Chief Justice of England, and two years later its youngest Lord Chancellor. Laymen ... will probably find the work entertaining and may be more inclined than experts to accept Helm's thesis that Jeffreys received a bad press from his Whig enemies." Colin Rhys Lovell, So. Cal. Law Rev. 40:742 (1967).

239

JOHNSON, ANDREW, Pres. U.S. Andrew Johnson; a study in courage, by Lloyd P. Stryker. N.Y., Macmillan, 1929. 881p. +
A27

This well written study of the controversial 17th president of the U.S. has been commended for the careful research it reflects.

240

JOHNSON, SAMUEL. Samuel Johnson by W. Jackson Bate. N.Y., Harcourt, Brace, Jovanovich, 1975. 646p.
A30.5

"The quintessential presentation of the life of Johnson and as a monument of genre. ... His closest American legal counterparts are Roscoe Pound and Chief Justice John Marshall ...(1) he represents an articulate, even brilliant, position for a Christian lawyer who believes that the ultimate values on which legal systems ought to be based are values revealed by God to man in scripture and theological teaching; and (2) he represents, to a wider group, the power and success that a thinker can obtain by the use of reason in applying values to concrete situations ... with what zest Johnson would take on the legal profession today." J.Allen Smith, Vanderbilt Law Rev. 32:1032 (1979).

241

____. Dr. Johnson and the English law, by Edward L. McAdam. [Syracuse, N.Y.] Syracuse Press [1951.] 209p.
A27

See No. 242

242

____. Dr. Johnson and the law, by Sir Arnold D. McNair. Cambridge, Univ. Press, 1948. 114p. +
A28

Samuel Johnson was deeply interested in law and had a predilection for the society of lawyers in a period of English legal history which is illuminated by such names as those of Hardwicke, Mansfield, Stowell and Blackstone. His reactions to the personalities and achievements of these great men are of absorbing interest. See Law Q. Rev. 65:384 (1949).

243

JOHNSON, WILLIAM. Justice William Johnson, the first dissenter; the career and constitutional philosophy of a Jeffersonian judge, by Donald G. Morgan. Columbia, Univ. of S.C. Press, 1954. 326p. +
A43.5, A58

Recommended as of particular local interest in South Carolina. Dean Prince, Univ. of S. C.

244

KENNEDY, FLORYNCE. Color me Flo; my hard life and good times. E.C., Prentice-Hall, 1976. 168p.
A43.5

An influential New York lawyer who participated in many public causes.

245

KENNEDY, ROBERT F. Kennedy justice by Victor Navasky. N. Y., Atheneum, 1971. 482p.
A72.5

"... an excellent study of the Justice Department under Robert F. Kennedy. [his relations with FBI's Hoover, Jimmy Hoffa, etc. are all explored]. Fred J. Naffziger, A.B.A.Jl 58:505 (1972).

246

KENT, JAMES. James Kent, a study in conservatism, 1763-1847, by John T. Horton. N.Y., Appleton [c1939.] 354p. +
A25.5, A45

James Kent was Justice of the Supreme Court of N.Y. for six years, Chief Justice for ten years, and thereafter Chancellor of N.Y. for nine years. He is listed by Dean Pound as one of the ten judges ranked first in American judicial history. He is also noted as the author of Kent's Commentaries on American Law. This biography is interesting and well documented.

247

KNOX, JOHN C. A judge comes of age. N.Y., Scribner's, 1940. 353p. +
A11

Experiences of a federal district judge. "He must be economist, scientist and sailor as well as lawyer." Interesting book with some good anecdotes. See Harvard Law Rev. 54:543 (1941).

248

LaFOLLETTE, ROBERT M. Robert M. LaFollette, June 14, 1855—June 18, 1925, by Belle Case LaFollette and Fala LaFollette. N.Y., Macmillan, 1953. 2 v. +
A28

This biography is of value in that it is also a deeply revealing study of American politics in that critical first quarter of the 20th century. It is an admirable documented, detailed, fast moving, interpretive narrative history of progressive politics and statesmanship in the U.S. from the mid-eighties to the mid-twenties with finely etched portraits of the leading actors in the political and economic scene. See Library J. 78:1681

249

LEE, ROBERT E. Robert E. Lee, by Douglas S. Freeman. N.Y., Scribner's, 1934-35. 4 v. +
A59

An excellent study not only of the leader of the Confederate armies, but also of the Civil War and its period.

250

LEIBOWITZ, SAMUEL S. Courtroom, the story of Samuel S. Leibowitz, by Quentin J. Reynolds. N.Y., Farrar, Straus, 1950. 419p. *+
A15, A22, A27, A36, A43, A43.5, A64, A71.5, A72

A study of the technique used by Leibowitz during his life in the criminal courtroom and a series of vignettes of the lives of the men and women he defended. [A43] A dazzling narrative of a thrilling professional career. Read this book. If you are a student of courtroom technique, you will learn much here. See Univ. Chicago Law Rev. 18:412 (1951).

[Nos. 251, 252 saved]

253

LEVY, NEWMAN. My double life. N.Y., Doubleday, 1958. 316p.
A29.5

"Within the pages of this book...are nuggets of wisdom wittily purveyed for the profession and the laity. ...[N]ot a book just for lawyers, ow writers, or musicians - its real charm is that it will absorb any reader who enjoys meeting a fascinating man who has led a full life." Roger Bryant Hunting, The Record 13:233 (1958).

254

LINCOLN, ABRAHAM, Pres., U.S. 1809-1858, by Albert J. Beveridge. Boston and N.Y., Houghton, Mifflin, 1928. 2v. *+
A28, A35, A61

Lincoln practised law at the Springfield bar for 25 years. He was considered a good lawyer. Although unfinished, this book is as important a work as Beveridge's life of Marshall. It is based on a wealth of documentation and original material.

255

____. Lincoln, the lawyer, by Frederick T. Hill. N.Y., Century, 1912. 334p. *+
A40, A44

A careful study of Lincoln the lawyer based on much original research.

256

____. Abraham Lincoln, the prairie years..., by Carl Sandburg. N.Y., Harcourt, Brace, [c1927.] 2 v. *+
A28, A35, A61

Sandburg presents an artistic description of Lincoln. See also his Abraham Lincoln: the war years (4 vols. 1939).

257

LYNN, CONRAD. There is a fountain; the autobiography of a civil rights lawyer. Westport, Conn., Lawrence Hill, 1979. 240p.
A35.5

"... Lynn for many years was the only Black lawyer handling political cases for Black people in the United States [this review discusses Lynn's participation in the

"Harlem Six" case, conscription cases, segregation, National Lawyers Guild, etc.]. L.B. Boudin, Vanderbilt Law Rev. 33:251 (1980).

258

MACMILLAN, HUGH PATTISON MACMILLAN, baron. A man of law's tale. The reminiscences of the Rt. Hon. Lord Macmillan. London, Macmillan, 1953. 378p. *+
A27, A43, A58

A superior legal mind here portrays his professional work and his many avocations without ostentation. His life is an example of what may be done in the profession through ability, industry and public spirit. [A43]

259

MADISON, JAMES, Pres., U.S. James Madison, by Irving Brant. Indianapolis, Bobbs, Merrill, [1941-1961] (v. 1—The Virginia Revolutionist; v. 2—The Nationalist, 1780-1787; v. 3—Father of the Constitution, 1787-1800; v. 4—Secretary of State, 1800-1809.; v. 5—The President, 1809-1812; v. 6—Commander in Chief, 1812-1836).+
A19, A28

A thorough and understanding biography of a leading theorist of the constitution. Mr. Brant has also written _The Bill of Rights, its origin and meaning_ (1965); _Impeachment, trials and errors_ (1972); and _Storm over the Constitution_ (1936).

260

____. James Madison, philosopher of the Constitution, by Edward M. Burns. New Brunswick, Rutgers Univ. Press, 1938. 212p. N.Y., Octagon Books, 1968. 240p.
A25.5

261

MAITLAND, FREDERIC W. The Frederic William Maitland Reader, by V. T. H. Delaney. N.Y., Oceana, 1957. 254p. (Docket Series No. 10.). *+
A3, A19, A27.5, A35, A41, A50, A55, A57.1

Maitland was probably the greatest English legal historian since Lord Coke. His literary style is very attractive. See No. 204 for annotation on this book.

262

____. Frederic William Maitland, Downing professor of the laws of England; a biographical sketch by H. A. L. Fisher. Cambridge, Univ. Press, 1910. 179p. +
A28

An inspiring sketch of a great English law teacher and historian. See Harvard Law Rev. 58:603 (1945).

263

MARSHALL, JOHN. John Marshall, a life in law by Leonard Baker. N.Y., Macmillan, 1974. 846p.
A35.5, A53, A57.1

"A sizeable share of Beveridge's [life of Marshall] outlined 'the times' in which Marshall lived...By contrast, Baker...concentrates instead on Marshall the man...What is lacking in Baker's development of the theme is a picture of John Marshall as a craftsman of the law, influencing the course of public policy by his choices on questions of the day...the book contains little synthesis of Marshall's constitutional doctrines...a book that is impressive in places...Beveridge's work remains the stronger overall..." [The review has a listing of books and articles about Marshall since Beveridge's biography] D. Grier Stephenson, Southern California Law Rev. 48:959 (1975).

264

____. The life of John Marshall, by Albert J. Beveridge. Boston and N.Y., Houghton, Mifflin, 1916-1919. 4 v. *+
A1, A2, A4, A6, A7, A8, A9, A14, A19, A21, A25, A27, A28, A30, A35, A39, A40, A41, A43, A43.5, A44, A49, A54, A56, A57, A59, A61, A62, A63, A67, A68, A71, A71.5, A72

Marshall was Chief Justice of the U.S. for 34 years (1801-1835). He is one of the ten judges ranked first in American judicial history by Dean Pound. This detailed biography of the famous Chief Justice is definitive and enables the student's understanding of the law to grow, as the law itself grew, in virgin soil. [A54] It is an American classic.

265

____. Chief Justice; John Marshall and the growth of the Republic, by David G. Loth. N.Y., Norton [1949.] 295p. *+
A27, A72

A well written, readable account, although little attempt is made too synthesize and interpret Marshall's career. See James A.Servies, Bibliography of John Marshall (1956).

266

____. The Marshall reader: the life and contributions of Chief Justice John Marshall, by Erwin C. Surrency. Bicentenary ed. N.Y., Oceana, 1955. 256p. (Docket Series, No. 3.). +
A3, A6, A31, A50, A57.1

A judicious selection from the mass of available material. See Jur. Rev. 1957, pt. 1:108. Contains life, decisions, speeches and other pertinent works by and about him.

267

MASON, JEREMIAH. Memoirs of..., by G. J. Clark. Boston, Boston Law Book Co. [c1917.] 491p. +
A28

This is a reprint of a privately printed edition of 1873. "If you asked me," once said Daniel Webster, "who is the greatest lawyer I have known, I should say 'Chief Justice Marshall,' but if you took me by the throat and pushed me to the wall,, I should say 'Jeremiah Mason'." See Lewis, Great Amer. Lawyers.

268

MEDINA, HAROLD R. Judge Medina, a biography, by Hawthorne Daniel. N.Y., W. Funk [1952.] 373p. +
A27

A biography of a former professor of law and leading federal judge who presided in the Communist Trial.

269

MILL, JOHN STUART. The life of John Stuart Mill, by Michael St. John Packe. N.Y., Macmillan, 1954. 567p. +
A19

An admirable biography of the great 19th century liberal, economist and philosopher. It carries the reader along like a first-rate novel, yet Mr. Packe never invents conversations or inner thoughts, but supplies documentation for all his statements. It throws entirely new light on Mill's character and supplements the material in Mill's autobiography. See Hazlitt, The Free Man's Library.

270

MILLER, SAMUEL F. Mr. Justice Miller and the Supreme Court, 1862-1890, by Charles Fairman. Cambridge, Mass., Harvard Univ. Press, 1939. 456p. *+
A27, A28, A41, A43.5, A45, A54, A59, A61, A64

This book gives an intriguing insight into the inner workings of the conference chamber of our highest tribunal. It is also a noteworthy biography of the judge and history of the court. [A54]

271

____. Samuel Freeman Miller by Charles Gregory. Iowa City, The State Historical Society of Iowa, 1907. 217p.
A25.5

272

MCKNOWN, DAVE R. The dean; the life of Julien C. Monnet. Norman, Univ. of Oklahoma Press, 1973. 294p.
A24.5

The biography of a successful practitioner who became Dean of the Oklahoma Law School. "... the human content of the story gives it universal appeal." A.A. White, Houston Law Rev. 12:293 (1974-5).

273

MORGAN, CHARLES JR. A time to speak. N.Y., Harper & Row, 1964. 177p.
A29.5

"After beginning the practice of law, Morgan represented many types of unpopular defendants: Negroes, students, ministers, workers for SNCC. ...He involved himself in causes which most Alabama lawyers would not have touched under any circumstances, and yet he was still considered of the moderates; he was trying very hard to establish a practice, to live with his family in a suburban community, to maintain his status as a member of Birmingham's middle class." David H. Jacobs, Conn. Bar Jl 39:480 (1965).

274

MURPHY, FRANK. Mr. Justice Murphy; a political biography by J. Woodford Howard. Princeton University Press, 1968. 578p.
A29.5

"...underlying [Justice] Murphy's work was a coherent, however roughhewn, jurisprudence, which is evidenced by much of the material in this book ... I cannot escape the conclusion that this is a major contribution to the literature on the American Supreme Court." Walter F. Murphy, Yale Law Jl 78:725 (1969).

275

____. Mr. Justice Murphy and the Bill of Rights by Harold Norris. N.Y., Oceana, 1965. 568p.
A29.5

"In format, the book is an edited volume containing over seventy opinions by the Justice, a few of his speeches, excerpts from commentaries, and introductory essays by the author which are designed to link these materials to current issues." J. Woodford Howard, Duke Law Jl 1966:866 (1966).

276

OLENDER, TERRYS T. For the prosecution: Miss Deputy D.A. Phila., Chilton, 1961. 380p.
A43.5

277

PARRY, SIR EDWARD ABBOTT. My own way; an autobiography ...London, Cassell [1932.] 319p. *+
A19, A27, A28, A35, A36

A humane English County Court Judge, who is much concerned with law in action, especially its effects on the poor. See Harvard Law Rev. 58:601 (1945).

278

PEPPER, GEORGE WHARTON. Philadelphia lawyer, an autobiography ... Phila., Lippincott [1944.] 407p. *+
A1, A8, A11, A19, A27, A28, A35, A36, A39, A43.5, A44, A49, A54, A56, A58, A59, A61, A63, A68, A71

A counterpart for the Partridge, Country Lawyer, story [see No. 899], being in this instance the autobiography of a successful city lawyer who had an eventful career at the bar and as a legislator. [A54] A delightful book, written with fluent, literary style. See Harvard Law Rev. 58:291 (1944). See also Arthur G. Hays [No. 208]

279

POLLOCK, SIR FREDERICK, bart. For my grandson; remembrances of an ancient Victorian....Lond., J. Murray [1933.] 232p. *+
A22, A27, A28, A35

Pollock is known not only for his text books on contracts and torts and his First Book of Jurisprudence and his collaboration with Maitland, but also for his correspondence with Justice Holmes. He was also the founder of the Selden Society and editor of the Law Quarterly Review. His "remembrances" vividly portray people, customs and events of the past.

280

POUND, ROSCOE. The life of Roscoe Pound: philosopher of law, by Paul Sayre. Iowa City, State Univ. of Iowa, 1948. 412p. Also published by Greenwood Press, 1974.
A29.5

See also David Wigdor, Roscoe Pound, philosopher of law (1974) [A57.1] See also index for other books and annotations on this famous American legal philosopher and former Dean of the Harvard Law School.

[Nos. 281 and 282 saved]

283

READING, RUFUS ISAACS, 1st marquis of. Rufus Isaacs, first Marquis of Reading,...by his son, the Marquis of Reading. N.Y., Putnam's, [c1940.] 2 v. *+
A72

Lord Reading made a great reputation in England as an advocate at a time when other great advocates flourished, such as Carson, Simons and F. E. Smith. He was a master analyst of difficult commercial and financial transactions.

284

____. Lord Reading and his cases: the study of a great career, by Derek Walker-Smith. N.Y., Macmillan, 1934. 400p. *+
A74

Herschel Brickell considers this "a grand book altogether."

285

RERAT, EUGENE A. The people's lawyer; the life of Eugene A. Rerat, by Paul A. Sevareid. Ross & Haines, 1963, 260p.
A48.5

286

RIIS, JACOB A. The making of an American, with an introd. by Theodore Roosevelt. N.Y., Macmillan, 1937. 284p. (First published in 1901). *+
A35, A59, A61

Riis was a journalist, author and reformer, particularly interested in slum clearance in N.Y. and elimination of conditions that bred crime therein. He became the enemy of politicians and a trusted friend of Theodore Roosevelt. He has been described as the "great emancipator" of the slums.

287

ROOT, ELIHU. Elihu Root and the conservative tradition, by Richard W. Leopold. Boston, Little, Brown, 1954. 222p. +
A19, A43.5

This is a study of the interaction between Elihu Root and history. His life is not stressed. Root is interesting to the legal profession as an example of one of the greatest American business lawyers in government service. See Harvard Law Rev. 68:743 (1955).

288

RUTLEDGE, WILEY. Justice Rutledge and the bright constellation, by Fowler V. Harper. Indianapolis, Bobbs-Merrill, 1965. 406p.
A43.5

"... an authorized biography drawn from the Rutledge papers, which have not otherwise been opened to the public. ...Much of the content is a series of essays by the author on those portions of the Constitution that most concerned Mr. Justice Rutledge, particularly those sections of the Bill of Rights which the author calls the Bright Constellation. included in these discussions are such matters as due process of law, freedom of speech and press, religious freedom and establishment, search and seizure, and the right to the assistance of counsel." Eugene Gressman, Michigan Law Rev. 64:166 (1965).

289

SCHWARTZ, HELENE E. **Lawyering.** N.Y., Farrar, Straus, & Giroux, 1976. 308p.
A35.5, A57.1

Ms. Schwartz has represented William Buckley, Abbie Hoffman, the Chicago Eight, and many others. She also recounts sexism in legal practice.

290

SEWALL, SAMUEL. Samuel Sewall of Boston; a biography of a chief justice, by Ola Elizabeth Winslow. N.Y., Macmillan, 1964. 235p.
A43.5

Judge Sewall presided over the infamous Salem witch trials. The State House in Boston contains a mural of Judge Sewall's public repentance for his role in the witchcraft trials. For other Boston episodes of legal significance, see Bander, The Path of the law, a lawyer's tour of Boston (1979).

291

SHAW, LEMUEL. The law of the Commonwealth and Chief Justice Shaw, by Leonard W. Levy. London, Oxford Univ. Press, 1957. 383p.
A43.5, A57.1

"During his term of office Chief Justice Shaw wrote more than 2,000 opinions in which he did much to mould not only the law of his own state, but also that of the other States in the Union. ...Professor Levy's book is to be welcomed as a contribution to American legal history which, unfortunately, has been neglected in the American law schools." A.L. Goodhart, Law Q. Rev. 74:140 (1958).

292

SHIRAS, GEORGE, Jr. Justice George Shiras, Jr., of Pittsburgh, Associate Justice of the U.S. Supreme Court, 1892-1903; a chronicle of his family, life, and times, by George Shiras, 3rd. Edited and completed, 1953, by Winfield Shiras. [Pittsburgh] Univ. of Pitts. Press [1953.] 256p. +
A27

A saga of a notable and substantial family. Four chapters are devoted to Justice Shiras' 10 1/2 years on the Supreme Court. Although he was not a great judge, nor a colorful one—the book is very interesting and we are wiser for this biography. See Yale Law Jl 63:431 (1954).

293

STONE, HARLAN F. Chief Justice Stone and the Supreme Court, by Samuel J. Konefsky, with a prefatory note by Charles A. Beard. N.Y., Macmillan, 1946. 290p. +
A28

Konefsky brings out the role of the Constitutional Judge. His book is of value as a descriptive analysis of constitutional development in the period from 1925 to 1945. See Harvard Law Rev. 49:305 (1945).

294

____. Harlan Fiske Stone: pillar of the law, by Alpheus T. Mason. N.Y., Viking, 1956. 914p. *+
A19, A43.5, A47, A62, A64, A67

A readable, authoritative and scholarly study of a Chief Justice of the U.S.

295

STORY, JOSEPH. Joseph Story and the American Constitution, by James McClellan. Norman, Univ. of Oklahoma Press, 1971. 413p.
A29.5

The author wrote this book primarily "to supply a basic philosophical and theoretical understanding of Justice Story's constitutionalism, ...but also to elevate a relatively obscure figure to his rightful place in American History." John F. Hagemann, South Dakota Law Rev. 17:523 (1972).

296

____. Justice Joseph Story and the rise of the Supreme Court, by Gerald T. Dunne. N.Y., Simon and Schuster, 1970. 458p.
A35.5

"...the first biography of Story...[the author] has given us much in a single volume, but a single volume is simply not enough. ...Dunne concludes that Justice Story made four major contributions to the development of American law, and these he made more as a scholar than as a judge deciding great cases. First were his treatises ... Second, he founded Harvard Law School ... Third, he taught American judges how to write judicial opinions ... And fourth, he carried the traditions of John Marshall forward onto the Taney court and thereby served as a modifying influence during what otherwise might have been an era of disruptive change." John Phillip Reid, N.Y.U. Law Rev. 46:1210 (1971).

297

STRONG, GEORGE TEMPLETON. Diary of..., edited by Allan Nevins. N.Y., Macmillan, 1952. 4 v. +
A19

Strong (1820-1875) was in active legal practice from

1841 until he retired from the bar in 1872. He was influential in refounding Columbia Univ. Law School in 1856. The diary brings this out as well as his reactions to public affairs, Civil War, art, literature, etc., of the period. See Columbia Law Rev. 53:586 (1953).

298

SUTHERLAND, GEORGE. Mr. Justice Sutherland, a man against the state, by Joel F. Paschal. Princeton, Princeton Univ. Press, 1951. 267p. +
A7, A27, A28, A43.5

A serious, sympathetic study of a leading conservative jurist, this biography fills a large need in the scholarship of recent American history. See U.S. Quarterly Bk. Rev. 7:341. Sutherland was called the workhorse of the Old Guard on the Supreme Court of the 1920's and 1930's.

299

TAFT, WILLIAM HOWARD. William Howard Taft; Chief Justice, by Alpheus Thomas Mason. N.Y., Simon and Schuster, 1964. 354p.
A43.5

"...reviews Taft's nine years as Chief Justice. [T]ells the story of Taft's long preparation in his years as Solicitor General, as circuit judge, as Governor of the Philippines, as Secretary of War, as President of the United States, and then, during a quiet interlude, as Kent Professor of Law at Yale." Arthur E. Sutherland, Harvard Law Rev. 79:222 (1965).

300

____. The life and times of William Howard Taft; a biography, by Henry F. Pringle. ...N.Y., Farrar & Rinehart, Inc. [c1939.] 2 v. +
A45

Robert Carr has written of this biography that the chapters on Taft's judicial career were necessarily somewhat secondary. Nonetheless, along with Fairman's Miller, this is one of the best biographical studies of a Supreme Court Justice.

301

TANEY, ROGER B. Without fear or favor; a biography of Chief Justice Roger Brooke Taney, by Walker Lewis. Boston, Houghton Mifflin Co., 1965. 556p.
A43.5

"...follows the pattern of a life and times...The ordinary citizen knows Taney as the Jackson stalwart of the Bank War and as the Chief Justice who read the Dred Scott decision. ...As the author shows, Taney hoped to keep the court clear of party politics, a task that proved difficult during the Jackson period and impossible during the hectic years of the slavery controversy." Aubrey C. Land, Maryland Law Rev. 26:97 (1966).

302

____. Roger B. Taney, by Carl B. Swisher. N.Y., Macmillan, 1935. 608p. *+
A1, A2, A7, A14, A19, A21, A27, A28, A30, A39, A41, A43.5A45, A54, A56, A59, A61, A63, A68, A71, A72

The best biography of this great Chief Justice which raises one's deep respect for Taney as a man, a statesman and a judge. [A54] A scholarly, but readable biography with emphasis on the political developments which shaped his career in politics and on the Supreme Court. [A39]

303

TRAIN, ARTHUR CHEYNEY. My day in court. N.Y., Scribner's, 1939. 520p.
A27, A28, A35, A36, A45, A61, A62, A64

The creator of Mr. Tutt was formerly a prosecuting attorney in N.Y.C. as narrated in his autobiography. His memoirs are highly entertaining. See Harvard Law Rev. 58:602 (1945).

304

ULMAN, JOSEPH N. A judge takes the stand. N.Y., Knopf, 1933. 289p. *+
A11, A12, A22, A23, A29, A35, A36, A38.5, A43, A44, A49, A64

A trial judge's first-hand account of what happened in his court room with shrewd comments. Recommended for 1st year students by Harvard, and then to be re-read in 2nd and 3rd years. Will be understood better then with legal background.

305

[VOELKER, JOHN DONALDSON]. Trouble-shooter; the story of a Northwoods prosecutor, [by] Robert Traver [pseud.] N.Y., Viking Press, 1943. 294p. *+
A44

Another well told collection of good stories of a lawyer's life. The experiences of a prosecuting attorney in the Northwoods are very instructive. [See also No. 928].

306

WAITE, MORRISON R. Morrison R. Waite; the triumph of character, by C. Peter Magrath. N.Y., Macmillan Co., 1963. 334p.
A24.5

"The principal aims of the author is to refute the common if not universal judgment that Waite was an indistinguished Chief Justice and a mediocre man, to assert that he was on the contrary 'a worthy successor to Marshall and Taney.'" Robert G. McCloskey, Harvard Law Rev. 77:1171 (1964).

307

WALDMAN, LOUIS....Labor lawyer. N.Y., Dutton, 1944. 394p. *+
A28, A35, A36, A59

Waldman was a specialist in labor law and this is a recital of his many battles.

308

WARREN, EARL. The memoirs of Earl Warren. N.Y., Doubleday, 1977. 394p.
A43.5, A48.5, A57.1

[list of biographies of justices] "...a far more detailed view behind the judicial curtain, and a more significant revelation of Warren himself, than heretofore has been available to students of the Court and this Chief Justice..." William F. Swindler, William and Mary Law Rev. 19:159 (1970). See also G. Edward White, Earl Warren: a public life (1982) and Bernard Schwartz, Super Chief: Earl Warren and his Supreme Court - a judicial biography (1983). These two books are reviewed by Dennis J. Hutchinson in Michigan Law Rev. 81:922 (1983). See also Jack H. Pollack, Earl Warren, the Judge who changed America (1979). [See also No. 2175].

309

WATROUS, JOHN C., def. The case of John C. Watrous, U.S. judge for Texas; a political story of high crimes and misdemeanors, by Wallace Hawkins. [Dallas] Univ. Press in Dallas, 1950. 109p. +
A28

Involves charges of dealing in fraudulent land certificates in Texas. Fine background material for the period.

310

WAYNE, JAMES M. James Moore Wayne, Southern unionist, by Alexander Lawrence. Chapel Hill, N.C., Univ. of N.C. Press, 1943. 250p. *+
A43

The story of a gentleman from Savannah who was elevated to the Supreme Court because of his political loyalty to Andrew Jackson. [A43]

WEBSTER, DANIEL.

Prof. Willis evaluates Webster as perhaps one of the two greatest constitutional lawyers of the U.S., stating that many of the arguments used by Marshall were made by Webster.

311

____....The devil and Daniel Webster, [by Stephen Vincent Benet]. N.Y., Farrar & Rinehart [1937.] 61p. *+
A27, A28, A35, A39, A43.5

The law student will find this of great interest. See Harvard Law Rev. 58:603 (1945). This is a fictionalized drama, yet it reflects the character, inspiration, and love of democracy of Daniel Webster. The story can be found in the anthology Law in Action [No. 867].

312

____. Daniel Webster, by Claude M. Fuess. Boston, Little, Brown, 1930. 2 v. +
A41, A43.5

This is considered to be one of the best biographies on Webster.

313

____. The Daniel Webster reader, edited by Bertha Rothe. N.Y., Oceana, 1956. 225p. (Docket Series No. 5.). *+
A3, A41, A50

A well-selected collection of source material on and by a great American statesman and constitutional lawyer. It contains his autobiographical sketch and specimens of his speeches, including his argument in the Dartmouth College Case and in McCulloch v. Maryland.

314

WELLMAN, FRANCIS LEWIS. Gentlemen of the jury; reminiscences of thirty years at the bar....N.Y., Macmillan, 1924. 298p. +
A45, A49

Wellman is noted for his Art of Cross-Examination and he has written this book "to acquaint jurors with the profound importance and dignity of their membership in ... trial by jury ... to open their minds to the fallacies of human testimony ...." The book, however, is more entertaining than instructive. See Ill. L. Rev. 19:714 (1925).

315

WIGMORE, JOHN HENRY. John Henry Wigmore; scholar and reformer, by William R. Roalfe. Evanston, Northwestern Univ. Press, 1977. 340p.
A21, A43.5

A famous professor, Dean, and legal scholar noted for his monumental set that is still published under the name of Wigmore on Evidence. Dean Wigmore and Justice Frankfurter squabbled over the Sacco-Vanzetti case.

316

WILLIAMS, MONTAGU S. Leaves of a life, being [his] reminiscences. N.Y., Macmillan, 1890. 2 v. +
A19

See annotation for No. 147.

317

WILLISTON, SAMUEL. Life and law; an autobiography. Boston, Little, Brown, 1940. 347 p. +
A11, A20

Williston on Contracts continues to be a leading treatise although Professor Williston is no longer here to guide its fortunes. Williston was noted as a teacher of law and as an inspiration for the thousands of students who studied under him. His thoughts, philosophy, and mode of life are well worth reading about. See Harvard Law Rev. 54:352 (1940).

318

WILSON, JAMES. James Wilson, founding father, 1742-1798, by Charles P. Smith. Chapel Hill, N.C., Univ. of N.C. Press for the Institute of Early American History and Culture [c1956.] 426p. +
A19, A43.5

Sanderson in his "Lives of the Signers" notes that a member of the Constitutional Convention of 1787 observed that in his opinion, the most able and useful members of the Convention were James Wilson and James Madison. Fiske calls Wilson one of the most learned jurists this country has ever seen.

319

WILSON, WOODROW. The Wilson reader, edited by Frances Farmer. N.Y., Oceana, 1956. 286p. (Docket Series No. 4.). +
A3, A41, A50, A57.1

Contains a good biography, selections from his more significant pronouncements, and appreciations and evaluations of his work and influence. Wilson's intellectual status and the importance of his presidency make this collection of considerable value. The book conveys a clear impression of the man and his achievements. See Jurid. Rev. 1957, Pt. I:108.

[Nos. 320-324 saved]

COLLECTIVE BIOGRAPHIES

325

BIRKENHEAD, Frederick Edwin Smith. Fourteen English judges. London & N.Y., Cassell & Co., 1926. 383p.
A74

The characteristics of the present work are precisely a charming style, a vivid fancy, exhaustive research. Each of these fourteen judges is here seen distinct with personality. They live as well as judge... Lord Macmillan.

326

DUNHAM, ALLISON, ed. Mr. Justice, edited [with] Philip B. Kurland. [Chicago] Univ. of Chicago Press. [1956.] 241p. *+
A22

Thumbnail sketches of Holmes, Marshall, Stone, Bradley, Brandeis, Sutherland, Hughes, Rutledge and Taney, all Supreme Court justices, written by "thinkers...who had acquired or attempted to acquire an understanding of a man called a Justice of the Supreme Court of the U.S." Each essay introduces the man in a way that the reader will be interested in finding out more about him.

327

FLANDERS, HENRY. The lives and times of the Chief Justices of the Supreme Court of the United States. Buffalo, Hein, 1971 [c.1891]
A43.5

An historical review of the times and the contemporaries of the judges presented such as John Jay, John Rutledge, William Cushing, Oliver Ellsworth, and John Marshall.

328

FRIEDMAN, LEON & FRED L. ISRAEL, eds. The Justices of the United States Supreme Court, 1789-1978; their lives and major opinions. N.Y., Chelsea House Publishers and Bowker & Co. 5 vols. A31.7

"...Biographical sketches of ninety-seven...Justices of the Supreme Court of the United States. Appended to each biography are two opinions, although occasionally there is but one and sometimes there are three, selected by the biographer as most representative of his subject's important judicial efforts." Philip B. Kurland, Michigan Law Rev. 69:778 (1971). The last Justice covered was Justice Stevens.

329

KENNEDY, JOHN F. Profiles in courage. N.Y., Harper, [c1956.] 266p. *+
A19, A22

Biographical vignettes of U.S. senators who have exhibited great moral courage in resisting pressures brought on them to submit to the interests of their constituents though against the national good. Exciting and stimulating reading.

330

LEWIS, WILLIAM D., ed. Great American lawyers; the lives and influences of judges and lawyers who have acquired permanent national reputation, and have developed the jurisprudence of the U.S. A history of the legal profession in America. Phila., Winston, 1907-1909. 8 v. +
A9, A19

Lewis offers more than a mere collection of biographical sketches — he also gives the development of our legal institutions and a grasp of the personality of the man and his times. Ninety-six leaders of the bench and bar from colonial days to the 20th century are so treated by outstanding lawyers and jurists.

331

MACDONELL, SIR JOHN, ed....Great jurists of the world. ... [with] Edward Manson...[and] introduction by Van Vechten Veeder ...with portraits. Boston, Little, Brown, 1914. 607p. +
A62

Although lacking many Anglo-American and important jurists, there still is nothing like it.

332

SEAGLE, WILLIAM. Men of law from Hammurabi to Holmes. N.Y., Macmillan, 1947. 391p. *+
A1, A3, A12, A14, A19, A20, A21, A23, A27, A29, A30, A39, A41, A43, A47, A56, A59, A63, A64, A68, A72

The life stories of 14 men who made legal history, written with great sensitivity to the role of law in modern society. [A39] Men selected are from 8 different countries over a period of 4000 years. These are splendid short studies of great jurists. Harvard recommends for 1st year students, to be re-read in 2nd and 3rd years.

333

SHIENTAG, BERNARD L. Moulders of legal thought. N.Y., Viking, 1943. 253p. *+
A28, A64, A71

Judge Shientag thoughtfully studies the opinions and writings of Judge Cardozo, Lord Mansfield, Sir Samuel Romilly, Sir Frederick Pollock, Lord Macmillan and Lord Wright. Paxton Blair has commented that "the study of the various essays in this volume will be an intellectual experience — rare and memorable." See Columbia Law Rev. 44:111 (1944).

334

UMBREIT, KENNETH B. Our eleven chief justices; a history of the Supreme Court in terms of their personalities. ...N.Y., Harper [1938.] 539p. *+
A22, A25.5, A45

An engaging book which tells the story of the lives of the Chief Justices from the standpoint of their inheritances and personal interests. Lawyers, generally should enjoy it. A good bibliography appended to the book suggests much worthwhile reading on the subject. See A.B.A.Jl 25:245 (1939).

335

VAN SANTVOORD, GEORGE. Sketches of the lives, times and

judicial services of the Chief Justices of the Supreme Court of the United States. 2d ed. Buffalo, Hein, 1977, c.1882. 740p.
A43.5

BUSINESS ORGANIZATIONS

340

BARNET, RICHARD J. and RONALD E. MILLER. Global reach; the power of the multinational corporations. N.Y., Simon and Schuster, 1974. 508p.
A72.5

"The authors have used the story of the multinational as a vehicle for expounding their ideological objections to capitalism. ...The authors contend that the [problem] created by the multinational companies ...poses a serious threat not only to our standard of living, but to our very survival ... Part I is concerned with the executives of the global companies ... Part II relates to the role of the global corporations in the developing countries ... [Part III the effects in the United States of the reorganization of the world economy into a Global Shopping Center and a Global Factory] ... exciting and alarming..." Michael J. McIntyre, Harvard International Law Jl 16:761 (1975).

341

EISENBERG, MELVIN ARON. The structure of the corporation. Boston, Little, Brown, 1976. 320p.
A31.7

"Next to government, the large corporation is probably the dominant economic and social institution in our society. ... Although [this book] neither raises all the questions nor furnishes all the answers, it moves us significantly toward a prescription of sound policy for corporate law. ... [The] most important chapters treat the role of management in corporate structure. ... [Eisenberg] finds the principal function of the board to be monitoring management, not giving advice, approving major transactions, or exercising control. The prime requirements of his model are independent directors and an adequate flow of information to the board." Donald E. Schwartz, Yale Law Jl 87:685 (1978). See also No. 1332 for the jurisprudential significance of the corporation.

CHRISTIANITY

345

AUGUSTINUS, AURELIUS, Bp. of Hippo. The City of God; translated by Marcus Dods; with an introd. by Thomas Merton. N.Y., Modern Library, [1950.] 892p. +
A59

Augustine represented the conflicting forces of antiquity (Cicero, Plotinus) and Christianity (Bible, Church fathers) and combined in himself the pagan and Christian currents and undercurrents of the first four centuries of Christianity. His work on The City of God marks the transition of Christianity from adolescence to maturity. It influenced radically the theology and philosophy, the political doctrines and economic precepts of the Middle Ages. Encyc. of Soc. Sci. II:314.

346

DRINAN, ROBERT F. Religion, the courts, and public policy. N.Y., McGraw-Hill, 1963. 261p.
A29.5

"Drinan catalogues the current areas of church-state controversy in the United States and proceeds, with admirable forensic talents, to proofs of the validity of the Catholic position as to each. Essentially, the proofs are of two different kinds. One is concerned with the details of legal controversies,, the cases and arguments with which courts must deal in order to resolve the litigation before them. The second is an appeal to what is obviously regarded as a higher command, a request for conduct that is not governed by the limitations of the first amendment of the Constitution." Philip B. Kurland, Harvard Law Rev. 77:1374 (1964)

347

PFEFFER, LEO. God, Caesar and the constitution; the court as referee of church-state confrontation. Boston, Beacon Press, 1975. 390p.
A57.1

A civil libertarian's approach to church and state.

CIVIL LAW

350

MERRYMAN, JOHN HENRY. THE civil law tradition; an introduction to the legal systems of Western Europe and Latin America. Stanford, Stanford Univ. Press, 1969. 172p.
A24.5

The author writes for "the general reader who wants to know what it is that binds together the legal systems of Western Europe and Latin America, and that distinguishes them from the legal systems of the Anglo-American world." Focus is on historical development, institutional arrangements, and official doctrine. Arthur T. von Mehren, Harvard Law Rev. 83:1954 (1970).

351

WATSON, ALAN. The making of the civil law. Cambridge, Harvard Univ. Press, 1981. 201p.
A24.5

See review by Charles Donahue, Jr. in Michigan Law Rev. 81:972 (1983).

CIVIL LIBERTIES

360

ABRAHAM, HENRY J. Freedom and the court; civil rights and liberties in the United States. 4th ed. N.Y., Oxford Univ. Press, 1982. 443p.
A43.5

A survey of the court's work with chapters on the "double standard," Bill of Rights, due process, freedom of expression, religion, and race.

361

BALDWIN, ROGER N. Civil liberties and industrial conflict. Cambridge, Mass., Harvard Univ. Press, 1938. 137p. +
A45

A stimulating discussion of trade unions, strikes, lockouts, etc., and civil liberties.

362

BARRETT, EDWARD L. The Tenney committee; legislative investigation of subversive activities in California. Ithaca, Cornell Univ. Press, 1951. 400p.
A28

This book by a professor of law at the University of California is an objective account of a legislative committee investigating communism in California whose activities have stirred up much comment. One of the problems considered is that of "witch hunts."

363

CHAFEE, ZECHARIAH, Jr. The blessings of liberty. Phila., Lippincott [1956.] 350p. * +
A67

The late Prof. Chafee objects to practices which are cutting down our personal liberties, under the cloak of a threat to our national security. He discusses the loyalty and security programs, legislative investigations, denial of passports and banning of books. Although you may not agree with him, his scholarly approach will make you think.

364

____. Free speech in the U.S. Cambridge, Mass., Harvard Univ. Press, 1941. 634p. * +
A1, A2, A8, A14, A19, A20, A27, A28, A30, A33, A35, A39, A40, A56, A61, A63

A definitive study of the legal aspects of free speech in the U.S., of great value and interest to the layman as well as the lawyer. The author was a professor of law at Harvard Law School. [A39]

365

COMMISSION ON FREEDOM OF THE PRESS. Government and mass communications, by Zechariah Chafee, Jr. Chicago, Univ. of Chicago Press, [1947.] 2 v. +
A27

Examines past and present relations between government and the press, radio and motion pictures, from the standpoint of the individual (libel laws), public decency (obscenity regulations) and other public policies sometimes conflicting with absolute freedom of the press (labor laws, anti-trust laws). This is used as a background for an exhaustive discussion of proposals to make mass communication media more responsive to public needs. See Michigan Law Rev. 46:285 (1947).

366

DORSEN, NORMAN. Frontiers of civil liberties. N.Y., Pantheon Books, 1968. 420p.
A29.5

"Dorsen's book serves, among other things, to show how long and varied is the list of civil rights in the United States. [The] book is set up in four sections that draw the contours of the civil rights field. [Those sections include:] basic questions about the ability of our legal institutions to make good the promises extended by our Federal Constitution, our professed intolerance of censorship and thought-suppression, the fairness of our legal processes, discrimination." Jon R. Waltz, N.Y.U.Law Rev. 44:443 (1969)

367

____, ed. The rights of Americans; what they are - what they should be. N.Y., Pantheon, 1971, c1970. 679p.
A43.5

The right to essential of life (Robert L. Carter, Graham Hughes, Philip G. Schrag, etc.); right to vote, etc. (Howard I. Kalodner, Thomas I. Emerson, Harry Kalven, etc.); right of privacy, use of drugs, etc. (Leo Pfeffer, Leonard Boudin, etc.); rights of criminals, mental patients, etc. (Anthony G. Amsterdam, Bruce J. Ennis, etc.); rights of women, students, aliens, etc. (W. van Alstyne, Roy Lucas, Edward J. Ennis, etc.).

368

DOUGLAS, WILLIAM O. An almanac of liberty. Garden City, N.Y., Doubleday, 1954. 409p. +
A19, A57.1

With a short half to a full page essay for each of the days of a year, commencing appropriately with July 4 and ending with July 3, Mr. Justice Douglas presents facts and events that explicitly tell the import of the struggle for liberty in English and American history and impliedly emphasizes that the pursuit of liberty is a continuous daily task. See A.B.A.J. 41:254 (1955).

369

____. Points of rebellion. N.Y., Random House, 1969. 97p.
A48.5

The case for dissent by the young by a great dissenter.

370

EMERSON, THOMAS I., ed. Political and civil rights in the U.S., a collection of legal and related materials [with] David Haber. Foreword by Robert M. Hutchins. Buffalo, Dennis. [1952.] 1209p. (The 1967 edition adds Norman Dorsen as editor. This set is maintained with supplements by a variety of authors.). * +
A8

A collection of materials dealing with such problems as security of the person, negro suffrage, academic freedom, separation of Church and state, racial and religious discrimination, fair judicial procedures and the various aspects of freedom of expression. Although intended primarily for law students and lawyers as a casebook for study in law school, much of the material is distinctly non-legal. Editorial notes and bibliographical references are very helpful. See Columbia Law Rev. 53:290 (1953).

371

ERNST, MORRIS L. The first freedom. N.Y., Macmillan, 1946. 316p. +
A28

Discusses the economic restraints by which our First Freedom is stifled. Mr. Ernst attempts to awaken Americans to the dangers of centralized irresponsibility in the newspaper, radio and moving picture industries. See Harvard Law Rev. 59:1016 (1946). Dated but still significant as to the thinking of a leading civil liberties advocate of another generation.

372

FORTAS, ABE. Concerning dissent and civil disobedience. N.Y., New American Library, 1968. 127p.
A31.7

"Fortas, a former Supreme Court Associate Justice, has concentrated on a moral duty of obedience to law. Dissent is possible in a democracy, but disobedience of law can go unpunished only where the law is unconstitutional or invalid, and hence no law at all. His essential thesis is that law, and the democratic society with which Fortas equates it, bestow great benefits on the individual, so that the individual in turn owes a duty of obedience to those laws." Donald H.J. Hermann, Calif. Law Rev. 57:1281 (1969).

373

FRAENKEL, OSMOND K. The rights we have, revised to include the most important decisions of the United States Supreme Court through 1973. 2d ed. N.Y., Crowell, 1974. 246p.
A31.7

Mr. Fraenkel was a great civil liberties lawyer.

374

FROMM, ERICH. Escape from freedom. N.Y. Harcourt, Brace, 1941. 305p. * +
A8, A36

A searching inquiry into the meaning of freedom for modern man, part of a broad study of the character structure of man in our culture. The author stresses the role of psychological factors in the social process, interpreting the historical development of freedom in terms of man's awareness of himself as a significant separate being. See Library J. 66:614.

375

GELLHORN, WALTER. Individual freedom and governmental restraints. Baton Rouge, La. State Univ. Press, [c1956.] 215p. +
A19

These lectures are devoted to three facets of the never ending swing of the pendulum between individual freedom and governmental restraints, namely, the activities of and changing attitudes towards the administrative proceses, restraints on book reading and finally the fencing in of the right to make a living. See A.B.A.Jl 43:535 (1957).

376

GLAZER, NATHAN. Affirmative discrimination; ethnic inequality and public policy. N.Y., Basic Books, 1975. 248p.
A29.5

"Professor Glazer builds his argument on the premise that affirmative action remedies for racial discrimination are unconstitutional, unnecessary, and counterproductive. ...He asserts that racial quotas will not solve the problems of pathology, drugs, crime, and welfare which plague lower-class blacks; rather, the quotas unnecessarily aid middle-class blacks who, he claims, were doing well before affirmative action programs were implemented." Derrick A. Bell, Jr., Emory Law Jl 25:879 (1976). See also his collection of essays, Ethnic dilemmas 1964-1982 (1983).

377

GRAGLIA, LINO A. Disaster by decree; the Supreme Court's decisions on race and the schools. Ithaca, N.Y., Cornell Univ. Press, 1976. 351p.
A57.1

"...not a history of the Brown decision, but rather an account of the evolving requirements of desegregation as imposed by Brown and its progeny. As the title to his volume suggests, Graglia is a sharp critic of those judicial decisions which move toward mandating racial assignments and racial balance in the public schools." James W. Ely, Jr., Houston Law Rev. 14:955 (1977).

378

HAIGHT, ANNE (LYON). Banned books, 387 B.C. to 1978. 4th ed. N.Y., Bowker, 1978 A.D.. 196p. +
A27

Considers the problem of censorship as it pertains to books with an exhaustive listing of books and events relating to this theme.

379

JENCKS, CHRISTOPHER. Inequality; a reassessment of the effect of family and schooling in America. N.Y., Basic Books, 1972. 399p.
A29.5

"Both educators and laymen are likely to take umbrage at Christopher Jencks' conclusion that equalizing educational opportunity will not significantly alter the degree of economic inequality among adults. Bristling with controversial findings, [this book] might portend a new philosophy on the purpose of education in modern society." The sophisticated statistical technique called path analysis was employed to draw the conclusions. Christopher Smith, Jl of Law and Education 1:189 (1973).

380

KLUGER, RICHARD. Simple justice; the history of Brown vs. Board of Education and Black America's struggle for equality. N.Y., Knopf, 1976. 787p.
A2.5, A20.5, A43.5, A49, A57.1, A57.7

"The subtitle of this book ... accurately describes the depths to which America's black population had fallen after the heady, promise-filled days of the Reconstruction Period, and their struggle to regain lost ground in the effort to achieve racial equality after the turn of the century." Robert A. Mautino, Western State Univ. Law Rev. 3:353 (1976).

381

KONVITZ, MILTON R. The Constitution and civil rights. N.Y., Columbia Univ. Press, 1947. 254p. +
A20

Civil rights here are rights of persons to employment, accommodations in hotels, restaurants and common carriers and other places of public accommodation and resort. It is of value as a reference book for its appendices bring out the various federal and state laws. See Calif. L. Rev. 36:148 (1948). Professor Konvitz was a noted legal author and his probing analysis of constitutional issues should not be neglected.

382

KONVITZ, MILTON R. and THEODORE LESKES. A century of civil rights. N.Y., Columbia Univ. Press, 1961. 293p.
A31.7

"... covers the ante bellum slave system in the South, the Reconstruction legislation; the interpretation and application of current federal and state civil rights laws, and analyzes the prospects for success in ending racial discrimination in the United States." Marshall W. Krause, Stanford Law Rev. 14:422 (1962).

383

LEVY, LEONARD W. Legacy of suppression; freedom of speech and press in early American history. Cambridge, Harvard Univ. Press, 1960. 353p.
A31.7

"...the work of a careful scholar as well as a creative thinker. Dean Levy has drawn upon recently published documents and has gone to considerable lengths to search out original materials on which to base his history of seditious libel as it relates to the Original Understanding of the first amendment's Framers. The truly new and important contribution of this work, however, is the author's own fresh and thoughtful analysis of evidence that has long been generally available." Stanford Law Rev. 13:991 (1961). [See also No. 462].

384

MARSHALL, BURKE. Federalism and civil rights. N.Y., Columbia Univ. Press, 1964. 85p.
A31.7

"On one level, the book is an analysis of a few of the problems that arise because the struggle for civil rights in the South has occurred within a federal system; on another level the book is a brief for the Government and, more specifically, for the policies of intervention and nonintervention adhered to by the Department of Justice in this struggle." Richard A. Wasserstrom, Univ. of Chicago Law Rev. 33:406 (1966)

385

MEIKLEJOHN, ALEXANDER. Political freedom. N.Y., Harper Bros., 1960. 166p.
A31.7

"...a philosophical study of the First Amendment's guarantee of freedom of expression...Part of Meiklejohn's book consists of articles and letters dealing with academic freedom, congressional committees, and the privilege against self-incrimination." [also a review of Charles L. Black, The People and the Court; Walter Gellhorn, American Rights; and Osmond K.Fraenkel, The Supreme Court and Civil Liberties]. Osmond K. Fraenkel, Notre Dame Lawyer 36:42 (1960-1).

386

MILLER, ARTHUR R. The assault on privacy; computers, data banks, and dossiers. Ann Arbor, Univ. of Michigan Press, 1971. 333p.
A24.5

"...a little book on a big and troublesome contemporary subject. Professor Miller has written a well-documented, tightly reasoned, and frightening analysis of the clash between individual privacy and information-gathering technology in a computer age. ...The extensive notes and selected bibliography alone are worth the price of the book." Bernard A. Berkman, Case Western Reserve Law Rev. 22:808 (1971). See also David Burnham, The rise of the computer state (1980).

387

MILTON, JOHN. Aeropagitica: a speech to the Parliament of England, for the liberty of unlicensed printing. (First published on Nov. 25, 1644.)—In many editions. An excellent abridgement is

available in The Tradition of Freedom, edited by Milton Mayer for The Fund for the Republic. N.Y., Oceana Publications, 1957. pp3-32. (Docket Classic). +
A27

The most popular and eloquent, if not the greatest, of all Milton's prose writings. It was published deliberately as unlicensed and unregistered, and was a remonstrance addressed to the parliament, as if in oration to them face to face, against the whole system of licensing and censorship of the press. See Encyc. Brit. 11th ed.—under Milton.

388

MYRDAL, GUNNAR. American dilemma; the Negro problem and modern democracy [with] Richard Sterner, Edward Mauritz and Arnold Rose. N.Y., Harper, 1944. 2 v. +
A20

Exhaustive and objective analysis, intelligently interpreted, of anthropological, cultural, social, economic, legal, political, educational and spiritual aspects of Negro minority set against background of the American creed. Dilemma between American ideals and social concepts and the actual behavior of white towards Negro (and vice-versa) represent "moral lag in the development of the nation." See Library J. 68:667.

389

NEWMAN, EDWIN S. The Freedom reader. N.Y., Oceana, 1955. 256p. (Docket Series No. 2). +
A3, A19, A50

An interesting and valuable collection of materials on civil rights and liberties as exemplified in the thoughts of statesmen (Truman, Eisenhower, Hoover); academic scholars (Griswold, Chafee, MacIver); judges (Holmes, Frankfurter, Hughes, Black, Warren); and others.

390

O'BRIAN, JOHN LORD. National security and individual freedom. Cambridge, Harvard Univ. Press, 1955. 84p.
A29.5

The author speaks in these lectures "not as a prophet scorned, but as a man, fundamentally conservative, imbued with humanistic ideals, who is deeply indignant at the violent departures from standards of decency and fair play that the loyalty and security program has brought with it. ... There has been established, he states, 'something like a new system of preventive law applicable to the field of ideas.'" Abe Krash, Yale Law Jl 65:565 (1956).

391

O'NEIL, ROBERT M. Discriminating against discrimination. Bloomington, Indiana Univ. Press, 1975. 271p.
A29.5

"In the narrow context of pupil selection in higher education, [this author] supports dual admission programs that will increase the representation of blacks and other minorities in higher education. A major portion of the book outlines the history of the Defunis litigation; the last one-third is simply a reprint of the decisions from the Washington Supreme Court and the United States Supreme Court." Mack A. Player, Georgia Law Rev. 11:251 (1976).

392

___. The price of dependency; civil liberties in the welfare state. N.Y., Dutton, 1970. 351p.
A29.5

"[This] aptly titled book tells a great deal about a major source of erosion of civil liberties in the United States: the increasing dependence of large classes of people upon government benefits. His conclusion [is] that our benefits systems, supplying support while undermining self-reliance, have failed to reconcile dignity and dependency..." John de J. Pemberton, Jr., Harvard Law Rev. 84:1960 (1971).

393

PAINE, THOMAS. The rights of man. (First published in 1791). In many editions and Modern Library edition. +
A59

This was in reply to Burke's Reflections on the Revolution in France. It had enormous circulation and effect. His style has dignity, force and temperance. Paine is also noted for his Age of Reason (1794-5) and Common Sense (1776).

394

PERRY, RICHARD L. and JOHN C. COOPER. Sources of our liberties ... Chicago, American Bar Foundation, 1959. Rev. ed. 1978. 466p.
A29.5

Magna Carta, Confirmatio Cartarum, The First Charter of Virginia, Ordinances of Virginia, Mayflower Compact, Colonial Charters, Declaration of Independence, state constitutions, Northwest Ordinance, etc. "...should have a prominent place on the reference shelf of every lawyer and jurist." Joseph E. Naron, Jr., So. Texas Law Jl 5:310 (1960).

395

SAFEGUARDING CIVIL LIBERTY TODAY; the Edward L. Bernays lectures of 1944 given at Cornell University by Carl L. Becker [and others]...and an address by Edmund Ezra Day. Ithaca, N.Y., Cornell Univ. Press, 1945. 158p. * +
A8, A39

A series of essays on the philosophical and practical aspects of civil liberties during the war years.

396

U.S. PRESIDENT'S COMMITTEE ON CIVIL RIGHTS. To secure these rights. The report of the President's Committee on civil rights ...N.Y., Simon and Schuster, 1947. 178p. * +
A8, A30

This committee inquired into whether and in what respect current law-enforcement measures and the authority and means possessed by Federal, state and local governments may be strengthened and improved to safeguard the rights of the people.

CIVIL PROCEDURE
See also PROCEDURE

410

BLUME, WILLIAM. American civil procedure. Englewood Cliffs, Prentice-Hall, 1955. 432p.
A24.5

"This is a small, elementary treatise on a very large subject; namely what remedies are available and what is the procedure for obtaining them. ...the problem of jury trial and the merger of law and equity, ...and the treatment of tests for taking a case from the jury... come to grips with specific problems...does not possess the clarity of purpose and the evenness of execution that characterize Clark's book and Millar's." James H. Chadbourn, Iowa Law Rev. 41:719 (1956).

411

FLEMING, JAMES JR. Civil procedure. Boston, Little, Brown, 1965. 672p.
A24.5

The author "keeps in steady focus the fact that it is the law student for whom he is writing, and his long years of teaching the subject have given him an unusual sensitivity to the problems that beset beginning students. ...the law teacher tackling a procedure course for the first time should consider Professor James required reading." Richard H. Field, Yale Law Jl 75:166 (1965).

412

FRANKLIN, MARK A. The biography of a legal dispute; an introduction to American civil procedure. Mineola, Foundation Press, 1968. 196p.
A65, A71.8

The libel case of Towle v. St. Albans from newspaper clipping to final judgment. An interesting excursion through litigation procedures.

413

FRIENDLY, HENRY J. Federal jurisdiction; a general view. N.Y., Columbia Univ. Press, 1973. 199p.
A24.5

"The flavor of Judge Friendly's thesis includes: (1) Diversity must go; that is ten thousand or more cases out the window. (2) The state prisoner cases should be in the state courts. (3) Stop all this injunction business on civil rights. (4) Quit putting federal courts into the 'protect the environment business.' (5) Send the seamen's, railroad workers', and longshoremen's personal injury business somewhere else. (6) Put patents and taxes into a special court. (7) Cut back on class suits. (8) Don't adopt the ALI proposals which would expand federal jurisdiction. (9) Eliminate overbroad federal criminal laws. (10) Over-all, retrench the federal jurisdiction." John P. Frank, A.B.A.Jl 59:466 (1973).

414

KARLEN, DELMAR. The citizen in court, litigant, witness, juror, judge. N.Y., Holt, Rinehart and Wilson 1964. 211p.
A43.5

A lucid account of court procedures for the educated layman by a former civil procedures teacher.

415

STERN, GERALD. The Buffalo Creek disaster. N.Y., Random House, 1976. 274p.
A1, A38.5

"...Stern's story is one of legal reckoning ... Representing more than 600 plaintiffs from over 4000 survivors (collapse of dams), Stern demanded 64 million dollars from Pittston....what is involved in a big-time law suit involving high claims, high power law firms, and the intricacies of disaster litigation. Clearly, he knows his law and trial practice, and these details provide a most fascinating 'read' for the lawyer...detailed description of the legal processes involved in prosecuting such a suit." J.D.F, Rev. of Law and Social Change 6:83 (1976).

CIVILIZATION

416

BARR, STRINGFELLOW. The pilgrimage of western man. N.Y., Harcourt, Brace, [1949.] 369p. +
A5

A philosophical approach to the subject of civilization.

417

BENEDICT, RUTH (FELTON). Patterns of culture. N.Y., Houghton, Mifflin, 1934. 290p. +
A36

A study of the civilization of the Zuni Indians, the natives of Dobu and the Kwakiutic Indians.

418

LEBOUTILLIER, JOHN. Harvard hates America. The odyssey of a born again American. South Bend, Ind., Gateway editions, 1978. 161p.
A72.5

A harvard business school student tried to do for Harvard what Buckley did for Yale.

419

SUMNER, WILLIAM G. Folkways: a study of the sociological importance of usages, manners, customs, mores and morals. Boston., Ginn & Co., 1907. 692p. +
A19

A valuable sociological summary in which is compiled a mass of anthropological data on the origin and evolution of social institutions.

COMMON LAW

See also ENGLISH AND ANGLO-AMERICAN LAW

420

GRISWOLD, ERVIN N. Law and lawyers in the United States; the common law under stress. Cambridge Univ. Press, 1964. 152p.
A43.5

"In giving this series of Hamlyn Lectures, Dean Griswold has left us greatly in his debt. He has shown us how judges in the United States have applied the spirit of the common law, and in so doing has shown us how we should draw on it ourselves in the problems that lie before us. We share a common heritage - the heritage of freedom under the law - and Dean Griswold is a most worthy exponent of it." Lord Denning, Harvard Law Rev. 80:916 (1967).

421

HOGUE, ARTHUR R. Origins of the common law. Bloomington, Indiana Univ. Press, 1965. 276p.
A24.5

"...designed as [an] introduction to the history of English law and presuppose[s] no knowledge of law or of legal history. ...The reader will acquire from it a sense of legal history in its social and political setting, and an indispensable acquaintance with the constitutional and legal development of early England that is of utmost importance in any further study of the field." Frederick G. Kempin, Jr., American Jl of Legal History 10:321 (1966).

422

LLEWELLYN, KARL N. The common law tradition: deciding appeals. Boston, Little, Brown, 1960. 565p.
A71.5, A71.8

"This is a remarkable book. ...The book is an elaborate and exhaustive study of the process of judicial decision at the appellate level, in so far, and only in so far, as it is or can be made apparent from the opinions written. It is, in other words, a penetrating study of the technique of writing opinions. ...It should be required reading for any judge." William L. Prosser, Jl of Legal Education 13:431 (1961).

423

MILSON, S.F.C. Historical foundations of the common law. London, Butterworths, 1969. 429p.
A36, A57.6

"In this book Professor Milson sets out to discuss two basic questions about [the common law] system. He formulates these as, first, 'what starts a legal system off, what causes customs to turn into reasoned law?' and secondly, 'how has it been so versatile and so durable? How can a system of law, a system of ideas whose hypothesis it is that rules are constant, adapt itself to a changing world?'" J. Levin, Modern Law Rev. 33:331 (1970).

424

NELSON, WILLIAM E. Americanization of the common law; the impact of legal change on Massachusetts society, 1760-1830. Cambridge, Harvard Univ. Press, 1975. 269p. A31.7

"This perceptive and deeply researched monograph adds a significant dimension to the corpus of knowledge about the transformation of American society which began with the American Revolutionary Era, as well as about the transformation of American law. Although the author prudently focuses on Massachusetts, he implies, with all due caution, that many of his Bay State findings might well be paralleled in other parts of the nation." Richard B. Morris, American Jl of Legal History 21:86 (1977).

425

SIMPSON, A.W.B. A history of the common law of contract; the rise of the action of assumpsit. Oxford, Oxford Univ. Press, 1975. 646p.
A57.6

"...The present work is the first of a projected two-volume series and carries the story to 1677, the date of the Statute of Frauds. For the first time students of the common law can hope for a reliable and reasonably complete doctrinal history of the common law of contracts. ... he has entirely passed over the official records of the courts ... makes conclusions beyond those his sources can support ... little attention was paid to policy matters or to explanations of legal change ..." Morris S. Arnold, Yale Law Jl 85:990. See also Professor Simpson's The rise and fall of the legal treatise; legal principles and the forms of legal literature, Univ. of Chicago Law Rev. 48:632 (1981).

COMMUNICATIONS

430

ASHMORE, HARRY S. Fear in the air; broadcasting and the first amendment: the anatomy of a Constitutional crisis. N.Y., W.W.Norton, 1973. 180p.
A29.5

"Yet notwithstanding the author's predilections, the book is a valuable and an eye-opening one, if only to identify and briefly chronicle the various factors which have contributed to the multi-faceted problems inherent in the interplay between broadcasting and government, today more so than ever." The conflict between the White House, the F.C.C., network and local stations administrators, and commentators. Contributions by F.C.C., bar and law professors.

COMMUNITIES

434

BANFIELD, EDWARD C. The unheavenly city revisited; a revision of the unheavenly city. Boston, Little, Brown, 1974. 358p.
A29.5

A revision of the author's 1970 treatment of city planning.

435

FISHER, ROBERT M., ed. The metropolis in modern life. Garden City, N.Y., Doubleday, 1955. 401p. +
A6

A symposium on world problems held at Columbia University. Participants were distinguished scholars and practitioners in the fields of sociology, economics, archaeology, law, engineering, medicine, religion and city planning. The past, present and future of the large city were considered. This is a condensation of, and commentary on their papers. See N.Y. Times, Feb. 6, 1955, p. 10.

436

MCDONALD, AUSTIN F. American city government and administration. 4th ed. N.Y., Crowell [1946.] 657p. +

A59

A standard text in its field for many years which covers the history of American city government, the growth of cities, the problems of the modern city, and the relationships among city and state and federal governments. The book also treats municipal administration and accompanying problems. See Rocky Mountain. Law Rev., 19:302 (1947).

440

DAVID, RENE and JOHN E.C. BRIERLEY. Major legal systems in the world today. London, Stevens & Sons, 1968. 508p.
A24.5

"...an English translation of the French edition which appeared in 1966. [Into this book] Professor David has distilled a lifetime's experience of teaching in the Paris Faculty the wider context of contemporary systems of law within which French law takes its proud and proper place." The major legal systems considered are the Romano-Germanic Family, the Socialist Laws, the Common Law and the "Religious and Traditional Laws" [Muslim, Hindu and African law]. L. Neville Brown, Law Q. Rev. 85:437 (1969).

441

HALL, JEROME. Comparative law and social theory. Baton Rouge, Louisiana State Univ. Press, 1963. 167p.
A43.5

"What in Professor Hall's views distinguishes the legal comparatist, even in his historical research, from other historians is that he is concerned with common legal concepts and common legal institutions, rather than with the individuality of historical events. ...The legal comparatist should emphasize the importance of the social context and the function of laws and institutions; he should construct a bridge from the states' laws to the social reality of law." Kenneth W. Graham, U.C.L.A. Law Rev. 12:682 (1965).

442

HAZARD, JOHN N. and WENCESLAS J. WAGNER, eds. Legal thought in the United States of America under contemporary pressures. Brussels, Etablissements Emile Bruylant, 1970. 639p.
A24.5

"Reports from the United States of America on topics of major concern as established for the VIII Congress of the International Academy of Comparative Law." W. Paul Gormley, Saint Louis Univ. Law Jl., 15:669 (1971).

443

LAWSON, FREDERICK H. A common lawyer looks at the civil law...with a foreword by Hessel E. Yntema. Ann Arbor, Univ. of Michigan Law School, 1953 [i.e., 1955.] 238p. +
A19, A43

This book was conceived in the grand traditions of the Roman law. Written in discursive, clear and simple language, it will serve as a source of continued inspiration to those students of Roman law who have been aware of its humanizing influence in world law. See St. John's Law Rev. 30:144 (1955).

444

McILWAIN, CHARLES H. Constitutionalism, ancient and modern. Rev. ed. Ithaca, N.Y., Cornell Univ. Press, 1947. 162p. +
A28

The theme of this work is the rise of the idea of limited government and it points to the deeply laid foundation of this conception in English mediaeval institutions and legal ideas. The 4th chapter is important. Entitled "Constitutionalism in the Middle Ages," it centers about Bracton's De Legibus [see also No. 1677] and the King's relation to the law. See Harvard Law Rev. 54:533 (1941).

445

SCHWARTZ, BERNARD, ed. The Code Napoleon and the common law world. ...N.Y., N.Y.U. Press, 1956. 438p. +
A24.5

As part of the sesquicentennial program commemorating the promulgation of the first great modern codification of the law - the French Civil Code or Code Napoleon - a series of lectures was delivered at N.Y.U. School of Law by a group of outstanding legal authorities. Recognizing that the importance of the code lay as much in its effect on the common law world as on the civil law, the theme stressed in these lectures was "what are the lessons for our system of an 150 years of the French Code?"

COMPREHENSION

See READING AND COMPREHENSION

450

CAVERS. DAVID F. The choice-of-law process. Ann Arbor, Univ. of Michigan Press, 1965. 336p.

A24.5

"In part the book ranges widely. It glances at the history of the subject beginning in the Italian city states of the Middle Ages. It comments on the roles of legislation, treaties and the federal courts. ... For the most part, however, the volume is a statement of the author's own preferences in the choice-of-law process." Elliott E. Cheatham, Vanderbilt Law Rev. 19:558 (1966).

451

NADELMANN, KURT et al, eds. XXth century comparative and conflicts law; legal essays in honor of Hessel E. Yntema. Leyden, Sythoff, 1961. 547p.

A24.5

"...the first group deals with the theory of comparative law, and is headed by Roscoe Pound's 'Passing of Mainstreetism,' ... civil lawyers are well represented in this section by Judge Marc Ancel and Professors Rene David and Andre Tunc ... Professor Valladao rightly stresses that uniform law cannot be steam-rollered ... Professor Nial's address on legal research and teaching ... Professor Schlesinger of Cornell outlines the procedure whereby 'the common core of various legal systems' can be considered ... (also Professor Zweigert on division of legal systems, Professor McWhinney on 'Toward the Scientific Study of Values in Comparative Law Research,' Professor Smith on occupiers' liability ... John P. Dawson on legal questions arising from risk; Professor Hazard, Professor Dainow, Professor Brutau on Catalan law; Dr. Szladits on comparative aspects of legal contracts; Dean de Sola Canizares deals with the question of subscription of company's capital ... Dr. Domke discusses the giving of awards without written opinions; Professor Kisch deals with the problem of harmonizing interpretations. Dr. Dolle discusses the difficult problem of the use of travaux preparatoires, Professor Battifol on questions of the law governing personal status, Professor Graveson on importance of judicial role in conflict of laws, Dr. Nadelmann deals with the problem of jurisdiction. Professor Egawa deals with divorce of foreigners in Japan; Professor Cavers on Restatement of Contracts; Professors Hancock and von Mehren deal with choice-of-law problems; Professor Ehrenzweig on characterisation in conflict; Professor Reese deals with agency in conflict of laws; Mr. Derenberg deals with the territorial scope and situs of trademarks, Mr. Kronstein deals with extraterritorial effects of anti-trust legislation. On public law problems Dr. Vera Bolgar, Mr. Eder, Mr Markose, Professor Rozmaryn and Professor Stein." B.A. Wortley, Int'l and Comparative Law Q. 11:307 (1962).

CONSTITUTIONAL HISTORY

See also HISTORY (ANGLO-AMERICAN)

460

BEARD, CHARLES A. The Republic: conversations on fundamentals. N.Y., Viking, 1943. 365p. * +
A28, A35, A61

This gives one of the best pictures of the governmental framework of American law. See Harvard Law Rev. 58:593 (1945).

461

BOWEN, CATHERINE DRINKER. Miracle at Philadelphia; the story of the Constitutional Convention, May to September, 1787. Boston, Little, Brown, 1966. 346p.
A49, A53

Ms. Bowen writes a highly interesting and dependable review of the founding of the United States Constitution.

462

BRANT, IRVING. The Bill of Rights. Indianapolis, Bobbs-Merrill, 1965. 567p.
A31.7

"Both of the books under review [also The Case for Liberty by Helen Hill Miller] suffer from the characteristic distortions of ritual history. ... Brant, on the other hand, asks interesting questions but must distort his material in order to find the answers he is looking for ... Brant seeks to rebut the contention of Leonard Levy in Legacy of Suppression [See No. 383] that the framers of the First Amendment adhered to a traditional understanding of freedom of the press, one which would permit prosecution for seditious libel. ... he greatly overstresses the importance of key individuals in understanding the developments of the past." Sanford Levinson, Yale Law Jl 76:249 (1966).

463

FARRAND, MAX. The fathers of the Constitution; a chronicle of the establishment of the Union. New Haven, Yale Univ. Press, 1921. 246p. +
A28

[Charles] Warren recommends this for "the story of the heated opposition to the Constitution which developed within a few months after its signature, and of the bitterly fought contests in the State Conventions which resulted in its ratification by 11 of the 13 states prior to August, 1788." See Warren, Making of the Constitution, p. 744 [see no. 472].

464

____. The framing of the Constitution of the U.S. New Haven, Yale Univ. Press, 1913. 281p. +
A28

One of the basic works on the Federal Convention of 1787. An epitome of the highlights of the Convention in narrative form, accurate and readable.

465

THE FEDERALIST. (First published 1787-1788—now in many editions. Modern Library, Everyman's Library, etc.). * +
A1, A2, A7, A14, A19, A22, A27, A39, A40, A41, A50, A56, A63, A68, A72

These papers, at once an exposition and a defense of the Constitution, were written mostly by Alexander Hamilton. A few only were the work of James Madison and John Jay. James Bryce says that they were "written at the very birth of the Union by those who watched its cradle and recorded the impressions and anticipations of the friends and enemies of the infant Constitution." [A39] Mr. Justice Marshall believed the opinion of the Federalist to be of great authority as a commentary on the U.S. Constitution. The edition edited by Clinton L. Rossiter is recommended. [A2.5]

466

GARRETY, JOHN A, ed. Quarrels that have shaped the Constitution. N.Y., Harper & Row, 1964. 276p.
A31.7

"... consists of sixteen essays by as many authors sketching the background to eighteen great decisions in constitutional history. ...The cases discussed (which extend from Marbury v. Madison to Brown v. Board of Education) are seen in terms of the personalities involved and the theme, if any, is that great constitutional doctrines originate in petty quarrels and become significant through the accident of historical circumstance." John Phillip Reid, New Hampshire Bar Jl 9:30 (1966).

467

KEIR, DAVID L. The Constitutional history of modern Britain, 1485-1937. London, A. & C. Black, 1948. 568p. +
A28

The story of the British Constitution based on available material at the time. Keir's approach is authoritative and his style very readable.

468

McLAUGHLIN, ANDREW C. A Constitutional history of the U.S. N.Y., Appleton Century, [1935.] 833p. +
A8, A28, A35, A57, A61, A68

This is considered a classic, excellent for the period through the election of Hayes, but rather sketchy thereafter. It is a storehouse of information on the development of the American Constitutional system.

469

____. The foundations of American Constitutionalism.... N.Y., N.Y.U. Press, 1932. 176p. Gloucester, P.Smith, 1972. +
A28

Commager believes McLaughlin shows extraordinary acumen in seizing on the basic factors that distinguish the American from other Constitutional systems. Emphasized here is the influence of New England ideas and principles.

470

RUTLAND, ROBERT A. The birth of the Bill of Rights, 1776-1791. Chapel Hill, Univ. of N.C. Press, [1955.] 243p. +
A19

Published for the Institute of Early American History and Culture, this is a competent chronicle of the events leading to the establishment of legal guarantees for personal freedom, starting with the English beginnings. A concluding chapter philosophizes concerning modern developments. The author, a journalist, covers only the chronological narrative of historical events and political struggles. See A.B.A.Jl 42:443 (1956).

471

VAN DOREN, CARL C. The great rehearsal; the story of the making and ratifying of the Constitution of the U.S. N.Y., Viking, 1948. 336p. * +
A28, A43.5, A72

Based on official records, Van Doren dramatically relates the day to day, hour to hour, story of what took place during the Constitutional Convention and what happened when the Constitution emerged from the secret convention and faced the struggle for ratification in state after state.

472

WARREN, CHARLES. The making of the Constitution....Boston, Little, Brown, 1929. [c1928.] 832 p. +
A40, A43.5, A45

A carefully prepared and skillfully presented account of the day- by- day work of the Convention of 1787. It makes conveniently available those records of the Convention without which an intelligent understanding of the Constitution is virtually impossible. See Harvard Law Rev. 50:997 (1937).

CONSTITUTIONAL LAW

480

ANASTAPLO, GEORGE. The Constitutionalist; notes on the First Amendment. Dallas, Southern Methodist Univ. Press, 1971. 826p.

"The Constitutionalist is a most unusual and prodigious feat of scholarship, a veritable tour de force, beautifully written...a search for the principles, spirit and tendency of the Constitution in the institutions and circumstances of the American people ... he regards the 'clear and present danger' test as unconstitutional ..." Philip Mullock, Jl of Legal Education 26:247 (1974). Professor Anastaplo was denied admission to the Illinois

Bar in 1957 for speaking his conscience to the Court's Committee on Character and Fitness. See New York Times, Sept. 11, 1983, p.30.

481

ASSOCIATION OF AMERICAN LAW SCHOOLS. Selected essays on Constitutional law....Chicago, Foundation Press, 1938. 5 v. in 4.
A6 +

Prof. Wright in the preface states "these thick volumes contain a collection which is invaluable to one who desires a closer acquaintance with the history and principles of American Constitutional law up to the time of the court struggle of 1937." Vol. 1, Book 1: Nature of the judicial process in constitutional cases; Vol. 2, Book 2: Limitations on governmental power; Vol. 3, Book 3: Nation and states; Vol. 4, Book 4: Administrative law; and Book 5: Taxation. Douglas B. Maggs, general editor.

482

____. Selected essays on constitutional law: 1938-1962. ... Edited by Edward L. Barrett, Jr. and Nathaniel L. Nathanson. St. Paul, West Publishing Co., 1963. 971p.
A24.5

"The four volume set of Selected Essays on Constitutional Law (1938) ... has now been supplemented by a new one volume edition for the period 1938-1962. ... it is a highly selective culling of largely current comment on some major themes of constitutional law ... There are 41 selections largely printed in full. ... Bibliographical notes and connective comment, however, would have helped mightily." Robert G. Dixon, Jr., Jl of Legal Education 16:473 (1964). Authors include Herbert Wechsler, T.R. Powell, Alexander Bickel, Henry M. Hart, and Paul Freund.

483

BEANEY, WILLIAM M. The right to counsel in American courts. Ann Arbor, Univ. of Michigan Press, 1955. 268p.
A31.7

"In a twenty page summary ... the difficulties in providing effective counsel for those without funds are strikingly outlined ... This book makes it clear that there remain ahead many battles to be fought under the banner of the right to counsel." Jack B. Weinstein, Columbia Law Rev. 56:454 (1956).

484

BEARD. CHARLES A. An economic interpretation of the Constitution of the United States. N.Y., Macmillan, 1913. 325p.
A29.5

A classic text which still arouses controversy.

485

BEDAU, HUGO ADAM. The courts, the Constitution, and capital punishment. Lexington, D.C. Heath, 1977. 505p.
A31.7

"While Bedau is not a neutral and detached academician, his book nevertheless reflects considerable insight and skill in the analysis of difficult issues which confront a democratic society still groping for an appropriate response to death penalty cases ... five major legal arguments proposed in support of abolishing the death penalty." C. Michael Abbott, Emory Law Jl 26:483 (1977). Mr. Bedau also edited Death Penalty in America: An Anthology. (3d ed. 1982).

486

BELL, DERRICK A. Race, racism and American law. Boston, Little, Brown, 1973. 1076p. 2d ed. 1980. 685p.
A29.5

"As I read Professor Bell's excellent treatise...I kept wondering why law professors have not published similar casebooks before. ...In addition to Part I ... which is basically a historical analysis during the time of slavery, Professor Bell covers ... the rights of citizenship, the right to education, the right to housing, the right to employment, and the right to justice ... a handy and invaluable reference book for the practicing lawyer in any civil rights litigation." A. Leon Higginbotham, Jr., Univ. of Pennsylvania Law Rev. 122:1044 (1974). Dean Bell also edited Shades of Brown: new perspectives on school desegregation (1980).

487

BERGER, RAOUL. Government by judiciary; the transformation of the Fourteenth Amendment. Cambridge, Harvard Univ. Press, 1977. 483p.
A57.1

"Berger finds a distressing pattern of judicial misconstruction and a concomitant usurpation of legislative prerogatives. ...Berger reserves much of his censure for the Warren Court ... Poor organization and burdensome reading detract from the presentation of Berger's ideas. ...a valuable addition to the literature on constitutional history and the fourteenth amendment." James W. Ely, Jr., Villanova Law Rev. 23:1187 (19778). Mr. Berger has also written Congress vs. the Supreme Court (1969)[A57.1], Executive Privilege; A Constitutional Myth (1974) [A57.1]; Impeachment; the Constitutional Problems (1973); Death Penalties (1982).

488

BERNS, WALTER. The First Amendment and the future of American democracy. N.Y., Basic Books, 1976. 266p.
A29.5

"His arguments are usually wrong, but he is the sort of man who helps us to find the truth as we are pushed to refute him ... Berns examines several areas of first amendment lore in attempting to prove his thesis [Supreme Court steadily eroding the conditions of civil liberty] ... one still can be skeptical of Berns' vision of the State as teacher of civic virtue." Peter Linzer, Jl of Urban Law 55:225 (1977). Mr. Berns is also the author of For Capital Punishment; Crime and Morality of the Death Penalty (1979); a thoughtful defense of the morality of capital punishment. See David O'Brien, Univ. of Florida Law Rev. 31:824 (1979).

489

BICKEL, ALEXANDER. The morality of consent. New Haven, Yale Univ. Press, 1975. 156p.
A57.1

"He discusses constitutionalism and the political process, citizenship, free speech and free press, civil disobedience, and the moral authority of the intellectual. ... Bickel views the Warren Court as having egregiously violated [the moral imperative] of restraint." Charles E. Ares, Arizona Law Rev. 18:482 (1976). Mr. Bickel is also the author of The Least Dangerous Branch (1963) and Politics and the Warren Court (1965). See Herbert Wechsler, Yale Law Jl 75:672 (1966).

490

BLACK, CHARLES L. Capital punishment; the inevitability of caprice and mistake. N.Y., W.W.Norton, 1974. 96p.
A29.5

"...a concise statement of the due process problems that persist in recent state statutes that purport to reinstate capital punishment without violating the dictates of a majority of the Court in Furnam ...the author sacrifices depth to achieve clarity for his lay audience." Michael Kuhn, Houston Law Rev. 13:212 (1975).

"The point of Capital Punishment is that the entire criminal process ... is riddled with arbitrariness and opportunity for mistake that can not be eliminated simply by introducing mandatory death sentences or purported standards for their imposition ... James M. Kramon, Harvard Law Rev. 88:1343 (1975).

491

BLACK, HUGO LAFAYETTE. A constitutional faith. N.Y., Knopf, 1968. 76p.
A24.5

"(1) The role of the courts in our constitutional system, (2) due process of law, and (3) the First Amendment ... he would much prefer to put his faith in the people and their elected representatives to choose the proper policies for their government to follow, leaving the courts only questions of constitutional interpretation and enforcement." Harold Norris, Wayne Law Rev. 15:960 (1969).

492

CAHN, EDMOND, ed. The Great Rights. N.Y., Macmillan, 1963. 242p.
A24.5

"... lectures delivered [at New York University School of Law] by Justice Black, Justice Brennan, Chief Justice Warren, and Justice Douglas ... valuable introductory chapters by Edmond Cahn and Irving Brant." Albert M. Bendich, California Law Rev. 51:651 (1963). Professor Cahn also edited Supreme Court and Supreme Law (1954) with contributions by Ralph F. Bischoff, Charles P. Curtis, John P. Frank, Paul A. Freund, and Willard Hurst. See review by Edwin M. Zimmerman, Columbia Law Rev. 1956:293 (1956).

493

CAPPALLETTI, MAURO. Judicial review in the contemporary world. N.Y., Bobbs-Merrill, 1971. 117p.
A24.5

"It is impossible to do justice to this book, short as it is, in a short review; but, in closing, attention must be called to the excellent discussion of the reasons that prevent most European systems of review, especially where their roles are important, from adopting our decentralized system." J.A.C.Grant, U.C.L.A. Law Rev. 21:1172 (1974). See also the book edited by this author, Access to justice and the welfare state (1981) reviewed in Michigan Law Rev. 81:1006 (1983).

494

CARR, ROBERT K. The Supreme Court and judicial review. Greenwood Press, 1970 (c.1942). 304p.
A43.5

"This volume implements effectively the fact that the Supreme Court is in politics and is subject to the same pressures ..." John J. George, 17 Temple Univ. Law Q. 206 (1942).

495

CARRINGTON, FRANK G. Neither cruel nor unusual; the case for capital punishment. New Rochelle, N.Y., Arlington House, 1978. 213p.
A29.5

"... It is not objective; ..." James Abourezk, Civil Liberties Rev. 5:101 (Jan./Feb. 1979). See also his The Victims (1975). [A57.1]. For a summary of the arguments for capital punishment, see John Kaplan, The problem of capital punishment, Univ. of Ill. Law Rev. 1983:555.

496

COHEN, MARSHALL, THOMAS NAGEL AND THOMAS SCANLON, Eds. Equality and preferential treatment; a philosophy and public affairs reader. Princeton Univ. Press, 1977. 209p.
A24.5

Owen Fiss (equal protection adjudication and desegregation decisions); Thomas Nagel (affirmative action); Judith J. Thomason (preferential hiring); Ronald Dworkin (equal protection clause); George Sher (reverse discrimination in employment). Kenneth W. Simons, Michigan Law Rev. 77:513 (1979).

497

CORWIN, EDWARD S. The Constitution and what it means today. [11th ed.] Princeton, N.J., Princeton Univ. Press, 1954. 340 p. 13th ed. revised by Harold W. Chase and Craig R. Ducat. 1973. 601p.
A6, A10, A20, A28, A33, A43, A45, A55, A67 * +

Professor Corwin was a noted constitutional scholar. A small guidebook or manual to the "tangled mazes of American Constitutional law problems." See Harvard Law Rev. 44:152 (1930). Dean Thormodsgard of Univ. of North Dakota recommends this for second year students. See also Corwin on the Constitution, Richard Loss, ed. (1981).

498

____. The doctrine of judicial review; its legal and historical basis, and other essays. Princeton, Princeton Univ. Press, 1914. 177p. +
A28

The point of view here is historical rather than legal. Many citations are given which will be of value to legal scholars. "Here and there are passages somewhat shocking to the lawyer." See Harvard Law Rev. 28:340 (1915).

499

CROSSKEY, WILLIAM W. Politics and the constitution in the history of the United States. Chicago, Univ. of Chicago Press, 1953. 2 vols.
A31.7

"This work is devoted to proving that ever since about 1800 the most important portions of the Constitution having to do with the distribution of power between state and nation have either been completely misunderstood or intentionally misconstrued ... more ingenious than persuasive ... stimulates differences of opinions ... [various reviewers] Northwestern Univ. Law Rev. 49:107 (1954). Volume 3 is The political background of the Federal Convention by William W. Crosskey and William Jeffrey, Jr. (1980) reviewed by Erwin Chemerinsky in Michigan Law Rev. 81:828 (1983).

500

DOUGLAS, WILLIAM O. We the judges: studies in American and Indian constitutional law from Marshall to Mukherjea. Garden City, N.Y., Doubleday, 1956. 480p. +
A19

Mr. Justice Douglas reviews the social and political developments of our concepts of governmental power and the rights of man in the last 150 years. He compares them with similar concepts in India.

501

DREYFUSS, JOEL and CHARLES LAWRENCE III. The Bakke case; the politics of inequality. N.Y., Harcourt, Brace, Jovanovich, 1979. 278p.
A1

A cause celebre occasioned by Mr. Bakke's challenging the quota system at the University of California at Davis. An exploration into affirmative action.

502

ECKHARDT, BOB and CHARLES L. BLACK. The tides of power; conversations on the American Constitution. New Haven, Yale Univ. Press, 1976. 225p.
A43.5

A law professor and Congressman discuss the interactions among the three branches of government.

503

ELY, JOHN HART. Democracy and distrust, a theory of judicial review. Cambridge, Harvard Univ. Press, 1980. 268p.
A2.5

"...Ely attempts to articulate a workable theory of judicial review consistent with the underlying democratic assumptions of our system. ...Ely argues for a 'participation-oriented, representation-reenforcing' approach to judicial review. [Ely's mode] may offer the best practical means of living with the imperfections of the existing order." Ralph U. Whitten, Creighton Law Rev. 13:1479 (1980). Also reviewed by James Fleming and Gerald T. Dunne in Michigan Law Rev. 80:652 (1982).

504

EMERSON, THOMAS I. Toward a general theory of the First Amendment. N.Y., Random House, 1966. 245p.
A24.5

"...[the author] has sought with care and precision to give rationality and systemization to the law governing free expression - the cognate rights of speech, press, petition, and assembly." Harold Norris, Jl Urban Law 45:210 (1967).

505

ERNST, MORRIS. The great reversals, tales of the Supreme Court. N.Y., Weybright & Talley, 1973. 212p.
A25.5

Cases in which the court overruled itself.

506

FUNSTON, RICHARD Y. Constitutional counterrevolution?: The Warren Court and the Burger Court: judicial policy making in modern America. N.Y., Wiley, 1977. 399p.
A43.5

An appraisal of the Warren Court's work on race relations, apportionment, and defendants' rights. Also considers obscenity and the Burger Court. For students and lay people.

507

GRAHAM, FRED P. The self-inflicted wound. N.Y., Macmillan, 1970. 377p.
A71.5

"...a survey of the Warren Court's criminal justice decisions in the 1960s." Decisions considered include Mapp v. Ohio, Gideon v. Wainwright, Douglas v. California, Malloy v. Hogan, Griffin v. California, Miranda v. Arizona, Benton v. Maryland, Pointer v. Texas, Wash. v. Texas, Klopfer v. N.Car., Duncan v. Louisiana, Robinson v. California, etc. William M. Beaney, Denver Law Jl 48:299 (1971).

508

GUNTHER, GERALD, ed. John Marshall's defense of McCulloch v. Maryland. Stanford Univ. Press, 1969. 214p.
A31.7

"...the war or words which raged between Chief Justice John Marshall and his states rights opponents..." R. Kent Newmyer, American Jl of Legal History 14:366 (1970).

509

HAND, LEARNED. The Bill of Rights. Cambridge, Harvard Univ. Press, 1958. 82p.
A31.7

"...a masterly discussion by a great judge on the Bill of Rights. It is a discriminating analysis and, as might be expected of him, the author frequently states views that are unorthodox. His lectures include: When a court should intervene, the fifth and fourteenth amendments, and the guardians." Albert J. Harno, Hastings Law Jl 10:229 (1958).

510

HUTCHESON, JOSEPH C. ...Law as liberator; the principle of democracy in America, the spirit of its laws. Chicago, Foundation Press, 1937. 201p. +
A45

See annotation for No. 15.

511

JENNINGS, SIR WILLIAM I. The law and the constitution. 4th ed. London, Univ. of London Press [1952.] 327p.
A8, A30

An eminently trustworthy exposition and criticism of the fundamental principles of the English constitution. See Law Q. Rev. 50:430.

512

KONEFSKY, SAMUEL J., ed. The Constitutional world of Mr. Justice Frankfurter; some representative opinions, selected and edited ....N.Y., Macmillan, 1949. 325p. +
A28

The editor has supplied some brief yet acute introductory comments to each opinion. Justice Frankfurter has been described as the "Apostle of judicial self-restraint."

513

KURLAND, PHILIP B. Politics, the constitution and the Warren Court. Univ. of Chicago Press, 1970. 222p.
A43.5

Professor Kurland has also written: Religion and the Law of Church and State and the Supreme Court (1962) reviewed by Norman Abrams in UCLA Law Rev. 11:169 (1963); and Mr. Justice Frankfurter and the Constitution (1971) reviewed by John D. French in Minnesota Law Rev. 57:423 (1972).

514

LEVY, LEONARD W. Against the law; the Nixon Court and criminal justice. N.Y., Harper, 1974. 506p.
A35.5

A comparison of the Nixon and Warren Courts. "[T]he author brings to his effort an extraordinary degree of intellectual integrity and professional expertise. His conclusions and his analysis, however, demonstrate that there can never be total objectivity. [a discussion of search and seizure cases follows.]" Edward R. Korman, Hofstra Law Rev. 4:549 (1976). Professor Levy has also written: Judgments; essays on American constitutional history (1972) reviewed by Henry J. Friendly in Columbia Law Rev. 73:179 (1973); and Origins of the fifth amendment (1968) reviewed by O. John Rogge in Michigan Law Rev. 67:862 (1969).

515

MCCLOSKEY, ROBERT G. The American Supreme Court. Chicago, Univ. of Chicago Press, 1960. 260p.
A27.5, A57.7

"Professor McCloskey treats constitutional history in terms of sweeping although well defined periods." Lawrence Parkus, Cornell Law Q. 46:658 (1961). Professor McCloskey has also written: Essays in Constitutional Law (1957) reviewed by Ernest R. Bartley in Univ. of Florida Law Rev. 10:240 (1957) and The Modern Supreme Court (1972) reviewed by Bradley C. Canon in Wisconsin Law Rev. 1973:313 (1973).

516

MILLER, ARTHUR SELWYN. The Supreme Court; myth and reality. Westport, Greenwood Press, 1978. 388p.
A31.7

"...a representative collection of essays ... seeks to reveal the many myths and realities which have combined to create an aura of mystery concerning the functions of the Court." Thomas J. Barrett, Loyola Law Rev. 25:433 (1979). Mr. Miller has also written Democratic dictatorship: the emergent constitution of control (1891); The Supreme Court and American capitalism (1968); Toward increased judicial activism: the political role of the Supreme Court (1982).

517

MILLER, CHARLES A. The Supreme Court and the uses of history. Cambridge, Harvard Univ. Press, 1969. 234p.
A31.7

"...the first monograph devoted to the detailed assessment of the use of history in the Supreme Court's decision-making process during the past half-century. ...His choice of five case studies, stretching from 1926 to 1964, is apt and comprehensive: the presidential removal power; the right of political expression; the

Minnesota mortgage moratorium ...; the sit-in cases of 1964; and the reapportionment of 1962-1964." Thomas G. Barnes, California Law Rev. 58:1251 (1970).

518

MOTT, RODNEY L. Due process of law; a historical and analytical treatise of the principles and methods followed by the courts in the application of the concept of the "law of the land." Indianapolis, Bobbs-Merrill Co. [c1926.] 702p. * +
A43.5, A72

The most important aspect of this book is its historical background. The book is lucidly written with considerable ease of style and is heavily documented. See Cornell Law Q. 12:423 (1926).

519

PERRY, MICHAEL J. The Constitution, the courts and human rights: an inquiry into the legitimacy of constitutional policymaking by the judiciary. N.H., Yale Univ. Press, 1982. 241p.
A31.7

See Richard B. Saphire's review, Making noninterpretationism respectable, Michigan Law Rev. 81:782 (1983).

520

POLLAK, LOUIS H., ed. The constitution and the Supreme Court; a documentary history. Cleveland, World Publishing Co., 1966. 2 vols.
A31.7

"...this compilation should provide a useful basis for high school courses in civics and college courses in constitutional law and government. ...substantial insight into the uses of law as our primary battleground for resolution of the twin social drives for stability and change and the uses of the Constitution and the Supreme Court as critical agencies for the constant rejuvenation and articulation of principle in our society." Sanford Jay Rosen, Univ. of Pennsylvania Law Rev. 115:646 (1967).

521

POWELL, THOMAS REED. Vagaries and varieties in constitutional interpretation. N.Y., Columbia Univ. Press, 1956. 229p.
A29.5

"...a suggestive and stimulating summary of the development of doctrine in his chosen field of emphasis along with a keen analysis of the process of judicial review which can be studied with profit by all who deal with Supreme Court law in any of its manifestations. [deals with national power to regulate and tax, intergovernmental relations, limits on state regulation of interstate commerce, and state taxation of interstate and foreign commerce.]" Edward L. Barrett, Jr., California Law Rev. 44:807 (1956).

522

REMBAR, CHARLES. The end of obscenity; the trials of Lady Chatterley, Tropic of Cancer, and Fanny Hill. N.Y., Random House, 1968. 528p.
A43.5

"[A] sensitive, lucid description of the judicial struggles of two notorious literary ladies (Lady Chatterly and Fanny Hill) and a cryptic restroom wall (Tropic of Cancer) ... It is also the limited autobiography of a provocative and interesting man, and a didactic tour de force of a frustrated school teacher." Thomas L. Shaffer, Notre Dame Lawyer 44:493 (1969). Mr. Rembar has also written The Law of the Land; The Evolution of Our Legal System (1980), which is an interesting book for beginning law students, and Perspective (1975).

523

ROBERTS, OWEN J. The court and the Constitution. Cambridge, Harvard Univ. Press, 1951. 102p. +
A43.5, A49

Three lectures by a late Supreme Court Justice entitled "Sovereignty and the Power to Tax," which traces the history of tax exemption; "Conflicts of Police Power" involving the distinction between "direct" and "indirect" effects on interstate commerce as a test of whether a subject might be governed by Congress under the Commerce Clause; and the "Fourteenth Amendment and its Implications." An interesting and stimulating book. See Harvard Law Rev. 65:1471 (1952).

524

RUTLEDGE, WILEY. A declaration of legal faith. Lawrence, Univ. of Kansas Press, 1947. 82p. * +
A40

The late Mr. Justice Rutledge states his faith in the legal principle and in the federal principle. The first section, from which the title is derived, should be required reading for every college student, law intended or otherwise. See N.Y.U.L.Q. Rev. 24:259 (1952). [See also No. 288]

525

ST. JOHN-STEVAS, NORMAN. Obscenity and the law. London, Secker and Warburg, 1956. 289p.
A24.5

"...This book pleads the cause of freedom of expression - not unlimited license of unqualified right, but relative freedom for the serious artist ... documents the thesis that obscenity laws are unworkable and historically have been so abused as to occasion more social harm than good..." Henry H. Foster, Jr., Jl of Legal Education 10:260 (1957).

526

SCHWARTZ, BERNARD. American Constitutional law. With a foreword by A. L. Goodhart. Cambridge [Eng.] Univ. Press, 1955. 364p. +
A19

The first 160 pages succinctly outlines the structure of American constitutional government stressing the bases of the system - a written constitution, judicial review, the separation of powers and the rule of law. Part II of the book entitled "Modern Developments" interestingly discusses current problems as Presidential prerogative and the Steel Seizure Case, the changing role of the Supreme Court and the Negro and the law. See A.B.A.Jl 42:61 (1956). Professor Schwartz has also published: A Commentary on the Constitution of the United States. Part I - The Powers of Government. 2 vols. (1963). Reviewed by Frederick Bernays Wiener, Northwestern Law Rev. 58:711 (1974). Part II - The Rights of Property (1965) reviewed by Thomas F. Bergin, Yale Law Jl 75:360 (1965). Part III - Rights of the Person. 2 vols. (1968). Reviewed by Paul W. Bruton, Univ. of Pennsylvania Law Rev. 118:325 (1969). He also wrote The Great Rights of Mankind; A History of the American Bill of Rights (1977). [A43.5] He also edited The Bill of Rights; A Documentary History. 2 vols. (1971) reviewed by Kenneth Graham, U.C.L.A. Law Rev. 19:343 (1971). Professor Schwartz has also written a biography of Chief Justice Earl Warren [see No. 2175]

527

STITES, FRANCIS N. Private interest and public gain; the Dartmouth College case. Univ. of Massachusetts Press, 1972. 176p.
A29.5

"...develops concisely the origin of the case in the College's early sectarian history, the constitutional issues which then emerged, the litigation through the New Hampshire courts, the famous appeal to the Supreme Court, and the significance of the decision for future contractual charter rights in American law ... It also demonstrates magnificiently why America has been so successful in entrusting to a court policy which in other nations have usually been resolved by quite different processes." Vincent E. Starzinger, Minnesota Law Rev. 57:1045 (1973).

528

SWISHER, CARL B. American Constitutional development. [Under the editorship of Edward McC. Sait] 2nd ed. Boston, Houghton, Mifflin [1954] 1145p. * +
A1, A2, A4, A7, A14, A19, A27, A28, A36, A39, A43.5, A55, A56, A59, A63, A72

An account of American Constitutional law as part of the economic and political history of the U.S. by a Professor of Political Science. Dean Thormodsgard recommends this work for 2nd year law students.

529

____. The growth of Constitutional power in the U.S. Chicago, Univ. of Chicago Press [1946.] 261p. +
A28

An analysis of the courts within our changing social structure. Presents a substantial amount of background material considering the problems of the courts today [1946] and in years to come. See Seckler-Hudson, Bibliography on Public Administration (1953 ed.).

530

TIEDMAN, CHRISTOPHER G. The unwritten constitution of the United States; a philosophical inquiry into the fundamentals of American Constitutional law. Buffalo, W.S. Hein, 1974 (c.1890). 165p.
A43.5

531

TRIBE, LAURENCE H. American constitutional law. Mineola, Foundation Press, 1978. 1202p.
A24.5

"...an innovative effort to infuse moral advocacy into legal scholarship, but it is also, in many places, a rather traditional hornbook. Although the book is generally accurate and often brilliant, its treatment of some issues is misleading and limited ... His analyses are useful and provocative but will also be impenetrable and treacherous for the uncritical student or judge." Robert F. Nagel, Univ. of Pennsylvania Law Rev. 27:1174 (1978).

CONTRACT LAW

NOTE: In substantive areas of law, law reviews are probably the best approach for analysis of specific topics. Occasionally, a symposium issue will provide an overview that is generally to be found only in treatises such as those listed below. See, for instance, The Symposium on Jurisprudential Perspectives on Contract in Valparaiso Univ. Law Rev. 17:613 (1983). The annotations in this book will also attempt to reveal seminal approaches to contract and other areas of the law. See for instance Kairys, _The Politics of law_ (1982) [See no. 624]. It should be added that hornbooks and casebooks are generally limited to explaining the law as it is and, obviously, are only occasionally represented in this book.

575

ATIYAH, PATRICK S. The Rise and Fall of Freedom of Contract. Oxford Univ. Press, 1979. 791p.
A31.7

"This volume will superbly serve the reader for whom it is an introduction to the subject; the specialist in the field will find in it an abundance of novel insight and provocative ideas. We have here a major scholarly contribution, and a splendid big book." See Barbara Black's review in Michigan Law Rev. 79:929 (1981). See also this author's "The legacy of Holmes through English eyes," which was based on a lecture given at Harvard Law School and is published in Boston Univ. Law Rev. 63:341 (1983).

576

DANZIG, RICHARD. The capability problem in contract law. Mineola, Foundation Press, 1978. 254p.

Principally, the author investigates the events leading up to and following litigation. His "scheme is to present the reported appellate opinion in the case, to follow the report with 'first questions,' then to provide supplementary comments delving into the trial phase of the case or into background facts, and to conclude with 'further questions.'" George C. Oldham, Michigan Law Rev. 77:949 (1979).

577

FRIED, CHARLES. Contract as promise; a theory of contractual obligation. Cambridge, Harvard Univ. Press, 1981. 162p.
A30.5

"Fried argues powerfully for a moral basis of contract law [as opposed to Holmes' view that one is free to break his contract if he chooses to pay damages]." Daniel Kornstein, The music of laws, p. 97 (1982).

578

FRIEDMAN, LAWRENCE M. Contract law in America; a social and economic case study. Madison, Univ. of Wisconsin Press, 1965. 280p.
A31.7

Quotes from the book: the devastating obsoleteness of legal education; [law schools] fail to teach the legal system as a whole, let alone the legal system as part of society; they teach disjointed fragments of a fragment; traditional course-work in contracts is outmoded; grappling with trivia; [the appellate decisions which form its subject matter] do not pose large issues. See Guenter H. Treitel, Univ. of Chicago Law Rev. 33:418 (1966).

579

GILMORE, GRANT. The death of contract. Columbus, Ohio State Univ. Press, 1974. 151p.
A49, A71.8

"The book represents an important contribution to the history of ideas about contract law. In it, Gilmore traces the birth, development, and reported death of the 'bargain' theory of consideration. ...contract is being absorbed into the mainstream of a more expansive theory of tort liability." Richard E. Speidel, Stanford Law Rev. 27:1161 (1975).

580

HAVIGHURST, HAROLD C. The nature of private contract. Evanston, Northwestern Univ. Press, 1961. 144p.
A31.7

"...takes the reader for a ride in a juristic spaceship from which he is able to look down upon the broad outlines of contract, spread out before him as a map....It does great credit to its author, and constitutes a valuable addition to his already imposing list of contributions to the law. George W. Gobel, Stanford Law Rev. 14:631 (1962).

581

KRONMAN, ANTHONY T. and RICHARD A. POSNER. The economics of contract law. Boston, Little, Brown, 1979. 274p.
A31.7

"The book is a compilation of essays, reprinted from a variety of journals, treating the economic implications of substantive concepts of contract law...the final chapter offers different views on freedom of contract and the role of economic analysis." C. Paul Rogers III, Harvard Law Rev. 93:1039 (1980). See also Daniel A. Farber, Contract law and modern economic theory, Northwestern Univ. Law Rev. 78:303 (1983).

582

MACNEIL, IAN R. The new social contract; an inquiry into modern contractual relations. N. Y., Yale Univ. Press, (1981). 164p.
A29.5

"It is a concept of contract that is neither the contract of positivist economics or law, nor on the other hand, either a restoration of the status of Henry Maine or the surrender to torts of Grant Gilmore." - Introduction: the case for relational contract law. See also this author's Values in contract: internal and external, Northwestern Univ. Law Rev. 78:340 (1983).

CORPORATION LAW

See also BUSINESS ORGANIZATION

600

REICH, CHARLES A. The greening of America. N.Y., Random House, 1977. 399p.
A29.5

"...Reich sees corporate life as a deadening, stultifying, pathless labyrinth. By working at what we want to work at, saying what we want to say, dressing as we care to dress, caring more for our life style than our livelihood, we will destroy that ole debil, the corporate state, and give society a new thrust and meaning...The Consciousness I-III ploy has the overtones of a fad word like middle class or high brow, or inferiority complex, or U and non-U ... an article meticulously expanded into a book..." Edward J. Bander, N.Y.U. Law Rev. 45:1145 (1970). The former Yale Law professor Reich has also written extensively for law reviews.

601

STONE, CHRISTOPHER D. Where the law ends; the social control of corporate behavior. N.Y., Harper and Row, 1975. 273p.
A36

"...a general criticism of existing laws designed to control corporate activity. ...he would design new laws ...make large corporations operate more responsibly in the public interest... On the whole this is an imaginative study. Kenneth A. Cohen, Virginia Law Rev. 62:259 (1976). For a global expansion of this topic, see his "On the moral and legal rights of nature, Bostonia (Boston Univ.) 29:July-Aug. 1983.

COURTS

See also Judiciary

610

ABRAHAM, HENRY J. The judiciary: the Supreme Court in the governmental process. 5th ed. Boston, Allyn and Bacon, 1980. 252p.
A27.5, A43.5

Mr. Abraham is also the author of _The Judicial Process; An Introductory Analysis of the Courts of the United States, England and France_. 3rd ed.(rev. and enl. 1975).

[611 saved]

612

BATOR, PAUL M., PAUL J. MISHKIN, DAVID L. SHAPIRO and HERBERT WECHSLER. Hart and Wechsler's the Federal courts and the Federal system. Mineola, Foundation Press, 1973. 1657p.

"...more than a mere teaching instrument for law students encountering for the first time the challenging problems generated by the co-existence of dual court systems exercising judicial power derived from different sovereignties. The veteran practitioner, the perplexed judge, the conscientious legislator - all have been able to turn to this book for help in overcoming their diverse difficulties." Carl McGowan, Columbia Law Rev. 74:1015 (1974).

613

CARTER, ALBERT T. A history of the English courts...being a 7th ed. of a history of English legal institutions. London and Toronto, Butterworth, 1944. 183p. +
A13, A28

A short, clear account of the history and present organization of the English court system. One of the best in the field.

614

CURTIS, CHARLES P. Lions under the throne. A study of the Supreme Court of the U.S., addressed particularly to those laymen who know more Constitutional law than they think they do and to those lawyers who know less. Bost., Houghton, Mifflin, 1947. 368p.
A21, A43.5, A62 * +

One of the best of the numerous books on the Supreme Court. [A21]. Not a history but rather a group of informal essays on the functions of the court and the Constitution in our system of government. See Vanderbilt Law Rev. 2:150 (1948).

615

ENSOR, ROBERT C. K. Courts and judges in France, Germany, and England. London, Oxford Univ. Press, 1933. 141p. * +
A8, A30

Expositions of the judicature of England, France and Germany written to enable English readers to compare theirs with two continental systems. A compact and complete picture is given. See A.B.A.Jl 20:40 (1934).

616

FLEMING, MACKLIN. The price of perfect justice; the adverse consequences of current legal doctrine on the American courtroom. N.Y., Basic Books, 1974. 196p.
A57.1

"It is the essence of Judge Fleming's theme that the American courts, particularly during the past twenty years, have striven towards an ideal of perfectability, both in procedure and in substantive law, with ruinous results to our society. ... under the guise of protecting the innocent ... the courts have provided endless possibilities for the shrewd and knowledgable attorney to engineer countless delays, and, in many instances, the eventual release of the guilty client." Billups P. Percy,

Tulane Law Rev. 49:736 (1974-5). See also his Of crimes and rights (1978). [A57.1]

617

FREUND, PAUL A. On understanding the Supreme Court. Boston, Little, Brown, 1951. 140p.; Greenwood Press, 1979. * +
A6, A20, A22, A42, A49, A64

Three essays—one analyzes the considerations and values which determine a judge's vote in a given case, another describes a liberal judge (Brandeis), and a third considers the position of the lower courts and counsel as affecting the work of the Supreme Court. The book exhibits clarity of thought and is written in superior English. See Harvard Law Rev. 63:1081 (1950).

618

HOROWITZ, DONALD L. The courts and social policy. Washington, D.C., Brookings Institution, 1977. 309p.
A31.7

"Horowitz' central thesis is that the very processes of adjudication that equip courts to resolve particular legal disputes ill-suit them for resolving general social problems. ...Ignoring the familiar question of whether judges should innovate, the author examines their ability to do so from both functional and empirical perspectives." J. Woodford Howard, Jr., Washington Univ. Law Q. 1978:833 (1978).

619

HUGHES, CHARLES E. The Supreme Court of the U.S.; its foundations, methods and achievements, an interpretation. N.Y., Columbia Univ. Press, 1928. 269p. * +
A6, A28, A35, A41, A45

Robert Carr considers this a valuable, very readable, and remarkably frank exposition of the work of the Supreme Court by a great judge.

620

HUGHES, GRAHAM. The conscience of the courts; law and morals in American life. N.Y., Doubleday, 1975. 324p.
A57.1

"To attempt to write about law and morals in American life in this era of American life is to enter a very large ocean about which some very complex and often seemingly unquenchable storms are seething. ...[this book] emerges as a pellucid, serenely impressive legal/philosophical work, but one that happens not to contain a central, cohesive philosophy." Ken Sutak, Brooklyn Law Rev. 42:603 (1976).

621

INSTITUTE OF JUDICIAL ADMINISTRATION. A guide to court systems [by Leon Schneider]. N.Y. [The author]. August 1957. 45 p. +
A19

Outlines, succinctly, simply, but authoritatively, "the judicial framework within which litigable disputes are resolved in the United States." Part I deals with the organization and jurisdiction of the federal courts, including specialized courts of the U.S. and territorial courts. Part II outlines the organization of state court systems generally, illustrated in Part III by the complex N.Y. system. A "Glossary" adds to the value of this little work. Updated in Fanny Klein, Federal and state court systems-a guide (1977). This guide has a chapter on legal research by Edward J. Bander which was subsequently englarged into Legal Education and Research Abridgment (1978).

622

JACKSON, ROBERT H. The struggle for judicial supremacy, a study of a crisis in American power politics. N.Y., Knopf, 1941. 361p. +
A45, A64

Robert Carr considers this a highly critical analysis of the Supreme Court with particular emphasis upon the New Deal years. Somewhat hurried and superficial but nontheless one of the most stimulating volumes on the subject.

623

____. The Supreme Court in the American system of government. Cambridge, Harv. Univ. Press, 1955. 92p. +
A43, A46, A56

The Godkin lectures at Harvard Univ. for 1955 by the late Mr. Justice Jackson dealing with the role of the Supreme Court in the American Constitutional democracy.

624

KAIRYS, DAVID, ed. The politics of law: a progressive critique. N.Y., Pantheon, 1982. 321p.
A29.5

These seventeen essays attempt to strip from American law the popular belief that our legal system consists of neutral rules designed to lead to justice. James A. McKenna III, A.B.A.Jl. 69:798 (1983). This book attacks legal education as oriented toward corporate American and the legal curriculum as a rationale for middle class perspectives. There are also Marxist interpretations of legal subjects. The essayists include Duncan Kennedy.

[625 saved]

626

MURPHY, WALTER F. Elements of judicial strategy. Chicago, Univ. of Chicago Press, 1964. 249p.
A24.5

"This book, written by a political scientist, is likely to annoy a good many lawyers. ...Conflict between lawyers and political scientists often arises over the subject of courts and judges." Martin Shapiro, Stanford Law Rev. 18:544 (1966).

627

POUND, ROSCOE ...Organization of courts. Boston, Little, Brown, 1940. 322p. +
A56

A history of the development of the American court system. Also pertains to the organization of courts and administration of justice in the United States and Great Britain.

628

VANDERBILT, ARTHUR T. Judges and jurors: their functions, qualifications and selection. Boston, Boston Univ. Press, 1956. 76p. (The Gaspar C. Bacon lectures on the Constitution of the U.S., 1955.) +
A19

These lectures, although intended primarily for graduate students in government, were designed also for the "general reader" as an aid in understanding "the functioning of a government operating under a written constitution and the workings of the judicial system under which we live" with a focus on the judicial system. The style is vigorous, effective and competent. See Northwestern Law Rev. 51:644 (1956).

629

WARREN, CHARLES. The Supreme Court in United States history ...New and rev. ed....Boston, Little, Brown [c 1926.] 1937. 2 v.
A4, A5, A6, A21, A28, A35.5, A49, A72 * +

An historic study of the Supreme Court in its political surroundings and of the effects which its decisions have produced in American politics. This is a classic work on the subject. Dean Havighurst believes it is a work with which you will eventually want to become familiar and you might make a beginning now. But you will probably get more out of it during the time you are studying Constitutional Law.

630

WENDELL, MITCHELL. Relations between the Federal and the state courts. N.Y., Columbia Univ. Press, 1949. 209p. +
A11

What is the governmental significance of judicial federalism? Federal and state court litigation offer clues as to the operation of the federal system. This study sets out to explore this area. See Va. L. Rev. 36:422 (1950).

CREATIVE THINKING

A large part of the work the law-trained man is called upon to do calls for problem-solving and sound judgment. This is true regardless of whether he devotes his life to the practice of law, to governmental administration, or to being a judge, legislator, teacher or scholar, or to some other endeavor. He will be called upon to create or give advice concerning an almost infinite number of relationships. [They] may range from a comparatively simple contract through tailoring a highly complex corporate structure to the needs of a business or non-profit organization. Any task to which he will be called can be done better if he possesses this power of creative thinking. Predicting the outcome of even routine litigation may involve considering whether a hitherto well-settled rule of law which is applicable would, in the light of the particular facts of the case, possibly be modified or reshaped to avoid unfairness and practical inconvenience. Here, the power to think creatively will often merge with critical understanding of human institutions and values with the latter serving as the necessary threshold to creative power. [A63].

a) Research. See also LEGAL RESEARCH AND METHOD [Nos. 1725 et seq.]

Creative power in thinking requires the development of skill in research or an awareness of sources and types of material, adaptation to particular use and methods of fact presentation. [A63].

Read the following:

650

GOODE, WILLIAM J. Methods in social research [with] P. K. Hatt. N.Y., McGraw-Hill, 1952. 386p. * +
A63

651

JAHODA, MARIE. Research methods in social relations, [with others]. N.Y., Dryden press, 1951. 2 v. * +
A63

b) Fact Completeness

Creative power in thinking requires the development of skill in fact completeness or willingness to recognize all facts, avoidance of preconception and fiction masquerading as fact, and disciplined ability to withhold judgment until all facts are "in." [A63].

Read the following:

652

JOHNSON, WENDELL. People in quandaries; the semantics of personal adjustment. N.Y., Harper, 1946. 532p. * +
A47, A63

c) Fact Differentiation

Creative power in thinking requires the development of skill in fact differentiation or an understanding of relevance of facts to particular issues, varying importance of different facts and relative persuasiveness of various facts. [A63].

Read the following:

653

HOVLAND, CARL I. Communication and persuasion; psychological studies of opinion change, [with] I. L. James and T. H. Kelley. New Haven, Yale Univ. Press, 1953. 314p. * +
A63

d) Fact Marshalling

Creative power in thinking requires the development of skill in fact marshalling or a reduction of masses of fact to manageable proportions and arrangement of facts in logical and convincing order. [A63].

Read the following:

654

CARTWRIGHT, DORWIN P. Group dynamics: Research and theory, [with] Alvin Zander. Evanston, Ill., Row, Peterson, [1953.] 642p. A63 * +

655

MacBURNEY, JAMES H. The art of good speech, [with] E. J. Wragge. N.Y., Prentice-Hall, 1953. 584p. * +
A63

e) Deductive Reasoning. See also Logic

Creative power in thinking requires the development of skill in deductive reasoning or use of the syllogism, spotting logical fallacies and avoiding conclusions flowing from inaccurate premises. A63.

Read the following:

656

BLACK, MAX. Critical thinking; an introduction to logic and scientific method. 2nd ed. N.Y., Prentice-Hall, 1952. 459p. * +
A63.

657

ROBINSON, DANIEL S. Principles of reasoning; an introduction to logic and scientific method. 3d ed. N.Y., Appleton-Century, 1947. 410p. * +
A63

f) Inductive Reasoning

Creative power in thinking requires the development of skill in inductive reasoning or experimental methodology, accuracy of observations, elimination of variables, determining the role of hypotheses and the conditions essential to valid generalization such as adequacy of sampling, strict limitation of conclusions by available reliable data. [A63].

Read the following:

658

DEWEY, JOHN. Logic, the theory of inquiry. N.Y., Holt, 1938. 546p. * +
A63

g) Reasoning by Analogy

Creative power in thinking requires the development of skill in reasoning by analogy involving methods of classification, gradation of relationships and finding resemblances which justify inferences of similarity. A63.

Read the following:

659

ALLPORT, GORDON W. The psychology of rumor, [with] Leo Postman. N.Y., H. Holt, [1947.] 247p. * +
A63

h) Critical Analysis

Creative power in thinking requires the development of skill in critical analysis or a disciplined skepticism in approach, thoroughness of inquiry and keenness of mind in cutting through to essentials. [A63].

Read the following:

660

BERELSON, BERNARD R., ed. Reader in public opinion and communication, [with] Morris Janowitz. Enlarged ed. Glencoe, Ill., Free Press [1953.] 611p.
A63

i) Constructive Synthesis

Creative power in thinking requires the development of skill in constructive synthesis or sytematic formulation of principles, meaningful organization of ideas and determining structural relationship of concepts. [A63].

Read the following:

661

STEBBING, L. SUSAN. THinking to some purpose. Harmondsworth, Middlesex, Eng., Penguin books, 1939. 244p.
A63

662

THOULESS, ROBERT H. How to think straight. N.Y., Simon & Schuster, 1950. [1939.] 246p.
A20

Mr. Thouless also wrote _Straight and crooked thinking_ (1930). See also Anthony Flew's _Thinking about thinking_ (1975) and E.R. Emmet's _The use of reason_ (1960). [A74]

j) Power of Decision

Creative power in thinking requires the development of skill in making decisions. This power of decision involves resolution of discoverable issues in the light of short and long term ends found preferable on explicitly identified and justified grounds. [A63].

Read the following:

663

BEARDSLEY, MONROE C. Thinking straight; a guide for readers and writers. N.Y., Prentice-Hall, 1950. 278p.
A63

CRIMINAL LAW and PROCEDURE
See also ADMINISTRATION OF JUSTICE

700

ALLEN, FRANCIS A. The borderlands of criminal justice; essays in law and criminology. Chicago, University of Chicago Press, 1964. 139p.

"...a graceful, witty and provocative book which has important implications for teaching and research in criminology and law...seven essays and speeches on [rehabilitative ideal, socialized justice, juvenile court, criminal responsibility, Garofolo's Criminology, review of Koestler's Reflections on Hanging.]." Anthony M. Platt, Hastings Law Jl 17:145 (1965).

701

BONNIE, RICHARD and CHARLES H. WHITEBREAK II. The marihuana conviction; a history of marihuana prohibition in the United States. Charlottesville, Univ. Press of Va., 1974. 368p.
A57.1

See also John Kaplan, The hardest drug; heroin and public policy (1983). Also H. Wayne Morgan, ed. Yesterday's addicts; American society and drug abuse 1865-1920 (1974) [A57.1]

702

THE CHALLENGE OF CRIME IN A FREE SOCIETY. Wash., D.C., GPO, 1967. 340p.

"In an astonishingly short period of time, with a dedication and a competence that is unrivaled in the field, James Vorenberg and his staff produced a report that, were it acted upon responsibly and steadily, would reduce fear, reduce suffering, and increase human happiness in this country. Norval Morris, Law and Society Rev. 277 (1968).

703

FRANK, JEROME and BARBARA FRANK. Not guilty. N.Y., Doubleday, 1957. 261p.
A48.5

"This book relates in brutally convincing detail the history of a number of cases in which innocent men have been found guilty of crime. [Judge Frank provides] sharp insights and deep perceptions, the shrewd and disturbing commentaries which cap each chapter, as well as the concluding chapter which evaluates our whole system of apprehension, investigation, and conviction." Columbia Law Rev. 58:284 (1958). See also Borchard, Convicting the innocent [See No.9].

704

FRANKEL, MARVIN E. Criminal sentences; law without order. N.Y., Hill and Wang, 1973. 124p.
A24.5

"...an excellent job of describing the various systems provided for the imposition of criminal sentences, and the faults and evils of each. Federal procedures are chiefly discussed, but the book includes suggestions which the author feels will alleviate some injustices that result from sentencing in both the state and the federal courts." George J. McMonagle, Cleveland State Law Rev. 23:190 ((1974). Mr. Frankel has also written, with Gary P. Naftalis, The Grand Jury; An Institution on Trial (1977) reviewed by Norval Morris, Yale Law Jl 87:680 (1978). Also Partisan justice (1978). See also Nigel Walker, Sentencing in a rational society (1972) and Rupert Cross, The English sentencing system (2d ed. by Andrew Ashworth, 1981) for two recommended English books on the topic. A74.

705

HALL, JEROME. Theft, law and society...with an introduction by K. N. Llewellyn....Boston, Little, Brown, 1935. 360p. * +
A7, A8

Book I (Basic Problems), traces the growth of the law of theft in the 18th century, discloses the construction of the substantive law as shown in the subject matter of larceny, and elaborates upon the function of technicality and discretion in criminal law administration. Book II (Contemporary Problems) directs attention to the questions of receiving stolen property and automobile theft and offers a proposed reform of treatment for petit larceny. See Harvard Law Rev. 48:1450 (1935).

706

HOOD, ROGER, ed. Crime, criminology and public policy; essays in honour of Sir Leon Radzinowicz. London, Heinemann, 1974. 635p.
A24.5

"...twenty-nine of Sir Leon Radzinowicz's friends and colleagues have contributed to this volume." Contributors include D.A. Thomas, D.G.T. Williams, Professor Greenawalt, Mr. Justice Steyn, Professor Nigel Walker, etc. P.R. Glazebrook, Cambridge Law Jl 35:336 (1976).

707

INBAU, FRED E. Lie detection and criminal interrogation [with] John E. Reid. 3d ed. Baltimore, Williams & Wilkins, 1953. 242p. +
A28

Written in non-technical language as a practical guide to law enforcement officers, particularly the criminal interrogator. A frank analysis and appraisal of lie-detection and criminal interrogation. See Tulane L. Rev. 23:591 (1949). A more recent book on this topic is David T. Lykken, _A tremor in the blood; uses and abuses of the lie detector_ (1981).

708

____. Self-incrimination: what can an accused person be compelled to do? Springfield, Ill., Thomas [1950.] 91p. +
A28

This interesting monograph deals with the limited proposition well established in the federal courts and most state courts that the privilege against self-incrimination applies only to the giving of testimony and does not extend to physical evidence. In this respect a good deal of helpful material is here collected. See Geo. Wash. Law Rev. 20:250 (1951).

709

KARLEN, DELMAR (in collaboration with Geoffrey Sawer and Edward M. Wise). Anglo-American criminal justice. N.Y., Oxford Univ. Press, 1967. 233p.
A29.5

"...observations and reactions which resulted from an interchange of experience in the area of criminal justice between judges and lawyers in the United States and England in 1963 and 1964... revealing the strengths and weaknesses of each." Richard M. Sims, Jr., Hastings Law Jl 20:1447 (1969).

710

MELTSNER, MICHAEL. Cruel and unusual; the Supreme Court and capital punishment. N.Y., Random House, 1973. 316p.
A57.1

"[captures] the essence and flavor of the arguments made to the Supreme Court.... Welsh S. White, Columbia Law Rev. 74:319 (1974).

711

MORRIS, NORVAL and COLIN HOWARD. Studies in criminal law. London, Clarendon Press, 1964. 270p.
A24.5

"...there is a conflation of articles by both authors in provocation and fear as defences in murder, and a chapter on insanity and automatism. [also strict responsibility and estoppel]." Glanville Williams, Cambridge Law Jl 137 (1965). Professor Morris also wrote The Future of Imprisonment (1974) reviewed by Christopher T. Bayley, Hofstra Law Rev. 4:161 (1975); and The honest politician' guide to crime control (with Gordon Hawkins 1970).

712

PACKER, HERBERT L. The limits of the criminal sanction. Stanford Univ. Press, 1968. 385p.
A47

"He develops a view of the criminal justice problem which leads him to counsel great caution in the use of the criminal sanction." Roger B. Dworkin Indiana Law Jl 44:493 (1969).

713

RADZINOWICZ, LEON. A history of English criminal law and its administration since 1750. N.Y., Macmillan, 1948. 3 vols.
A74

A scholarly and detailed history of English criminal law presented as an historical narrative. Vol. 1 is concerned with the chaotic criminal law of the eighteenth century. Vol. 2 is concerned with The Enforcement of the Law. Vol. 3 is concerned with the abortive proposals for reform. See C.K. Allen, Law Q. Rev. 73:260 (1957). See also this author's Crime and justice (3 vols. 1977); and Ideology and crime (1966).

714

SCHAEFER, WALTER V. The suspect and society. Evanston, Northwestern Univ. Press, 1967. 99p.
A24.5

"[the author] suggests that the privilege against self-incrimination should be rested on a rational rather than an allegedly historical base. [the reviewer cites Traynor, Friendly, Wechsler, Bickel, Learned Hand]. Philip B. Kurland, Univ. of Chicago Law Rev. 34:704 (1967).

715

STEPHEN, SIR JAMES FITZJAMES. A history of the criminal law of England. N.Y., Research and Source Work Series No. 71, 1964. 576p.

"...an exact reproduction of the London edition of 1883 now makes it readily available to libraries and scholars." J.A.C.Grant, U.C.L.A. Law Rev. 14:372 (1966). When this book appeared in 1883 it was considered the best modern history of English criminal law. Though parts of it are obsolete today, it still one of the best histories of its kind.

716

SZASZ, THOMAS S. Law, liberty, and psychiatry... N.Y., Macmillan, 1963. 281p.
A43.5

The author espouses the "radical view that no punishment is morally retributive or reformative or deterrent, [and he] advocates abolishing the insanity defense altogether and convicting the mentally ill along with everyone else whenever they violate the law." Ronald P. Wertheim, Columbia Law Rev. 1964:977 (1964). See also this author's Psychiatric slavery (1977). See also his The age of madness; the history of involuntary mental hospitalization presented in selected texts. Ed. by Dr. Szasz (1974).

717

WEINREB, LLOYD L. Denial of justice; criminal process in the United States. Free Press, 1977. 177p.
A43.5

Preface: "This book is about the criminal process in operation: not the rules of law so much as who actually does what and how, and what the consequences are." The author is critical of our system and recommends the establishment of the office of an investigating magistracy. He also has interesting ideas on the privilege against self-incrimination.

CRIMINOLOGY
See also MENTAL DISORDERS

725

ABRAHAMSEN, DAVID. Who are the guilty? N.Y., McGraw-Hill, 1952. 340p. * +
A8

This book although perhaps less sophisticated than some others, fairly represents the ideas of a number of modern psychiatrists writing and working in the field of crime. They believe all criminals are mentally abnormal, their crime fills emotional needs: the emotions they respond to are deeply repressed, and these repressed emotions, rather than any rational influences, are the prime movers of criminal behavior. See Lawyers Guild Rev. 12:155 (1952).

726

ATTICA; The official report of the New York State Commission on Attica. N.Y., Bantam Books, 1972. 532p.
A24.5

"What is lamentable about the Commission Report is its failure to propose detailed alternatives that could avoid future Atticas [prison riot]. ...This is the most detailed and accurate description of what goes on in today's prison that I have ever read." John J. Buckley, Boston Univ. Law Rev. 53:255 (1973). Robert B. McKay, former Dean of the N.Y.U. School of Law was Chairman of this Commission appointed to investigate the causes and effects of the prison riot in Attica that began on Sept. 8, 1971.

727

BARNES, HARRY E. New horizons in criminology; the American crime problem, [with] Negley K. Teeters...foreword by Frank Tannebaum ...N.Y., Prentice-Hall, [c1947.] 1069p. +
A28

One of the most complete surveys ever to be undertaken in the field of American criminology. Has a wealth of information based on much source material and is very readable.

728

BATES, SANFORD. Prisons and beyond. N.Y., Macmillan, 1936. 334p. * +
A35, A61

"The end and aim of a penal system is the protection of

society." This book reviews our present methods of punishment to see how far they contribute to that ultimate object. See Harvard Law Rev. 50:712 (1935). See also Nigel Walker, Punishment, danger and stigma (1980). [A74]. See also James B. Jacobs, New perspectives on prison and imprisonment (1983).

729

BROMBERG, WALTER. Crime and the mind, an outline of psychiatric criminology. Phila., Lippincott, [1948.] 219p. * +
A8

A psychiatrist who has had many years of experience dealing with prisoners considers the legal and social environment of the criminal. He also describes in detail the special type of psycho-therapy needed in the treatment of criminals. His style is pleasing.

730

CLARK, RAMSEY. Crime in America. N.Y., Simon and Schuster, 1970. 346p.
A48.5

"There is nothing new, just old polemics [on death penalty, marihuana, wiretapping, FBI]." William J. Schafer III, Arizona Law Rev. 12:846 (1970]. "... describes with vivid candor and his typical low-keyed dialogue, the causes of crime in America." Joseph H. Hill, Akron Law Rev. 4:238 (1971).

731

GLUECK, SHELDON. After-conduct of discharged offenders... [with] Eleanor T. Glueck ...London, Macmillan, 1945. 114p. +
A28, A43.5

A summary and critique of the many Glueck studies in the field of criminology and penology. A small but dynamic book posing tough questions. "If we are confused by the problem of juvenile delinquency, what about the offenders who never grow up?" See Harvard Law Rev. 58:1099 (1945).

732

____. Crime and correction. Cambridge, Mass., Addison-Wesley Press, 1952. 288p. * +
A8, A35

Eleven papers written over a period of 25 years, brought together by a continuity of theoretical development. Covered are subjects such as analysis of various approaches to the problem of crime causation, the intricacies of the administration of criminal justice, psychiatry and criminal law, peno-correctional treatment, crime prevention and an able discussion of the Nuremberg Trials and aggressive war. All these problems are currently important and the lawyer and law student should be aware of them.

733

___. Unraveling juvenile delinquency, [with] Eleanor Glueck. N.Y., Commonwealth Fund, 1950. 399p. (Harvard Law School Studies in Criminology). +
A28

This is essentially a study of the biological, psychological, education, social and juvenile characteristics of 500 persistently delinquent boys as compared with 500 non-delinquents. It is a notable advancement in our understanding of the mechanisms of crime and delinquency. See Harvard Law Rev. 64:1022 (1951).

734

PHILLIPSON, COLEMAN. Three criminal law reformers: Beccaria, Bentham, Romilly ...London, Dent.; N.Y., Dutton, 1923. 344p. +
A45, A62, A74

The greatest service rendered by Romilly was his determined and persistent struggle to reform the sanguinary, antiquated criminal code of England. Three of the greatest criminal law reformers of all time belong to this era. Beccaria of Italy whose fame is based upon his formulation of scientific principles of penology, Bentham the great student of law reform, and Romilly who fought in the legislative halls to secure legislation to carry into effect the principles which all three advocated. See Shientag, Molders of Legal Thought, p. 205 (1943).

735

RADZINOWICZ, LEON. The modern approach to criminal law [with] J.W. Cecil Turner. London, Macmillan, 1945. 511p. +
A28

Consisting of essays on various aspects of criminal law and penology, it contains contributions by some of the foremost English authorities. The lawyer who is seriously interested in the administration of criminal justice will find much in this excellent volume to make him pause, such as a disillusioning essay on the jury and the mental element in crimes at common law. See Harvard Law Rev. 59:156 (1945).

[736 saved]

737

SILBERMAN, CHARLES E. Criminal violence, criminal justice. N.Y., Random House, 1978. 540p.
A57.1

The effect that poverty and racial oppression have on crime. An examination of criminal justice, juvenile justice, and correction. But see Mark G. Kelman's criticism of "liberal and conservative criminology." Stanford Law Rev. 31:527 (1979).

738

TALLANT, ROBERT. Ready to hang—seven famous New Orleans murders. N.Y., Harper, 1952. 241p. +
A28

The author is excellent as a reporter of seven true crimes that occurred in New Orleans from 1883 to 1933.

739

VAN DEN HAAG, ERNEST. Punishing criminals; concerning a very old and painful question. N.Y., Basic Books, 1975. 283p.
A57.1

An attempt to explore all the ramifications of punishment. A discussion of retribution, justice and the utilitarian need for punishment. Also the causes of crime: poverty, race, mental illness, and addiction. Also chapters on the deterrent effect of crime and statistical data. A final section on the types of punishment including corporal punishment, death penalty, fines and prison.

740

VOLLMER, AUGUST. The police and modern society. Berkeley, Univ. of Calif. Press, 1936. 253p.
A45

Police responsibilities and the author's opinions about their implications in "modern society," are discussed. The author had a long, distinguished career as a police officer.

741

WILSON, JAMES Q. Thinking about crime. Rev. ed. N.Y., Basic Books, 1983. 280p.
A29.5

Myths about our conceptions of crime, an analysis of how we deal with drugs and the death penalty, and a discussion of courts and corrections. The author suggests that we abandon our ideological conceptions and "test our theories rather than fund our fears." (p.208).

CROSS EXAMINATION

See THE TRIAL AND ITS PRELIMINARIES

ECONOMICS

See also HUMAN INSTITUTIONS AND VALUES; POLITICAL THEORY AND POLITICAL ECONOMY

750

ACKERMAN, BRUCE A. Private property and the constitution. New Haven, Yale Univ. Press, 1977. 303p.
A31.7

"Ackerman's grand claims for the difference that philosophy makes, which immply at least a partial ability to avoid the problems of collapse and indeterminancy, fail. ...[the book] is filled with novel insights about philosophy, compensation law, state action, and judicial roles." Philip Soper, Columbia Law Rev. 1979:44. Professor Ackerman has also written Economic foundations of property law (1975) and Social justice in the liberal state (1980), the latter being reviewed in Michigan Law Rev. 80:72 (1982).

751

ADAMS, GEORGE P., Jr. Competitive economic systems. N.Y., Crowell, 1955. 516p. * +
A8

An analysis of capitalism, socialism, fascism, and communism. Each system is examined as a going concern in a particular historical and sociological context. The author stresses the mutual competition of these systems in the world today and exposes the elements common to all the systems discussed.

752

AYRES, CLARENCE E. The theory of economic progress. Chapel Hill., Univ. of N.C. Press, 1944. 317p. +
A59

The author thinks about economic problems in terms of the economic life process. For the price theory of value he substitutes a conception of value drawn from technology itself from which he derives the policy of abundance. He is positive in his convictions and thinks very little of most other economists—yet he is interesting and scholarly and the book is well worth reading. See Ann. Am. Acad. 236:206.

753

BRANDEIS, LOUIS D. Business—a profession; with preliminary chapters regarding the author by Ernest Poole, Felix Frankfurter and James C. Bonbright. Boston, Hale, Cushman, Flint, 1933. 374p. * +
A6.5, A35

First published in 1914. The entire field ranging from trusts to monopolies and from organized labor and efficiency to life insurance and transportation monopoly, is surveyed by a leading attorney, who later became Associate Justice of the U.S. Supreme Court, with pungent criticisms here and there, along with suggestions for improvement and reform. Read the last essay, at least, "Opportunities in the law." See Boston Transcript, May 31, 1933, p. 2.

754

FERGUSON, J. M. Landmarks of economic thought. N.Y., Longmans, Green, 1938. 295p. +
A59

A useful, readable and agreeable short history of economic thought, stressing the contributions of the leading thinkers. Prof. Ferguson apparently intended his volume to serve both for the general reader and as a textbook. It has the virtues of straight forwardness, balance and impartiality. See Hazlitt, <u>The Free man's library,</u> p. 70.

755

GALBRAITH, JOHN KENNETH. The affluent society. Boston, Houghton Mifflin, 1969. 2d ed. rev. 333p. also N.Y., New American Library, 3d ed. rev. 1978. 275p.
A48.5

Mr. Galbraith has also written <u>Economics and the Public Purpose</u> (1973). [A72.5]; and <u>The New Industrial State</u> (3d rev. ed. 1978). [A72.5]. He is a leading spokesman for liberal causes and is generally at opposite poles with William F. Buckley.

756

GEORGE, HENRY. Protection or free trade; an examination of the tariff question, with especial regard to the interests of labor....N.Y., Doubleday, Page, 1912. 335p. +
A5

One of the books that have most influenced my overall attitude toward life. Dean Woodbridge.

757

HANEY, L.H. History of economic thought. N.Y., Macmillan, 1911 [etc.] 1949. 957p. +
A59

A critical account of the origin and development of the economic theories of leading thinkers in the leading nations. Prof. Haney wrote of the totality of economic thought and in doing so provided the student with the most comprehensive text for the study of this subject available in the fifties.. See Hazlitt, The Freeman's library, p. 8.

758

HAYEK, FRIEDRICH AUGUST VON ...The road to serfdom; with a foreword by John Chamberlain. Chicago, Univ. of Chicago Press [1944.] 250p. +
A59

Henry Hazlitt writing in the N.Y. Times, Sept. 23, 1944, held this book to be one of the most important of our generation. It restates for us the issue between liberty and authority with the power and vigor of reasoning that John Stuart Mill stated the issue for his own generation in his great essay "on liberty." It is an arresting call to all well-intentioned planners and socialists, to all those who are sincere democrats and liberals at heart, to stop, look and listen. See also the author's The Constitution of liberty (1960) and Law, legislation and liberty (vol. 1: Rules and order, 1973; vol. 2: The mirage of social justice, 1976). And see Robbins, Politics and economics (1963).

759

HILL, IVAN. The ethical basis of economic freedom. Chapel Hill, N.C., American Viewpoint, 1976. 427p.
A72.5

A diverse collection of essays that covers Vietnam, Watergate, stuent unrest, corporate bribes, moral codes, etc.

760

KIRKLAND, EDWARD C. A history of American economic life. 3d ed. N.Y., Appleton-Century-Crofts, [1951.] 740p. * +
A8, A35, A57, A59, A61, A68

A moving narrative of American development from colony to commonwealth, from commonwealth to nation and from nation to empire. The author often succeeds by a few deft phrases in revealing the technique of a process or mechanism that has changed the life of men. See America 47:551. This is primarily a textbook history of agriculture, commerce, industry, finance, etc.

761

LYNCH, DAVID ...The concentration of economic power. N.Y., Columbia Univ. Press, 1946. 423p. * +
A8

An analysis of the testimony presented before the Temporary National Economic Committee (TNEC) established in 1938—at the request of President Roosevelt for an investigation of the concentration of economic power in American industry and its effect upon the decline of competition.

762

MARSHALL, ALFRED. Principles of economics. 8th ed. London, Macmillan, 1920. 871p. (First published in 1890.) +
A7, A59

This book has had an immense influence and will remain a standard work for many years to come. It shows a pronounced reaction from the severe individualism of most of the early economists and whilst no one would belittle its value in focusing and clarifying earlier thought, one may doubt whether the ultimate verdict of economists will regard the reaction that it heralded as entirely good. See _The Philosophy of Individualism: A bibliography_ (1927).

763

MISES, LUDWIG VON. Human action. New Haven, Yale Univ. Press, 1949. 889p. +
A19

One of the most uncompromising and most rigorously reasoned statements of the case for capitalism that has yet appeared. If any single book can turn the ideological tide that has been running in recent years so heavily toward statism, socialism and totalitarianism, _Human Action_ is that book. It should become the leading text of everyone who believes in freedom, in individualism, and in the ability of a free-market economy to outdistance any government-planned system. See Newsweek, Sept. 19, 1949.

764

POSNER, RICHARD A. Economic analysis of law. Boston, Little, Brown, 1972. 415p. 2d ed. 1977. 572p.
A36, A49

"...a substantial intellectual achievement, but it is not lacking in faults...the reader is warned that the book is sometimes over-simplified, parochial and anachronistic; it demands the most critical reading the reader can give it. Paul D. Carrington, Univ. of Illinois Law Forum 1974:187. Judge Posner has also written The economics of corporation law and securities regulation (with Kenneth E. Scott, 1980), and The economics of justice (1981).

765

SIMONS, HENRY C. Economic policy for a free society. Chicago, Univ. of Chicago Press, 1948. 353p. * +
A8, A59

As an economic theorist, Simons was far from first rate; his originality lay in the realm of phrase-making rather than that of thought. No one, however, could deny Simon's disinterestedness, or the depth of his desire for a better and freer society. He had a deep concern for freedom and a suspicion of concentrated power. See N.Y. Times, Aug. 1, 1948.

766

TAUSSIG, FRANK W. Inventors and money-makers... N.Y., Macmillan, 1930. 138p. * +
A35

Taussig is a leading economist. This book consists of lectures on some relations between economics and psychology.

767

____. Principles of economics. N.Y., Macmillan, 1912. 2 v.
A35, A59 * +

A fine picture of classical doctrines. It remains an important part of economic literature—as it has been for over a quarter of a century. See T. F. Haygood in Southern Economic Journal, 1940. Characterized by an exquisite sanity and lucidity. See N.Y. Times, 1925.

768

TAWNEY, RICHARD H. The acquisitive society. N.Y., Harcourt, Brace [c1920.] 1921. 188p. * +
A35

A profound and brilliant treatment by a socialist thinker.

769

VEBLEN, THORSTEIN B. The theory of a leisure class; an economic study of institutions, with a foreword by Stuart Chase. N.Y., Modern Library, [c1934.] 404p. (First published in 1899.)
A59 +

Veblen was an American economist and social philosopher. The general purpose of this book and of the others he wrote was to present from different angles, an evolutionary analysis and a critique of the existing economic system, which he conceived of as essentially a price system, a pecuniary economy rather than as a system of capitalism or as a system of individualism and laissez-faire. See Encyc. of Soc. Sci. under Veblen.

ENGLISH and ANGLO-AMERICAN LAW

800

CONFERENCE ON THE FUTURE OF THE COMMON LAW. The future of the common law. Cambridge, Harvard Univ. Press, 1937. 247p.
A45

The critical judgments of able and experienced jurists as to the present and the future of the common law.

801

DAWSON, JOHN P. The oracles of the law. Ann Arbor, Univ. of Michigan Law School, 1968. 520p.
A32, A43.5

"...a study of the nature and extent of the contribution that case law has made to the legal systems of England, Rome, France, and Germany. ...Many comparative references also concern American practice....Only a master could present the result of such wide and profound research in so elegant and readable a style, illuminated with wit and adorned with memorable and quotable gems..." T.B.Smith, Harvard Law Rev. 82:490 (1968). Professor Dawson has also written Gifts and promises; continental and American law compared (1980).

802

DENNING, ALFRED THOMPSON, LORD. The discipline of law. London, Buttersworth, 1979. 331p.

"...about law reform - the necessity of reshaping the

principles laid down in the nineteenth century to meet the needs of the twentieth. It discusses seven branches of English law [including abuse of ministerial powers, problems of locus standi, abuse of 'group' powers, rules of costruction, the doctrine of promissory estoppel, liability for negligent statements, and the doctrine of precedent.]" Lord Denning has also written The due process of law (1980); and What next in the law (1982).

803

HARDING, ALAN. A social history of English law. Baltimore, Penguin Books, 1966. 503p.
A71.5

"... a broad panorama of English legal history from 597 to the middle of the twentieth century." G.G. Kempin, Jr., American Jl of Legal History 10:321 (1966). Mr. Harding has also written The law courts of medieval England (1973).

804

JENKS, EDWARD. The book of English law, as at the end of the year 1952. 5th rev. ed., by D. J. L. I. Davies. London, Murray [1953.] 347p. +
A6

A concise, accurate treatise covering the field of English civil law.

805

KINNANE, CHARLES H. A first book on Anglo-American law. 2d ed. Indianapolis, Bobbs-Merrill, [1952.] 810p. +
A4, A25, A28, A43, A56

Describes the function, origin, nature and history of law and the organization of American courts, American legal procedure and remedies.

806

KIRALFY, ALBERT K. R. The English legal system. 2d ed. London, Sweet & Maxwell, 1956. 404p.
A19

Designed to give beginners their first view of English law and legal institutions. Good historical background adds perspective to the discussion. Chapter 3 on sources is quite well done. A 6th edition was published in 1978.

807

LUNT, DUDLEY C. The road to law....N.Y., McGraw-Hill, 1932. 281p.
A45

By use of the case method, sugar coated with interesting facts, the author attempts to teach the lay reader the law in the first-year law books. It also describes the work of judges and lawyers—but does not show the human or social considerations that enter into decisions. See A.B.A.Jl 19:37 (1937).

808

MORTENSON, ERNEST. You be the judge ... London, N.Y., Longmans, Green, 1940. 451p. +
A28

The purpose of this book is to give the layman a general idea of the principles of the law. The style is lively and entertaining showing by illustration how the principles work. The author uses quiz games making the reader apply what he has learned to the decision of real controversies. The reader becomes the judge—hence the title. See A.B.A.Jl 26:915 (1940).

809

POLLOCK, SIR FREDERICK, bar. The genius of the common law ...N.Y., Columbia Univ. Press, 1912. 141p. +
A28

A critical study of certain characteristics of the common law which only an accomplished legal historian, a master of the modern law, and a professor of jurisprudence could have written. See Holdsworth, Some Makers of English law, p. 287.

810

RADCLIFF, GEOFFREY. The English legal system [with] Geoffrey Cross. 3d ed. London, Butterworth, 1954. 440p. +
A31.7

A beginner's book, well arranged and agreeably written which gives a short history of English legal institutions and an account of the existing organization of English courts of law.

EQUITY

811

MAITLAND, FREDERIC W. Equity, also, the forms of action at common law... ed. by A. H. Chaytor ...and W. J. Whittaker ... Cambridge [Eng.] Univ. Press, 1936. 92p. +
A11, A37

These lectures were designed for law students. Principles are clearly stated and the lectures on the forms of action at common law give an insight into the way in which the common law has developed.

812

NEWMAN, RALPH A. Equity in the world's legal systems; a comparative study. Brussels, Establissements Emile Bruylant, 1973. 652p.
A31.7

"The thirty-three essays contained in this tribute to Rene Cassin discuss the concepts of equity, by whatever name known in the major legal systems of the world including ancient Hebrew, Roman Law, Catholic Canon Law ...In addition, there are essays on the philosophy and theory of equity, universality of equity, equity in international law, natural law and equity, and the Editor's own final essay on the general principles of equity." S. Houston Lay, California Western International Law Jl 4:397 (1974).

EVIDENCE

815

MAGUIRE, JOHN MacARTHUR. Evidence; common sense and common law.... Chicago, Foundation Press, 1947. 251p. +
A6

Prof. Maguire discusses the controversial problems of trial evidence and makes practical suggestions for elimination of the inconsistencies of the rules of evidence.

816

MORGAN, EDMUND M. Some problems of proof under the Anglo-American system of litigation. N.Y., Columbia Univ. Press, 1956. 207p. +
A19, A56

Carpenter Lectures for 1955 on the function of procedural rules, including evidence, in the administration of justice in jury trials. [A56] A brilliant summation of Prof. Morgan's prior commentary which has ranged over practically the entire law of evidence. J. Faulknor, Ann. Survey. Am. Law 1956:525.

817

MUNSTERBERG, HUGO. On the witness stand; essays on psychology and crime ...with foreword by Charles S. Whitman ...N.Y., Clark Boardman, [1923] 1941. 268p.
A40

The possibilities of the application of psychology to law, mainly in the acquisition of evidence, is considered here. Many illustrative references add interest to the book, particularly the example of creating a scene in a classroom and asking each student to describe what he saw.

818

OSBORN, ALBERT S. Questioned document problems, the discovery and proof of the facts. 2d ed....Introd. by Dean Roscoe Pound ...Albany, Boyd Printing, 1946. 569p. * +
A12, A23, A29, A35, A62

A fascinating account by a famous handwriting expert. He analyzes his methods of detecting forgeries with pen and typewriter and of disclosing other frauds. Illustrated with many photographs. Recommended by Harvard for 1st year students and then to be reread in 2nd and 3rd years-greater knowledge of the law will then add to understanding of the book.

819

WIGMORE, JOHN H. The principles of judicial proof; or the process of proof as given by logic, psychology, and general experience and illustrated in judicial trials....2d ed. Boston, Little, Brown, 1931. 1056p. * +
A35

830

____. ____. 1st ed. 1913. 1179 p. * +
A35

A collection of famous trials such as the Lizzie Borden case and other materials to illustrate puzzling problems of fact, with comments by a great legal writer. One of the most delightful books in a law library. The 2d ed. in 1931, is less interesting because of extensive omission. See Harvard Law Rev. 58:598 (1945). Dean Wigmore, of course, is the author of Wigmore on Evidence, a monumental treatise presently kept up-to-date by legal scholars who have not retained the renaissance quality of the original.

FAMILY LAW
See PERSONS

FICTION, PLAYS, POETRY, etc.
See also LAW AND LITERATURE

Many works were recommended in this field—so many—in fact, that the editors found it necessary to delete some of the obvious ones.

A faculty-alumni committee of The University of Kansas City School of Law chose certain classics as part of a list of great literature with which it is particularly important that lawyers be acquainted. This is in furtherance of the goal that "first of all, a lawyer ought to be an educated man." In this group it recommended among others:

No. 821 - Shakespeare's Hamlet, Merchant of Venice, Macbeth, Julius Caesar, Richard III.

All of the classic Greek plays.

No. 822 - The Rubaiyat of Omar Khayyam.

No. 823 - The Odes of Horace

No. 824 - The Epigrams of Martial

No. 825 - The Satires of Juvenal

No. 826 - The works of Balzac

No. 827 - The works of Mark Twain (Samuel Clemens)

831

ANDERSON, MAXWELL. Winterset; a play. N.Y., Sloane Assoc. [1935.] 104p. * +
A7, A22, A27, A39, A43.5

A great American tragedy. Anderson depicts a possible aftermath of the Sacco-Vanzetti case with Mio, the son of one of the executed men attempting to clear his father of the guilt attached to him. Issues of faith, justice and integrity are considered.

832

ANOUILH, JEAN. Antigone. [many editions]
A49

This play raises the basic question of the source and the authority of the law. Mr. Anouilh is also the author of The Lark (1956) translated by Christopher Fry. [A43.5].

833

AUCHINCLOSS, LOUIS. The great world and Timothy Colt. Boston, Houghton, Mifflin, 1956. 285p. * +
A8, A19, A38.5, A43.5, A71.5

A young N.Y. lawyer with ideals becomes disillusioned and reverts to the other extreme, wrecking his career and marriage. Excellent characterizations are given of Colt's clients and members of his law firm and their families. See also Benjamin Kaplan's review in Harvard Law Rev. 70:1132 (1957). Other books written by the author and recommended are: The Partners (1974) reviewed by G. Edward White in A.B.A.Jl 60:1020 (1974). [A35.5]; and Powers of Attorney (1963). A35.5, A43.5, A53, A71.5. For a less Jamesian but well-crafted picture of the law, read the stories of Lowell B. Komie, Judges chambers (A.B.A. 1983). Loie Fenerle recommends them for first year students. Commentator (N.Y.U.), September 22, 1983, p.6.

834

____. Law for the Lion. Boston, Houghton Mifflin, 1953. 279p.
A8 * +

A divorce is the central theme here. The author's knowledge of law is expertly handled. The book is considered as "lively reading and takes a good whack at false living and false gods."

835

BALZAC, HONORE DE. Eugenie Grandet. London, J. M. Dent, N.Y., Dutton [1907.] 229p. (First published in 1833; in many editions.) A27, A39, A61 * +

See annotation for No. 836.

836

____. The rise and fall of Cesar Birotteau. London, Dent, 1896. 348p. (First published in 1837; in many editions.). * + A27, A39, A61

F. Loesch writing in Ill. L. Rev. 1:465, states that "Balzac is the greatest judge of human nature after Shakespeare. I think I learned more of human nature (outside of my own experience) from Balzac than I have from any other author except Shakespeare." He particularly recommends numbers 835, 836.

837

BARTH. JOHN. The floating opera. N.Y., Avon, 1965, 1956. 272p. N.Y., Appleton-Century-Crofts, 1956. 280p. A25.5

"... the cerebral maunderings of Todd Andrews, a lawyer who is a reincarnated version of Laurence Sterne's uninhibited Tristram Shandy. ..." Siegfried Mandel, N.Y. Times Book Rev., Aug. 26, 1956, p.27.

838

BASSO, HAMILTON. View from Pompey's Head. Garden City, N.Y., Doubleday, 1954. 409p. * + A8

A literary claim is investigated in a Southern town by a N.Y. lawyer who formerly lived there. A mystery of disappearing funds is cleared up in "a loquacious, unhurried, pleasant-toned story," chosen by the Literary Guild.

839

BLAUSTEIN, ALBERT P., ed. Fiction goes to court; favorite stories of lawyers and the law selected by famous lawyers. [1st ed.] N.Y., Holt [1954.] 303p. * + A7, A8, A27

The Library Journal has recommended this book for all public libraries, dormitory and open shelf collections of colleges and universities. Stories by M.D. Post, Arthur Train, A.P. Herbert, John Galsworthy, O, Octavus Roy

Cohen, Irwin S. Cobb, R. McDaniel, A.A. Milne, William Faulkner, Irwin Shaw, R.H. Davis, Harry Glingsberg, Marc Connelly, S.V. Benet, J.R. Parker, C.O. Skinner, and E.S. Gardner.

840

BOK, CURTIS. Backbone of the herring....N.Y., Knopf, 1941. 302p. * +
A7, A11, A22, A25.5, A27, A28, A35, A36, A39, A43, A44, A64

Fictionalized account of a trial judge's attempt to do justice by searching out the character of the litigants. Interwoven with the recital of the cases are the judge's meditations on the meaning of justice. Read also Judge Bok's Star Wormword (1959).

841

____. I too, Nicodemus. N.Y., Knopf, 1946. 349p. * +
A1, A7, A8, A14, A19, A27, A28, A36, A39, A43, A43.5, A54, A56, A62, A63, A64, A67

Gives a cross section of the array of situations that a trial judge meets in his work and must solve somehow. The cases are fascinating and superbly narrated. [A43].

842

BOLL, HEINRICH. The lost honor of Katherine Blum. N.Y., McGraw-Hill, 1975. 142p.
A43.5

"The contrast between the American and the German systems of law with respect to the rights of defendants, on the one hand, and the attitude toward freedom of the press versus the rights of the accused, on the other hand, make the book particularly interesting to an American lawyer." Bruce R. Rockwood, A.B.A.Jl 63:35 (1971).

843

BOLT, ROBERT. A man for all seasons. N.Y., Random House, 1962. 163p.
A2.5

A solid dramatization of St. Thomas More's involvement in politics and religion when to lose meant losing your head.

844

BOTEIN, BERNARD. The prosecutor, a novel. N.Y., Simon & Schuster, 1956. 273p. * +
A8, A19, A64

"I have tried to capture the color and the glory and the crackling excitement of a prosecuting office." This statement by Judge Botein, the author, aptly summarizes this excellent story of a ruthless Ass't District Attorney. It has authentic background, because the author was himself a distinguished special investigator and prosecutor.

845

BRIEUX, EUGENE. The red robe. (In C. H. Whitman, Representative modern dramas. [1936, 1940.]) * +
A7, A27

The leit motif in this play is the warping effect of ambition on justice. A French peasant accused of murder is remorselessly and unfairly prosecuted by one who desires to attain the red robe of a judge.

846

BURGESS, ANTHONY. A clockwork orange. N.Y., W.W.Norton & Co., 1963. 184p.
A29.5

"The novel...is set in a near future utopia that has all but eliminated the standard economic causes of crime. Nevertheless, gangs of young hoodlums roam the streets ...beating, robbing, and raping. ...Alex, the gratuitously vicious leader of one of these gangs, narrates the story. Thus it is significant that when the State, through conditioning, cures Alex of his propensity to do evil it also 'cures' him of his ability to appreciate music." John T. Anderson, American Jl of Criminal Law 1:249 (1972). The moving picture is also a harrowing experience.

847

CECIL, HENRY, pseud. According to the evidence. N.Y., Harper, 1954. 216p. * +
A8, A19

See annotation for No. 850.

848

____. Brothers in law. N.Y., Harper, [c1955.] 275p. * +
A8, A19

"The misadventures of a neophyte embarking upon his career at the English Bar." Leo E. Lloyd, A.B.A.Jl 42:538 (1956). In the same vein is Daughters in Law (1961) reviewed by Elmer M. Million, Albany Law Rev. 26:376 (1962). See also annotation for No. 850.

849

____. Much in evidence. London, Michael Joseph [1957.] 192p.
A8, A19

See annotation for No. 850.

850

____. No bail for the judge. N.Y., Harper, 1952. 181p.
A8, A19

A wonderful sense of humor, a charming and skillful literary style, an accurate knowledge of law and administration of justice in England, characterize the works of Henry Cecil. You must become familiar with Colonel Brain, "undoubtedly the greatest character in fiction." See also Full Circle (1948). [A74]

851

CHESTER, GIRAUD. The ninth juror. N.Y., Random House, 1970. 205p.
A27.5, A57.7

"... the report of the experience of one juror, starting with the voir dire and continuing through the trial to the verdict ... the book is an affirmation of the justness of our system of criminal procedure." James R. Greenfield, Conn. Bar Jl 45:94 (1971).

852

[CLARK, ALFRED A. G.] Tragedy at law, by Cyril Hare [pseud.] London, Faber & Faber [1942.] 290p. * +
A27, A44, A74

A mystery novel of English judicial life. The law involved is accurately presented and the climax contains an ingenious legal point. See also the author's That yew tree's shade (1954) and When the wind blows (1950,1976). See the New Republic, July 30, 1977 for a fine profile of Mr. Hare, as well as Harry Stephen Keeler, Dashiell Hammett, William Haggard, Jacques Futrelle, Ngaio Marsh, Earl Derr Biggers, Arthur W. Upfield and Rex Stout. P.D. James could be added to this Pantheon of detective story writers.

853

CLARK, WALTER VAN T. The ox-bow incident. N.Y., Random House, 1940. 309p. * +
A12, A22, A23, A29, A35.5, A43

This fine novel of the West gives expression to the forces leading to an orderly system of law in a frontier community. [A12]. Harvard recommends this for 1st year students and worth rereading in 2nd and 3rd years to ascertain how much more you can get out of it with a legal training. The film, starring Henry Fonda, is a stark tragedy of a posse committing murder in the name of justice.

854

COE, CHARLES F. Pressure. N.Y., Random House, 1951. 186p.
A8 * +

An unsuccessful lawyer becomes involved with a criminal organization. Mr. Coe, who is a lawyer, tells a lawyer's story—precise and well worked out. In spite of a somewhat old-fashioned style, it is a story as modern as the Kefauver hearings. See N.Y. Herald Tribune Book Rev. S. 9 '51.

855

COLLINS, WILKIE. The woman in white. [in many editions]
A53

Estate planning at its most criminal. Collins was called to the bar in 1851, but decided on writing as a career. He collaborated with Dickens on several works. He is considered as the first English novelist to write detective stories.

856

____. The moonstone. [in many editions]
A53

The curse of the gem.

857

COZZENS, JAMES G. ...The just and the unjust. N.Y., Harcourt, Brace, [1942.] 434p. * +
A1, A7, A8, A12, A14, A19, A23, A27, A27.5, A28, A29, A34, A35, A36, A38.5, A39, A41, A43, A43.5, A44, A49, A56, A57, A57.1, A57.7, A61, A63, A64, A68, A71.5

The best account in fiction of the daily life of ordinary lawyers. It tells something of what really happens in office work and in trials. [A12]. The book is exciting reading and is also a competent introduction to the problems of evidence and strategy in a trial involving murder. [A43]. Harvard recommends this for 1st year students and worth rereading in 2nd and 3rd years to ascertain how much more you can get out of it with a legal training.

858

____. By love possessed. N.Y., Harcourt, Brace and Co., 1957. 570p.
A38.5, A49, A53

"Perhaps the most rewarding aspect of the novel is that it integrates profound questions of law, ethics and morals into a background which is not on the one hand Elizabethan and therfore archaic, or on the other hand that of unique tribe of judicial specialists, but rather the not extraordinary life of a believable modern attorney." John P. MacArthur, Buffalo Law Rev. 7:339 (1957-8).

859

CRICHTON, MICHAEL. The great train robbery. N.Y., Knopf, 1975. 266p.
A43.5

A reconstruction of the celebrated robbery of gold bullion by a gang organized by a Victorian gentleman of substance if not form.

860

DICKENS, CHARLES. Bleak House. (First published in 1852. Available in many editions.) * +
A2.5, A6, A7, A21, A27, A28, A35, A35.5, A36, A43, A43.5, A47, A61, A71.5, A74

One theme of this story is the monstrous injustice and even ruin that could be wrought by the delays in the Old Court of Chancery which defeated all purposes of a court of justice. The case is that of Jarndyce v. Jarndyce in which an indecisive judge let a suit drag on for twenty years. [A43]. See also the Holdsworth book on Dickens [No. 1640].

861

____. Great expectations. (First published in 1861. Available in many editions.) * +
A7, A27, A39, A61

The Old Bailey Court House and its surroundings plays an important role here.

862

____. The posthumous papers of the Pickwick Club. (First published in 1837—available in many editions.) * +
A7, A8, A12, A19, A27, A28, A29, A35, A36, A39, A43, A43.5, A61, A71.5, A74

The most famous lawsuit in fiction is Bardell v. Pickwick. Do not be too discouraged by the case as it represents an exaggeration of the situation more than a century ago. This gives you a vivid impression of the situation before modern reforms—which still leave considerable room for progress, with which you may some day be able to help. [A12]. Can be understood better in 2nd and 3rd years, if reread then. The Bardell case can be found in Prosser's Judicial Humorist [No. 761].

863

DOSTOEVSKY, FEODOR M. Crime and punishment. (First published in 1866—now available in many editions.) * +
A8, A27, A39, A43.5, A61

A great classic story of an impoverished, sensitive intellectual who believed he was above moral law. It is interesting, too, to follow the use of psychology in police investigation of crime.

864

DOYLE, SIR ARTHUR CONAN. Sherlock Holmes, memoirs and adventures. (First published in 1891—now available in many editions.) * +
A8

A collection of short stories of the "adventures" of the famous amateur detective Sherlock Holmes, as told by his friend Dr. John Watson. Sherlock's deductive powers and his knowledge of science and English law serve him in good stead in the solution of his detective problems.

865

DREISER, THEODORE. An American tragedy. (First published in 1925—now available in various editions.) * +
A27, A39, A61

Involves social inequality and lack of privilege and how they affect a young man. An interesting trial scene is one of the book's dramatic features. The book is based on an actual case. See the section on Dreiser and Darrow in Law and American literature [No. 1512], p. 88.

866

FAST, HOWARD. The American. N.Y., Grosset & Dunlap, 1977. 311p.
A53

Based on the life of John Peter Altgeld, a Governor of Illinois at the time of Darrow.

867

[FULLER, EDMUND] ed. Law in action, an anthology of the law in literature; ed. by Amicus Curiae with an introd. by Roscoe Pound. N.Y., Crown publishers [1947.] 408p. * +
A21, A27, A28, A41, A43, A43.5, A57.1

Something new in the way of anthologies. Its operative principle of selection is to show what the layman thinks of law. Law is the state, or state authority and law in action is the interaction of state and individual upon each other. Liberty, morals, justice and crime are the aspects from which this interaction is viewed. The compiler in his selection has tempered drama with comedy, realism with fancy. See N.Y.U.L.Q. Rev. 23:566 (1948).

868

GALSWORTHY, JOHN. The Forsythe saga. (First published in 1922—now available in various editions.) * +
A27, A35, A39, A61, A74

A well known work of fiction. The leading character is an office lawyer. There are two divorce cases, the second of which recounts at length the examination of witnesses and the observations of the judge. See Harvard Law Rev. 58:603 (1945).

869

____. Plays (Strife; Justice; Loyalties.) (In various editions.) * +
A7, A27, A35, A39

Galsworthy's collected plays appeared in 1929. Justice (1910) and Loyalties are of particular interest. The first asks whether criminal law is just; the second presents a lawyer's ethical dilemma. See Harvard Law Rev. 58:603 (1945). Also The Silver box (1909) [A74].

870

GILBERT, SIR WILLIAM S. Trial by jury [with] Sir Arthur Sullivan. (First presented in London in 1875. Available in various editions.) +
A27, A39, A71.5, A74

This is a satire on a breach of promise action. It is believed that Gilbert was influenced by the trial of Bardell v. Pickwick of Dickens' Pickwick Papers fame. Gilbert practised law too, and it is possible that the play reflects his own reaction to legal procedure.

871

GODWIN, WILLIAM. Caleb Williams. (First published in 1794—now available in various editions.) * +
A43.5

Reflects 18th century English law which leaned so heavily in favor of the wealthy landowners as against the poorer citizens. It also describes prison life during the long time Caleb had to await his trial.

872

GROSS, FRED LOUIS. What is the verdict? N.Y., Macmillan, 1944. 311p. * +
A8

Based on actual cases, a former president of the N.Y. State Bar Association relates a series of hypothetical cases with the purpose of explaining some of the problems of the law. Pleasant reading with a warm sense of humor.

873

HABERMAN, HELEN (LIEBMAN). Justice is a woman. N.Y., Prentice-Hall, [1947.] 360p. * +
A8

A story about a lawyer practising in N.Y., stimulating to the mind. Note the chapter involving a condemnation case before the Court of Appeals.

874

HAMILTON, BRUCE. Hanging judge. N.Y., Harper, [1948.] 250p.
A54 * +

This novel of suspense concerning a British judge who is tried and convicted for murder receives its impact from the judge's own reputation as a particularly severe "adminstrator of justice." [A54].

875

HARDY, THOMAS. Tess of the D'Urbervilles. (First published in 1891—available in various editions.) +
A5

This is a modern classic typifying how fate influences the lives of people. Dean Woodbridge states that it is one of the books that most influenced his overall attitude toward life.

876

HARRINGTON, WILLIAM. Which the justice, which the thief? Indianpolis, Bobbs-Merrill, 1963. 288p.
A53

A 92 year old judge relates the case of an armed robbery.

877

HAWTHORNE, NATHANIEL. The scarlet letter. (First published in 1850—available in various editions.) * +
A8, A43.5

Dean Wigmore once wrote "what lawyer can afford to be ignorant of the never-fading scenes in The Scarlet Letter." See Ill. L. Rev. 2:576 (1908).

878

HELLMAN, LILLIAN. Scoundrel time. Boston, Little, Brown, 1976. 163p.
A53

Ms. Hellman's memoir of the witch-hunting, black-listing years of the 1950s, and her involvement with them. She testified before the House UnAmerican Activities Committee unlike a small coterie of Hollywood writers who paid a penalty of contempt for exhibiting their own.

879

HIGGINS, GEORGE V. The friends of Eddie Coyle. N.Y., Knopf, 1972. 183p.
A53

The criminal scene in Boston as dialogued by a former district attorney.

880

HOBSON, LAURA Z. Gentlemen's agreement. N.Y., Simon & Schuster, 1947. 275p. * +
A8

A powerful and well told novel on the subject of anti-semitism. A young American journalist poses as a Jew for a short period of time.

881

HUGO, VICTOR. Les miserables. (First published around 1880. Now available in many editions.) * +
A8, A47

Chosen by a faculty-alumni committe of Univ. of Kansas City School of Law for reasons given at the beginning of this section.

882

IBSEN, HENRIK. An enemy of the people. N.Y., Dutton, 1911.
A43.5

A powerful drama depicting the reactions of a town's solid citizens to the threat of bankruptcy should they inform tourists that their water system is suspect.

883

JACKSON, FELIX. So help me God, a novel. N.Y., Viking Press, 1955. 310p. * +
A8

A novel concerning a N.Y. lawyer, not a communist, who writes anonymously to a Congressional Committee accusing himself of being a member of the Party, in order to show how difficult it is for an innocent man to prrove his innocence once he has attracted the attention of the Committee. See New Yorker 31:169.

884

KAFKA, FRANZ. The trial; translated by Edwin and Willa Muir. N.Y., Knopf, [c1937.] 297p. +
A27, A39, A43.5

First published in 1925, this is considered to be a "powerful and provocative" book, containing humor and fantasy. Kafka is arrested for a crime he knows nothing about. It is a symbolic tale and apparently a commentary on a legal system whose leaders are convinced they are right.

885

KEMMELMAN, HARRY. The nine mile walk. N.Y., Putnam, 1967. 186p.
A53

Is academic advancement and publication in learned journals a basis for a motive to commit murder? That and other stories.

886

LAWRENCE, JEROME and ROBERT E. LEE. Inherit the wind. N.Y. Bantam, 1960 (c.1955). 115p.
A29.5

A fictional account of the Darrow/Bryan confrontation in the Scopes creationism trial.

887

LEE, HARPER. To kill a mocking bird. Phila., Lippincott, 1960. 296p.
A2.5, A6.5, A35.5, A43.5, A49

A seering account of race, rape, and revenge in pre-King South that ends in an emotionally laden trial scene. The film, starring Gregory Peck, was a moving drama.

888

LEWIS, SINCLAIR. Arrowsmith. N.Y., Harcourt Brace, 1925. 448p. * +
A8, A40

First published in 1924. Lewis considers the American medical profession, castigating its desire for publicity, the commercial aspects of the fashionable clinic, the political corruption in the field of public health. A doctor can find salvation in medical and scientific research, he believes. See also A.J. Cronin's The Citadel.

889

____. Cass Timberlane; a novel of husbands and wives. N.Y., Random House, [c1945.] 390p. +
A27

An attack on the smugness and cruelty of small town life. Mr. Lewis is best known for his seering attack on the bourgeoisie, Babbitt (1922).

890

LIPSKY, ELEAZOR. Lincoln McKeever. N.Y., Appleton-Century-Crofts, 1953. 309p. * +
A8, A27

A land grant case in New Mexico involving a clash between Anglo-Saxon and Spanish cultures is the main theme here. As a lawyer, Lipsky handles the trial scenes very well.

891

MANKIEWICZ, DON M. Trial. N.Y., Harper. [c1955.] 306p. * +
A27, A43.5, A61

A realistic picture of Communist exploitation of the trial of a young Mexican for rape and murder. The place is a West Coast city where racial prejudice makes a verdict of guilty highly probable, a situation seized on by the Communists. See Booklist 51:161.

892

MARBUT, Ann. Bill of particulars. N.Y., David McKay, 1955. 304p. * +
A8

Nancy Cameron decides to carry on the family tradition

of the practice of law despite much opposition. The action takes place in a small town in Pennsylvania. She succeeds. The authoress is a lawyer and writes pleasantly of small town life and legal cases.

893

MELTSNER, MICHAEL. Short takes. N.Y., Random House, 1979. 244p.
A29.5

"Blurring the line between fiction and nonfiction, it's hardly a novel in the usual sense - the turbulent professional life cycle of a sensitive young lawyer, baptized by the fire of the real world, fitfully unravels in a stream of consciousness style." A.B.A.Jl 66:984 (1980). The author was Dean of the Northeastern School of Law.

894

MELVILLE, HERMAN. Billy Budd. (Written around 1891, available in various editions.) * +
A22, A27, A38.5, A39

An impressed American seaman is taken aboard a British warship in 1797. There, although his actions are exemplary, he arouses the animosity of a superior petty officer, eventually resulting in his court-martial and hanging under circumstances which make him almost saintly. See Charles A. Reich, The tragedy of justice in Billy Budd, Yale Rev. 56:368 (1967). And do not neglect Bartleby the scrivener: a story of Wall Street. See Peter Baida, Wall Street Jl, Oct. 31, 1983, p. 30.

895

NOWINSON, MARIE L. Legacy of Gabriel Martel. N.Y., Appleton-Century-Crofts, 1950. 311p.
A8

A father of four children, who is a lawyer, is influenced in his career by the precepts of Christian ethics. In doing so, his children's lives are affected. There are many accounts of his legal cases. This is an inspiring, religious novel.

896

OSBORN, JOHN JAY, JR. The Associates. Boston, Houghton- Mifflin Co., 1979. 270p.
A6.5, A57.1

"Instead of aged Ivy League classrooms, the confrontations now occur in the starkly modern offices of Bass & Marshall [where] excellence is measured strictly by your clients and money. And associates striving desperately for partnership are cannon fodder to be ruthlessly exploited, then cast aside to a corporate law department." Jeremy C. Shea, A.B.A.Jl 65:776 (1979).

897

____. The paper chase. Boston, Houghton-Mifflin Co., 1971. 181p.
A6.5, A35.5

One can perhaps divide the student body at any major law school into three broad types: the whizzes, who perform exceptionally well in class or on exams either as a result of natural endowment or acquisition of 'inside dope' from upperclassmen; the playboys and jokers...and the grinds, who read all assigned material and operate on the belief that constant preoccupation with study and review are necessary for and result in success in law school. Osborn has written a book about the grinds." Donald H.J. Hermann, Wisconsin Law Rev. 1972:634.

898

PARKER, JAMES REID. Attorneys at law, Forbes, Hathaway, Bryan & Devore. Garden City, N.Y., Doubleday, Doran, 1941. 247p. * +
A8, A27

These stories appeared originally in the New Yorker magazine and pertain to the daily activities of a Wall Street law firm. The big corporation lawyers are held up to ridicule in an inoffensive way. You get the authentic ring of steel on stone and see the honest sparks fly. See N.Y. Herald-Tribune Books—N. 16 '41.

899

PARTRIDGE, BELLAMY. Country lawyer....N.Y., Whittlesey House, McGraw-Hill, [c1939.] 317p. * +
A1, A2, A6, A8, A11, A14, A19, A23, A25.5, A27, A28, A29, A30, A35, A36, A39, A40, A43, A54, A56, A59, A61, A63, A67, A68, A72

An uplifting account of the pleasant variety of work and recreation which falls to the lot of the old-fashioned lawyer in a small town. [A54]. See also Pepper, Philadelphia lawyer (1944) for a big city practice [No. 278].

900

PATON, ALAN. Cry, the beloved country; a story of comfort in desolation. N.Y., Scribner's, 1948. 278 p. * +
A22

A distinguished novel about racial unrest in South Africa written by a minister.

901

PECK, DAVID W. The Greer case, a true court drama. N.Y., Simon & Schuster, 1955. 209p. +
A19, A43.5

A fascinating case involving a claim to a valuable estate by a "natural" heir.

902

POWELL, RICHARD. The Philadelphian. N.Y., Scribner, 1956. 376p.
A29.5

The ingredients for a Philadelphia lawyer. See Edward J. Bander, Woe unto you, novelists! A.B.A.Jl 45:925 (1959) for an appraisal of this and other novels about lawyers.

903

RABELAIS, FRANCOIS. Gargantua and Pantagruel. (Written around 1533 to 1567. Available in many editions.) +
A47

Rabelais' theme is that the true meaning of life can be ascertained by experiencing as much as possible. Earthy, gay and prodigious eaters and drinkers, dominate the story. Chosen by a faculty-alumni committee of University of Kansas City School of Law for reasons given at the beginning of this section. The legal profession receives its share of satire.

904

RADIN, MAX. The day of reckoning. N.Y., Knopf, 1943. 144p.
A54

Though cast in the form of a dramatic play, this book is a searching discourse on the nature of law. It seeks to determine on what legal grounds the actions of Hitler and his associates can be tried for crimes and punished accordingly. See Harvard Law Rev. 56:1338 (1945).

905

RATTIGAN, TERENCE. The Winslow boy [with two other plays]. London, Pan Books, 1950. 251p. +
A27

This play is based on an actual case involving the Archer-Shee family and the famous advocate Lord Carson. A young lad is dismissed for petty theft from the Royal Naval Academy, and his father makes a long gallant fight to reinstate him and establish his innocence. It is the classic theme of a person wrongfully accused and justice conquering in the end. This play is reprinted in London's The World of Law [No. 1509].

906

RICE, ELMER L. Counsellor-at-law, a play in three acts. N.Y.[etc.] S. French, [c1931.] 1940. 298p. +
A7, A27, A39

First produced in 1931, it involves a busy city lawyer and the problems with which he is confronted as part of his daily routine. From humble, immigrant peasants, the attorney has risen to society ranks the hard way—and at times by some shady methods. One of these tricks is brought to light by a society lawyer who doesn't like him. This brings out the dramatic climax.

907

____. On trial. (In Burns Mantle, Best Plays of 1909-1919 ...N.Y., Dodd, Mead, 1933.) +
A7, A27, A39

First played on Broadway in 1914. The center of the action is a courtroom during a murder trial with flashbacks to
The trial scenes are dramatic and tense.

908

SARTRE, JEAN PAUL. The flies [In No Exit and Three Other Plays] N.Y., Vintage Books, 1982.
A29.5

"...law schools have been sluggish [to] stimulate student initiative, inspire creative thought ...so otherwise lacking in the standard legal curriculum...In The Flies, Sartre grapples with the illusive quality of free will and the problem of assigning responsibility and blameworthiness to one who commits an act and to the environment and person that have laid the groundwork for that act." American Jl Criminal Law 1:133 (1972).

909

SCOTT, SIR WALTER. Guy Mannering [in many editions]
A74

Based on the Annesley case. Other books by Scott that are recommended are The Heart of Midlothian and Red Gauntlett. [A74]

910

SHAW, GEORGE B. St. Joan. (In various editions.) * +
A22, A27

This is considered to be Shaw's most important play. It depicts Joan standing for freedom of conscience against the decrees of the established Church. Shaw accurately follows the trial procedure of the period.

911

SNOW, CHARLES PERCY. The affair. N.Y., Scribner, 1960. 374p.
A53

One of Mr. Snow's Strangers and Brothers novels. See also his _Two cultures; and a second look_ (1969) about the difficulty of communication between the scientist and the artist.

912

SOLMSSEN, ARTHUR R.G. The comfort letter, a novel. Boston, Little, Brown, 1975. 328p.
A29.5

The Philadelphia firm of Conyers and Dean, and its dealings with a conglomerate. An accuratte portrayal of a firm involved in corporate law.

913

TAKATA, TIMOTHY. The last exam; a novel. Roslyn Heights, N.Y., Libra, 1977. 120p.
A43.5

A novel about the bar exam.

914

TEY, JOSEPHINE. [pseudonym of Elizabeth Mackintosh] The daughter of time. N.Y., Macmillan, 1952. 204p.
A53

Detective stories have long been standard fare for a lawyer's leisure hours. Ms. Tey is considered one of the better in this genre. Here, she speculates on whether Richard III murdered the little Princes. See also annotation for No. 852.

915

____. The franchise affair. N.Y., Macmillan, 1948. 238p.
A53

A country solicitor is enmeshed in a criminal action hinging on whether to believe a fifteen year old girl or two eccentric old ladies.

916

THACKERAY, WILLIAM MAKEPEACE. Pendennis...1849 [in many editions]

Thackeray entered the Middle Temple...and his experience there is pictured in Chapter 29. See Williams, The Study of Law (1982) p.228. [A74]

TRAIN, ARTHUR C.

Arthur Train is the author of the "Tutt" series. The "Tutt" stories are well-known for their charm and entertainment based on a great variety of legal situations solved by the perspicacity and legal learning of an "old-fashioned" successful practitioner of the law.

917

____. The adventures of Ephraim Tutt, attorney and counsellor-at-law. N.Y., Scribner's 1930. 751p. * +
A28, A37, A66, A71.5, A72

918

____. Blind goddess. N.Y., Grosset & Dunlop, 1926. 338p.
A28, A66 * +

919

____. By advice of counsel, being adventures of the celebrated firm of Tutt and Tutt....N.Y., Scribner's, 1921. 267p. * +
A28, A66

920

____. The confessions of Artemas Quibble....onetime practitioner in the N.Y. criminal courts, together with an account of the divers wiles, tricks, sophistries, technicalities, and sundry artifices of himself and others of the fraternity, commonly yclept "shysters." ...N.Y., Scribner's 1922. 227p. * +
A28, A43.5, A54, A66

921

____. Mr. Tutt at his best, a collection of his most famous cases. N.Y., Scribner, 1961. 357p.
A28

See also Mr. Tutt's case book (with an introduction by John H. Wigmore 1936) which includes a legal analysis of each of Mr. Tutt's "most celebrated trials."

922

____. Mr. Tutt comes home. N.Y., Scribner's, 1941. 341p.
A8, A66, A71.5 * +

923

____. Mr. Tutt finds a way. N.Y., Scribner's, 1945. 241 p.
A8, A28, A43, A66, A71.5 * +

924

____. Mr. Tutt takes the stand; a collection of Mr. Tutt's most celebrated trials. N.Y., Scribner's, [1936.] 290p. * +
A43, A66, A71.5

925

____. Tut, tut! Mr. Tutt. N.Y., Scribner's, 1923. 315p. * +
A28, A35, A66, A71.5

926

____. Tutt and Mr. Tutt....N.Y., Scribner's, 1921. 304p. * +
A27, A28, A35, A39, A61, A64, A66, A71.5, A72

927

____. Yankee lawyer, the autobiography of Ephraim Tutt....N.Y., Scribner's 1943. 464p. * +
A6, A8, A11, A12, A23, A28, A29, A36, A41, A43, A66

"By all means read Arthur Train's stories of Mr. Tutt if you have not already done so." [A21]. See also Mr. Train's review of this book, Yale Law Jl 52:945 (1943).

928

TRAVER, ROBERT [VOELKER, JOHN D.]. Anatomy of a murder. N.Y., St. Martin's Press, 1958. 437p.
A25.5, A35.5, A49, A53, A57.7, A71.5

"...so smacks of reality it is difficult to believe it entirely a product of the juridical mind at play...deadly duel between two capable advocates under the watchful eye of a superbly competent trial judge..the trial is an ideal and an idealized one...it is symbolical of the possible grandeur of the adversary system...Jack R. Wahlquist, Texas Law Rev. 36:553 (1958). This book has also been adaapted for a play by Elihu Winer (1964), and was also a successful film. [A43.5]. Judge Voelker's book The Jealous Mistress (1968) has also been recommended. [A71.5]. His Laughing whitefish (1958, 1983) is based on the true story of a contract between mining officials and an Indian Chieftan and whether American law or Indian custom should prevail.

929

TROLLOPE, ANTHONY. Orley Farm, with an introd. by Henry S. Drinker. N.Y., Knopf, 1950. 729p. (First published in 1862.)
A27, A35, A39, A74

This is a will case with a notable cross-examination. Trollope was not a lawyer, and his success in handling a legal plot as involved as any of Dickens' is quite remarkable in spite of a number of legal errors which have been criticized by lawyers. The technical and ethical deviations of Trollope's lawyers are commented upon in the introduction. See Jl Am. Jud. Soc. 34:94 (1955-6). In his novel, Phineas Redux, Trollope introduces us to a plot involving a fascinating trial scene and a great criminal lawyer. [A53].

930

TUROW, SCOTT. One L; an inside account of life in the first year at Harvard Law School. N.Y., G.B.Putman, 1977. 300p.
A6.5, A21, A35.5, A38.5, A43.5, A48.5, A57.7, A71.8

"...an evocative retelling of the first year of law school. From the initial mystery and confusion, through the depths of Socratic terror, the heights of intellectual intoxication, and the many convolutions between, to the relief and wonder at the end, the book presents a believable and gripping narrative of the experience of the beginning law student. It should be on the reading list of every person planning on or considering the possibility of attending law school....Steve Pepper, Arkansas Law Rev. 31:529 (1977). This and the Osborn book have inspired spinoffs such as Katherine A. Davis Roome's The Letter of the Law (1979) about the tortuous ritual of the second-year law review writing competition.

931

URIS, LEON. QB VII. N.Y., Doubleday, 1970. 504p.
A29.5

"This is the story of a British libel action...the theme is vengeance, powered by the implacable hatred of the Jews for those who destroyed so many of their people in Hitler's Germany. ...The trial gets off to an exciting start, but its length tests the attention span of the reader..." Walker Lewis, A.B.A.Jl 57:800 (1971).

932

VIDAL, GORE. Burr; a novel. N.Y., Random House, 1973. 430p.
A49

Law, lawyers and politics in early America, in which Burr is made out to be a delightful scoundrel.

933

WARREN, ROBERT P. All the king's men. N.Y., Bantam, 1946. 464p. * +
A8

This was a Pulitzer Prize winner on the career of a

Southern governor, obviously one like the late Gov. Huey Long of Louisiana. A brilliant novel involving politics and careers in government.

934

WARREN, SAMUEL. Ten thousand a year. (In many editions. approx. 1086p.) +
A27, A28, A39, A58, A74

A mid-nineteenth century novel reflecting English political, social and professional life of the period. The story is based on an action in ejectment when the practice of the English courts was very formalized. Contains may interesting and amusing descriptions of lawyers and their ways. See A.B.A.Jl 20:699 (1934).

935

[WIENER, PHILIP.] The Gay sisters, by Stephen Longstreet [pseud.]...N.Y., Random House [1942.] 306p. * +
A8

A story involving the three Gay sisters who inherited a fortune and what lawyers, courts and trust corporations were able to do with it over a period of twenty years or so. It was also made into a Gay Nineties Bleak House type movie with Barbara Stanwyck.

936

WILLIAM, BEN AMES. Leave her to heaven. N.Y., Houghton, 1944. 429p. * +
A27, A28, A35, A39, A61

Psychological novel in which the character of a despicable woman is the motivating force. Even after her suicide, which she arranged to resemble murder, her evil influence was not ended. See Book Rev. Dig. 1944 :815.

937

WOUK, HERMAN. The Caine mutiny court-martial. (In the Best Plays of 1953-1954.) * +
A7, A8, A27, A39, A43.5, A61

The play based on the novel has a dramatic, tense, trial scene of a court-martial—excellently presented. Also a film.

FINANCE

1000

BRANDEIS, LOUIS D. Other people's money, and how the bankers use it....New ed. with foreword by Norman Hapgood. N.Y., Frederick A. Stokes, 1932. 233p. * +
A1, A8, A14, A19, A27, A39, A56, A63

The most influential of the late Justice Brandeis' nonjudicial writings which criticizes in a popular style the financial practices of corporations and anticipates certain of the New Deal reforms. [A39].

FOREIGN AFFAIRS

See also INTERNATIONAL LAW

1115

BAILEY, THOMAS A. A diplomatic history of the American people. 4th ed. N.Y., F.S. Crofts & Co., 1950. 937p. * +
A8, A57, A68

Treats external relations of the U.S. from colonial times to the present, showing how our foreign policy has always reflected American public opinion and domestic forces. This is a highly readable book.

FORENSIC ENGLISH

See also RHETORIC; LANGUAGE

1116

BRYANT, MARGARET M. English in the law courts; the part that articles, prepositions and conjunctions play in legal decisions....N.Y., Columbia Univ. Press, 1930. 312p. +
A27

274 cases are considered. The interpretations are literal, suggested by fact based on intent, or common meaning.

1117

DICKERSON, REED. Materials on legal drafting. St. Paul, West, 1981. 425p.
A24.5

A fascinating collection of material that could serve as a basis for a course on legal writing. The Seth S. Searcy III bibliography (p. 164) is a succinct annotated list of books on style, usage and grammar.

1118

GEORGE, JOYCE J. Judicial opinion writing handbook. Buffalo, Hein, 1981. 150p.
A24.5

An exhaustive exploration into all aspects of opinion writing with innumerable examples. Includes items on how to write an opinion, structure, judgments, effective writing, appellate writing, tables, footnotes, bibliography, appendices, etc.

1119

MILLER, GEORGE L. On legal style. In 43 Kentucky Law Journal 235-273. (1955). +
A19

A clear, concise, entertaining and highly recommended brief outline on legal literary style. Miller's comments on sentence structure, parallelism in comparison, punctuation and common errors and barbarisims are of real value to the law student or lawyer.

1120

PHILBRICK, FREDERICK A. Language and the law; the semantics of forensic English. N.Y., Macmillan, 1949. 254p.
A27, A49

Written particularly for judges and lawyers on the semantics of forensic English. Considered is the influence words may exert on the law and legal thinking. The book is "illustrative rather than didactic" and hence contains exemplary judicial opinions. Four famous cases are also analyzed based on the principles he enunciates. See Michigan Law Rev. 47:871 (1949).

1121

STATSKY, WILLIAM P. Legal research, writing, and analysis. 2d ed. St. Paul, West, 1982. 167p.
A29.5

Reprinted from Introduction to paralegalism; perspectives, problems, and skills (2d ed. 1982). Pictures and texts that spoon feed the user in the use of law books.

GOVERNMENT and POLITICS

See also HUMAN INSTITUTIONS AND VALUES - Political Organization of Societies under

1130

APPLE, R.W. Jr. The White House transcripts. N.Y., Bantam Books, 1973. 877p.
A72.5

"Recorded presidential conversation to the Committee on the Judiciary of the House of Representatives by President Richard Nixon."

1131

BARTH, ALAN. Government by investigation. N.Y., Viking Press, 1955. 231p.
A31.7

"...Congressional investigations running wild. ...He is justly alarmed at three tendencies: the usurpation of executive power, the legislative trial, and the censorial inquest into ideas. [discusses Sen. McCarthy, the trials of Owen Lattimore and Virginia Durr, House Un-American Activities Committee.]" Will Maslow, Yale Law Jl 1217 (1955).

1132

BINKLEY, WILFRED E. President and Congress....N.Y., Knopf, 1947. 312p. +
A59

A study of the powers of the President and his relation to the legislature with historical background.

1133

BROGAN, WILLIAM D. Government of the people; a study in the American political system...with a foreword by Professor Harold J. Laski. N.Y., Harper, 1944. 415p. * +
A8, A30

Brogan is forced to admit that "there is an elasticity in the American system that is hard to fit into the rigid categories of textbooks and decisions." He is now almost as staunch a defender of that system (for Americans) as he was a critic before. It is too bad that this book has not been thoroughly revised to point up Brogan's new thesis. See N.Y. Times, S' 10 '44, p. 10.

1134

____. Politics and law in the United States. Cambridge [Engl.] Univ. Press, 1941. 127p. * +
A8, A28, A35

Brogan is an English political scientist with an extraordinary gift for understanding and illuminating the woof of constitutional principles and the warp of political tactics in the fabric of democratic history. He gives us a remarkably readable and able account of our own constitutional history in this small volume. He traces the accretions of custom and usage which have been added to our written constitution and proves that our system is not as inflexible as is sometimes assumed. See Nation 153:460.

1135

CORWIN, EDWARD S. The Presidency today [with] Louis W. Koenig. N.Y., N.Y.U. Press, 1956. 138p. +
A19

Most useful in its examination of the sources and nature of presidential powers. It also provides a brief but valuable restatement of the case for a new type of cabinet that will include legislative leaders as well as heads of executive and administrative agencies. There is a similar examination of problems of presidential election and succession. See N.Y. Times, May 13, 1956.

1136

CUMMINGS, HOMER S. Federal justice; chapters in the history of justice and the federal executive [with] Carl McFarland....N.Y., Macmillan, 1937. 576p. +
A62

White considers this the principal secondary historical work on the attorney general and an excellent work.

1137

de GRAZIA, SEBASTIAN. Political community: a study of anomie. Chicago, Univ. Chicago Press, 1948. 258p. +
A59

Prof. de Grazia discusses past and present cultures in relation to man's need for beliefs, and the effect of community changes of opinion or organization on man. It is a plea for a more idealistic society, in opposition to current tendencies toward disintegration. See Current Hist. 16:35.

1138

DIMOCK, MARSHALL. The executive in action. N.Y., Harper, 1945. 276p. +
A59

Based on his experience as an executive in establishing the manning organization of the Merchant Marine in World War II, the author contends that there is very little difference between management in government and in business. He then proves it.

1139

GROSS. BERTRAM M. Legislative struggle; a study in social combat. N.Y., McGraw-Hill, 1953. 472p. +
A59

The problem is put in its proper context of international crises, political power struggles, personalities, social objectives, propaganda and the pressure groups. The present relationships between the Executive and Congress receive excellent treatment. Does an excellent job of making the American political scene meaningful to students. See Current Hist. 25:131.

1140

KEY, VALDIMER O. Politics, parties, and pressure groups. 2d ed. N.Y., T. Y. Crowell [1947.] 767p. * +
A8, A59

A college textbook which extends the field covered in most courses on political parties by including pressure groups and also a discussion of violence and education as political techniques. See Book List 44:250.

1141

LEBEDOFF, DAVID. Ward number six. N.Y., Scribner, 1972. 179p.
A72.5

Concerns election of 1968.

1142

MACHIAVELLI, NICOLO. The prince, and the discourses; with an introduction by Max Lerner. N.Y., Modern library [1950.] 340p.* +
A8, A59

Machiavelli's (b. 1469) merit consists in having been the creator of the experimental science of politics—in having observed facts, studied histories and drawn consequences from them. The peculiarity of Machiavelli's genius lay in his artistic feeling for the treatment and discussion of politics in and for themselves, without regard to the immediate situation. See Encyc. Brit. 11th ed. Italian Literature.

1143

MERRIAM, ROBERT E. Going into politics [with] Rachel M. Goetz. N.Y., Harper, 1957. 216p. +
A19

This is a book on how to get into politics—how to make your voice and opinion count as a citizen under our form of government. The approach is practical and should be of particular interest to law students. Lawyers today should carry on the grand tradition of the 19th century when they were so influential in government and civic affairs. Some current books with the same intent are Ralph Nader, Action for change, a student's manual for public interest organizing (1971); and Kenneth Norwick, Lobbying for freedom in the 1980s (1975).

1144

MUMFORD, LEWIS. The culture of cities. N.Y., Harcourt, 1938. 586p. +
A59

This book is worth the formidable undertaking of reading it, for he has amassed a huge amount of information on the growth and life of cities and has not lost himself in the facts. See New Statesman & Nation 16:742

1145

OLIVER, FREDERICK S. Alexander Hamilton, an essay on American union....N.Y., Putnam's, 1912. 502p. * +
A35, A59

This is an evaluation of Hamilton's work and the founding of the federal government by an original thinker about politics. See Harvard Law Rev. 58:595 (1945). Channing considered this a moderate English view of the founding of the Federal government.

1146

RATHER, DAN and GARY PAUL GATES. The Palace guard. N.Y., Harper & Row. 1974. 326p.
A72.5

A fascinating behind-the-scenes account of the Nixon administration and the men who ran it, and the country, before the Watergate disaster.

1147

ROSSITER, CLINTON L. The American presidency. N.Y., Harcourt, Brace [1956.] 175p. +
A19

What are the powers and limitations of the American president? They are discussed here with historical commentary and the modifications made by Roosevelt, Truman and Eisenhower. The author believes in presidential strength and his analysis is highly intelligent and stimulating. Professor Rossiter also edited a recommended edition of The Federalist Papers (1961) [A2.5]

1148

SMITH, THOMAS V. The legislative way of life. Chicago, Univ. of Chicago Press, 1940. 101p. +
A59

The author, Congressman at the time, and a university professor, writes here of the nature and philosophy of legislative government in a democracy, and in particular of American legislatures and legislators, their shortcomings as well as their achievements and possibilities. See Book Rev. Dig. 1941 :837.

1149

WARREN, CHARLES. Congress, the Constitution and the Supreme Court. Boston, Little, Brown, 1925. 308p. +
A45

Should Congress or the Supreme Court determine questions of constitutionality? Warren believes it should be the Supreme Court.

1150

WILLS, GARY. Inventing America; Jefferson's Declaration of Independence. N.Y., Doubleday, 1978. 398p.
A25.5

A critical examination of the "three" Declarations of Independence.

HISTORY (ANGLO-AMERICAN)

See also CONSTITUTIONAL HISTORY; LEGAL HISTORY

1175

ADAMS, JAMES T. Epic of America. Bost., Little, Brown, 1937. 446p. * +
A8, A22, A57, A68

A wise historian has sketched in our national history with broad strokes and interpreted the various elements and the qualities of character that have gone into its making. See Book Rev. Dig. 1931 :7.

1176

ALLEN, FREDERICK L. The big change: America transforms itself, 1900-1950. N.Y., Harper [1952.] 308p. +
A20

The author is of the opinion that there has been a great change in the U.S. in the fifty years from 1900 to 1950. He maintains that those critical and those in favor of the American way of life speak in cliches of things which no longer exist and proceeds to prove his point. See Library J. 77:1393.

1177

BEARD, CHARLES A. A basic history of the U.S. [with] Mary R. Beard. N.Y., The New Home Library, 1944. 508p. * +
A8, A57, A68

The Beards were the foremost historians of their day. They portray vividly how our great society came into being, how and why it developed, and what physical, social, military, political, economic, intellectual and spiritual events and circumstances produced the American civilization in which we now live and work. See School & Society 60:95.

1178

____. The rise of American civilization [with Mary R. Beard....N.Y., Macmillan, 1954. 2 v. in 1, rev. and enl. * +
A1, A2, A14, A19, A27, A35, A39, A41, A56, A59, A61, A62, A63, A68, A72

Brilliant and suggestive, this famous work represents a landmark in American historiography. [A39]. It is an important and popular political-economic story shrewdly and concisely written.

1179

CHEYNEY, EDWARD P. An introduction to the industrial and social history of England. N.Y., Macmillan, 1927. 386p. * +
A8, A57, A68

You will enjoy reading this book.

1180

CHURCHILL, SIR WINSTON L.S. A history of the English-speaking peoples. N.Y., Dodd, Mead, 1956. 4 vols. [published in paperback in 1983] +
A19

With a historical sense, which unerringly chooses the significant highlight and with a consummate power of pen, Sir Winston makes each period of British history as alive, as important, and as stirring as if it were but yesterday's Battle of Britain. See Christian Science Monitor, April 26, 1956. For a biography of Mr. Churchill, see the multivolume set by Randolph Churchill and Martin Gilbert (Vol. 6, Finest Hour, 1939-1941 (1983).

1181

COMMAGER, HENRY S., ed. The heritage of America [with] Allan Nevins. Boston, Little, Brown, 1939. 1152p. * +
A27, A35, A59, A61

Collection of first-hand materials on American history and life. Famous documents and speeches, accounts by eye-witnesses of events and scenes.

1182

GREEN, JOHN R. A short history of the English people....N.Y., E. P. Dutton, 1934. 2 v. (reprint). * +
A8, A27, A35, A57, A61, A68

This is the first popular history of the English people—interesting and well written.

1183

MOODY, JOHN. The railroad builders: a chronicle of the welding of the states. New Haven, Yale Univ. press, 1919. 385 p.
A35, A59, A61 * +

A fascinating, journalistic account of the planning and building of the great American railroad systems that spanned and eventually bound together the nation.

1184

MORISON, SAMUEL E. The growth of the American Republic, [with] Henry Steele Commager. [4th ed.] N.Y., Oxford Univ. Press, 1951. 2 v.
A59

Modern scholarship at its best, offering a picture of the full life of a people at work, at play, at school, in politics, etc. The judgments offered are sane and fair. The style is much better than usual in this field. See Books, N. 30 '30. p. 16. For an informal, illustrated and delightful history, see Mark Sullivan, Our Times: the history of the U.S., 1900-1925 (4v. 1926).

1185

RANDALL, JAMES G. The civil war and reconstruction. N.Y., D. C. Heath & Co., 1937. 959p. +
A59

An excellent summary history of the Civil War and Reconstruction period based on thorough research. The style is highly readable.

1186

SCHLESINGER, ARTHUR M. The age of Jackson. Boston, Little, Brown, 1945. 577p. +
A28, A59

This is not merely a history of a Presidential administration, it is an exhaustive inquiry into Jacksonian democracy as an intellectual as well as a political-philosophic movement. See New Yorker 21:89.

1187

TOYNBEE, ARNOLD J. A study of history. (Abridgment of v. 1-6) by D. C. Somervell. London, Oxford Univ. Press, 1947. 617p. +
A59

An excellent abridgment of a classic work of a great professional historian and publicist. Toynbee is very learned and so is his "History."

1188

TREVELYAN, GEORGE M. English social history; a survey of six centuries, Chaucer to Queen Victoria....London, N.Y., [etc.] Longmans, Green, 1942. 628p. * +
A28, A35, A61

By social history, Trevelyan means "negatively...the history of a people with politics left out....The daily life of the inhabitants of the land in past ages." The Nation (v. 156:387) describes the book as "stimulating and fascinating reading as well as a useful corrective for an overdose of materialist interpretation."

1189

____. History of England. New and enl. ed. Lond., Longman's, Green, [1948.] 756p. * +
A28, A35, A61, A62, A72

An excellent account by a great historian.

1190

TURNER, FREDERICK J. The frontier in American history. N.Y., Holt, 1920. 375p. (First published in 1893). * +
A35, A61

Sets forth in the clearest possible manner the view of American expansion which has inspired all of Prof. Turner's work. Among all American historians no one has so fully caught the meaning of the frontier in our national development. See R. of Rs. 63:110.

HUMAN INSTITUTIONS and VALUES

See also ECONOMICS; PHILOSOPHY; POLITICS and ECONOMIC THEORY

Lawyers must develop insight into rather than merely information about the institutions and values with which man is concerned. One pursuing a legal career encounters all sorts of these institutions under circumstances in which his conduct necessarily shapes the conduct of others in their value choices: Examples are marriage and the conduct of parties to it; business and the actions of sellers and buyers, stockholders and directors, employers and employees [etc.]. The lawyer is a force in the operation and shaping of these institutions. It is vital that he perform his work in the choice of preferable means and ends. This insight comes from intensive study for a substantial period of an area such as the nature of man and the physical world of which he is a part; the economic systems of societies; the political organizations of societies; the democratic processes in Western societies; the social structures of societies and the cultural heritages of Western societies: rather than from attemppts to skim all the large areas listed. "Study" includes dealing with people in these contexts and reflecting upon the experience thus gained. [A63].

1200

BOORSTIN, DANIEL J. Democracy and its discontents; reflections on everyday America. N.Y., Random House, 1974. 136p.
A57.1

Mr. Boorstin has been characterized as having an "ability to bring familiar information into fresh combinations ... [and] to draw out unexpected and suggestive findings." See the review of his Discoverers (1983) by E.E. Morison in the N.Y. Times Book Rev., Nov. 23, 1983, p.1.

1201

CALABRESI, GUIDO and PHILIP BOBBITT. Tragic choices. N.Y.,, W.W.Norton Co., 1978. 252p.
A36

"Their purpose is to define the nature of the tragic choices our kind of society confronts, as deeply rooted egalitarian and humanistic values come into conflict with the fact of scarcity [The choices are the competitive market approach, the accountable political approach, the lottery, and the customary or evolutionary approach.]" W.W. Rostow, Texas Law Rev. 56:1507 (1978).

1202

FORER, LOIS G. The death of the law. N.Y., David McKay Co., 1975. 353p.
A57.1

"...the author ruminates about the failure of the legislature, the executives, the police, the courts...the lawyers, the judges, the law itself, and most importantly, the people. ...lack of respect, the inadequate salaries, and the scathing criticism, contempt and abuse to which a judge is subjected." Gerald D. McClellan, Family Law Q. 10:93 (1976).

1203

MURRAY, JOHN COURTNEY. We hold these truths; Catholic reflections on the American proposition. N.Y., Sheed and Ward, 1960. 336p.
A24.5

"...[an] outline of a public philosophy of law as the background for a discussion of a series of practical and vital problems which threaten the unity and perhaps the survival of America...." Joseph T. Tinnelly, Catholic Lawyer 7:270 (1961).

1204

NOONAN, JOHN T., JR. The morality of abortion; legal and historical perspectives. Cambridge, Harvard Univ. Press, 1970. 287p.
A24.5

Contributors: Paul Ramsey, James M. Gustafson, Bernard Haring, George Huntston Williams, John M. Finnis, David Louisell. See Charles P. Kindregan, Fordham Law Rev. 39:567 (1971).

1205

PATERSON, MERRILL D., ed. Democracy, liberty and property; the state constitutional conventions of the 1820s. Indianapolis, Bobbs-Merrill, 1966. 452p.
A72.5

Selections from the texts of debates of three constitutional conventions: Mass., N.Y., and Va.

1206

WASSERSTROM, RICHARD A. Philosophy and social issues. South Bend, Univ. of Notre Dame Press, 1980. 187p.

"...a model for rational discussion of controversial current issues...racism and sexism, preferential treatment, the obligation to obey the law, punishment and responsibility in war, ...reasoning is free from dogmatism and empty rhetoric [also Bakke, H.L.A.Hart, Herbert Morris, sex and autonomy]. Thomas E. Hill, Jr. U.C.L.A. Law Rev. 28:135 (1980). The author has also published The judicial decision (1961) and edited Morality and the law (1971).

a) The nature of Man and the Physical World of which He is a Part.

The lawyer should gain insight in the stimuli which move him to action, internal and external limitations upon the development of understanding and reason, man's ability to plan conduct and the function of value choices in his planning. [A63].

Read the following for this purpose:

1207

KLUCKHORN, CLYDE. Mirror for man; the relation of anthropology to modern life. N.Y., McGraw-Hill, 1949. 313p. * +
A63

1208

KRECH, DAVID. Theory and problems of social psychology [with] R. S. Crutchfield. N.Y., McGraw-Hill, 1948. 639p. * +
A63

b) The Economic Systems of Societies.

The lawyer should gain insight of theoretical foundations, imperfection in practice, business patterns, the function of governmental processes in economic control. [A63].

Read the following for this purpose:

1209

GAMBS, JOHN S. Man, money, and goods. N.Y., Columbia Univ. Press, 1952. 339p. * +
A63

1210

SCHUMPETER, JOSEPH A. Capitalism, socialism, and democracy. 3d ed. N.Y., Harper [1950.] 431p.
A63

c) Political Organizations of Societies.
See also GOVERNMENT AND POLITICS

The lawyer should gain insight into basic theories, modern complexities, the relation of politics to law. [A63].

Read the following for this purpose:

1211

BALDWIN, RAYMOND E. Let's go into politics. N.Y., Macmillan, 1952. 179p. * +
A63

1212

VOEGELIN, ERIC. New science of politics. Chicago, Univ. of Chicago Press, 1952. 193p. * +
A16, A63

d) The Democratic Processes in Western Societies.

Insight, especially into responsiveness of governmental policy to popular will, art of compromise, role of education and discussion, functions of majorities and minorities, methods of reconciling competing interests, requirements for participating effectively in world society, degree of efficiency self-government permits; and an awareness of moral values inherent in these processes. [A63].

Read the following for these purposes:

1213

ARNOLD, THURMAN W. The symbols of government. New Haven, Yale Univ. Press [1941.] 278p. * +
A8, A24, A27, A45, A63

A delightful book that has lost nothing with time. The chapter on theories about legal theory is ideal for providing perspective on what law is all about. Also chapters on jurisprudence, economics, government, criminal law, trial by combat, and courts.

1214

POSTON, RICHARD W. Democracy is you; a guide to citizen action. N.Y., Harper, 1953. 312p. * +
A63

e) The Social Structures of Societies.

Awareness of functions of individuals and groups such as the family and churches, implications of the service state, governmental processes in social control, and control of the atypical person. [A63].

Read the following:

1215

CUBER, JOHN F. Problems of American society; values in conflict, [with] R. A. Harper. N.Y., Holt, 1951. 496p. * +
A63

1216

MAYO, ELTON. The social problems of an industrial civilization. Boston, Grad. School of Business Admin., Harvard Univ., 1945. 150p. * +
A63

f) Cultural Heritages of Western Societies.
See also PHILOSOPHY.

This area includes philosophy and ethics and is concerned with awareness of freedom for the individual, traditions of humility, brotherhood and service, inevitability of change and the art of peaceful, orderly adaptation to change. [A63].

Read the following:

1217

ORTON, WILLIAM A. The liberal tradition; a study of the social and spiritual conditions of freedom. New Haven, Yale Univ. Press, 1945. 317p. * +
A63

1218

VOGT, VON OGDEN. Cult and culture; a study of religion and American culture. N.Y., Macmillan, 1951. 269p. * +
A63

INSURANCE LAW

1225

CALABRESI, GUIDO. The costs of accidents; a legal and economic analysis. New Haven, Yale Univ. Press, 1970. 340p.
A36, A49

"Today there are legal scholars...who believe that over a broad range of subjects they will make greater progress utilizing the theories and empirical procedures of the social sciences than continuing to depend exclusively on the methods of traditional legal scholarship....I conclude [in opposition to the author] that the fault system need not entail an intolerable problem of secondary costs."

1226

GREEN, LEON. Traffic victims. Evanston, Northwestern Univ. Press, 1958. 127p.
A29.5

"...seeks to demonstrate the obsolescence and futility of common law jury trials and liability insurance as a remedy for traffic casualties, and advocates compulsory comprehensive loss insurance as a substitute." Eugene M. Wypyski, Fordham Law Rev. 27:473 (1958).

1227

O'CONNELL, JEFFREY and ROGER C. HENDERSON. Tort law, no-fault and beyond. N.Y., M. Bender, 1975. 939p.
A17.6, A24.5

"...Professor O'Connell...has now turned his attention to developing materials for the education of law students about no-fault." Leslie Steven Rothenberg, University of Illinois Law Forum 1977:719. See also Professor O"Connell"s Ending Insult to Injury (1975) reviewed by Walter J. Blum, Univ. of Chicago Law Rev. 43:217 (1975);

and The Injury Industry and Remedy of No-Fault Insurance (1971) reviewed in Georgia Law Rev. 6:453 (1972).

INTERNATIONAL LAW and RELATIONS

1235

BOWETT, D. W. The law of international institutions. 3d ed. London, Stevens, 1975. 382p.
A31.7

A dated but concise text on the United Nations, the International Court of Justice, etc.

1236

BRIERLY, JAMES L. The law of nations; an introduction to the international law of peace. 5th ed. Oxford, Clarendon Press, 1955. 331p. * +
A1, A2, A8, A14, A15, A19, A27, A30, A39, A56, A61, A63, A68, A72

A brief but extremely clear and penetrating introduction to the problems of international law. The author is Professor of International Law at Oxford University. [A39].

1237

Cambridge essays in international law; essays in honor of Lord McNair. Dobbs Ferry, Oceana, 1965. 186p.
A31.7

"...questions involving the organization or operation of United Nations bodies...[deals with International Court of Justice, concept of nullity and illegality in the actions of international organizations, British consular conventions, decision-making process by international organizations, voting]. The authors are [D.W.Bowett, Sir Gerald Fitzmaurice, C. Wilfred Jenks, R.Y.Jennings, E.Lauterpacht, Clive Parry and Sir Francis Vallet]. James N. Hyde, American Jl of International law 61:218 (1967).

1238

FENWICK, CHARLES G. International law. 3d ed. N.Y., Appleton-Century-Crofts. [1948.] 744p. * +
A55

Recommended for third year law students. [A55]. This is one of the best standard texts on the subject.

1239

FISHER, ROGER. Points of choice. Oxford, Oxford Univ. Press, 1978. 89p.
A31.7

"...the importance of international law to rational and perceptive decision in international affairs...the power of international law to promote national goals, including the goal of a more stable international political environment..." Alfred P. Rubin, Michigan Law Rev. 77:336 (1979). Mr. Fisher also wrote Getting to yes; negotiating agreements without giving in (with William Ury 1981)

1240

FRIEDMANN, WOLFGANG, LOUIS HENKIN and OLIVER LISSITZYN, eds. Transnational law in a changing society; essays in honor of Philip C. Jessup. N.Y., Columbia Univ. Press, 1972. 324p.
A31.7

[authors include] Judge De Visscher, Chief Justice Elias, Wilfred Jenks, Ambassador El-Erian, Judge Lachs, Francis Deak, Professor Henkin, Judge Jiminez de Arechaga, J.E.S.Fawcett, Professor Bastid. See Brunson MacChesney, American Jl of International Law 67:352 (1973).

1241

HENKIN, LOUIS. How nations behave. N.Y., Praeger, 1968. 324p. 2d ed. N.Y., Columbia Univ. Press, 1979. 400p.
A31.7

"...a judicious and wise book on the role international law plays in the behavior of states. ...Henkin's quiet but firm statement that international law, like all law, is a set of norms for compliance, that it pervades all inter-state relations, and that states on the whole behave in accordance with it is most convincing." Stanley Hoffman, Columbia Law Rev. 1969:533 (1969). [The second edition] incorporates the teachings of world politics during the momentous decade from 1968-1978...he reaffirms his thesis..." Michigan Law Rev. 78:820 (1980).

1242

JESSUP, PHILIP C. Transnational law. New Haven, Yale Univ. Press, 1956. 113p. (Storrs lectures on jurisprudence, 1956.) +
A6

In "transnational law" Mr. Jessup has chosen a new term to denote the body of law concerned with relations between individuals, corporations and governments when the transaction involved crosses national boundaries. He attacks current theories of the scope of jurisdiction or sovereign authority. See Harvard Law Rev. 70:950 (1957). See also Gross, Transnational essays on international law and organizations (2 v. 1983) for a collection of essays on the United Nations, research in international law, etc. For a competent handbook on international law materials, see The Jl of International Law and Economics, Vol. 15, No. 1 (1981).

1243

LARSON, ARTHUR. When nations disagree; a handbook on peace through law. Baton Rouge, Louisiana State Univ. Press, 1961. 251p.
A31.7

"...Starting with the premise that many international disputes...contain justiciable issues and could therefore be settled on the legal level, Mr. Larson inquires into the accessibility of a body of world law, the existence of legal machinery to apply it, the acceptance by states of such machinery, and their compliance with adverse decisions." Peter Hay, University of Pittsburgh Law Rev. 23:820 (1962).

1244

MCDOUGAL, MYRES S. and Associates. Studies in world public order. New Haven, Yale Univ. Press, 1960. 1058p.
A31.7

"...a collection of some of the products of McDougal's prolific pen. ...it makes available the most comprehensive statement of McDougal's prescription for 'policy-science' jurisprudence." Arthur S. Miller, Jl of Public Law 10:158 (1961). See also his Law and Minimum World Public Order (with Florentino P. Feliciano) (1961) reviewed by Edward Hambro in California Law Rev. 50:745 (1962).

1245

NUSSBAUM, ARTHUR. A concise history of the law of nations. Rev. ed. N.Y., Macmillan, 1954. 376p. +
A59

An erudite and charmingly written survey of the great writers on international law and a perceptive analysis of their doctrinal disputes. About half of the volume deals also with the practice of states. Bibliographical annotations are valuable. See Cornell L. Q. 39:553 (1954).

1246

OPPLER, ALFRED C. Legal reform in occupied Japan; a participant looks back. Princeton Univ. Press, 1976. 345p.
A43.5

"... an essentially defensive, platitudinous reminiscence that tells us little not already known about the famous but still superficially reported 'experiment in directed political change.' ... the vast reforms he supervised have stood the test of time reasonably well. ... personal odyssey is fascinating..." Chalmers Johnson, Am Jl of Comparative Law 25:189 (1977).

1247

WRIGHT, QUINCY. A study of war. Chicago, Univ. of Chicago Press, 1942. 2 v. +
A59

This should be considered as a work of reference to ascertain the origin of wars, how they were fought and what they resulted in or accomplished. It is a huge and very comprehensive study of the history, causes, nature and control of war. See also Michael Walzer, Just and unjust wars; a moral argument with historical illustrations (1977) reviewed by Richard Wasserstrom, Harvard Law Rev. 92:536 (1978).

JUDICIARY

See also COURTS

1275

ABRAHAM, HENRY J. Justices and Presidents. N.Y., Oxford Univ. Press, 1974. 298p.
A24.5

"A political history of appointments to the Supreme Court...brief sketches of the Justices make them human and real personalities..." Robert H. Birkby, Emory Law Jl 23:1047 (1974).

1276

ALDISERT, RUGGERO J. The judicial process; readings, materials, and cases. St.Paul, West, 1976. 948p.
A1

"...edited selections from the best writings of our country's jurisprudents, interlaced with instructive opinions and the author's penetrating comments and incisive queries. [Holmes, Cardozo, Pound, Jerome Frank,

Jerome Hall, Karl Llewellyn, Learned Hand, Harlan F. Stone, Charles D. Breitel, Kenneth Culp Davis, Ronald Dworkin, Robert A. Leflar, Edward H. Levi, Roger J. Traynor, Harry W. Jones, etc.] Morris L. Weisberg, A.B.A.Jl 63:1080 (1977).

1277

ASHMAN, CHARLES R. The finest judges money can buy. L.A.,Nash Publishing Corp., 1973. 309p.
A57.1

"...seventy four short case histories of specific judges, past and present, who have engaged in reprehensible activities. ...sarcastic, overly cute style of expression which becomes annoying..." Kenneth A. Manaster, Santa Clara Lawyer 15:256 (1974). But see review by Melvin Belli in N.Y.Times, Nov. 18, 1973, p.42 and column by John Leonard in N.Y.Times Book Review, Dec. 14, 1973, p.31 as to self-interest behind Mr. Belli's request he review this book.

1278

BALDWIN, SIMEON E....The American judiciary. N.Y., The Century Co., 1905. 403p. (The American state series.) +
A36

Dean Pound recommends this book for the study of the organization and jurisdiction of the courts. Also of value in understanding the judicial function.

1279

BARTH, ALAN. Prophets with honor; great dissents and great dissenters in the Supreme Court. N.Y., Knopf, 1974. 254p.
A35.5, A57.1

"...an appeal to the brooding spirit of the law, to the intelligence of a future day!...Discussed are Plessy v. Ferguson, Olmstead v. U.S., Minersville School District v. Gobitis, Betts v. Brady, Colegrove v. Green and Dennis v. U.S...." Christopher R. Kelly, Howard Law Jl 18:870 (1975).

1280

BECKER, THEODORE, ed. The impact of Supreme Court decisions. N.Y., Oxford Univ. Press, 1969. 213p.
A31.7

"...(1) Congress and the President, (2) the lower courts, (3) state and local government and politics, and (4) public opinion. ...worthy of widespread academic attention and use." William Gangi, Utah Law Rev. 1972:321.

1281

BICKEL, ALEXANDER M. The least dangerous branch; the Supreme Court at the bar of politics. Indianapolis, Bobbs-Merrill, 1963. 303p.
A35.5, A47, A49

"...[a critique of Bickel's principal of the court's 'passive virtues'] Mark DeWolfe Howe, Harvard Law Rev. 77:579 (1964).

1282

BLAUSTEIN, ALBERT B. and **ROY M. MERSKY.** The first one hundred Justices; statistical studies on the Supreme Court of the United States, Hamden, Conn., Archon Books, 1978. 102p., App.
A31.7

Ratings of the Justices, Justices who did not serve though nominated, tabulation of opinions, etc. See Woodford L. Gardner, Jr., 67 Kentucky Law Jl 268 (1978-9)

1283

CECIL, HENRY. The English judge. London, Stevens & Sons, 1970. 177p.
A29.5

"'...just what the average English judge is, from what background he comes, how he conducts himself, and what his qualifications are...'" Walter P. Armstrong, A.B.A.Jl 59:350 (1973).

1284

COVER, ROBERT M. Justice accused; antislavery and the judicial process. New Haven,Yale Univ. Press, 1975. 322p.
A38.5, A57.1

"...Cover explores this theme by examining the response of American judges of the antebellum era to the statutes which protected and fostered slavery, raising more general issues of the judiciary's proper role." Richard S. Kay, Harvard Civil Rights-Civil Liberties Law Rev. 12:219 (1977).

1285

DEVLIN, RT. HON. PATRICK. The judge. Oxford, Oxford Univ. Press, 1979. 207p.
A24.5

"...an inquiry into the place of the judge in the political life of the country. ...He admonishes judges in crisp terms about their obligations to judicial form and precedent." J. Skelly Wright, Stanford Law Rev. 33:179 (1980). See also Henry J. Friendly's review in Michigan Law Rev. 79:634 (1981).

[No. 1286 saved]

1287

GOULDEN, JOSEPH. The benchwarmers; the private world of the powerful Federal judges. N.Y., Ballantine Books, 1974. 375p.
A43.5, A57.1

"[the author] has managed to depict the good and the bad in federal judges in his exceptionally readable book...[subjects include judicial selection, Southern District of New York, District of Columbia district court, and a look at when the system flops]" James G. France, Washington University Law Q. 1975:262.

1288

JACKSON, DONALD DALE. Judges; an inside view of the agonies and excesses of an American elite. N.Y., Atheneum, 1974. 433p.
A36, A38.5, A57.1

"...an immensely readable and thoroughly enjoyable series of miniportraits of ordinary men placed in positions of power, each of whom has his own notion of what a judge should be and how justice should be dispensed." Allan Ashman, A.B.A.Jl 60:897 (1974).

1289

JAMES, HOWARD. Crisis in the courts. N.Y., McKay, 1967. Rev. ed., 1971. 267p.
A48.5

An investigative reporter's findings after a countrywide inspection of state court systems. An indictment of our court structure for which a solution must be found. Chapters on judges, juveniles, lawyers, sentencing, delay, etc. While the names may change, the problem persists.

1290

Judicial clerkships; a symposium on the institution. Vanderbilt Law Rev 26:1123 (Nov. 1973).
A6.5

Articles by P.R. Baier, E.A. Wright, G.R. Smith (a primer of opinion writing for clerks), T.J. Lesinski and N.O. Stockmeyer, Jr. (prehearing research), F.G. Hamley (sample instructions to law clerks), R.J. Aldisert (duties of law clerks).

1291

LIDE, LANNEAU du RANT. The trial judge in South Carolina. Columbia, Univ. of South Carolina Press, 1953. 114p. +
A11, A58

Recommended as of particular local interest for South Carolina by Dean Prince of Univ. of S.C. School of Law.

1292

LUMMUS, HENRY T....The trial Judge....Three lectures delivered at the Law School of Northwestern Univ. ...Chicago, Foundation Press, 1937. 148p.
A45, A62

The qualities, duties, conduct and selection of the trial judge are considered. These subjects are discussed in a manner calculated to awaken public consciousness to the daily problems involved in the administration of justice. Recorded here are the practical experiences of an active member of the bench. See Brooklyn L. Rev. 7:407 (1948). See also Frank M. Coffin, <u>The ways of a judge; reflections from the Federal Appellate Bench</u> (1980). See review by E.J.Bander, Suffolk Univ. Law Rev. 15:546 (1981). For a list of books on the judicial experience, see L.D.Shubow's review, Massachusetts Law Rev. 66:95 (1981).

1293

NOONAN, JOHN T., JR. Persons and masks of the law; Cardozo, Holmes, Jefferson, and Wythe as makers of the masks. N.Y., Farrar, Straus and Giroux, 1976. 206p.
A49, A57.1

"[law people] are bad historians in part because of the masks of the law...the rules and reasons must be understood, and can only be understood by knowing something about the persons who made the rules and gave the reasons..." Thomas Ehrlich, American Jl of Legal History 21:351 (1977).

1294

ROCHE, JOHN P. Courts and rights; the American judiciary in action. N.Y., Random, 1961. 2d ed. 1966. 143p.
A43.5

"... examination of American judiciary and its relationship to our history, politics, and mores ... aimed primarily at the uninitiated university student." William B. Gould, Univ. Detroit Law Jl 41:342 (1964).

1295

SCIGLIANO, ROBERT G. The courts: a reader in the judicial process. Boston, Little, Brown, 1962. 504p.
A57.1

The courts as policy making bodies and the persons involved in the process.

1296

SIMON, JAMES F. The judge. N.Y., David McKay, 1976. 209p.
A57.1

"... we are given the Monday through Friday viewpoint of what one human being feels when he controls the liberty and sometimes the life of another ... clearly written, quick paced, and thought provoking." S. Sbarbaro, A.B.A.Jl 63:492 (1977).

1297

STRICK, ANNE. Injustice for all, how our adversary system of law victimizes us and subverts true justice. Penguin, 1978. 282p.
A43.5

An attack on methods lawyers use to win cases with copious cites from known and unknown authors. She criticizes professional ethics, the fiction of the impartial judge or jury, and has unoriginal suggestions for the improvement of the system. She recounts her experiences in trying cases.

1298

WHITE, G. EDWARD. The American judicial tradition; profiles of leading American judges. N.Y., Oxford Univ. Press, 1976. 441p.
A43.5, A47, A48.5, A57.1

John Marshall; Kent, Story, and Shaw; Roger Taney; Miller, Bradley, and Field; Cooley and Doe; John Marshall; Harlan I; Holmes, Brandeis; Hughes and Stone; Robert Jackson; Cardozo, Learned Hand and Frank; Roger Traynor; Frankfurter, Black, Warren and Harlan...Good bibliographical essay.

1299

WILKIN, ROBERT N. The judicial function and industrial and international disputes....Charlottesville, Va., Michie, 1948. 91p.
A68 +

An interesting historical analysis of the function of the judiciary from ancient times through early English history and the middle ages. Linking it with the present, the author favors the use of judicial procedures for the settlement of industrial and international disputes. See Arb. Jl n.s. 4:235 (1949).

JURISPRUDENCE and PHILOSOPHY OF LAW
SEE ALSO PHILOSOPHY

1325

ALLEN, CARLETON K. Law in the making. 5th ed. Oxford, Clarendon Press, 1951. 626p. * +
A8, A24, A30, A38, A39, A74

An admirable study of the origin and development of Anglo-American law by a then Professor of Jurisprudence at the University of Oxford. [A39]

1326

ASSOCIATION OF THE BAR OF THE CITY OF NEW YORK. COMMITTEE ON POST-ADMISSION LEGAL EDUCATION. Jurisprudence in action; a pleader's anthology, [by] Ames and others ...N.Y., Baker, Voorhis, 1953. 494p. * +
A1, A2, A8, A14, A19, A27, A28, A35, A39, A43, A53, A54, A56, A63, A68

A collection of essays and addresses dealing with the broader aspects of law and its philosophy. [A56] Some of the articles are of a more practical aspect as Shientag on cross-examination. As some of the authors represent some of the outstanding names in law, a listing follows: Law and morals (J.B. Ames), Law and literature (B.N. Cardozo) State law in the Federal courts (C.E. Clark), Law and scientific method (M.R. Cohen), A better theory of legal interpretation (C.P. Curtis), The argument of an appeal (J.W. Davis), The ratio decidendi of a case (A.L. Goodhart), Contribution of an independent judiciary to civilization (L.Hand), Cardozo's Nature of the Judicial Process (A.Hand), Holt and Mansfield (W.S. Holdsworth), The path of the law (O.W. Holmes), The ethics of advocacy (H.P. MacMillan), A prologue to a history of English law (F.W. Maitland), Judicial caution and valor (F.Pollock), Do we need a philosophy of law (R.Pound), The permanent problems of the law (M.Radin), Cross-examination - a judge's viewpoint (B.L. Shientag), F.W. Maitland (P.Vinogradoff).

1327

AUSTIN, JOHN. The Province of jurisprudence determined and the uses of the study of jurisprudence. Introd. by H.L.A. Hart. Editors: Isiah Berlin, Stuart Hampshire, Richard Woolheim. London, Weidenfeld and Nicolson. 1954. 393p.; N.Y., Humanities Press, 1965. 396p.
A31.7

"It is to be hoped, however, that [law teachers] will not be tempted to recommend it again for serious study by the law student. [Austin] defined a legal rule in terms of action - it was a command by a commander who was obeyed." Note: The review has a critique of Austin and Hart. B.E. King, Cambridge Law Jl 1955:123 (1955).

1328

BARKUN, MICHAEL. Law without sanctions; order in primitive societies and the world community. New Haven, Yale Univ. Press, 1968. 180p.
A43.8

"Whatever the reservations, Barkun's thoughtful, scholarly and spirited book will contribute to the reformulation of traditional questions whose unsatisfactory solution has emasculated many schools of jurisprudence and generations of legal advisers, many of whom have not thought that they were practicing law at all." Harold D. Lasswell, American Jl of Int'l Law 63:646 (1969).

1329

BASTIAT, FREDERIC. The law. [Translation by Dean Russel]. Irvington-on-Hudson, N.Y., Foundation for Economic Education, 1950. 75p. * +
A8

Bastiat gained a great reputation for his Economic Sophisms published 1843-1850. The Law was published in 1850 and is one of his most famous pamphlets. "Law," he maintains, "is solely the organization of the individual's right of self-defense which existed before law was formalized. Law is justice." But the law has been perverted, and applied to annihilating the justice it was supposed to maintain. Protectionism, socialism and communism are all forms of legal plunder. See Henry Hazlitt, Free Man's Library, a descriptive and critical bibliography. (Princeton, Van Nostrand, 1956, p.39).

1330

BECKER, LAWRENCE C. Property rights; philosophic foundations. London, Routledge & Kegan Paul, 1977. 135p.
A24.5

"Professor Becker bases his conclusions on two versions of the labor theory originated by John Locke, on a utilitarian theory, and on a brief argument for a political liberty to own as much as possible, provided that others can still make a living. ...Becker criticizes 'welfare economics' as virtually equivalent to the complete cancellation of property rights. ...It is interesting nevertheless for its appraisal of the Hohfeldian concepts utilized in the Restatement and in Professor Powell's great treatise on real property. ...Although I do not agree with Professor Becker's objective, which is to justify selfish and absolute property, his book may be good ammunition for those who do agree with him." John P. Rooney, Suffolk University Law Rev. 12:1069 (1978).

1331

BENTHAM, JEREMY. Of laws in general. Ed. by H.L.A. Hart. London, Athlone Press, 1970. 342p.
A24.5

H.L.A.Hart's version of Bentham's Of Laws in General differs from Everett's Limits of Jurisprudence Defined in more than name. ...the nature of statutes, and the difference between the civil and penal law. ...despite the helping hand of Bentham (and his ilk) we cannot rid our law of such 'imperfections.' ...Bentham also seems to believe that every single rule of law (of any importance) has a civil part and a penal part ...In Anglo-American law of today it is possible to differentiate five basic types of law (1) the penal, (2) law defining and providing remedies for private grievances (3) administrative-regulatory ...(4) law ordering the conferral of substantive state benefits such as welfare ...and (5) law facilitating and protecting private arrangements." Robert S. Summers, Univ. of Toronto Law Jl 21:445 (1971).

1332

BERLE, ADOLF A. The modern corporation and private property ...[with] Gardiner C. Means ...Chicago, Commerce Clearing House, [c1932.] 396p. N.Y., Harcourt, Brace & World, 1968. Rev. ed. 380p.
A8, A25.5, A30, A43.5, A45 * +

The learned authors have drawn into stark relief three challenges with which modern corporate organization confronts the highly industrialized countries. Julius Stone believes it is the most penetrating study in sociological jurisprudence which the English-speaking world has yet produced. See Stone's Province and Function of Law, p.638 [No. 1420].

1333

BLOM-COOPER, LOUIS and GAVIN DREWRY, eds. Law and morality; a reader. London, Gerald Duckworth & Co., 1976. 265p.
A24.5

"To the perennial interest of arguments over moral values in and of the law ...shows the importance of setting such arguments in a historical context. ...As to the topics covered, they are somewhat restricted and predictable - punishment, capital and corporal, sexuality, family and fecundity, sanctity of life, obscenity, religion." Neil MacCormick, Law Q. Rev. 96:151 (1980).

1334

BODENHEIMER, EDGAR. Jurisprudence, the philosophy and method of the law. Rev. ed. Harvard Univ. Press, 1974. 463p.
A25.5, A43.5, A49

"... a critical examination of the history of the philosophy of law from Plato to McDougal and Lasswell ... nature and functions of the law ... sources and techniques of the law ... bias toward natural law ... rare gift for lucidity and compression." W.H. McConnell, McGill Law Jl 22:341 (1976). Professor Bodenheimer has also written Philosophy of responsibility (1980).

1335

BOORSTIN, DANIEL J. The mysterious science of the law; an essay on Blackstone's Commentaries, showing how Blackstone, employing eighteenth century ideas of science, religion, history, aesthetics, and philosophy made of the law at once a conservative and a mysterious science ...Cambridge, Harvard Univ. Press, 1941. 257p. Beacon Press, 1958. +
A43.5, A49.

The book is subtle, ingenious, witty and learned, presenting Blackstone against the intellectual background of the 18th century. Boorstin believes Blackstone a typical child of the 18th century and eager to show that the English law was indeed a science, that is to say, a rationally coherent body of facts. See Yale Law Jl. 51:519 (1942). See also No. 1200 for additional books by this author.

1336

BRANDEIS, LOUIS D. The living law. In Illinois Law Rev. 10:461 (1916). +
A52

Made a profound and permanent impression on me when I was a law student. Prof. Wm. P. Murphy, Univ. of Miss.

1337

CAHN, EDMOND. The moral decision; right and wrong in the light of American law. Bloomington, Indiana Univ. Press, 1956. 342p. Reissued in 1981. * +
A7, A19, A43.5, A64, A57.1, A66

Here is a book about law that the general reader can enjoy. Prof. Cahn writes for everybody who cares to see how judges' minds operate. And nobody interested in ethical problems should miss his examples of the reciprocity between morals and law, or his fresh and sensitive insights into human relationships. Every topic begins with an actual case, cogently stated, which raises a fascinating ethical problem. Then come several pages of thoughtful discussion of the problem leading into wise reflections on the topic. See N.Y. Times Bk. Rev., Oct. 23, 1955.

1338

____. The sense of injustice, an anthropocentric view of law. N.Y., N.Y.U. Press, 1949. 186p. +
A19, A28, A43.5, A47

For those who esteem conceptual analysis combined with an amazing sweep of well-integrated knowledge and a sensitiveness to the integrity of the living person, this book is a boon. Here is a fine consideration of justice that justifies the ways of the law in the lives of men. See Tulane Law Rev. 24:512 (1950). See also Lenore L. Cahn, ed. Confronting injustice; the Edmund Cahn reader (1966). [A38.5]

1339

CAIRNS, HUNTINGTON. Law and the social sciences. Foreword by Roscoe Pound. N.Y., Harcourt, Brace, 1935. 279p. +
A20, A36

The value of this book lies in its summarization of large fields of social sciences and helpful bibliographies. It is an attempt to effectuate a rapport between social science and the law on the basis of scientific methodology. See Columbia Law Rev. 50:1093 (1936).

1340

____. Legal philosophy from Plato to Hegel. Baltimore, Johns Hopkins Press, 1949. 583p. +
A20, A28, A41, A42

Between the first chapter (Philosophy as Jurisprudence) and the last (Jurisprudence as Philosophy) are 13 independent and self-contained essays, each expounding, with conscientious scrupulousness, a classic philosopher's theory of law. The book also presents a thesis concerning the future direction which legal philosophy should take. Columbia Law Rev. 49:286 (1949).

1341

CALAMANDREI, PIERO. Procedure and democracy ...Foreword ...by Edmond Cahn. [N.Y.], N.Y.U. Press, 1956. 104p. +
A19, A47

In many respects Prof. Calamandrei was the greatest Italian of the Twentieth Century. The book has flashes of humor and charm of style, but there is also deep passion and penetrating insight. He expresses an intrepid democratic faith and a reasoned discerning optimism. His discussion of procedural reform is challenging and stimulating. See N.Y.U. Law Center Bulletin, Fall, 1956.

1342

CARDOZO, BENJAMIN N. The growth of the law. New Haven, Yale Univ. Press, 1924. 145p. * +
A6.5, A8, A10, A20, A27, A27.5, A45, A49, A71.5, A72

Cardozo considered this a supplement to his "Nature of the Judicial Process." (See No. 1343).

1343

____. The nature of the judicial process. New Haven, Yale Univ. Press, 1921. 180p. * +
A6, A6.5, A7, A8, A10, A20, A21, A24, A25.5, A26, A27.5, A28, A33, A35, A35.5, A36, A38.5, A40, A43, A43.5, A45, A46, A47, A48, A49, A51, A61, A62, A71.5, A71.8, A72, A74

Concerns law making by judicial decision and the elements of the mental process utilized in ascertaining the "ought" law for the operative fact situation. [A24] Will require a real effort on your part to read with comprehension but it is recommended that you try. Should then be read several times again after progress in law school studies has been made. Dean Havighurst. See also No. 1345. "[This books is] the type that can be read critically by the well informed ... or casually for practical benefit and general satisfaction by the more nearly average reader." Neil W. Schilke, William and Mary Law Rev. 3:219 (1961).

1344

____. The paradoxes of legal science. N.Y., Columbia Univ. Press, 1928. 142p. +
A6, A20, A28, A33, A45

The relation between justice and law is here discussed. The legal process must be one of compromise and concordance. Dean Harrison of Alabama recommended it for law students as distinguished from prelaw.

1345

____. Selected writings ...ed. by Margaret E. Hall, with a foreword by Edwin W. Patterson. N.Y., Matthew Bender [1975,1947.] 456p. +
A1, A2, A3, A6, A10, A11, A12, A14, A19, A23, A27, A28, A29,A30, A38, A39, A41, A43.5, A44, A49, A54, A56, A57, A63, A64, A66, A67, A68, A72

The penetrating philosophical writings of the late Justice. The best and most important is "The Nature of the Judicial Process." This is well worth reading before you come to law school and again after you get there. You may be interested in finding how much more you get out of Cardozo's essays after you have had some legal training. [A12]

1346

CARPENTER, WILLIAM SEAL. Foundations of modern jurisprudence. N.Y., Appleton, 1958. 230p.
A43.5

The nature and development of early legal institutions with discussions of natural law, Roman law, forms and methods of trial, and trends in jurisprudence.

1347

CARTER, LIEF. Reason in law. Boston, Little, Brown, 1979. 258p.
A24.5

An attempt to explain the legal process to lay people, to compensate for law professors only writing for law professors, and to fill the lacunae in the legal thinking of lawyers, judges and law professors. Chapters on legal reasoning, statutory interpretation, common law, reason and the constitution, law and reason.

1348

CICERO, MARCUS TULLIUS. De legibus libri tres. (In various editions—Loeb Classical Library tr. Keyes.) +
A68

Cicero was the leading spirit in Roman legal philosophy. He holds this position as the intermediary of the traditional philosophy of Greece, which he made accessible to his generation and adapted to the conditions of Roman law. In his method he was influenced by the Stoic philosophers. To him the highest good was to live according to nature. The highest virtues were the Stoic ones of prudence, justice, magnanimity and temperance. See Berholzheimer, World's Legal Philosophers, p. 87.

1349

COHEN, MORRIS R. Law and the social order; essays in legal philosophy. N.Y., Harcourt, Brace [1933.] 403p. +
A1, A7, A8, A14, A19, A20, A24, A27, A30, A39, A43.5, A45, A49, A56, A63, A67, A72

A collection of stimulating essays by one of the greatest of contemporary American philosophers, dealing with the methods of solving legal problems, law and social change, legal institutions such as contract and property, and contemporary legal philosophy. [A39]

1350

____, ed. Readings in jurisprudence and legal philosophy, [with] Felix S. Cohen. N.Y., Prentice-Hall, 1951. 944p. 2d ed. Boston, Little, Brown, 1979. 109p. * +
A8, A20, A42, A49

Considered as less difficult for a beginner to understand. Dean Fenn, Univ. of Fla. See also Felix S. Cohen, Ethical systems and legal ideals, an essay on the foundations of legal criticism (1933, 1959).

1351

____. Reason and law; studies in juristic philosophy. Glencoe, Ill., Free Press [1950.] 211p. N.Y., Macmillan, 1961. +
A28, A35.5, A38, A43.5, A64

Some of these pieces are addressed to philosophers,

some are book reviews and some are historical in approach, but not one will be without interest to those concerned with the purposes of law. Two chapters, "Moral Aspects in the Criminal Law," and "Absolutism in Law and Morals" can be recommended as definitive in their scope. See Tex. L. Rev. 29:281 (1950).

1352

COWAN, THOMAS A., ed. The American jurisprudence reader. N.Y., Oceana, 1956. 254p. (Docket Reader No. 8.) * +
A3, A24, A35, A41, A57.1

The editor, a former Professor of Law at Rutgers University, presents the cream of modern American writing on jurisprudence under the three heads of Philosophical, Analytical and Sociological Jurisprudence. It adds up to an impressive corpus of thinking about law in which the juristic quality challenges comparison with anything in Europe. See Jurid. Rev. n. s. 2:109 (1890).

1353

DEVLIN, PATRICK. The enforcement of morals. London, Oxford Univ. Press, 1965. 139p.
A43.5

This book is Lord Devlin's response to the "1957 Wolfenden Report recommending that homosexual practices in private between consenting adults should no longer be a crime." His testimony before the Wolfenden Committee was, in part, "if there is no danger of corruption ...[he did] not think that there is any good the law can do that outweighs the misery that exposure and imprisonment caused to addicts who cannot find satisfaction in any other way of life." J.L. Montrose, Univ. of Toronto Law Jl 16:455 (1966).

1354

DWORKIN, RONALD. Taking rights seriously. Cambridge, Harvard Univ. Press, 1977. 293p.
A29.5

"Legal reasoning is, whatever else it may be, an observable phenomenon: it actually goes on in the world. For anyone seriously interested in this phenomenon - as an empirical student of, a participant in, or one who philosophizes about the activities of the institutions in which it occurs - Professor Dworkin's writings of the past few years are essential. [This book] collects those writings." John Griffiths, N.Y.U. Law Rev. 53:1124 (1978). Professor Dworkin's articles in law reviews, New

York Review of Books and elsewhere on quotas, Justice Douglas, are always thoughtful, controversial, and citeable. For a critique of Dworkin, see Aleksander Peczenik, Taking laws seriously, Cornell Law Rev. 68:660 (1983).

1355

EHRENZWEIG, ALBERT A. Psychoanalytic jurisprudence; on ethics, aesthetics, and law-crime, tort, and procedure. Dobbs Ferry, Oceana, 1971. 395p.
A11.5

"This is an exciting book, written in a colorful style that reveals an artistic temperament ... [legal systems, comparative jurisprudence, punishment, views on justice, battle between natural law and positivistic jurisprudence] the reviewer believes there is too much emphasis on Freudian 'truths'." Edgar Bodenheimer, Michigan Law Rev. 71:203 (1972).

1356

FEINBERG, JOEL and HYMAN GROSS, eds. Philosophy of law. Dickenson, 1975. 2d ed. Belmont, Cal., Wadsworth, 1980. 630p.
A31.7

Selections from Aquinas, Austin, Kelsen, Ross, H.L.A. Hart, Lon L. Fuller, Roscoe Pound, Dworkin, Aristotle, Rawls, Graham Hughes, Packer, Bentham, etc. Chapters on law, liberty, justice, responsibility, and punishment. Also selections from case law. The authors also edited Justice: selected readings (1977) and Philosophical perspective: selected readings (1977).

1357

FINNIS, JOHN MITCHELL. Natural law and natural rights. N.Y., Oxford Univ. Press, 1980. 425p.
A2.5

An introduction to natural law by one rooted in analytical jurisprudence. Discusses natural law in relation to justice, rights, authority, law, obligation, and unjust law.

1358

FRANK, JEROME. Law and the modern mind. N.Y., Coward-McCann [1949.] 368p. N.Y., Anchor, 1963. * +
A1, A2, A3, A7, A8, A12, A14, A19, A20, A23, A25.5, A27, A28, A29, A30, A33, A35.5, A36, A38, A39, A40, A43, A43.5, A49, A54, A56, A57, A63, A68, A74

A pioneer study, sometimes rash but always provocative, dealing with the relationship between psychology and the law. The late author was an eminent practitioner, law teacher, and Federal Court of Appeals Judge. [A39] One of the important iconoclastic books for lawyers and law students. First year students should read it and then reread it in 2nd and 3rd years. Legal training will give a better understanding. [A12].

1359

FRIED, CHARLES. Right and wrong. Cambridge, Harvard Univ. Press, 1978. 226p.
A24.5

The author "aims to develop an account of what a good person should and should not do, rather than, say, to analyze moral language. He concentrates on personal moral choice; though he treats briefly such issues as fair contributions to the community, his is not in the main concerned to outline basic institutions for a just society. ...Fried holds that a lawyer may choose clients in any way he wishes and may assist a client in a spiteful lawsuit. ...Fried seems to endorse what might be styled a boundary-line conception of morality. ... His chief critical target is utilitarianism..." Stephen R. Munzer, Michigan Law Rev. 77:421 (1979).

1360

FRIEDMANN, WOLFGANG G. Legal theory. 5th ed. N.Y., Columbia Univ. Press, 1967. 607p.
A25.5

A broad based survey from the Greek philosophers to the realist movement. This book can be opened at "Holmes" or "Pragmatic positivism," etc. and guarantee fifteen minutes of intellectual stimulation.

1361

FRIEDRICH, CARL J., ed. Authority. Cambridge, Harvard Univ. Press, 1958. 234p.
A31.7

"Given the historical antecedents of the topic of authority and the erudition of the contributors to this symposium, one might predict that here is another academic exercise in the splitting of hairs that have been split before - often by the same authors - and that the tag called 'authority' will be pinned to a fantastically varied assortment of twigs on the tree of definition. The prediction is, of course, a sure thing. ...Plainly, this symposium has overcome the tribulations that normally attend such a composite effort in sufficient degree to deserve our thanks." Harold D. Lasswell, Yale Law Jl 68:393 (1958).

1362

____. The philosophy of law in historical perspective. Chicago, Univ. of Chicago Press, 1958. 253p.
A25.5

"...the volume presents a broad-guaged analysis of some central problems of legal philosophy - first and primarily from a historical, subsequently from a systematic viewpoint - rather than a detailed introduction to the history and present status of the general theory of law." Edgar Bodenheimer, Michigan Law Rev. 57:628 (1959). Professor Friedrich also edited Rational Decision (1964), one of a series of volumes (this was NOMOS VII) published by the American Society of Political and Legal Philosophy. This book was reviewed by Mary Ellen Caldwell, Natural Law Forum 10:275 (1965). Professor Friedrich and John W. Chapman edited NOMOS VI, Justice (325) which was reviewed by Charles Perelman, Natural Law Forum 9:122 (1964).

1363

FULLER, LON L. The law in quest of itself; ...a series of three lectures ... delivered at the Law School of Northwestern Univ. ... in April, 1940. Brooklyn, Foundation Press, 1940. 147p.
A24, A48.5, A49, A68 * +

A readable perspective on the role of authority in the ordering, adjusting, or resolving of overlapping rights and values - interacting with the body politic. [A24] Professor Fuller's "The Case of the Speluncean Explorers" in Harvard Law Rev. 62:616 (1949), an imaginary opinion written in a future century is one of the most commented on pieces ever written for a law review. [A47] For those interested in the philosophical underpinnings of Professor Fuller (the is and ought of the law), see Kenneth I. Winston, ed. The principles of social order; selected essays ...(1981). This book also contains a bibliography of Professor Fuller's writings that include his reflections on teaching, bar exams, and ethics. A biography of Professor Fuller by Robert S. Summers has been announced for 1983 or 1984 publication.

1364

____. Legal fictions. Stanford, Stanford Univ. Press, 1967. 137p.
A35.5

"...The republication in 1967 of what Lon Fuller wrote more than thirty-five years before provides much nourishing food for thought concerning our whole legal, political and social environment as well as serving as a lucid account of the concept of legal fictions. ...This book should be read and re-read not only by those whose primary endeavors fall within the realm of law but by all who profess to have inquiring minds." Univ. Law Forum 1967:847 (1967).

1365

____. The morality of law. New Haven, Yale Univ. Press, 1964. 195p.
A6.5, A25.5, A27.5, A43.5, A57.7, A71.5

"Professor Fuller begins by drawing a very important distinction in systems of morality - the difference between a 'morality of duty' ... and a 'morality of aspiration.' ...In essence, Professor Fuller's position is that once a particular function or end of law is chosen, the physical environment, the nature of man and the institutional structure force choices as to how that end or function is to be achieved and this becomes a natural law governing the way the end must be sought." B. McDowell, Boston Univ. Law Rev. 44:587 (1964).

1366

GOLDING, M.P. Philosophy of law. Englewood Cliffs, Prentice-Hall, 1975. 133p.
A43.5

"The explicit aim of this eminently readable little book is to 'introduce the student to legal philosophy and to stimulate his own thinking.' Alongside this runs an implicit aim, namely, to convince the student 'of the intellectual and practical significance of [legal philosophy].'" Roger Brownsword, Modern Law Rev. 39:603 (1976).

1367

GRAY, JOHN CHIPMAN. The nature and sources of the law, ...2nd ed., from the author's notes, by Roland Gray. N.Y., Macmillan, 1921. 384p. * +
A1, A7, A8, A14, A19, A27, A30, A36, A38, A39, A41, A42, A56, A63, A68, A72

An analysis of the nature of law and the factors which contribute to its development. The author was a member of the faculty of Harvard Law School. [A39] Holdsworth has said of Gray that he was a great lawyer, a great teacher, and as his books show, a great legal philosopher.

1368

GUEST, A. G., ed. Oxford essays in jurisprudence. London, Oxford Univ. Press, 1961. 292p.
A24.5

"This collection of essays merits the serious attention of all American lawyers claiming an interest in jurisprudence. The essays are sometimes brilliant, invariably stimulating and generally well-written. But more important than these attributes, is that for the first time, the American reader is presented with a genuine cross-section of the jurisprudential thought current in modern Oxford." R.B. Stevens, Tulane Law Rev. 36:183 (1961).

1369

HACKER, P.M.S. and **J. RAZ**, eds. Law, morality, and society; essays in honour of H.L.A.Hart. N.Y., Oxford Univ. Press, 1977. 313p.
A24.5

"The sixteen papers include several concerned primarily with Hart's legal philosophy, especially as developed in The Concept of Law (1961). I have selected two themes in Hart's legal philosophy for closer examination: ...legal rules ... and ... rights. ...D.N.MacCormick ... develops a powerful critique of Hart's 'will' theory of legal rights." Stanley L. Paulson, Michigan Law Rev. 77:484 (1979).

1370

HAINES, CHARLES G. The revival of natural law concepts; a study of the establishment and the interpretation of limits on

legislatures with special reference to the development of certain phases of American Constitutional Law ... Cambridge, Harvard Univ. Press, 1930. 388p. +
A68

A scholarly discussion of the development and influences of theories of natural law from Graeco-Roman time to the present. Also developed is the influence of natural law in the construction of written constitutions in the U.S. See Univ. of Pennsylvania Law Rev. 80:149 (1931-32).

1371

HALL, JEROME. Living law of democratic society. Indianapolis, Bobbs-Merrill [1949.] 146p. * +
A28, A43.5, A49, A72

In this scholarly volume, new twentieth century concepts of law are discussed with many illustrations and in a readable style. Brought out is the significance of these concepts for a democratic society. See N.Y.U.L. Rev. 25:937 (1950). Professor Hall also authored Foundations of Jurisprudence (1973). [A25.5, A43.5]

1372

HARDING, ARTHUR L., ed. Origins of the natural law tradition. Dallas, Southern Methodist Press, 1954. 96p. +
A68

In studying natural law one must begin with definitions. Here four different ideas of natural law which have bulked large in our legal history are defined and outlined. The four theories have been presented in terms of their principal expositors: Cicero, with his transcending synthesis of the Aristotelian man and the Stoic cosmology; St. Thomas Aquinas with his Hellenized adaptation of traditional Jewish-Christian Theology; Richard Hooker who provided an intellectual bridge between the neo-classical natural law of Bracton and the rationalist natural rights doctrines of the 17th century; and Herbert Spencer, who constructed a sort of natural law on the basis of the natural laws of biological existence as propounded by Charles Darwin. See Preface. Mr. Harding also edited The Rule of Law (1961).

1373

HART, H.L.A. The concept of law. Oxford, Clarendon Press, 1961. 263p.
A2.5, A49

"Even though the book is primarily an essay in analytical jurisprudence, it moves, in many of its parts, very close to the borderlines which separate analytical jurisprudence from legal sociology on the one hand and philosophical jurisprudence on the other, and it crosses these borderlines at a number of points." Edgar Bodenheimer, U.C.L.A. Law Rev. 10:959 (1963). Professor Hart also wrote Punishment and Responsibility (1968) reviewed by Franklin S. Longan, Gonzaga Law Rev. 4:365 (1969). He also authored, with A.M. Honore, Causation in the Law (1978,1959).

1374

____. Law, liberty and morality. Stanford, Stanford Univ. Press, 1963. 88p.
A38.5, A43.5, A71.5, A74

The case against using criminal law to enforce morality.

1375

HOHFELD, WESLEY N. Fundamental legal conceptions as applied in judicial reasoning, and other legal essays ...ed. by Walter Wheeler Cook ...New Haven, Yale Univ. Press, 1923. 420p. Republished by Yale in paperback in 1964. +
A28, A38

This work attracted wide attention. Hohfield attempted what had often in recent decades been attempted by others - to isolate the basic types of legal relationship and to give each side of each relation a name suitable in itself and agreeable, so far as possible to the usages of professional parlance. His solution quickly gained wide adherence in all quarters, especially among law teachers, judges, and even economists. See Law, A Century of Progress II:207 (1937). See also John A. McMenamin, Villanova Law Rev. 10:407 (1965).

1376

HOLLAND, SIR THOMAS E. The elements of jurisprudence. 10th ed., N.Y., Oxford Univ. Press (Amer. branch), 1906. 443p. +
A18

One of the greatest difficulties of the beginning student is to orient himself in the law. Among other things, this involvles an understanding of the relationship of one course to another. This, in turn, involves a classification of the law and at this point Holland will prove useful. Dean Reppy.

1377

HOLMES, OLIVER WENDELL, Jr. The common law. Boston, Little, Brown, 1881. 422p. (many editions) +
A1, A2, A3, A7, A8, A10, A11, A14, A19, A20, A24, A26, A27, A28, A30, A33, A34, A38, A40, A41, A42, A43, A48, A49, A54, A55, A56, A63, A66, A68, A71.5, A72, A74

The classic account of the great formative ideas of English law. [A56] Beginners in the law may find some of it an intellectual challenge. [A54] Recommended for third year law students. [A42] No jurist has stirred the emotions of the legal fraternity as much as Justice Holmes. See Y. Rogat, Mr. Justice Holmes, a dissenting opinion, Stanford Law Rev. 15:254 (1963); also symposia in Univ. of Chicago Law Rev. 31:(Winter 1964); also Hofstra Law Rev. 10:(Spring 1982), particularly the Touser article at page 673. See also P.S. Atiyah, The legacy of Holmes through English eyes, Boston Univ. Law Rev. 63:341 (1983). An article could easily be compiled on the number of ways scholars have attempted to discredit Justice Holmes.

1378

INTERPRETATIONS OF MODERN LEGAL PHILOSOPHIES; essays in honor of Roscoe Pound, edited with an introduction by Paul Sayre. N.Y., Oxford Univ. Press, 1947. 807p. +
A42

A symposium of 38 articles on many aspects of the philosophy of law, written with a competence and authority that make them a veritable treasure of juristic thought. The essays should be pondered in the law schools and by members of the profession. See Can. B. Rev. 27:126 (1949). The authors are C.K. Allen, E. Balogh, Bustamante, Cairns, Chroust, Cossio, Cowan, del Vecchio, Eggleston, J. Frank, M. Franklin, A.L. Goodhart, Gutteridge, J.Hall, W.E. Hocking, W. Jaeger, J.W. Jones, H.Kelsen, A.Kocourek, M.M. Laseron, V.Lundstedt, C.H. McIlwain, A.Mendizabel, A.Meyendorff, K.Olivecrona, E.W. Patterson, E.Martinez, Max Radin, Max Rheinstein, L.R. Siches, Helen Silving, P.A. Sorokin, Julius Stone, N.S. Timasheff, A. von Mehren, R.West, P.H. Winfield, and Lord Wright.

1379

JENKS, EDWARD. The new jurisprudence ...London, J. Murray, [1933.] 290p. +
A40

Dr. Jenks is a humanist and a historian. Without neglecting the ethical aspect, therefore, he devotes his principal attention to a system of law as a chapter in the history of institutions and as a topic in sociology. See Law Q. Rev. 50:126 (1939).

1380

JONES, HARRY W. The efficacy of law. Evanston, Northwestern Univ. Press, 1969. 117p.
A31.7

"Professor Jones provides guidelines - in the form of tentative hypotheses - that will be invaluable to the sociology of law and theoretical jurisprudence alike. As a successor to Llewellyn, Patterson and company in the realm of responsible American Legal Realism, Professor Jones emphasizes the crucial distinction between 'paper rules' and 'real rules.'" E. Hunter Taylor, Jr., Georgia Law Rev. 4:432 (1970).

1381

KADISH, MORTIMER R. and **SANFORD** H. **KADISH.** Discretion to disobey; a study of lawful departures from legal rules. Stanford, Stanford Univ. Press, 1973. 241p.
A24.5

A philosopher and a lawyer argue that there are occasions "when the refusal to obey the directives of a legal system is in fact sanctioned by that legal system and perhaps even part of our legal obligation. ..." George C. Christie, California Law Rev. 62:1289 (1974).

1382

KELSEN, HANS, ed. What is justice; justice, law and politics in the mirror of science: collected essays. Berkeley, Univ. of California Press, 1957, 1971. 397p.
A43.5

"... the common thread that they deal with the problems of justice and their relation to religion, law, politics, and science ... our desire to argue with the Pure Theory of Law is, however, but a testimonial to its compelling importance." A.H. Campbell, Law Q. Rev. 74:441 (1958).

1383

LEISER, BURTON M. Liberty, justice and morals: contemporary value conflicts. N.Y., Macmillan, 1973. 436p.
A57.1

Sections on: Lord Devlin and the enforcement of morals, homosexuality, contraception and abortion, divorce, marijuana, obscenity and pornography, punishment, death penalty, the ethics of truth, civil disobedience, war crimes, and crimes against humanity.

1384

LUCEY, REV. FRANCIS E. Natural law and American legal realism; their respective contributions to a theory of law in a democratic society. In Geo. L.Jl 30:493 (1942). +
A68

The purpose of this article is summed up by the author. "The main problem here is Realism versus Scholastic Natural Law, so often confused with the Pseudo-Natural Law of 19th century American jurisprudence, that philosophy which decapitated the sound philosophy of the founding fathers."

1385

MAINE, SIR HENRY JAMES S. Ancient law. (New ed., rev. by Sir Frederick Pollock. Toronto, Carswell, 1930. 440p. (In many editions.) 1963 Beacon Press edition. * +
A1, A2, A7, A8, A14, A27, A30, A39, A41, A42, A43.5, A49, A54, A56, A59, A63, A68, A72, A74

One of the 19th century classics; this is a pioneer study of the relationship between the development of society and law, with a now famous emphasis on the interdependence of liberty, progress, and freedom of contract. [A39] Dean Fenn considered this as less difficult for a beginner to understand.

1386

MODERN THEORIES OF LAW. London, Oxford Univ. Press, H. Milford, 1933. 229p. +
A4

An attempt to coordinate jurisprudence with the other social sciences by a series of lectures delivered to students of the Faculty of Law of the University of

London. Lawyers, political scientists, sociologists and others, expounding on legal theory. Some of the best minds in the English academic world contributed. See Harvard Law Rev. 47:721 (1934).

1387

MORRIS, CLARENCE, ed. The great legal philosophers; selected readings in jurisprudence. Phila., Univ. of Pennsylvania Press, 1959. 571p.
A24.5

"... consists of lengthy extracts from the writings of twenty-two men whose works ought to be considered by all students working in this field [legal philosophy]. The book is intended for use in a course in jurisprudence in a law school. [authors extracted include Pound, Savigny, Hegel, Ihering, Ehrlich, Dabin, Hobbes, Locke, Montesquieu, Hume, Rousseau, Kant, Bentham, Mill]. Stanley D. Rose, Tulane Law Rev. 33:928 (1959).

1388

MORRIS, HERBERT, ed. Freedom and responsibility; readings in philosophy and law. Stanford, Stanford Univ. Press, 1961. 547p.
A31.7

The editor "has collected a great number of readings from works in philosophy, psychology, and law in order to suggest possible meanings for the basic terms used in discussing freedom and responsibility. ...[T]here must be a host of practitioners, teachers, and judges who need just this type of material to give depth to their thinking about the practical and very much alive issues of freedom and responsibility." Stanley D. Rose, Rutgers Law Rev. 16:488 (1962).

1389

MURPHY, CORNELIUS F., JR. Modern legal philosophy; the tension between experiential and abstract thought. Duquesne Univ. Press, 1978. 241p.
A43.5

Chapters on analytical jurisprudence, the advent of sociology, the pure theory of law, the pursuit of justice, and the problem of natural law.

1390

MY PHILOSOPHY OF LAW; credos of sixteen American scholars ...Boston, Boston Law Book Co. [1941.] 321p. * +
A11, A28, A43, A49, A54, A56, A64

Joseph W. Bingham, Morris R. Cohen, Walter Wheeler Cook, John Dewey, John Dickinson, Lon L. Fuller, Leon Green, Walter B. Kennedy, Albert Kocourek, K.N. Llewellyn, Underhill Moore, Edwin W. Patterson, Roscoe Pound, Thomas Reed Powell, Max Radin, and John H. Wigmore. These credos tend to emphasize the inadequacy of law as precedent and to enlarge the reader's feeling of the relation of justice to the lawyer's everyday practice in which he must protect his client and the public from the law's foibles. [A54]

1391

NEWMAN, RALPH A., ed. Essays in jurisprudence in honor of Roscoe Pound. Indianapolis, Bobbs-Merrill, 1962. 670p.
A31.7

"The editor has grouped the essays into three categories, whose titles are self-explanatory: 'The Foundations of Law,' 'Concepts of Jurisprudence,' and 'The Impact of Jurisprudence on the Living Law.' ...[A] significant tribute is found in the multitude of citations to Pound's own work - a remarkable tribute indeed when one notes the scope and variety of subjects covered." Robert N. Covington, Vanderbilt Law Rev. 16:491 (1963).

1392

NOZICK, ROBERT. Anarchy, state and utopia. N.Y., Basic Books, 1974. 367p.
A57.1

"...an important and wide ranging book that is bound to have a significant impact on moral and political philosophy. Nozick is primarily interested in questions concerning the justification of the state and its coercive activity, but in his discussion of these issues he deals with a great variety of problems in normative moral theory. The author approaches his topic from the perspective of the libertarian and anarchistic traditions ..." Houston Law Rev. 12:1186 (1975).

1393

OAKESHOTT, MICHAEL. On human conduct. Oxford, Clarendon Press,1975. 326p.
A29.5

"The book consists of three essays: 'On the Understanding of Human Conduct' - a theoretical understanding proper to a philosopher, not a psychological or sociological analysis; 'On the Civil Condition' - a title reflecting the author's long absorbtion in Hobbes; and 'On the Character of a Modern European State' - an analysis, in terms explicated throughout the work, of political theory and practice from the late Middle Ages to our own day." Law Q. Rev. 92:122 (1976).

1394

PATTERSON, EDWIN W. Jurisprudence; men and ideas of the law. Brooklyn, Foundation Press, 1953. 649p. +
A6, A41, A49

Presents concisely and clearly with ample illustrations, the ideas and theories about law in general which have been and are most influential in American law. Sketches personality and social setting of the men who have contributed influential ideas. Professor Patterson was also the author of Law in a Scientific Age (1963). [A43.5]

1395

PEKELIS, ALEXANDER H. Law and social action; selected essays, edited by Milton R. Konvitz. Ithaca, Cornell Univ. Press, 1950. 272p. +
A43

A posthumous volume in which Pekelis discusses the problem of evolution in the judicial and legislative process, the problems of legal control over the major centers of monopolistic power in the U.S. and the concrete problems involved in implementing the Bill of Rights. The essays all reflect a stimulating freshness. See N.Y.U. L. Rev. 26:727 (1951).

1396

PENNOCK, J. ROLAND and JOHN W. CHAPMAN, eds. Due process. N.Y., N.Y.U. Press, 1977. (NOMOS XVIII). 362p.
A31.7

"Ultimately, the most interesting thing about this volume for comparativists may be its testimonial to America's continued love affair with its judiciary."

[Charles Miller on the American Constitutional Tradition; Geoffrey Marshall on Due Process in England; Edmund L. Pincoff, Due Process, Fraternity, and a Kantian Injunction; David Danelski, Due Process in a Nonlegal Setting: An Ombudsman's Experience; David Resnick, Due Process and Procedural Justice; Frank Michelman, Formal and Associational Aims in Procedural Due Process; and Thomas C. Grey, Procedural Fairness and Substantive Rights. Also essays by Gerald Kramer, Arthur Kuflik, and

Richard Epstein.] The American Jl of Comparative Law 26:656 (1978).

1397

____. The limits of law. (NOMOS XV). N.Y., Lieber-Atherton, 1974. 276p.
A31.7

David J. Daniels, William L. McBride, Julius Cohen, June Louis Topp, Kent Greenwalt, Sergio Cotta, Michael A. Weinstein, Graham Hughes, Alan Dershowitz, Stephen Wasby, Michael D. Bayles, Donald H. Regan, Kenneth M. Dolbeare, Jerome Hall, Hugo Adam Bedau and Victor G. Rosenblum. See A. McBride, Saskatchewan Law Rev. 41:208 (1976). Some other titles in this series are Anarchism (1978), Coercion (1972), Compromises in ethics law and politics (1979 Nomos 21), Ethics, economics and the law (1982 Nomos 24), Human rights (1981 Nomos 23), Liberal democracy (1983 Nomos 25), Political and legal obligations (1970 Nomos 12), Privacy (1971 Nomos 13), Voluntary associations (1969 Nomos 11).

1398

PLATO. Gorgias. [in many editions]

Is it dishonorable to be a lawyer? [A49] Should a student participate in moot court if he doesn't believe in the argument given him? What are the limits in your obligation to represent a client? If you object to the Socratic method, do not blame Langdell or Harvard Law School - blame Socrates.

1399

POLLOCK, SIR FREDERICK, bart. A first book of jurisprudence for students of the common law ...6th ed. London, Macmillan, 1929. 376p. +
A13, A71.5

Addressed to readers who have laid the foundation of a liberal education and are beginning the study of law, it considers ideas underlying discussion in lay language and also deals with sources of the English law, the history of law reporting and the authority of decided cases. Note: This essay is included in Jurisprudence and Legal Essays (1961). [A43.5, A71.5] "The evidence is cumulative that Pollock had no great social vision. He was a lawyer and a good one - but in a narrow vein." Stanley D. Rose, Vanderbilt Law Rev. 15:1350.

1400

POUND, ROSCOE. The formative era of American law. N.Y., P. Smith, 1950 [c1938.] 188p. +
A43.5, A45, A56, A71.5

Four lectures on the study of legal theory and the development of law in this country between the Revolution and the Civil War. An interesting and valuable introduction to the study of juristic theory and legal agencies. See Ore. Law Rev. 30:191 (1950-1). Dean Pound lists his choice "of the ten judges who must be ranked first in American judicial history (p.4). For a current list, see Bernard Schwartz, The judicial ten: America's greatest judges, So. Ill. Univ. Law Jl 1979:405 (1979). For the best and worst current judges, see The American Lawyer, July/August 1983. But for a criticism of this rating practice, see Tom Goldstein's appraisal of The American Lawyer in the Columbia Law Rev. 83:1351, 1356 (1983). And see David R. Currie's The Most Insignificant Justice, A Preliminary Inquiry, Univ. of Chicago Law Rev. (to be published late 1983).

1401

____. An introduction to the philosophy of law. Rev. ed. New Haven, Yale Univ. Press, 1954. 201p. * +
A1, A2, A7, A8, A14, A19, A20, Aa25.5, 27, A30, A35.5, 36, A38, A39, A42, A43.5, A45, A49, A54, A56, A63, A68, A72

An excellent introduction to legal theory by the late Dean of the Harvard Law School. [A39] It is clear and concise dealing with the philosophy of law from the Greek period through the Roman and Medieval down to the present, always exhibiting a wealth of learning.

Dean Fenn considers it less difficult for a beginner to understand.

1402

____. Law and morals. 2d ed. Chapel Hill, Univ. of N.C. Press, 1926. 144p. * +
A24, A40, A45

This is one of Prof. Pound's ingenious and stimulating critical-historical studies. His theme is the succession of different views held by judges and publicists during the past century as to the relation of law to morality. See Law Q. Rev. 41:108 (1926).

1403

____. The spirit of the common law. Boston, Marshall Jones Co. [1921.] 224p. * +

A6.5, A8, A10, A12, A13, A15, A23, A28, A29, A33, A35, A36, A38, A43, A43.5, 45, A49, A50, A54, A55, A57, A61, A62, A68, A71.5, A72

Brilliant lectures in which Dean Pound places the common law on trial but finds it can successfully weather its indictments for extreme individualism and its tendency to impose duties and liabilities upon men as members of groups or classes, independently of their individual will. [A54] Don't worry if you don't get it all - reread in 2nd and 3rd years - your greater background in law will give you better understanding.

1404

____. Social control through law ...New Haven, Yale Univ. Press [etc.]. 1942. 138p. * +

A8, A24, A64

An excellent orientation of the law and its present position in our society as it is seen by a foremost legal philosopher. See Harvard Law Rev. 56:680 (1943).

1405

____. The task of law ...Lancaster, Pa., Franklin and Marshall College [c1944.] 94p. +

A49

What is the task of the law? Is it to translate the divine commands into the language of humans or is it to give the will of the sovereign enforceable expression? This question and others are answered by Dean Pound with great historic and critical scholarship. See Harvard Law Rev. 57:922 (1944). For a bibliography of the extensive writings of Dean Pound, see Franklyn C. Setaro, _A bibliography of the writings of Roscoe Pound_ (1942).

1406

RADCLIFFE, LORD. The law and its compass. Evanston, Northwestern Univ. Press, 1960. 99p.

A29.5

"...For an American reader the penetration of this new classic of the law - a work not one whit inferior in imagination and idealism to Cardozo's _The Nature of the Judicial Process..._" Charles E. Wyzanski, Jr. Northwestern Univ. Law Rev. 55:503 (1960).

1407

RADIN, MAX. The law and Mr. Smith ...Indianapolis, Bobbs-Merrill [c1938.] 333p. * +
A8, A20, A28, A39, A43, A54, A64, A71

A popular and entertaining treatment of the nature of the law and the development of legal institutions. The author is a late Professor of Law. [A39] For another excellent treatment of this type see Lon Fuller, The Anatomy of the Law (1968) [No. 2133]. For an interesting treatment of Professor Radin, read G. Edward White, Earl Warren, a public life (1982).

1408

____. Law as logic and experience. New Haven, Yale Univ. Press, 1940. 171p. * +
A8, A28, A40, A72

Prof. Radin considers two texts - the dictum of Coke, J., "Reason is the life of the law" and the opinion of Holmes, J., "The life of the law has not been logic: it has been experience." Although this volume does not purport to be a serious contribution to legal philosophy, it is full of mellow wisdom, gracious erudition, thought provoking phrase and human sympathy. See Harvard Law Rev. 54:711 (1941).

1409

RATCLIFFE, JAMES M. The good samaritan and the law. N.Y., Doubleday, 1966. 300p.
A24.5

Includes reprint of Ames" 'Law and Morals,' and essays by Professors Gregory, Tunc, Dawson, Zeisel, Waller, Gusfield, Rudolf; and Alan Barth, Antony Honore, and Dr. Freedman. See William Samore, Albany Law Rev. 31:393 (1967).

1410

RAWLS, JOHN. A theory of justice. Cambridge, Harvard Univ. Press, 1971. 607p.
A2.5, A35.5, A36, A38.5, A47

"...It is not often we get a book like this one ... similar in scope and ambition to the great books of Spinoza, Locke, and Kent. ...almost exclusively concerned with the justice of individual actions, persons, or policies ...second, he is concerned to describe an ideally just basic structure as it would operate if everyone always acted justly and discharged the duties imposed by the basic theory as opposed to 'partial compliance theory.'" Joel Feinberg, Yale Law Jl 81:1004 (1972). "...the paramount conclusion is that justice, in the final analysis, depends on our feelings and inclinations." Erwin Neumeier, Mississippi Law Jl 47:827 (1976).

1411

REDDEN, KENNETH R. An introductory survey of the place of law in our civilization. ...Charlottesville, Va., Michie, 1946. 272p.
A43, A56 +

The book's purpose is to provide, in an introductory survey form "the means whereby the college student may see the 'law' not as a foreign, unintelligible aspect of his society ... but rather as a fluid set of working principles responsive to the fluctuating needs of society."

1412

REUSCHLEIN, HAROLD G. Jurisprudence, its American prophets: a survey of taught jurisprudence. Indianapolis, Bobbs-Merril [1951.] 527p. 1971 reprint. +
A7, A25.5, A43, A43.5, A49, A56, A68

Survey of the course of American legal thought in terms of the men who did the thinking. [A56] From Wythe to Cooley, Benthamites, Langdell, Ames, Pound, Vanderbilt, Hohfeld, Realists (Rodell, J. Frank), neo-scholastics (Hutchins, et al), F.S.C. Northrop, Cardozo, Fuller, and a host of others. Biographical list of authors with their major accomplishments.

1413

RODENBECK, ADOLPH J. The anatomy of the law; a logical presentation of the parts of the body of the law ...Boston, Little, Brown, 1925. 292p. * +
A54

A noteworthy attempt at placing the law into scientific arrangement, worthwhile reading on an objective which is impossible of practical attainment. [A54].

1414

RODES, ROBERT. The legal enterprise. Port Washington, N.Y., Kennikat Press, 1967. 181p.
A2.5

"To sum up, the ultimate purpose of the legal enterprise is to protect and support the personal fulfillment of individual persons. ...This teleological content provided by human nature is what I have in mind when I use the term natural law" (p.121) The book discusses different schools of jurisprudence, the "just law" doctrine, and a critique of Hart.

1415

ROMMEN, HEINRICH A. The natural law, a study in legal and social history and philosophy; tr. by Thomas R. Hanley. St. Louis, B. Herder Book Co., 1947. 290p. +
A25

A scholarly presentation which traces the development of the idea of natural law from its early expression in Greece and Rome down through its mature development in the writings of the scholastics. There is also an interesting discussion on morality and law. See Temple Law Q. 23:255 (1950).

1416

ST.JOHN-STEVAS, NORMAN. Life, death and the law; law and Christian morals in England and the United States. Bloomington, Indiana Univ. Press, 1961. 375p.
A43.5

"The entire text is well-documented, while retaining a lively and graceful literary style. We do not often see the appearance of a volume which is so rewarding to the reader who wishes to look behind and beyond law to discern its roots and goals." Thomas J. O'Toole, Villanova Law Rev. 7:160 (1961).

1417

SHKLAR, JUDITH N. Legalism. Cambridge, Harvard Univ. Press, 1964. 246p.
A31.7

"...a brilliant and forceful attack on some of the fundamental concepts which have created and which perpetuate the isolation of law from other kinds of social theory, especially political science. ..." Thomas J. O'Toole, Georgetown Law Jl 53:854 (1965).

1418

SIMPSON, A.W.B., ed. Oxford essays in jurisprudence. Second series. Oxford, Oxford Univ. Press, 1973. 804p.
A31.7

Includes Honore, Finnis, Simpson, MacCormick, Hacker, Hart (on Bentham's benefit theory of legal rights, Dworkin (taking rights seriously), Marshall, Tapper, Raz. "... linguistic subtlety and refinement which have come to be recognised as the hall-marks of the present day Oxford philosopher ... so much learning and dexterity has been deployed in engendering a rather arid product ... perhaps jurisprudence and legal theory are too important to be left to the legal philosophers." Lloyd of Hampstead, Law Q. Rev. 90:130 (1974).

1419

SIMPSON, SIDNEY P. Cases and readings on law and society, [with] Julius Stone and M. Magdalena Schoch, St. Paul, West Pub. Co., 1948-49. 3 v.
A42

This is an invaluable source book of excerpts from books dealing with society in all its more vital aspects, of extracts from decided cases and of relevant portions of codes and statutes bearing upon the same subject. Numerous footnotes refer to large numbers of other works and articles and this documentation is remarkably extensive. See Modern Law Rev. 13:385 (1950).

1420

STONE, JULIUS. The province and function of law; law as logic, justice and social control; a study in jurisprudence. ...Sydney, Associated General Publications, 1946. 918p. * +
A64, A67

The most comprehensive and thorough survey of the important theories of or about law which has thus far appeared in English. The selected documentation of the footnotes, the full bibliography, and an index of 77 pages, make it an invaluable reference work to the literature in the field. See Columbia Law. Rev. 47:330 (1947). Mr. Stone also wrote _Social Dimensions of Law and Justice_ (1966) reviewed by A.S.Miller and A.W. Scheflin in American Univ. Law Rev. 16:359 (1967). Mr. Stone also wrote _Legal system and lawyers' reasonings_ (1964).

1421

SUMMERS, ROBERT, ed. Essays in legal philosophy, Berkeley,Univ. of California Press, 1971. 307p.
A31.7

Includes Ronald Dworkin, A.M.Honore, Herbert Morris, Glanville Williams, Anthony Kenny, J.R.Lucas, Graham Hughes, M.P.Golding, Gerald MacCallum Jr., Richard A. Wasserstrom. See Hilliard A. Gardiner, Brooklyn Law Rev. 38:834 (1972).

1422

TWINING, WILLIAM. Karl Llewellyn and the realist movement. London, Weidenfeld and Nicolson, 1973. 574p.
A31.7

Covers the Realist Movement and the life of Llewellyn - his life, writings, commentaries on his writings, and an account of his work on the Uniform Commercial Code. See Grant Gilmore, American Jl of Comparative Law 22:812 (1974). Mr. Twining (along with David Miers) wrote How to do things with Rules: A Primer of Interpretation (1976). [A48.5]

1423

UNGER, ROBERTO MANGABIERA. Knowledge and politics. N.Y., Free Press, 1975. 336p.
A29.5

"...Unger's account of the ideal self represents no advance beyond Marx ... misconstrues the ideals of political, social, and economic justice on the model of personal love ... Unger's ideas of communitarian purposes would have difficulty in accounting to the right of privacy ..." David A.J. Richards, Fordham Law Rev. 44:873 (1976). Mr. Unger also wrote Law in Modern Society (1977). [A47].

1424

VINOGRADOFF, SIR PAUL. Common sense in law. Revised by J. G. Hanbury. 2d ed. London, G. Cumberledge, Oxford Univ. Press, 1946. 192p. +
A6, A36

Considers legal rights and duties and the sources of the rules which the courts enforce as law; an admirable little sketch. See Guide to Historical Literature.

[1425 saved]

JURY

1426

JOINER, CHARLES W. Civil justice and the jury. Englewood Cliffs, Prentice-Hall, 1962. 238p.
A29.5

"...should give the layman an accurate picture of what trial by jury is all about and encourage him to participate in its functioning. It will provide an excellent summary for law students and lawyers of fact and argument in support of retention and improvement of not only a time-honored institution, but one which plays a current and functionally valuable role in the administration of the rule of law." James P. Whyte, William and Mary Law Rev. 4:248 (1963).

1427

KALVEN, HARRY JR. and HANS ZEISEL. The American jury. Boston, Little, Brown, 1966. 559p.
A43.5

"The main inquiry of the book is to answer the question where do trial by judge and trial by jury lead to divergent results in American criminal trials?" Dickson Phillips, Cornell Law Q. 52:1037 (1967). Another volume of the Jury Project of the Univ. of Chicago is Rita James Simon, The Jury and the Defense of Insanity (1967) reviewed by Edward M. Wise in N.Y.U. Law Rev. 43:603 (1968). Ms. Simon also edited The Jury System in America; a critical overview (1975) reviewed by Merritt Lane, Jr. in A.B.A.Jl 62:568 (1976). See also Reid Hastie, Steven D. Penrod and Nancy Pennington, Inside the jury (1983).

LABOR

1428

BLOOM, GORDON F. Economics of labor and industrial relations, [with] Herbert R. Northrup. Phila., Blakiston, 1950. 749p. * +
A8

It combines in a very satisfactory manner the institutional and the theoretical approach to an understanding of the problems relating to employer-employee relations. Deals with union structure and government, management and industrial relations, industrial jurisprudence, wage determination, collective bargaining and a theoretical discussion of wage-employment relations. See Virginia Law Rev. 37:3537 (1951).

1429

GREGORY, CHARLES O. Labor and the law; rev. and enl. ed. ...N.Y., Norton [c1949.] 523p. 3d ed. with Harold A. Katz. N.Y., Norton, 1979. * +
A8, A43

Written probably for the lay reader, it is complete and technical enough to give necessary information to the general practitioner and to give even the specialist some help. See Columbia Law Rev. 47:167 (1947).

1430

HARPER, F. A. Why wages rise. Irvington-on-Hudson, N.Y., Foundation for Economic Education, 1957. 124p. +
A19

Almost the only book which deals directly and in detail with the question whether trade unions can raise real wages generally. Somewhat oversimplified, but cogent.

1431

HAYS, PAUL R. Labor arbitration; a dissenting view. New Haven, Yale Univ. Press, 1966. 125p.
A31.7

Judge Hays asks many questions "in a manner well calculated to affright and enrage those who unquestioningly accept arbitration as a superior, indeed irreplaceable, institution. ...[T]here is a definite if unwelcome twinge in the abdomen which occurs on reading Judge Hays' skillful and effective destruction of Mr. Justice Douglas' view of the parties' expectations of arbitrators." Thomas G.S.Christensen, Stanford Law Rev. 19:671 (1967).

1432

PETRO, SYLVESTER. The labor policy of the free society. N.Y., Ronald [1957.] 339p. +
A19

Sets forth the structure of labor law during the fifties and the underlying social, legal, economic and political principles. It then makes proposals designed to correct defects in our laws which emerge when current rules are measured against the basic principles of our society. A successful attempt to bring to bear upon the problems of labor relations the insights to be derived from the law, economics and political science. H. Hazlitt, writing in Newsweek, May 13, '57, p. 100 considers it to be "the best analysis of the law of labor relations that has yet appeared. ...It deserves to be widely quoted and studied."

1433

STAGNER, ROSS. The psychology of industrial conflict. N.Y., John Wiley & Sons, 1956. 550p. * +
A8

Written for advanced students in psychology and other social sciences this is a discussion of basic psychological factors involved in labor and management negotiations and strikes. In the conclusion there is an analysis of psychological steps necessary to establish union-management cooperation and industrial peace. See Library Jl 81:1533.

LANGUAGE

See also FORENSIC ENGLISH; RHETORIC; READING AND COMPREHENSION

Language is the lawyer's working tool. He must be able, in the drafting of legal instruments, to convey meaning clearly and effectively. In oral and written advocacy he must be capable of communicating ideas convincingly and concisely. In reception no less than in expression, language is fundamental as the lawyer's medium of communication. For the lawyer must be able to grasp the exact meaning of factual statements and legal instruments, to catch the fine points of legal reasoning and argument, and to comprehend the technical materials which constitute the body of the law. To acquire sufficient capacity for communication calls for extensive practice in all phases of the art. Truly, the law-trained man, if he is to perform effectively the tasks expected of him, must be a precisionist in the use of language. [A63].

The lawyer should have a skill in detecting deceptiveness of language: emotionally-charged words, catch phrases, hidden meanings of words, empty generalizations. Read the following for this purpose:

1450

BARZUN, JACQUES. Simple and direct. N.Y., Harper & Rowe, 1975. 212p.
A11.5

A no nonsense approach to writing clearly. An excellent listing of troublesome words and phrases and where they are discussed in the text.

1451

CHASE, STUART. Power of words, [with] Marian T. Chase. N.Y., Harcourt, Brace, 1954. 308p. + A27

1452

____. Tyranny of words. N.Y., Harcourt, Brace, 1938. 396p.
A7, A12, A23, A29 +

One of the principal works on semantics. See also annotation for the Hayakawa book [No. 1458].

1453

ELBOW, PETER. Writing without teachers. N.Y., Oxford Univ. Press, 1973. 196p.
A29.5

1454

EWING, DAVID W. Writing for results in business, government, and the professions. N.Y., Wiley, 1974. 406p.

1455

FLESCH, RUDOLF F. The art of readable writing. Foreword by Alan J. Gould. N.Y., Harper [1949.] 237p. +
A27, A28, A63

See also his _How to Write Plain English; A Book for Lawyers and Consumers_ (N.Y., Harper & Row, 1979) which was reviewed by Bob Giesbrecht in Manitoba Law Jl 10:487 (1980): "Flesch gives many examples of the pitfalls which beset the writer of legal documents, by showing first, the original, lawyer's version of a document, and then his own Plain English version. ...[His] Plain English translations of American taxing statutes are nothing short of amazing. ...Throughout the book, Flesch pokes gentle fun at the way lawyers write. He points out some common faults and, also, how writing style can be improved. The light, entertaining style and the many examples should make Flesch's suggestions easy to follow." Mr. Flesch is also known for his mathematical formula for sentence structure that has been adopted in some Plain Language statutes. [See also No. 2063].

1456

FREEMAN, MORTON S. The grammatical lawyer. Philadelphia, ALI/ABA, 1979. 350p.
A24.5

"This is not a systematic guide to the rules of word usage and grammar. It is, rather, a provocative potpourri of illustrative cases of proper and improper usage, punctuation, and syntax." Robert K. Emerson, A.B.A.Jl 66:82 (1980). The book is a collection of columns from the _Practical Lawyer._ It has a good index. See also Gertrude Block, _Effective legal writing, a style book for law students and lawyers_ (2d ed. 1983); John C. Dernbach and Richard V. Singleton II, _A practical guide to legal writing and legal method_ (1981).

1457

GOLDFARB, RONALD L. and **JAMES C. RAYMOND.** Clear understanding, a guide to legal writing. N.Y., Random House, 1982. 172p.
A29.5

One of the few books on legal writing that you can read profitably in a couple of hours. One's opinion of books on style and writing should be offered cautiously as critics on the art of writing are a vicious breed.

1458

HAYAKAWA, SAMUEL I. Language in thought and action, [with] B. H. Pillard. N.Y., Harcourt, Brace, 1949. 307p. * +
A8, A12, A23, A27, A27.5, A29, A43, A57, A63, A68

Experience has shown that a good deal of difficulty in law, and especially in the first year study of law, lies in a lack of understanding of the functions of language and of the relation of language to thought. There are a number of books in this field, including Ogden and Richards, The Meaning of Meaning [See No. 1463]; Vaihinger, The Philosophy of As If [See No. 1469]; and Stuart Chase, The Tyranny of Words [See No. 1452]. The Hayakawa book is particularly recommended because it is fairly simple, very readable and yet not glib. This is an extensive revision of an earlier excellent book by Hayakawa entitiled Language in Action. Many law students have found the two books to be of real help in understanding legal problems. [A12].

1459

LEACOCK, STEPHEN B. How to write. N.Y., Dodd, 1943. 261p.
A63 * +

Mr. Leacock was an outstanding humorist of his time and the attribute of humor can have a leavening effect on the art of legal writing.

1460

MELLINKOFF, DAVID. The language of the law. Boston, Little, Brown, 1963. 526p.
A11.5

"After some preliminaries, definitions, and a bit of a preview, there comes a lengthly history of the language of our profession. The languages of various peoples have played upon our current Anglo-American product: Vikings, Norsemen, Celts, Anglo-Saxons, Normans, and especially, Romans and the French. Among other interesting items the author traces to this mongrel heritage is our professional quirk of pairing synonyms coming from different language sources, such as 'will and testament,' 'breaking and entering', etc. ...Certainly [the book] is most delightful." Walter Probert, Stanford Law Rev. 16:767 (1964). See also his Legal writing: sense and nonsense (1982) which has excellent appendices.

1461

MILLER, CASEY and KATE SWIFT. The handbook of nonsexist writing. N.Y., Barnes & Noble, 1980. 134p.
A29.5

This book is an antidote to those speakers who facetiously announce that when they use the word "man" it is to embrace "woman".

1462

NEWMAN, EDWIN. Strictly speaking. N.Y., Bobbs-Merrill, 1974. 265p.
A49

"...a collection of examples of linguistic deficits and excesses - trite phrases, cliches, jargon, improper diction, incorrect grammar. The most disturbing characteristic of these examples is their familiarity. Because of it, the reader cannot always identify the error which Newman wishes him to see." U.C.L.A. Law Rev. 22:981 (1975). Mr. Newman followed this with another collection of examples not to follow called A Civil Tongue (1977). See also the 'On language' column of William Safire in the magazine section of the Sunday New York Times; also John Ivan Simon, Paradigms lost, reflections on literacy and its decline (1980).

1463

OGDEN, C. K. The meaning of meaning. N.Y., Harcourt, Brace, 1945. 363p. +
A12, A23, A27, A27.5, A29

See annotation for Hayakawa [No. 1458].

1464

PHILBRICK, F. A. Understanding English; an introduction to semantics. N.Y., Macmillan, 1942. 209p. +
A10

A closely reasoned study in semantics.

1465

PROBERT, WALTER. Law, language and communication. Springfield, Thomas, 1972. 376p. A24.5

"He is trying to equip students with a contextual technique for exploring the place of linguistic statements in the legal and social process." Harold D. Lasswell in the Foreword. Communication theory applied to law, how to read a case, fact, fancy, and interpretation.

1466

QUILLER-COUCH, SIR ARTHUR T. On the art of writing. N.Y., Putnam, 1916. 320p. +
A28

1467

SQUIRES, LYNN B. and MARJORIE DICK ROMBAUER. Legal writing in a nutshell. St. Paul, West, 1982. 294p.
A24.5

See also Rombauer's Legal problem solving: analysis, research and writing (4th ed. 1983).

1468

STRUNK, WILLIAM JR. The elements of style. Rev. by E.B.White. 3d ed. N.Y., Macmillan, 1979. 85p.
A24.5

The standard short text on style, which, if not read previously, is a must for law students.

1469

VAIHINGER, HANS. The philosophy of "as if"; a system of the theoretical, practical and religious fiction of mankind. Translated by C. K. Ogden. N.Y., Harcourt, Brace, 1924. 370p. +
A12, A23, A29

See annotation for No. 1458.

1470

WEIHOFEN, HENRY. Legal writing style. 2d ed. St.Paul, West, 1980. 332p.
A11.5

For someone to begin a book in 1980: "For the lawyer more than most men..." shows a lack of style that could turn off a large part of his potential users. Includes chapters on law school and bar examinations, oral argument, and briefs.

1471

WYDICK, RICHARD C. Plain English for lawyers. Caroline, Academic Press, 1979.
A24.5

Reprinted from California Law Rev. 66:727 (1978).

[Nos. 1472-1474 saved]

The lawyer should also have a developed sensitivity to fluidity of language: varying meanings of words in different times and contexts, shades of meaning. He should also be aware of interpretive problems and hazards in use of ambiguous terms. [A63] Read the following for this purpose:

1475

BOWEN, CATHERINE (DRINKER). The lawyer and the King's English. [Phila., Brandeis Lawyers' Society, 1951.] 28p. +
A27

Mrs. Bowen comments on the dualistic attitude of some lawyers concerning the use and abuse of language. Lawyers and authors have something in common: to be articulate, to speak out by the tongue, by script or by print.

1476

GOLDBERG, ISAAC. The wonder of words: an introduction to language for everyman ...N.Y., Appleton-Century, 1938. 485p. * +
A63

1477

GOWERS, SIR ERNEST ARTHUR. Plain words; a guide to the use of English. London, H. M. Stat. Off., 1948. 94p. +
A28

An excellent and literate guide.

1478

GREEVER, GARLAND. The century collegiate handbook, [with others] 3d ed. N.Y., Appleton-Century-Crofts, 1950. 460p. * +
A38

Please do not be insulted when you see this. Many college graduates come to law school deficient in the English language, and its use. This small book will give you an excellent review of the clear and complete sentence, grammar (what you have forgotten), diction, spelling, punctuation, and composition. [A38]. And, of course, do not neglect Henry W. Fowler, A dictionary of modern English usage. 2d ed. rev. by Sir Ernest Gowers (1963).

1479

OPDYCKE, JOHN B. Say what you mean; everyman's guide to diction and grammar. N.Y., Funk, 1944. 681p. * + A63

1480

PYLES, THOMAS. Words and ways of American English. N.Y., Random House, 1952. 310p. * +
A63

LAW and LITERATURE

See also ANECDOTES... and FICTION...

1500

BLOM-COOPER, LOUIS. The law as literature; an anthology of great writing in and about the law. London, The Bodley Head, 1961. 451p.
A74

"In some 450 pages this books sets out 33 extracts from judicial and other writings on law. ...The material is grouped under six headings: prosecution and defence; the courtroom scene; on law; on lawyers; from the bench; and crime and punishment. ...on any view this must in the main be accounted a sound selection [comparison with London's book] ...[includes] Wellman's version of Sir Charles Russell's cross-examination of Pigott; Robert H. Jackson's closing speech at Nuremberg; Plato's account of Socrates' address to the jurors; and Gandhi's plea for the severest penalty on his conviction for sedition ... Patrick Duncan's statement in answer to a charge of seditious libel ... Richard Carlile's account of his trial for blasphemy ... Sir Richard Muir's notes for his opening speech at the Crippen trial ... Boswell's Johnson ...Auden's Law Like Love ... Harman L.J., Lord Atkin, Maule, J., Younger, J., Lord Sumner, Eeve. J., and Stable J. For America, Holmes J., Learned Hand J., Brandeis J., Jerome Frank J., Douglas J., and Jackson J. R.E.Megarry, Law Q. Rev. 79:287 (1963). See also the author's _The language of the law_ (1965).

1501

CARDOZO, BENJAMIN N. Law and literature and other essays and addresses ...N.Y., Harcourt, Brace [c1930.] 190p. +
A45, A49

The first real analysis of the literature of the bench. Judge Cardozo, one of America's outstanding judicial stylists at the time brought to this task the rare combination of legal and literary learning. See Calif. L. Rev. 19:654 (1931).

1502

DAVENPORT, WILLIAM H., ed. Voices in court; a treasury of the bench, the bar and the courtroom. N.Y., Macmillan, 1958. 588p.
A27.5

"...anthology ranging from letters to trials and opinions and from history and biography to novels, essays and short stories. He directs it, as he says, at lawyers, judges, men of law in any capacity, and laymen interested in the law." Elliott E. Cheatham, Hastings Law Jl 11:228 (1959). See also Davenport's Readings in legal literature, A.B.A.Jl 41:939 (1955) and 43:813 (1957).

1503

DAVIS, CUSHMAN K. The law in Shakespeare. Wash., D.C., Washington Law Book Co. [1883.] 303p. +
A28

Selection of quotations from Shakespeare coupled with reference to legal source records. Before the flowering of law reviews, lawyers were more inclined to write about literary topics. See Record of the Bar Association of the City of N.Y. 19:325 (1964) for a bibliography on Shakespeare and the law. See also Edward J. Bander, Shakespeare for the law student, Duquesne Univ. Law Rev. 5:53 (1966).

1504

GEST, JOHN M. The lawyer in literature ...Boston, Boston Book Co., 1913. 249p. +
A28, A46

Includes essays on the law and lawyers of Charles Dickens, Sir Walter Scott and Balzac, on the writings of Coke, the influence of Biblical texts in English law, and on the historical method of studying law. Dean Wigmore's interesting preface points up the practical advantage to a lawyer of an acquaintance with literature. See Harvard Law Rev. 27:193 (1944). See also Richard H. Weisberg, Wigmore's "legal novels" revisited: new resources for the expansive lawyer, Northwestern Univ. Law Rev. 71:17 (1976). For a survey of legal humor, see Edward J. Bander, Legal humor dissected, Law Library Jl 75:289 (1983).

1505

GREEN, ADWIN W. Inns of court and early English drama. Oxford, Oxford Univ. Press, 1931. 199p.
A24.5

"... a fascinating book ...follow the transition from the revels to the masque and from the masque to drama." Harvard Law Rev. 45:423 (1932).
A43.5

1506

HENSON, RAY D., ed. Landmarks of the law. Boston, Beacon Press, 1963. 461p.
A43.5, A71.5

The author "has provided both the general reader and the trained practitioner with an opportunity to acquire a variety of articles aptly illustrating what the author characterizes as the 'rich treasury' of the law. ...[with] a few exceptions, this is not light reading. ... [S]elections by such legal philosophers as Holmes, Pound, and John Dewey [can be found]." Marx X. Leopold, Dickinson Law Rev. 68:232 (1964).

1507

KEETON, GEORGE W. Shakespeare and his legal problems, ...with a foreword by the Rt. Hon. Lord Darling. London, A. & C. Black, 1930. 239p. +
A28

These studies will be found instructive and interesting by readers who know their Shakespeare but are not learned in the law, by lawyers who want an occasion for improving their knowledge of Shakespeare and sharpening their wits and by Shakespearean students of all sorts. See Law Q. Rev. 46:522 (1930). See also Keeton, Shakespeare's legal and political background (1967) [A74], and Owen Hood Phillips, Shakespeare and the lawyers (1972).

1508

LAW IN LITERATURE. A series of articles in Calif. State Bar Jour. 13: (1938). +
A28

"A "popular" commentary on Bardell v. Pickwick, Dickens, Trial of Eugene Aram, Law in Song and Verse, Tyranny of Words in the Field of Law, and Junious Writes a Letter to Blackstone.

1509

LONDON, EPHRAIM, ed. The world of law; a treasury of great writing about and in the law, short stories, plays, essays, accounts, letters, opinions, pleas, transcripts of testimony, from Biblical times to the present. N.Y., Simon & Schuster, 1960. 2 vols.
A27.5, A43.5, A49, A57.1, A71.5

Includes complete Rattigan's _The Winslow Boy._ [A71.5]

1510

NICE, RICHARD W., ed. Treasury of the rule of law. 2d ed. Totowa, N.J., Littlefield, Adams & Co., 1965. 553p.
A27.5

Items from the Code of Hammurabi, Torah, Twelve Tables, Justinian, Bentham, Magna Carta, Civil Rights Act - 59 items in all.

1511

THE OLD YELLOW BOOK. Sources of Browning's "The Ring and the Book," a new translation with explanatory notes and critical chapters upon the poem and its source, by John Marshall Gest... Phila., Univ. of Pennsylvania Press, 1925. 699p. +
A28

An explanation of the actual facts of the case, and the law applicable to them and a vindication of the practice of the Roman secular authority and the competence of the legal profession against Browning's grotesque presentment. In doing so Judge Gest has made a serious contribution to our knowledge of the modern civil law as developed in Italy in the later Renaissance period. See Law Q. Rev. 41:469 (1925).

1512

SMITH, CARL S., JOHN P. MCWILLIAMS, Jr., and MAXWELL BLOOMFIELD. Law and American literature. N.Y., Knopf, 1983. 177p.
A29.5

Essays on the trial in American fiction, law and lawyers in American popular culture, American writers and the law. The book covers law and language, Melville's _Billy Budd,_ Cooper, Dreiser, etc.

1513

WHITE, JAMES P. The legal imagination; studies in the nature of legal thought and expression. Boston, Little, Brown, 1973. 986p.
A57.1

"... effective handling of both legal and non-legal sources ... stimulate the kind of thinking that rarely surface in the law school classroom. ...[includes topics such as death, how the law talks about people, how a statute works, lawyer-like arguments, judge's role, etc. Excerpts from cases, Shakespeare, Jane Austen, Melville, etc. See Richard Weisberg, Columbia Law Rev. 74:327 (1974).

1514

WINDOLPH, FRANCIS L. Reflections of the law in literature. Phila., Univ. of Pennsylvania Press [1956, 1970] 83p. * +
A19, A64

Three essays on Trollope, Browning and Shakespeare and the law, informally written with wit and learning. The Author analyzes the knowledge and approach to law as reflected in Trollope's _Phineas Redux,_ Shakespeare's _The Merchant of Venice_ and Browning's _The Ring and the Book._ He relates the legal points involved to moral and ethical issues.

LAW REFORM

See ADMINISTRATION OF JUSTICE

LEGAL AID

1550

BRAKEL, SAMUEL J. Judicare: public funds, private lawyers and poor people. Chicago, A.B.F., 1974. 145p.
A6.5

The American Bar Foundation has published a number of monographs on this subject. Check the card catalog in your law school library.

1551

BROWNELL, EMERY A. Legal aid in the U.S.; a study of the availability of lawyers' services for persons unable to pay fees. Foreword by Harrison Tweed, introd. by Reginald Heber Smith. Rochester, N.Y., Lawyers Co-operative, 1951. 333p. +
A6

This is part of the Survey of the Legal Profession of the American Bar Association and indicates some deficiencies in legal aid in this country—especially in the criminal courts. The report gave an accurate evaluation of legal aid in this country at that time. It also pointed up the need for a more comprehensive program of legal aid for those who need it.

1552

HARRISON, GORDON. The public interest law firm; new voices for new constituencies. N.Y., Ford Foundation, 1973. 40p.
A57.1

Public interest law firms grew out of the ferment of the sixties.

1553

MAGUIRE, JOHN MacARTHUR. The lance of justice; a semi-centennial history of the Legal Aid Society, 1876-1926 ...Cambridge, Harvard Univ. Press, 1928. 306p. * +
A35

Law has always been weak where it touches the poor. Lawyers have a special responsibility to give it new strength at this point. This book tells something of what can be accomplished and how. See Harvard Law Rev. 58:599 (1945). Of course, legal aid has now expanded into legal service, government programs, attorney fees under the Civil Rights Acts so that another semi-centennial history would be in order.

1554

NADER, LAURA, ed. No access to law; alternatives to the American judicial system. N.Y., Academic Press, 1980. 540p.
A31.7

This book covers complaint handling, the handling of a specific warranty complaint, trade associations, Better Business Bureaus, department store complaints, California Department of Insurance, ghetto complaints, San Francisco Consumer Action, labor unions, mass media complaint managers, etc. See review by Bryant G. Garth, Michigan Law Rev. 81:984 (1983).

LEGAL EDUCATION

See also STUDY OF LAW

1575

ALLEN, FRANCIS A. Law, intellect, and education. Ann Arbor, Univ. of Michigan Press, 1979. 123p.
A31.7

"...the most confident statement of the nature and purpose of American legal education to appear since questioning and serious criticism gathered force in the 1970s. ...The author undertakes to defend legal education from what he sees to be the potentially corrosive effect of developments beyond the borders of the university community. ...The substance of student criticism is never really presented." Gene R. Shreve, Vanderbilt Law Rev. 33:822 (1980).

1576

AMERICAN BAR ASSOCIATION. Section on Legal Education and Admissions to the Bar. Review of Legal Education. Chicago, annual
A6.5

A statistical listing of pertinent data of law schools such as enrollment, day or evening school, etc.

1577

ASSOCIATION OF AMERICAN LAW SCHOOLS and the Law School Admission Council. The Pre-Law handbook. Indianapolis, Bobbs-Merrill, annual
A6.5

Official information and data on law schools such as LSAT admission scores, where to apply for admissions, etc.

1578

BELLOW, GARY and **BEA MOULTON.** The lawyering process; materials for clinical instruction in advocacy. N.Y., Foundation Press, 1978. 1128p.
A31.7

"The heuristic approach to clinical education as a method in law study is the conceptual framework [for this book]. ...to stimulate students to think about ways of looking at particular tasks and relationships involved in lawyering. ...problems of conformity and values in being a lawyer ... [is the] lawyer's role inherently dishonest ... chronology of lawyer work from the initial relationship with a client through trial ... Can a lawyer be a good person?" J. Eric Smithburn, Arizona State Law Jl 1980:237.

1579

BERMAN, HAROLD, ed. Talks on American law. Rev. ed. N.Y., Vintage, 1971. 312p.
A71.5

Berman on legal history, J.P. Dawson on judges, Lon L. Fuller on adversary system, B. Kaplan on trial by jury, L.Hall on criminal law, Paul Freund on Supreme Court,

R.Fisher on free speech, A.E. Sutherland on race, L.L. Jaffe on administrative law, S.S. Surrey on tax, A. Cox on labor, L.Loss on corporations, P.Areeda on antitrust, R. Braucher on UCC, W.B. Leach on property, F.I. Michelman on housing, E.N. Griswold on legal profession, D.F. Cavers on legal education, Milton Katz on international law, Berman on philosophy.

1580

BOYER, BARRY B. and **ROGER C. CRAMPTON**, American legal education; an agenda for research and reform, Cornell Law Rev. 59:221 (1974).
A29.5

A frequently cited work that discusses, among other things, the "problems of boredom and disengagement which seem to plague traditional law teaching." [p.281]

1581

GILLERS, STEPHEN, ed. Looking at law school, a student guide from the Society of American Law Teachers. N.Y., Taplinger, 1977. 235p.
A2.5, A35.5, A38.5, A43.5, A48.5, A57.1, A57.7, A71.8

"...a compilation of essays written by law professors ... for the prospective law student. ...law school application process, first-year curriculum, and various ethical and social problems that pervade the entire three years of law school and the years of legal practice beyond." Joseph P. Tomain, N.Y.U. Law Rev. 53:692 (1978). Irving Younger also provides his views on what a good examination answer should contain. Also, course descriptions by A.R. Miller, R.L. Bard, L.L. Weinreb, C.J. Berger, J.O. Connell, and P. Bender. See also Elizabeth Dvorkin, Jack Himmelstein, and Howard Lesnick, Becoming a lawyer; a humanistic perspective on legal education and professionalism (1981).

1582

GRISWOLD, ERWIN. Legal education: 1878-1978, A.B.A.Jl 64:1051 (1978).
A29.5

A summary of developments beginning with the origin of the Association of American Law Schools and covering the case system, evening law schools, clinical programs, etc.

1583

HABER, DAVID and **JULIUS COHEN**, eds. The law school of tomorrow; the projection of an idea. New Brunswick, Rutgers Univ. Press, 1968. 240p. A1

"This is a report of a symposium which brought together some of the finest minds in legal education, jurisprudence, law practice and related areas." Covers: law as a phase of the humanities and as a subject of the behavioral sciences; directions for research, empirical and nonempirical, the training of the practitioner. Charles P. Kindregan, Suffolk Univ. Law Rev. 4:615 (1970).

1584

HARNO, ALBERT J. Legal education in the U.S.; a report prepared for the Survey of the Legal Profession. San Francisco, Bancroft-Whitney, 1953. 211p. * +
A15, A24, A52, A72

Will give you some idea on what law school is like.

1585

LASSWELL, HAROLD D. Legal education and public policy. Professional training in the public interest, [with] M. S. McDougal. In Yale Law Jl 52:203 (1943). * +
A24

The directive thrusts in the maintenance of the parallelism between the concepts of law and the concepts of morality, and the role of the lawyer therein are considered in this article. [A24]

1586

PACKER, HERBERT L. and **THOMAS EHRLICH.** New directions in legal education; a report prepared for the Carnegie Commission on Higher Education. N.Y., McGraw-Hill, 1972. 384p.
A24.5

The author's conclusion is that "the nature of legal education has been to train students in some basic fundamentals (analysis, legal theory, the general substantive map, etc.) only and that as a result the law school graduate generally is not competent to do anything very well. Experience is the real teacher of specific tasks..." Abraham S. Goldstein, Yale Law Jl 82:1092 (1973).

1587

ROTH, GEORGE J. Slaying the law school dragon. N.Y., Dodd, Mead, 1980. 184p.
A35.5

Chapters on how to study for class, a quick look at contracts, torts, crimes, property; how to act in class, exams, briefs, how to get clients, interesting listing of law review articles relevant to courses given at law school.

1588

SELIGMAN, J. The high citadel. Boston, Houghton Mifflin, 1978.262p.
A48.5

Originally, a Ralph Nader project, this history of the Harvard Law School has as its purpose the advocacy of a more clinically oriented curriculum at Harvard Law School. See Edward J. Bander' review in Suffolk Univ. Law Rev. 13:1579 (1979), particularly footnote ten that lists the various publications that have rated law schools. On this note, see also Scott van Alstyne, Ranking the law schools; the reality of illusion? American Bar Foundation 3:649 (1982); and see the Los Angeles Daily Jl, Nov. 1, 1982 for a critique of the Gourman Report on Graduate and Professional Schools, a maverick publication that simply rates schools.

1589

WHITE, JAMES B. Talk to entering students. Chicago, Univ. of Chicago Law School, 1977.
A43.5

LEGAL ESSAYS and ADDRESSES

Glanville Williams has an excellent paragraph on essays in his Learning the law (11th ed. 1982). [A74], calling to mind Bacon, Selden, Lamb, Hazlitt, Maitland, John Buchan and others.

1601

AMERICAN BAR ASSOCIATION. The lawyer's treasury; an anthology selected by the board of editors from articles ... representative of the best to appear in the forty-year history of the American Bar Association Journal. Ed. by Eugene C. Gerhart. Indianapolis, Bobbs-Merrill, 1956. 520p. +
A19

The editors are of the opinion that these articles by some of the leaders of the bar "will readily reveal to the reader why lawyers are properly regarded as members of a learned profession." Characteristic of the articles selected are: "Tribute to Country Lawyers," [See No. 1942] by Mr. Justice Jackson; "The Argument of an Appeal," [See No. 82] by John W. Davis; "The Romance of Law," by Lord Buckmaster and "The Five Functions of a Lawyer," by the late Chief Justice Vanderbilt.

1602

BECK, JAMES M. May it please the court ... edited by O. R. McGuire ... Atlanta, Harrison, 1930. 511p. * +
A40, A72

The author was a distinguished Solicitor-General of the U.S., and an authority on Constitutional law and history. This book contains a collection of his more important public addresses. It discloses a brilliance of oratory and vigor of imagination such as is seldom attributed to gentlemen of the "modern school" of public affairs. See Harvard Law Rev. 44:154 (1930). But see Justice Holmes' view of Beck's oratory in Edward J. Bander's Justice Holmes ex cathedra (1966) p. 207.

1603

BLUMBERG, ABRAHAM S. The scales of justice. 2d ed. New Brunswick, Transaction Books, 1973. 315p.
A27.5, A57.7

1604

COHEN, FELIX S. The legal conscience, selected papers. New Haven, Yale Univ. Press, 1960. 505p.
A43.5

Book I: Logic, law, ethics; Book II: The Indian's quest for justice; Book III: The philosophy of American democracy.

1605

FRANKFURTER, FELIX. Law and politics: [his] occasional papers [from] 1913 [to] 1918, edited by Archibald MacLeish and E.F. Prichard, Jr. ...N.Y., Harcourt, Brace [c1939]. 352p. * +
A20, A28, A35, A43, A45, A54, A71.5

These papers by [the then] Professor Frankfurter, apply ethical ideals of the law to a wide range of subjects. They show the author's wide range of interests, his vivid and accurate intelligence and his devotion of thought and study over many years, to the subjects he discusses. One valuable section of the book deals with three great justices of the Supreme Court, in an attempt to define the elements of judicial greatness: Holmes, Brandeis and Cardozo. See Law Q. Rev. 57:280 (1941). See also his Of law and men, 1939-1945; papers and addresses of Felix Frankfurter (Philip Elman, ed. 1956). This volume includes essays on Chief Justices Fuller, White, Taft, Hughes and Stone. Also tributes to Holmes, Brandeis, Cardozo, Hughes, Stone, Jackson, Roberts, and Learned Hand. Also, "John

Marshall and the judicial function," and "The judicial process and the Supreme Court." [A6.5, A27.5, A57.7, A71.5]. See also Paul A. Freund, Harvard Law Rev. 70:568 (1957).

1606

FREUND, PAUL A. On law and justice. Cambridge, Harvard Univ. Press, 1968. 259p.
A71.5

Part I-The Courts and the Constitution; Part II-The Pursuit of Justice; Part III-Appreciations: A Gallery of Justices (Brandeis, Frankfurter, Learned Hand, etc.). "[T]here is much food for talk and thought in these essays. It is not surprising that students of all ages hearing Professor Freund think they hear the small still voice of the Constitution." Louis Henkin, Harvard Law Rev. 82:1193 (1969).

1607

FRIENDLY, HENRY J. Benchmarks. Chicago, Univ. of Chicago Press, 1967. 324p.
A71.5

"...leaves the reader with a deep admiration for Judge Friendly as a man, as a literary craftsman, and as a judge. His writings are marked by a constant search for a rational and consistent view of society and the role of law. ...law-making functions of legislatures and courts ...problems of federal administrative agencies ...proper relationship between state and federal law ... the Supreme Court's use of the Bill of Rights ...four great judges (Holmes, Brandeis, Learned Hand, and Frankfurter)." Manuel F. Cohen, Michigan Law Rev. 66:1307 (1968).

1608

HAAR, CHARLES M., ed. The golden age of American law. N.Y., George Braziller, 1965. 533p.
A43.6

This anthology of the legal literature of the forty years before the Civil War "includes extracts from legal treatises, periodicals, judicial opinions, courtroom addresses, and a wide range of nonlegal sources." 33 Univ. of Chicago Law Rev. 867 (1966). Topics covered are the legal profession, public law, law and reform, law and economic development, and the search for legal identity.

1609

HAND, LEARNED. The spirit of liberty; papers and addresses collected and with an introd. and notes by Irving Dillard. N.Y., Knopf, 1952. 262 p. 3d ed. 1960. 310p.; 3d ed. enlarged. 1960. 310p. * +

A6, A13, A25.5, A27.5, A28, A62, A64, A67, A71.5

After forty years as District and Court of Appeals Judge, here is a book reflecting Judge Hand's exposition of the abiding faith in our traditions it has been his genius to expound eloquently and analyze philosophically. In it we get his views of democracy, the nature of society, the function of the judge, the need for tolerance and the importance of morals in public life. See A.B.A.Jl 38:586 (1952). Each address is a characteristic bit of self-expression with a literary style that charms. See Yale Law Jl. 62:135 (1952).

1610

HARRIS, RICHARD. Freedom spent. N.Y., Little, Brown, 1976. 460p.

A43.5

"...a collection of articles on three separate cases ... Charles James, an English teacher who was fired for wearing a black armband at school during the November, 1969 Vietnam Moratorium. ...The second case involved the scope of protection granted by the Fourth Amendment's prohibition of unreasonable searches and seizures ...The third case involved two radical feminists, Ellen Grusse and Terri Turgeon, who were questioned by F.B.I. agents searching for ... two radicals ... for alleged role in a 1970 Boston bank robbery." Bruce Plenk, Jl of Contemporary Law 4:137 (1977).

1611

HURST, J. W. Law and social process in United States history. Ann Arbor, Univ. of Michigan Law School, 1960. 361p.

A43.5

"In these five essays, Professor Hurst considers what law has meant in the experience of people in the United States. His approach is at once philosophical, anthro-political, and historical. ...a fine contribution for all who are interested in the factors which affect our societal operations." Hilliard A. Gardiner, American Jl of Comparative Law 10:488 (1961).

1612

MACMILLAN, HUGH PATTISON MacM., baron. Law and other things ...Cambridge [Eng.]. Univ. Press, 1937. 283p.; Freeport, N.Y., Books for Libraries Press, 1971. +
A45

A series of essays which give most interesting sketches of the contacts between law and politics, ethics, religion, history, letters and language. All these essays illustrate the width of the knowledge which a complete lawyer must possess. See Law Q. Rev. 54:287 (1938).

1613

ROSTOW, EUGENE V. The ideal in law. Chicago, Univ. of Chicago Press, 1978. 305p.
A43.5

"...a collection of disparate essays ... the demands of blacks for social justice, civil disobedience, the lawyer-client relationship, monopoly and restraint of trade, the responsibility of corporate management, the obligations of the national community to the international legal order, and so on ... the case for an ideal element in law clearly has not here been made...." Julius Cohen, Columbia Law Rev. 78:1731 (1978).

Professor Rostow also wrote _Planning for Freedom; the Public Law of American Capitalism_ (1959) reviewed by Miriam Theresa Roney in Catholic Lawyer 11:85 (1965); and edited _Is Law Dead?_ (1971). The latter contains material by Christopher D. Stone, Robert Paul Wolff, Ronald Dworkin, Hannah Arendt, Charles Dyke, David M. Potter and Gideon Gottlieb. See Francis A. Allen's review in Michigan Law Rev. 79:766 (1972).

1614

SELDEN, JOHN. Table-talk. Ed. by Edward Arber. Phila., A. Saifer, 1972, 1868. 120p.
A43.5

A collection of notable remarks over a period of twenty years and covering a wide range of topics. The Selden Society, which publishes invaluable material on early English legal history, is named for him.

1615

SIMES, LEWIS M. Public policy and the dead hand ... Ann Arbor, Univ. of Michigan Law School, 1955. 168p.
A29.5

Lectures on the Rule Against Perpetuities, rules against accumulation, and the power to perpetuate control through gifts to charity. See review by Austin Wakeman Scott, Stanford Law Rev. 8:765 (1956).

1616

SUTHERLAND, ARTHUR E., ed. Government under law. Cambridge, Harvard Univ. Press, 1956. 587p.
A24.5

A Conference to do honor to Chief Justice John Marshall. "[The book] concentrates on the subject of government under law rather than on the life or work of the great Chief Justice. ...With government under law as the central theme, the several lectures were organized in terms of four sub-themes - government as the protector of the people against the government; government under law in time of crisis; the meaning of due process today; and the value of constitutionalism today." Carl Brent Swisher, Virginia Law Rev. 43:623 (1957).

1617

WYZANSKI, CHARLES E. JR. Whereas - a judge's premises: essays in judgment, ethics, and the law. Boston, Little, Brown, 1965. 312p.
A43.5

"... The Judge has read prodigiously, has thought deeply, and writes English better than almost any lawyer who regularly tries to. ...[essays on Learned Hand, Augustus Hand, C.J. Stone, Nuremberg trials, Justice Brandeis, freedom of association, Justice Holmes, First Amendment, etc.] John P. Frank, Yale Law Jl 75:365 (1965).

LEGAL ETHICS
See PRACTICE OF LAW

LEGAL HISTORY

See also HISTORY (ANGLO-AMERICAN) and
ANCIENT and PRIMITIVE LAW

1625

AMES, JAMES B. Lectures on legal history. Cambridge, Harvard Univ. Press, 1913. 553p. +
A18

Prof. Ames was a legal historian of note and he

considers here with great scholarship such topics as the Salic and Anglo-Saxon courts, substantive law before Bracton, the common law actions and similar topics. See also annotations for Thomas A. Street [No. 1675].

1626

BAKER, JOHN HAMILTON. An introduction to English legal history. 2d ed. London, Butterworths, 1979. 477p.
A57.6

1627

BILLIAS, GEORGE NATHAN, ed. Law and authority in Colonial America; selected essays. Barre, Mass., 1965. 208p.
A31.7

Essayists include Mark DeWolfe Howe, George L. Haskins (dower rights); L. Kinvin Wroth (admiralty courts); Herbert Alan Johnson, Joseph H. Smith, Willcomb Washburn, Clifford K. Shipton; Darrett Rutman, John D. Cushing, Hillel Zobel, Edward H. Levi, Paul A. Freund, Herbert Wechsler, Richard Martin, and L. Tammelo. See Neal W. Allen, Albany Law Rev. 30:182 (1966).

1628

BRYSON, WILLIAM HAMILTON. Equity side of the Exchequer; its jurisdiction, procedures, and records... London, Cambridge Univ. Press, 1975. 217p.
A57.6

Mr. Bryson also edited _The Virginia Law Reporters before 1880_ (1977). [A57.6]

1629

FIFOOT, CECIL HERBERT S. English law and its background ...London, C. Bell, 1932. 279p. +
A40

An introduction to English law written for the student who is interested in delving deeper into the historical approach of the author. See also the author's _Frederic William Maitland; a life_ (1971), and _Letters of Frederic William Maitland_ (1965).

1630

____. History and sources of the common law: tort and contract. London, Stevens, 1949. 446p. + A28

A collection of material for the study of legal history, intended principally for the use of law students. The development of contract and torts law is traced from their sources with explanatory notes and extracts from the sources.

1631

____. Law and history in the nineteenth century. London, Quaritch, 1956. 24p. (Selden Society lecture, 1956.) +
A19

A delightful, charming essay by an understanding scholar.

1632

FLAHERTY, DAVID H., ed. Essays in the history of early American law. Chapel Hill, Univ. of North Carolina Press. 534p.
A31.7

"...Thorp L. Wolford's insipid summary of the contents of The Laws and Liberties of 1648 ...Julius Goebel's monumental study of the influence upon early Plymouth of the ...local customs of seventeenth-century England ...[the articles] appear as originally printed, lengthy footnotes and all." John Phillip Reid, Buffalo Law Rev. 19:717 (1970).

1633

FLEMING, DONALD and **BERNARD BAILYN**, eds. Law in American history. Boston, Little, Brown, 1971. 677p.
A27.5, A43.5

Essays by Byron White, James W. Hurst, R.M. Brown, Charles A. Miller, David H. Flaherty, Stanley N. Katz, Morton J. Horowitz, Harry N. Scheiber, Robert Stevens, Jerold Auerbach, John Elliff. The book covers race, morals, eminent domain, legal education, civil rights, and vigilantism.

1634

FRIEDMAN, LAWRENCE M. A history of American law. N.Y., Simon and Schuster, 1973. 655p.
A21, A27.5, A36, A43.5, A47, A49, A57.1, A57.6, A71.5

"The author has been a pioneering and innovative contributor to the monographic literature of the field [of American legal history]; he has emphasized the historical antecedents of substantive areas of American law; he has attempted to modernize the discipline of legal history by introducing to it the analytical techniques of the social sciences; and he is a charter member of the school of thought currently dominant among American legal historians. His History illustrates his functions in each of these capacities. Accordingly, it provides a starting point for an analysis of the present state of American legal history." G. Edward White, Virginia Law Rev. 59:1130 (1973). This book won the Order of the Coif Triennial Book Award in 1976.

1635

A GENERAL SURVEY of events, sources, persons and movements in continental legal history, by various European authors. Boston, Little, Brown, 1912. 754p. (The Continental Legal History Series, pub. under the auspices of the Association of American law schools.)
A16 * +

This suggestion was made by Dean Hebert, Louisiana State, for the purpose of providing a more balanced selection in the list of philosophical selections and to give some indication of the Roman legal culture.

1636

GILMORE, GRANT. The ages of American law. New Haven, Yale Univ. Press, 1977. 154p.
A2.5, A38.5, A43.5, A49

"Professor Gilmore's elegant set of lectures is primarily meant to describe what has by now become a standard periodization of American legal history. The first period, roughly between the Revolution and the Civil War, he calls the Age of Discovery. The second period, the Age of Faith, existed until around World War I. And for the past half century we have been laboring under the burden of the Age of Anxiety." Morton J. Horwitz, Buffalo Law Rev. 27:47 (1978).

1637

HASKINS, GEORGE LEE. Law and authority in early Massachusetts. N.Y., Macmillan, 1960. 298p.
A31.7

"...a study of the nature of law during the first twenty years of the history of the Massachusetts Bay colony - from 1630 to 1650. ...a colonizing effort following the voyages of discovery, which have been plentiful in the Massachusetts area." William F. Swindler, Indiana Law Jl 35:528 (1960).

1638

HICKS, FREDERICK C. Men and books famous in the law ...with an introduction by Harlan F. Stone ...Rochester, N.Y., Lawyers Co-operative, 1921. 259p. * + A43.5, A64

Traces in the broadest outline the lives of a few law writers, and more especially the story of their legal writings, the inception, production and vicissitudes of works which for the most part have become classics in legal literature, such as Cowell's Interpreter, Lord Coke's Reports, Blackstone's Commentaries, Kent's Commentaries and others. See Harvard Law Rev. 35:354 (1922).

1639

HIGGINBOTHAM, LEON A. JR. In the matter of color; race and the American legal process: the Colonial Period. N.Y., Oxford Univ. Press, 1978. 512p.
A31.7

"...traces the first chapters of the legacy sketched by Justice Marshall (in his separate opinion in the Bakke case). Beginning in 1619 with the first record of the arrival of blacks in the American colonies, Judge Higginbotham chronicles in unrelenting detail the role of the law in the enslavement and subjugation of black Americans during the colonial period ...a meticulous and well-documented review of the laws and judicial decisions which defined the special status of blacks, free and slave, during the colonial period." Harvard Law Rev. 92:1391 (1979).

1640

HOLDSWORTH, SIR WILLIAM S. Charles Dickens as a legal historian ...New Haven, Yale Univ. Press, 1928. 157p. +
A28

No two books outside the bounds of technical law are more worth reading for law students than Pickwick Papers (See FICTION) and Bleak House (See FICTION). Even a trained lawyer, however, is puzzled by some of the legal points brought up by Dickens, because they fortunately have passed forever out of the realm of living law. Prof. Holdsworth has performed a valuable service to lawyers and laymen alike in explaining these obscurities. See Harvard Law Rev. 42:286 (1928).

1641

____. Essays in law and history...ed., by A. L. Goodhart and H. G. Hanbury. Oxford, Clarendon Press, 1946. 302p. * +
A28

The constitutional historian, the international lawyer, the real property expert, the common law practitioner, the civilian and even the general reader will each find something to his taste. It is a book to browse in and enjoy at leisure. See Law Q. Rev. 64:120 (1948).

1642

____. A history of English law ...London, Methuen, Boston, Little, Brown, 1965. 17 vols. +
A7

This is a "storehouse of accurate learning," the only complete history of the English law in detail. It can be used as an accurate reference tool for a better understanding of some of the more difficult historical developments. See Edward A. Jenks, [No. 1650].

1643

____. Some makers of English law; the Tagore lectures, 1937-1938 ...Cambridge [Eng.] The Univ. Press, 1938. 308p. +
A45, A62

A series of biographical sketches tied together by the thread of chronology which becomes a panorama extending over seven centuries, a paradoxical pageant of continuity and change. Commented on are the authors of the five books which "stand out pre-eminently in the history of English law - Glanvil, Bracton, Littleton, Coke and Blackstone. See Harvard Law Rev. 52:1384 (1939).

1644

____. Sources and literature of English law. Oxford, Press, 1925. 274p. +
A18

Lord Justice Atkin has written of this book, "I know of no work of this size which deals so completely and in such perspective with the manifold sources of the English law." See also note for Winfield, [No. 1681].

1645

HOLT, WYTHE, ed. Essays in Nineteenth-Century American legal history. Westport, Greenwood Press, 1976. 735p.
A43.5

"This volume is a compilation of some of the best and more recent essays, notes, and reviews in American legal history from the ratification of the Constitution to 1900. ... [T]hese articles are a truly significant academic contribution to the field of legal history. The 23 articles are grouped into four general topics: schools of historical thought, substantive and procedural issues, constitutional questions, and subject matter relating to the legal profession itself." James L. Clayton, Jl of Contemporary Law 4:309 (1978).

1646

HONNOLD, JOHN, ed. The life of the law; readings on the growth of legal institutions. N.Y., Free Press of Glencoe, 1964. 581p.
A43.5, A71.5

"In the de-emphasis of history, legal educators have felt a sense of loss that runs far beyond mere nostalgia for an earlier time. An appreciation for the historical process as it effects the law is widely considered to be valuable for a better understanding of the legal process. Professor Honnold has attempted to provide such an appreciation." Frederick G. Kempin, Jr., Univ. of Pennsylvania Law Rev. 113:628 (1965). Includes O.W. Holmes, Maitland, Blackstone, Holdsworth, Pound, Bentham, D.D. Field, Cardozo, etc. Sections on the English heritage, the new world, codification, Restatements, judges, legislature, the bar, civil law, etc.

1647

HORWITZ, MORTON J. The transformation of American law, 1780-1860. Cambridge, Harvard Univ. Press, 1977. 356p.
A43.5, A49

"This is a first-rate monograph which will become a staple resource not only of legal scholars but of general historians concerned with the growth of the economy and related aspects of political and social structure in the United States. Six chapters trace shifts in key public policies between 1780 and 1860 mainly embodied in the common law of contract and property and in the statute law of franchises, eminent domain and private credit." Willard Hurst, American Jl of Legal History 1977:175.

1648

HOWARD, A. E. DICK. The road from Runnymeade; Magna Carta and constitutionalism in America. Charlottesville, Univ. Press of Virginia, 1968. 533p.
A57.1

"Dean Howard has chosen a grand theme, and he seems to possess the qualities of mind, style, and experience to execute it grandly." Leonard W. Levy, Michigan Law Rev. 68:370 (1969).

1649

HURST, JAMES W. The growth of American law: the law makers. Boston, Little, Brown, 1950. 502p. * +
A6, A11, A24, A27.5, A28, A36, A39, A43, A43.5, A46, A49, A54, A55, A56, A57.1, A62, A64, A67, A71.5

A pioneering attempt to evaluate in broad terms the contributions to the development of American law made by its five chief formative agencies: the legislatures, the courts, the conventions and other constitution-giving institutions, the bar and the executive-administrative branch. [A54] Covers the period 1790-1940. Professor Hurst has also written _Law and Social Order in the United States_ (1977) which was reviewed by James W. Ely, Jr. in Vanderbilt Law Rev. 31:227 (1978).

1650

JENKS, EDWARD. A short history of English law from the earliest times to 1933. 4th ed. London, Methuen & Co., 1934. 465p. +
A7, A18, A27.5, A30, A40, A54, A72

This and Plucknett's _Concise History_ [See No. 1666], appear to be the best short accounts of the English law; for greater detail and scope the student should consult Holdsworth's _History of English Law._ [See No. 1642] Dean Reppy.

1651

KEMPIN, FREDERICK G. Legal history; law and social change. Englewood Cliffs, Prentice-Hall, 1963. 117p.
A43.5

Professor Kempin has also written _Historical Introduction to Anglo-American Law in a Nutshell._ 2d ed. (1973). [A43.5]

1652

KUTLER, STANLEY I. Privilege and creative destruction, the Charles River Bridge case. N.Y., Lippincott, 1971. 191p.
A29.5

"...attempts to show in the microcosm of one case the practical application of two theories of legal development in the nineteenth century. Using the _Charles River Bridge_ Case as a vehicle, the author applies the release of energy theory conceived by James Willard Hurst to the nineteenth century legal system in the United States, and develops the idea that the law in the nineteenth century was a positive force being used to unlock the energy of an essentially virgin country." M.M.M., Alabama Law Rev.

24:249 (1972). Mr. Kutler has also written The American inquisition, justice and injustice in the cold war (1982), Judicial power and reconstruction politics (1968), The Supreme Court and the constitution; readings in American constitutional history (1977), and edited John Marshall (1972).

1653

LIEBERMAN, JETHRO K. Milestones! 200 years of American law; milestones in our legal history. St. Paul, West, 1976. 422p.
A43.5, A49

Marbury v. Madison, Warren and the Warren Court, U.S. v. Richard Nixon, Miranda Case, Brown v. Board of Education, Dred Scott decision, Social Security Act, Dartmouth College Case, In re Gault, Schecter Poultry Case, Baker v. Carr, Marshall and the Marshall Court, Gideon v. Wainwright, Fourteenth Amendment, Erie v. Tompkins, Mapp v. Ohio, McCulloch v. Maryland, and Roe v. Wade. See Joseph H. Smith, Detroit College of Law Rev. 1977:747 (1977).

1654

LOVELL, COLIN R. English constitutional and legal history; a survey. Oxford, Oxford Univ. Press, 1962. 580p.
A43.5

A beginners text that follows English constitutional theory from its beginnings. Includes sample entries from the Year Books.

1655

MAITLAND, FREDERIC W. A sketch of English legal history, [with] Francis C. Montague. N.Y., Putnam's 1915. 229p. * +
A6, A28, A36, A43.5, A54

Emphasizes the machinery by which law is made rather than development of law in particular internal branches; it considers the dooms, the assizes, the jury, Magna Charta, Parliament and Chancery, with valuable notes and commentary.

1656

____. Selected historical essays chosen ... Helen M. Cam. Cambridge, Selden Society, 1957. Boston, Beacon Press, 1962. 277p.
A71.5

See also ...Selected essays, ed. by H.D. Hazeltine, G. Lapsley, and P.H. Winfield (1936).

1657

MARKE, JULIUS J. Vignettes of legal history. South Hackensack, Rothman, 1965. 337p.

A29.5, A31.7

Vintage cases analyzed and interpreted. Marbury v. Madison, the saga of Gideon Olmstead, McCulloch v. Maryland, Wheaton v. Peters, Luther v. Borden, Dred Scott case, Lincoln and civil liberties, ex parte McCardle, the Slaughter-House cases, habeas corpus, judicial torture, trial of William Penn, Peter Zenger, Writs of Assistance, trial by battle, benefit of clergy, impeachment of Justice Chase, Bracton, Fortescue, legal dictionaries, and Year Books.

1658

____. Vignettes of legal history, second series. South Hackensack, Rothman, 1977. 274p.

A29.5, A31.7

"[Professor Marke] has interwoven anecdotal and biographical materials, drawn from contemporary newspapers, journal reports, memoirs, diaries, biographies, commentaries, court reports, and trials into perceptive and lively recountings of our judicial past. ... The book is enjoyable and educational reading for all, whether attorney or educated layman, and will be a valuable addition to any collection of legal materials, regardless of size." Roy M. Mersky, Texas Law Rev. 56:147 (1977). Chapters on Gibbons v. Ogden, Martin v. Hunter's Lessee, Dartmouth College case, Blackstone, Commonwealth v. Selfridge, Inns of Court, the Serjeant-at-law, Lord Mansfield, the right to have a fool for a client, and Justice Holmes.

1659

MILLER, PERRY. The life of the mind in America. N.Y., Harcourt, Brace & World, 1965. 338p.

A27.5

"The first section, 'The Evangelical Basis,' treats the American's quest for the 'sublime' through the medium of the revival. ...[T]he second section, 'The Legal Mentality,' [discusses] evidence culled from a variety of interesting sources [which] is textually analyzed, though a great many lengthy quotations somewhat mar the continuity in places. ...A third section suggests the clash of theoretical and applied science." Peter Karsten, Wisconsin Law Rev. 1967:567 (1967).

Mr. Miller also edited The Legal Mind in America: From Independence to the Civil War (1962). A27.5, A57.7

1660

MORRIS, RICHARD B. Studies in the history of American law. 2d ed. Phila., J.M.Mitchell, 1959. 285p.
A43.5

Early history of American law, land, women's rights, tortious acts, bibliographic chapter. "The Studies as a comprehensive approach to a huge problem, may well have been born before its time." R.B. Stevens, Univ. of Detroit Law Jl 38:106 (1960).

1661

NEW YORK UNIVERSITY SCHOOL OF LAW. Law; a century of progress, 1835-1935. Contributions in celebration of the 100th anniversary of the founding of the School of Law of New York Univ. ...[Edited by Alison Reppy] N.Y., N.Y.U. Press, 1937. 3 v. +
A18, A19, A43, A56

This is a survey of 100 years development of the substantive law in America. It should be read with the Field Centenary Essays [See PROCEDURE section, No. 2002] which is a survey of 100 years development of the procedural law in America. The two considered as a single work give a fair view of the chief developments in America over the last century. Dean Reppy. For the following century see American law: the third century...ed. by Bernard Schwartz (1976) [See No. 1950].

1662

OLIVER WENDELL HOLMES DEVISE HISTORY OF THE SUPREME COURT OF THE UNITED STATES. Volume I: Julius Goebel, Jr., Antecedents and beginnings to 1801. N.Y., Macmillan, 1971. 864p.
A24.5

""...The background of American constitutionalism through the experience under the Articles of Confederation; the Constitutional Convention, the ensuing debate over ratification, and the framing of the Bill of Rights; and the early legislation affecting the judiciary and the initial experience of the circuit courts and of the Supreme Court." Herbert L. Packer, Stanford Law Rev. 25:107 (1972).

1663

___. Vol. II. Foundations of power: John Marshall, 1801-15. N.Y., Macmillan, 1981. 687p.
Part one - by George Lee Haskins. A24.5

Part two - by Herbert A. Johnson.
A24.5

1664

____. Vol. V: Carl B. Swisher, The Taney period 1836-64. N.Y., Macmillan, 1974. 1041p.
A24.5

"Swisher has done little more than merely expand, to great length, Charles Warren's chapters on the Taney Court. Indeed, this work bears no indication that it was published in the 1970s rather than the 1950s. ...It's strengths, while real, are not enough to sustain it through the banality of the political interpretations that Swisher offers and the parochialism of his emphasis on politics." Mark V. Tushnet, Catholic Univ. Law Rev. 25:681 (1976).

1665

____. Vol. VI: Charles Fairman, Reconstruction and reunion; 1864-1888, Part I. N.Y., Macmillan, 1971. 1481p.
A24.5

"By placing the Court in its proper institutional setting in dealing with the Southern response to Congressional Reconstruction, Fairman has made a fine and probably lasting contribution to the scholarship of the era. Beyond this, one does not know much more about the individual Justices at page 1489 than he did at page one. An effort to synthesize the materials and place the Court in some sort of perspective could have diminished the consequences of this omission, but the author offers no such synthesis." L.A. Powe, Jr., Texas Law Rev. 50:1468 (1972).

1666

PLUCKNETT, THEODORE F. T. A concise history of the common law. 5th ed. London, Butterworths, 1956. 746, 56p. * +
A1, A2, A7, A8, A10, A18, A19, A27, A28, A30, A39, A40, A41, A49, A50, A54, A55, A%6, A59, A63, A68, A71.5, A72

One of the best short histories of the growth of the law in England. See also the Jenks book [No. 1650]. The book as it now is seems to fulfill two functions. The text itself gives an exposition for the learner and the notes provide the more advanced user with up-to-date information about legal literature and research. See Jl Soc. Pub. Teachers of Law, n.s. 4:55 (1957). Dean Thormodsgard recommended it for first year law students.

1667

POLLOCK, SIR FREDERICK, bart. The history of English law before the time of Edward I. [with] Frederic William Maitland ...2d ed. Cambridge, Univ. Press, Boston, Little, Brown, 1911. 2 v. + A7, A43.5, A49, A71.5

This is a monumental work which has given us a new perspective of the origins of early English law. Holdsworth believes that this history, plus Blackstone, plus Dicey's Law and Opinion, give us an adequate account of the whole course of English legal history.

1668

POTTER, HAROLD. A short outline of English legal history. 4th ed., rev. and enl., London, Sweet & Maxwell [etc., etc.] 1945. 256p. + A28

More of an introduction to English legal history keyed to the interests of advanced law students rather than beginners. See also A.K.R. Kiralfy, Outlines of English Legal History (5th ed. 1958).

1669

POUND, ROSCOE. Interpretions of legal history ...N.Y., Macmillan, 1923. 171p. +
A38, A45, A68

Pound's main theme is the juristic and philosophical interpretation of the history and principles of legal systems; and over that theme he throws the spell of his accurate and extensive learning in law, history, science, philosophy and literature. By his skill in the handling of the materials and by the force of his alert active mind he gives liveliness and vigor to the subject. See Hazeltine's Preface.

1670

___, ed. Readings on the history and system of the common law, [with] Theodore F. T. Plucknett ...3d ed. ...Rochester, Lawyers Co-operative Publishing, 1927. 731p. * +
A13, A49, A54, A71.5

One of the classics on the history and development of the common law on which the Anglo-American legal system is founded. [A54] Of value, too, in studying English common law in the newer states.

1671

RADIN, MAX. Handbook of Anglo-American legal history ...St. Paul, Minn., West Publishing Co., 1936. 612p. * + A10,A13,A30

An encyclopedic rather than discriminating approach - does not select subjects but rather covers the common law as part of a single story with English law rather than as an epilogue to it. See Harvard Law Rev. 50:1335 (1937).

1672

SCHWARTZ, BERNARD. The American heritage history of the law in America. N.Y., American Heritage Publishing Co., 1974. 383p.
A31.7

"[T]o those members of the bar and the general public who seek, to adopt the words of Terence Rattigan, 'legal history without tears,' this volume will be of interest and value." Joseph H. Smith, New York Law Forum 21:141 (1975). This book was also published, without illustrations, by McGraw Hill (1974). [A43.5]. See also his Reins of power, a constitutional history of the United States (1963), a sweeping introduction to constitutional law for the observant citizen.

1673

SEAGLE, WILLIAM. The quest for law [reprinted in 1946 as "The History of Law"]. N.Y., Knopf, 1941. 439p. * +
A1, A14, A15, A19, A27, A28, A39, A43, A47, A49, A54, A56, A59, A63

A searching and suggestive study of primitive, archaic and modern societies and their characteristic forms of law; some of the history should be taken with caution. [A39] This is a "brilliant" book on the history of law - a lively presentation, never over-technical and always attractive. See Columbia Law Rev. 42:500 (1942).

1674

SHIRLEY, GLENN. Law west of Fort Smith; an authentic history of frontier justice in the old Indian territory. N.Y., Henry Holt, 1957. 333p.
A57.1

"...focus is Judge Parker's court and Parker is its hero. That would necessarily be true of any account of law and order during the 1870s and 1880s in what is now eastern Oklahoma, because at that time and place Judge Parker was 'the law,' and enforcement of the law was by the marshals and deputy marshals of his court, 'the men who rode for Parker.' ...[N]o one can fully understand the legal system which we have in Arkansas or Oklahoma today unless he knows also of the system as it operated when this was a frontier. ... Robert A. Leflar, Arkansas Law Rev. 11:459 (1957). See also this author's West of hell's fringe, crime, criminals and the Federal peace officers (1978). [A57.1] Also Jack Gregory and Rennard Strickland, eds. Hell on the border, he hanged eighty-eight men (1971). [A57.1]

1675

STREET, THOMAS A. The foundations of legal liability; a presentation of the theory and development of the common law. Northport, N.Y., Edward Thompson Co., 1906. 3 v. * +
A18, A67

This is a remarkable historical study of the ideas at the back of delictual and contractual liability, and as a necessary part of that history, of the law of those actions by the working of which the principles of that liability were ascertained. See Holdsworth, Historians of the Law, p. 105.

The third volume of Street contains the most readable and yet accurate statement on the common law actions now available for the first year student. After reading Street, he may then consult Ames Lectures on Legal History [See this topic, No. 1625] which treats the common law actions in a shorter and more technical fashion. Dean Reppy.

1676

STRICKLAND, RENNARD. Fire and the spirits, Cherokee law from clan to court. Norman, Univ. of Oklahoma Press, 1975. 260p.
A48.5, A57.1

1677

THORNE, SAMUEL. Bracton on the laws and customs of England. Edited by George E. Woodbine. Translated, with revisions and notes by Samuel E. Thorne. Cambridge, Harvard Univ. Press, 1968. Vol. 1, 422p.; Vol. 2, 449p.; Vol. 3, 824p.; Vol. 4, 756p. A24.5

"...a reissue of the untranslated edition produced between 1915 and 1942 by G.E. Woodbine of Yale, to which Professor Thorne has added a translation 'with revisions and notes.' ...First printed four hundred years ago ... What Bracton had done was to produce a comprehensive account of English law, something that nobody else was even to attempt for half a millenium. ...for the history of the common law, of law generally, Bracton is uniquely valuable." S.F.C.Milsom, Harvard Law Rev. 84:756 (1971). "It is instructive to read (or re-read) Maitland first and then turn to Thorne;..." M.J.Prichard, Cambridge Law Jl 37:167 (1978).

1678

WALSH, WILLIAM F. A history of Anglo-American law. ...2d ed. Indianapolis, Bobbs-Merrill [c1932.] 477p. * +
A10, A28, A42, A49, A72

A reprint of this book contains a foreword by Dean Niles, dated 1950.

Prof. Walsh dealt with secondary sources - but he did make a real contribution with this book. He was able to view the historical panorama through the eyes of a student. He develops a subject so that students can understand and remember it. Although the book is not light reading, it is written so that a student will get a maximum benefit for the time which he devotes to it. A beginning law student could not make a better start than by reading this unpretentious but sound little book. See foreword by Dean Niles.

1679

WATSON, ALAN. Society and legal change. Edinburgh, Scottish Academic Press, 1977. 146p.
A31.7

See Richard L. Abel's review in Michigan Law Rev. 80:785 (1982).

1680

WILLIS, HUGH E. Introduction to Anglo-American law ... Bloomington, Ind., Indiana Univ. Press, [c1931.] 272p. * +
A43, A44

Helpful in understanding better the true function and therefore the proper direction for the development of our legal system. See Harvard Law Rev. 40:927 (1927).

1681

WINFIELD, PERCY H. The chief sources of English legal history ... Cambridge, Harvard Univ. Press, 1925. 374p. +
A18, A28

A beginning student should know where to secure short, succinct and accurate statements as to sources of English legal history, and Holdsworth's, Sources and Literature of English Law [See this topic, No. 1644] and Winfield are both authoritative and readable. Dean Reppy.

1682

WORMSER, RENE A. The law; the story of lawmakers and the law we have lived by, from the earliest times to the present day. N.Y., Simon & Schuster, 1949. 609p. +
A28, A42

Considered as less difficult for a beginner to understand. Dean Fenn. Republished by Simon & Schuster in 1962. [A43.5]

1683

ZANE, JOHN M. The story of law ... with an introd. by James M. Beck ...N.Y., Ives Washburn [c1927.] 486p. +
A28, A45, A71

Very readable, but incorrect on occasion. Gives a broad, dramatic sweep to the development of law. See Harvard Law Rev. 41:930 (1928).

1684

ZOBEL, HILLEL B. The Boston Massacre. N.Y. Norton Press, 1970.372p.
A29.5

"...a brilliant study of all aspects of the background, the event and the subsequent trials, clearly and concisely presented for specialists as well as the general public. ...The mythology of the Massacre has always emphasized the problem of the lawyer's duty to take unpopular cases, as reflected in the courage of John Adams in defending Captain Preston and the eight British troops who were indicted for murder by the Boston Grand Jury." Joseph C. Sweeney, Fordham Law Rev. 39:174 (1970).

LEGAL PROCESS

The following books represent a departure from both horn book and case book law. Law school curriculum committees tried to fill the gap between specific subject courses, such as Procedure, Contracts, etc., and the law as a process. These books combined legal history, politics, jurisprudence, legislation and other significant but neglected areas that law students should not ignore. The success or failure of this approach will be left to others.

1700

GARRISON, LLOYD K., AUERBACH, CARL A., et al. The legal process; an introduction to decision making by judicial, executive and administrative agencies. San Francisco, Chandler, 1961. 915p.
A43.5

1701

HART, HENRY M. JR. and **ALBERT M. SACKS.** The legal process: basic problems in the making and application of law. Tentative ed. Cambridge, 1958. Loose leaf.

1702

JACOB, HERBERT. Justice in America; courts, lawyers and the judicial process. 3d ed. Boston, Little, Brown, 1978. 247p.
A43.5

1703

MCLAUCHLAN, WILLIAM P. American legal processes. N.Y., Wiley, 1977. 218p.
A43.5

1704

MERMIN, SAMUEL. Law and the legal system; an introduction. Boston, Little, Brown, 1973. 339p.; 2d ed. 1982. 462p.
A35.5, A43.5, A57.1

An overview of the law illustrated by a case involving rape and the right of privacy from complaint to appeal. Also contains tips on law study, etc. [See also No. 2139].

1705

SIGLER, JAY A. An introduction to the legal system. Dorsey, 1968. 248p.
A48.5

LEGAL RESEARCH and METHOD

See also CREATIVE THINKING—a) RESEARCH;
see also STUDY OF LAW

1725

DOWLING, NOEL T. Materials for legal method [with] Edwin W. Patterson and Richard R. B. Powell. 2d ed, by Harry W. Jones. Brooklyn., Foundation Press, 1952. 607p. +
A6, A38, (Chap. 1, 2, 3, 6, 7 only); A69

Designed primarily to give the beginning student in law an understanding of the methods by which lawyers in their various kinds of professional work ascertain and determine what is the law. In other words upon the study of professional techniques, rather than upon the study of law as an aspect of organized society. See Preface.

1726

JACOBSTEIN, J. MYRON and ROY M. MERSKY. Fundamentals of legal research. Mineola, Foundation Press, 1981. 614p.
A1

See also their Legal research illustrated (1981). [A71.8] See also Morris L. Cohen and Robert Berring, How to find the law (1983). See also Edward J. Bander, Legal aids, Student Lawyer, Nov. 1981, p.52 for an iconoclastic evaluation of legal research texts.

1727

LEVI, EDWARD H. An introduction to legal reasoning. [Chicago] Univ. of Chicago Press [1949]. 74p. * +
A6.5, A20, A24, A27.5, A28, A38, A38.5, A43, A43.5, A48.5, A49, A51, A54, A57.7, A71.5, A71.8, A72

The author points out that legal reasoning operates by example; e.g., reasoning from case to case. He illustrates his "introduction" by the analysis of illustrative case, statute and constitutional material. [A54].

1728

LLEWELLYN, KARL N. The normative, the legal and the law jobs: the problem of juristic method. Yale L. Jl 49:1355 (1940). * +
A24

Treats the directive thrusts in the maintenance of the parallelism between the concepts of law and the concepts of morality, and the role of the lawmen therein. [A24].

1729

PRICE, MILES O. Effective legal research; a practical manual of law books and their use [with Harry Bitner and Shirley Raissi Bysiewicz]. 4th ed. Boston, Little, Brown, 1979. 643p. +
A15

This is the most comprehensive, basic manual on legal research methods. Will be of more value if reread in 2nd and 3rd year of law school. This 1958 evaluation holds true for the new edition.

1730

RE, EDWARD D. Brief writing and oral argument. 5th ed. Dobbs Ferry, Oceana, 1983. 434p.
A24.5

Reflects the sophisticated understanding and professionalism of a Federal Judge, a professor of law, and a legal scholar. Part I: Legal writing. Part II: Trial briefs and memoranda of law. Part III: Appellate brief writing. Part IV: Oral argument. Part V: Legal citator. Forms for appellate briefs, opinion letter, memoranda of law, trial memorandum.

1735

BENTHAM, JEREMY. An introduction to the principles of morals and legislation ...Oxford, Clarendon Press [etc., etc.] 1907. 378p. Also edition by J.H. Burns and H.L.A. Hart. London, Athlone Press, 1970. 343p. +
A7, A59

The limitations of Bentham's moral and social philosophy have not greatly impeded the value of his juristic thought. For as he himself so clearly points out, jurisprudence and legislation are concerned only with a limited sector of morality. Bentham's assessment of human motives and actions in terms of interests formed a powerful foundation for the science of legislation. See G. W. Keeton, Jeremy Bentham and the Law (1948, 1970) p.232.

1736

DICKERSON, REED. Fundamentals of legal drafting. Boston, Little, Brown, 1965. 203p.
A11.5

See this author's Materials on legal drafting (1981). [See No. 1117]. See also James Willard Hurst, Dealing with statutes (1982); and Guido Calabresi, A common law for the age of statutes (1982). For a short, practical text, see Gwendolyn B. Folsom, Legislative history; research for the interpretation of laws (1979). For a list of books on legal research in the various states, see Morris L. Cohen and Robert Berring, How to find the law (8th ed. 1983).

1737

TAYLOR, TELFORD. Grand inquest; the story of congressional investigations. N.Y., Simon and Schuster, 1955. 358p.
A31.7

"An enormous amount of intellectual effort has been directed in recent years at the problems presented by hyperactive congressional investigation committees. Some of the resulting articles and books have been most helpful; others have been obfuscating rant. Mr. Taylor's book is unquestionably entitled to a place among the leaders of the former group." Michael I. Sovern, Columbia Law Rev. 56:144 (1956).

LOGIC

See Also CREATIVE THINKING; subheads; Deductive Reasoning and Inductive Reasoning

1745

DESCARTES, RENE. A discourse on method. N.Y., Dutton, 1951. 287p. (Everyman's library). +
A59

While Descartes (French 17th century philosopher) made almost no direct contribution to the strictly social sciences, through the boldness of his rationalistic method he became one of the great figures in their history. His rejection of final causes meant that the study of social phenomena was to focus on their necessary connection and the mechanism by which they are actually brought into being; and this can be achieved only by close and precise observation and vigorous logical or mathematical calculation. See Encyc. Soc. Sci. under Descartes.

1746

HUME, DAVID. A treatise on human nature; being an attempt to introduce the experimental method of reasoning into moral subjects. Cambridge, Cambridge Univ. Press, 1938. 3 v. +
A59

This is the most complete exposition of Hume's philosophical conception and the first thorough-going attempt to apply the fundamental principles of Locke's empirical psychology to the construction of a theory of knowledge and as a natural consequence, the first systematic criticism of the chief metaphysical notions from this point of view. See Encyc. Brit. 11th ed.

1747

JAMES, WILLIAM. Pragmatism (first published in 1907 - available in various editions). +
A7, A59

Pragmatism as a method of inquiry was developed by James. The current trend of the physical sciences is largely in the direction of James' view of the nature of things. The social sciences on the contrary have moved away from it. See Encyc. of Soc. Sci.

1748

MILL, JOHN STUART. System of logic. N.Y., Longmans, Green, 1925. 2 v. +
A59

First published in 1843. Mill aspired after a doctrine of method such as should satisfy the needs of the natural sciences, notably experimental physics and chemistry as understood in the first half of the 19th century, and mutatis mutandis, of the moral sciences naturalistically, construed. It marked a fresh state in the history of empiricism. See Encyc. Brit. 11th ed. under Logic.

1749

SCHOPENHAUER, ARTHUR. The art of controversy. (In his Essays. Translated by T. Bailey Saunders, N.Y., Wiley Book Co. [n.d.]). +
A47

Schopenhauer is ironical in this essay of approximately 42 pages. He considers logic and dialectic as well as stratagems. Some of his stratagems in debate or argument are decidedly "under the belt" in attack.

MEDICAL JURISPRUDENCE

1760

ALLEN, RICHARD C., ELYCE ZENOFF FERSTER and **JESS G. RUBIN**, eds. Readings in law and psychiatry. Baltimore, Johns Hopkins Univ. Press, 1975. 828p.
A31.7

"...a magnificent collection of readings, commentary, and editorials, replete with information for both practicing psychiatrists and lawyers." Robert L. Sadoff, Villanova Law Rev. 21:1007 (1976). The book has four sections: basic concepts in psychiatry, the psychiatrist and psychologist in a legal setting, the psychiatrist and the civil law, and the psychiatrist and the criminal law.

1761

HARRIS, RICHARD O. A sacred trust. N.Y., New American Library, 1966. 218p.
A48.5

"The story of America's most powerful lobby - organized medicine - and its forty-five year multi-million dollar fight against public health legislation."

1762

KESSLER, GAIL. Judgment; a case of medical malpractice. N.Y., Mason/Charter Publishers, 1978. 153p.
A31.7

A malpractice case told from the plaintiff's point of view.

1763

POLSKY, SAMUEL. The medico-legal reader. N.Y., Oceana, 1956. 256p. (Docket Series No. 6). +
A3, A35, A41, A50

Contains reading materials for law-medicine programs. The collected essays cover the interrelations of law and medicine, law and the mind and practical aspects such as personal injury matters. Medical science in criminal cases and legal regulations of medical practice are also brought out. The materials collected are of a high quality. See Jl Leg. Ed. 9:270 (1956).

MENTAL DISORDERS
See Also CRIMINOLOGY

1775

HART, BERNARD. The psychology of insanity ...4th ed. N.Y.,Macmillan, 1931. 191p. * +
A35

Popular instructive book. Compare with Myerson, A Psychology of Mental Disorders [See No. 1776]. The points of disagreement are instructive. See Harvard Law Rev. 58:597 (1945).

1776

MYERSON, ABRAHAM. The psychology of mental disorders. N.Y., Macmillan, 1927. 135p. * +
A35

OBSCENITY and THE LAW

1780

SCOTT, GEORGE R. "Into whose hands," an examination of obscene libel in its legal, sociological and literary aspects. London, G. C. Swan [1945.] 236p. + A28

The author tries to prove that the obscenity law is of more importance than to regulate publication of books or painting of pictures - but rather strikes deeper - at the very foundation of freedom. [See also No. 525].

1790

GOLDSTEIN, JOSEPH, ANNA FREUD and **ALBERT J. SOLNIT.** Before the best interests of the child. N.Y., Free Press, 1979. 288p.
A31.7

"The critical questions are how much of a role should the state have, who should exercise this role, and what powers should the state have to alter parental care. In a system that starts with a preference for family autonomy, it must be decided ...' What ought to be established ... before the best interests of the child can be invoked over the rights of parents to autonomy, the rights of children to autonomous parents, and the rights of both parents and children to family privacy.'" Michael S. Wald, Michigan Law Rev. 78:645 (1980).

1791

____. Beyond the best interests of the child. N.Y., Free Press, 1973. 170p.
A31.7

"...three distinguished social science professionals have crafted out of evident compassion for the child a brief yet subtle program for the law's resolution of [child custody] cases. ...[The authors] insist that the child's perspective must be controlling in any judicial proceedings to decide custody issues." Peter L. Strauss and Joanna B. Strauss, Columbia Law Rev. 74:996 (1974).

1792

KATZ, SANFORD N. When parents fail; the law's response to family breakdown. Boston, Beacon Press, 1971. 251p.
A31.7

"...a small book which examines an area perhaps even more obscure and less rigorously investigated than the juvenile criminal system. He looks into the law's reaction to the child who is not properly cared for within his own nuclear family. That his book succeeds in making some sense out of this area of the law is probably due more to his own analytical ability than to the state of the law itself." Catholic Univ. Law Rev. 23:435 (1973).

PHILOSOPHY

See also HUMAN INSTITUTIONS AND VALUES, JURISPRUDENCE AND PHILOSOPHY OF LAW; POLITICAL THEORY AND POLITICAL ECONOMY

1800

COHEN, MORRIS R. Reason and nature; an essay on the meaning of scientific method. N.Y., 1931. Dover Publications, 1978, 1959. 470p. A20 +

Throws additional light upon the doubtful and difficult problems connected with the nature of "reason" in all fields, including that of law. See Columbia Law Rev. 31:725 (1931).

1801

DURANT, WILLIAM J. The story of philosophy; the lives and opinions of the greater philosophers. N.Y., Simon & Schuster, 1926. 577p. +
A59

The essential thought of the great philosophers from Plato to John Dewey is presented in such a way as to make it human and readable. Many quotations are included from the writings of the chosen philosophers. See Book Rev.Dig. 1926:203.

1802

HEGEL, GEORG WILHELM F. Hegel's philosophy of right, tr. with notes by T. M. Knox ...Oxford, Clarendon Press, 1942. 382p. * +
A8

Hegel has exercised great influence. His philosophy of the relations of individual and state has laid the foundation for the ascendancy of the state over the individual and in combination with his ideas on the intermediate function of the cooperation between individual and state has directly influenced modern Fascist ideas on the coporate totalitarian state. See W. Friedman, Legal Theory, p. 78 [No. 1361]. (See also JURISPRUDENCE).

1803

KANT, IMMANUEL. Critique of pure reason, with an introd. by the translator, J. M. D. Meiklejohn, and a special introd by Brandt V. B. Dixon ...Rev. ed. N.Y., Colonial Press [1900.] 480p. +
A7, A59

More than any other philosopher of the late 18th century, except perhaps Leibniz, Kant was attentive to the results of the scientific exploration of nature. In this work he presents the categories and formulas through which all phases of existence could be known in thought. His subject was - what is thinkable. See Dunning, Hist. of Pol. Theory, p. 131.

1804

LOCKE, JOHN. An essay concerning human understanding ...N.Y., Dutton, 1947. 2 v. +
A59

Not the least of the interest we have in Locke's philosophy today is due to its vast influence on practical affairs. It is clear that his basic ideas are at the root of much of the political theory of the 18th century and too, inspired the framers of the Declaration of Independence and the architects of the French Revolution. See Cairns, Legal Philosophy from Plato to Hegel, p. 336 [No. 1340].

POLITICAL THEORY and POLITICAL ECONOMY

See also ECONOMICS; HUMAN INSTITUTIONS AND VALUES; PHILOSOPHY

1825

ARISTOTELES. The Politics of Aristotle, translated, with an introduction, notes ...by Ernest Barker ...Oxford, Clarendon Press [1948.] 411p. +
A59, A68

This contains valuable, systematic expositions of Aristotle's political thought. Aristotle was the great humanist and scientist of antiquity.

1826

ARNOLD, THURMAN W. The folklore of capitalism. New Haven, Yale Univ. Press, 1937. 400p. * +
A1, A7, A8, A12, A14, A19, A20, A23, A27, A27.5, A29, A36, A39, A43, A43.5, A45, A56, A57, A63, A68, A74

This is a penetrating, though often exaggerated analysis of our legal and economic life written by a man who was a lawyer, mayor, state legislator, law teacher, ass't. atty-general in charge of anti-trust matters, and a federal judge. This is worth rereading in 2nd and 3rd years. You may be interested in finding how much more you get out of it after you have had some legal training. [A12].

1827

BECKER, CARL L. The Declaration of Independence, a study in the history of political ideas ...N.Y., Harcourt, Brace [c1922.] 286p. * +
A1, A2, A14, A19, A22, A27, A28, A35, A39, A43.5, A56, A59, A61, A63, A67, A68

A penetrating and brilliant study of the document and what went into its making. [A39].

1828

BERLE, ADOLF A. The 20th century capitalist revolution. N.Y., Harcourt, Brace [1954]. 192p. +
A6, A43.5

The central theme of the book is that the affairs of persons on earth inevitably depend on justice. Berle also stresses that the large corporation has become one of the chief instruments for carrying into effect social reforms in response to certain community demands. See N.Y.U. Law Rev. 30:734 (1935).

1829

BOULDING, KENNETH E. The organizational revolution, a study in the ethics of economic organization; with a commentary by Reinhold Niebuhr. N.Y., Harper [1953]. 286p. +
A7

A Quaker economist accounts for the economic, political and social forces behind the tremendous growth of labor, farm and business organizations in the U.S. and then takes up the ethical problems this raises for its citizens. Niebuhr answers with a critical rebuttal followed by a discussion carried on by economists, psychologists and sociologists. See Booklist 49:231.

1830

CASSIRER, ERNST. The myth of the state. New Haven, Yale Univ. Press [etc.] 1946. 303p. * +
A8

A posthumous book concerned with the collapse and resuscitation in Western civilization of myth as a bond of social cohesion and a basis for organized activity. The author concludes that the sense of inability to solve problems was the matrix for the rebirth of all-embracing myth in our day, and its use by totalitarian, especially Nazi, leadership. See Am. Pol. Sci. Rev. 41:331.

1831

COKER, FRANCIS W. Readings in political philosophy ...N.Y., Macmillan, 1938. 717p. +
A45

Contains selections from the great political philosophers with a selected bibliography at the end of each chapter. The choice of material is good.

1832

EASTON, DAVID. Political system; an inquiry into the state of political science. N.Y., Knopf, 1953. 320p. * +
A8

In this important book an able young political theorist endeavors with considerable success to show that American political theorists generally are today making very little contribution to political science, to indicate the reasons for their failure, and to suggest what he thinks they need to do. See Am. Pol. Sci. Rev. 47:862.

1833

EBENSTEIN, WILLIAM. Man and the state; modern political ideas. N.Y., Rinehart [1947.] 781p. +
A59

Presents the major political ideas of modern Western civilization in the original sources, with commentary thereon. Judicious selection of material, deficient however, in that representative Catholic politcal thought is not included. See Am. Pol. Sci. Rev. 41:1209 (1947).

1834

FRANKFURTER, FELIX. The public and its government. New Haven, Yale Univ. Press [etc.] [c1930.] 170p. * +
A28, A35, A45, A61, A71.5

The central inquiry of the book is to discover what has happened to democracy as a theory of political organization. How far has our development been diverted from the democratic basis? How adequate is democracy under modern conditions? The book is charming and eloquent. See Harvard Law Rev. 44:478 (1931).

1835

HARRIS, RICHARD. Justice; the crisis of law, order and freedom in America. N.Y., Dutton, 1970. 268p.
A48.5

"...The book is about the Nixon Administration, in particular the President's campaign strategy, his selection for Attorney General, his first year in office and the implications Mr. Harris sees from the campaign and early performance." Edwin H. Wolf, Buffalo Law Rev. 20:347 (1971).

1836

HEILBRONER, ROBERT L. The wordly philosophers. The lives, times and ideas of the great economic thinkers. N.Y., Simon & Schuster, 1953. 342p. +
A36

The author shows and does so very brilliantly how the theories of the economists reflect their times. The book thus becomes a kind of running comment upon the varied fortunes and crises of the capitalist system, and the fate of capitalism actually becomes its central theme. See N.Y. Times, Aug. 2, 1953, p.6.

1837

HOBBES, THOMAS. Leviathan. London, J. M. Dent, N.Y., Dutton [n.d.] 392p. +
A7, A59

Hobbes, a younger contemporary of Coke, was a philosopher who combined great learning with extraordinary powers of logical analysis. He was the first Englishman to explain the doctrine of sovereignty. In Leviathan he considers the object of sovereignty. This he finds in an original permanent social compact whereby man submits to the authority of the individual in return for repression of anarchy. See Law Q. Rev. 37:276 (1921).

1838

KIRK, RUSSELL. The roots of American order. La Salle, Ill., Open Court, 1974. 534p.
A57.1

Our antecedents from Mt. Sinai to Massachusetts Bay, Solon, Aristotle, Cicero, Christianity, Leviathan, Locke, Tocqueville, Montesquieu, Blackstone, Burke, Federal Constitution, Lincoln. Pages 505-516 has a chronology of events depicted in book. The volume provides a fleeting glimpse of Western civilization.

1839

LASKI, HAROLD J. The American democracy, a commentary and interpretation. N.Y., Viking Press, 1948. 785p. +
A7

This book tests the American achievement by standards accepted throughout the Western world and then gives reasons to persuade that our ideals can no longer find even partial recognition in the institutions of capitalism. It attempts to strike at the placid assumptions of American liberalism. See Harvard Law Rev. 62:338 (1948).

1840

____. Politics. Phila., Lippincott, 1931. 160p. +
A59

A primer on politics which considers the nature of the state, its place in society, its organization and its relation to international society. This is "so charmingly, so lucidly, so suggestively" presented that "the book is a sparkling literary presentation of the more fundamental problems of political science." See Am. J. Soc. 37:494.

1841

____. Studies in law and politics ...New Haven, Yale Univ. Press, 1932. 299p. +
A8, A39, A42

A collection of stimulating essays by the noted English political scientist and socialist. Some of the essays are historical, others have to do with English politics, while others discuss such problems as judicial review, the appointment of judges and constructive contempt. There are also essays on political and legal theory which are concerned primarily with the relationships between law, justice and the state. [A39].

1842

LASSWELL, HAROLD D. The analysis of political behavior; an empirical approach. London, K. Paul Trench, Trubner, [1948.] 314p.
A59 +

A compilation of articles from 1932 to 1948 for those who would like to make a survey of the ideas and approaches used by an American pioneer in the field of psycho-politics. The examples are dated, but not the ideas. See Pol. Sci. Q. 64:299.

1843

LEFCOURT, ROBERT, ed. Law against the people. N.Y., Vintage Books, 1971. 400p.
A29.5

"... the purpose ... is to demystify the law, tell it as it is, and lay the groundwork for challenging the law and changing it." Robert C. Berry, Jl of Legal Education 25:617 (1973). The author, William Kunsler and Arthur Kinoy are among the essayists. See also Mr. Kinoy's Rights on trial, the odyssey of a people's lawyer (1983).

1844

LOCKE, JOHN. Two treatises on government. (First published 1689, now available in various editions). * +
A7, A8

The second treatise of government was considered by Pollock as probably the most important contribution ever made to English Constitutional law by an author who was not a lawyer by profession. It presents a systematic, constructive theory of state and government. The first part need not be read as it is more of an attack on Filmer's "Patriarcha."

1845

MacIVER, ROBERT M. The modern state. Oxford, Clarendon Press, 1926. 504p. +
A45

A study of the state as it is when theory and practice are related. A good historical sketch traces the growth of the state through successive phases based on changing conditions. See New Stateman 27:646.

1846

____. The web of government. N.Y., Macmillan, 1947. 498p.* +
A8, A36

A notable contribution to the field of political theory. An analysis of the perplexing problems with which the nation state is confronted in our contemporary national and international society. See Law Q. Rev. 65:393 (1949).

1847

MARITAIN, JACQUES. Man and the state. Chicago, Univ. of Chicago Press [1951.] 219p. * +
A16, 159

Examined here is the idea of a democratic charter by which free men might live in peace. Maritain applies his philosophy of natural law to society and politics. He is lucid, persuasive and systematic. See Am. Pol. Sci. Rev. 45:899.

1848

MARX, KARL. Das Kapital. (In many editions—See Modern Library edition). * +
A8, A59

To understand communist polemics, it is important to be familiar with the thoughts of its founder Karl Marx (1818-1883) as exemplified in one of his main works - Das Kapital. Here he applies the so-called materialistic conception of history in the discovery of developmental laws of modern capitalistic economy. See Encyc. of Soc. Sci. For critical discussions of Marx's Theories of Value cf. A.D. Lindsay, Karl Marx's Capital (1925) Chs. III and IV.

1849

MERRIAM, CHARLES E. The new democracy and the new despotism. N.Y., McGraw Hill, 1939. 278p. +
A59

Study of the conflict of democracy and despotism in the world. Most of the discussion centers around the objectives of democracy and the means for realizing to a greater extent these objectives.

1850

____. On the agenda of democracy. Cambridge, Harvard Univ. Press, 1941. 135p. +
A8, A35, A57, A68

Merriam recommends a streamlining of the administrative process, with full power entrusted to a responsible and accountable executive, using the latest methods of a scientific management. They include a modernizing of the legislative process, with legislators avoiding technical detail, but relying on technical advice while airing principles and policies in constant deliberation and keeping a watchful eye on administration. This is the "agenda" by which democracy can serve its purpose.

1851

MILL, JOHN STUART. Elements of political economy. (First published 1848, now in many editions). +
A59

An attempt by the intellectual leader of the Benthamite school to bring accepted economic doctrines into harmony with the aspirations of the best people among the working classes. Mill achieved great distinction with this book.

Government is made by the public for their social well being.

1852

____. On liberty. (First published 1859, now in many editions). +
A59, A74

In his essay "On Liberty," Mill considers the limits of the authority of society over the individual and outlines the sphere of freedom for the several portions of the community. See Fritz Berolzheimer, World's Legal Philosophies (N.Y., A.M.Kelly, 1968, p. 141.).

1853

MISES, LUDWIG VON. Socialism. New Haven, Yale Univ. Press, 1951. 599p. +
A19

The most devastating analysis of socialism yet penned. Mises restates his case sometimes, but he conducts his argument in a masterly fashion. This is an economic classic of our time. See H. Hazlitt, N.Y. Times, Jan. 9, 1938.

1854

MONTESQUIEU, CHARLES L. deS., baron de la Brede. The spirit of laws. (First published in 1749—now in many editions.) An excellent abridgment is available in The Tradition of Freedom, edited by Milton Mayer for the Fund for the Republic. N.Y., Oceana publications, 1957. pp.35-193. (Docket Classic). * +
A8

A very influential book - especially on the minds of the founders of the American republic form of government. Montesquieu interprets the term "Esprit des Lois" as "the several relations which the law may have with various interests" which he then studies - especially the relation of the law "with the nature and principle of every form of government - the judicial, the legislative, and the executive." Here we have the formulation of the doctrine of checks and balances. Read particularly the part dealing with the English government.

1854a

MORE, SIR THOMAS, SAINT. Utopia. (In many editions). * +
A8

Published early in the reign of Henry VIII, More's Utopia was a satire of a cultivated mind and refined spirit upon the society of which he was a part, says Dunning. Although admired by the legal profession it should be noted that More banished lawyers from his utopia. See also E.E. Reynolds, The life and death of St. Thomas More (1968).

1855

MORGANTHAU, HANS J. Scientific man vs. power politics. Chicago, Univ. of Chicago Press, 1946. 245p. * +
A8

The principal thesis here is that grave dangers lurk in the assumption that since the methods of the physical sciences have yielded a considerable amount of reliable predictions, and of control of physical nature, those methods will be equally successful if applied to matters social. Despite its glaring faults, Judge Jerome Frank recommends this book as a valuable antidote to the pernicious pseudo-rationalism of many so-called social scientists and many legal thinkers. See Univ. of Chicago Law Rev. 15:462 (1948).

1856

NORTHROP, FILMER S. The meeting of East and West; an inquiry concerning world understanding. N.Y., Macmillan, 1946. 531p. * +
A59

An analysis of the philosophical, economic and religious beliefs of America, Europe and Asia. The purpose: to arrive at a synthesis of values. See Library J. 71:918.

1857

PARRINGTON, VERNON L. Main currents in American thought; an interpretation of American literature from the beginning to 1920. [N.Y., Harcourt, Brace, 1927-30.] 3 v. +
A59

A fresh and original interpretation of the more influential tendencies in American thought and sentiment from Colonial days to the Civil War. See Outlook 146:418. Justice Holmes objected to Parrington following the suggestion of Beard that really the adoption of the Constitution was due to moneyed interests. See Holmes' letter to Dr. Wu, June 21, 1928.

1858

PASSERIN d'ENTREVES, ALESSANDRO. Medieval contribution to political thought; Thomas Aquinas, Marsilius of Padua and Richard Hooker. Oxford, Univ. Press, 1939. 148p. +
A59

To the author, the history of political thought is "first and foremost, the history of the attempts to solve the problem of political obligation." He thus endeavors to understand the efforts of generation after generation of thinkers to reach a solution of problems which, as philosophical problems, remain unaltered, and necessarily lead us away from the proper place of history into the realm of values. See Times [London] Lit. Sup., May 27, 1939. p.318.

1859

PLATO. The Dialogues. (In many editions). +
A59, A68

These dialogues illustrate the originality of one of the most imaginative of Greek philosophers. Plato's concept of law was very broad. Law was the product of reason, indentifiable with reason. Almost all his "dialogues" comment on some aspect of law.

1860

____. The Republic. (In many editions). * +
A8, A20, A68

Dunning in his Hist. of Political Ideas states that this is Plato's greatest work. Both the substance of his thought and the form in which it is expressed have fascinated all succeeding generations and have stimulated endless imitation. Plato's object in formulating the conceptions of a state in which justice prevails was to discover by analogy the philosophical idea of justice in the individual man.

1861

ROUSSEAU, JEAN JACQUES. The social contract and discourses. London, Dent, N.Y., Dutton, 1920. 287p. (First published 1762; now in many editions). +
A59

Contains Rousseau's ideas on man and society. His arguments seem convincing although we cannot say he reasons well. His books gave the first signal of a universal subversion, and were as fatal to the Republic as to the Monarch. See Lord Acton, Essays on Freedom and Power, p. 266.

1862

SCHLESINGER, ARTHUR M. JR. The imperial presidency. Boston, Houghton Mifflin, 1973. 505p. A72.5

The changing concept of the role of the presidency as expounded by a noted historian who was active politically during the Kennedy administration.

1863

SMITH, ADAM. The wealth of nations. (First published in 1776, now in many editions.) See Modern Library ed. 1937. 2 v. +
A7, A59

The first systematic book on political economy. It is also the first powerful plea for commercial freedom. The difficulty of the work which Smith set himself to do can scarcely be overrated. A society founded on custom had given way to a society founded on competition, but the operation of the new economic force had never been explained. See Maitland, Collected Papers I:99.

1864

SPENCER, HERBERT. The man versus the state. 1884. (Many editions.) Caldwell, Idaho, Caxton Printers, 1940. 213p. +
A19

One of the most powerful and influential arguments for limited government, laissez-faire and individualism, ever written. Hardly less important in its bearing on individualism, is Spencer's Social Statics, published in 1850. See Hazlitt's The Free Man's Library.

1865

TOCQUEVILLE, ALEXIS C. H. M. C. de. Democracy in America. The Henry Reeve text as revised by Francis Bowen...foreword by Harold J. Laski. N.Y., Knopf, 1945. 2 v. (First published in 1835, now in many editions). * +
A2.5, A19, A22, A57.1

One of the best books ever written about America, and the most penetrating ever written about democracy. It won instant acclaim. Its central theme is that democracy has become inevitable; that it is with certain qualifications desirable; but that it has great potentialities for evil as well as good, depending upon how well it is understood and guided. The greatest danger that threatens democracy is its tendency toward the centralization and concentration of power. See Hazlitt's The Free Man's Library. His comments on the role of the legal profession in the United States are interesting.

POLITICS

See GOVERNMENT AND POLITICS, POLITICAL THEORY and POLITICAL ECONOMY

—

PRACTICE OF LAW and THE LEGAL PROFESSION

For background reading in this field, Dean Phillips of Columbia suggests the bibliography in Appendix III of Professor Elliot E. Cheatham's Casebook on The Legal Profession (1955). (See this topic).

1875

AMERICAN BAR ASSOCIATION. Code of professional responsibility. Chicago, 1975.
A24.5

It "is a useful point of departure [for a] body of critical discourse on basic problems affecting the sense of purpose of the legal profession." Charles Frankel, Univ. of Chicago Law Rev. 43:874 (1976). Codes of professional and judicial conduct can be found in the current issue of the Martindale-Hubbell Law Directory. They are also included in the American Bar Association data bank in Lexis, a legal research computer.

1876

____. General Practice Section. How to find the courthouse, a primer for the practice of law. Chicago, 1978.
A57.1

1877

____. Getting started; the first years of law practice. [Chicago.] 1948. 16p. +
A29.5

1878

____. Look before you leap; finding your place in the legal profession. [Chicago.] 1951. 13p. +
A41

1879

____. Professional responsibility; a guide for attorneys. Chicago, A.B.A. Press, 1978. 350p.
A25.5

1880

____. Section on International Law. Career opportunities in international law. Chicago, [latest edition]
6.5

1881

____. Standing Committee on Professional Utilization and Career Development. Non-legal careers; new opportunities for lawyers. Chicago [latest ed.]
A6.5

1882

AMERICAN BAR FOUNDATION. The 1971 lawyer statistical report. Ed. by Bette Sikes, Clara N. Carson and Patricia Gorai. Chicago, 1972. A29.5

1883

AMERICAN TRIAL LAWYERS FOUNDATION. Ethics and advocacy - final report. 1978 Annual Chief Justice Earl Warren Conference on Advocacy in the United States. Wash., D.C., 1978. 99p.
A25.5

1884

ASBELL, BERNARD. What lawyers really do; six lawyers talk about their life and work. N.Y., P.H.Wyden Co., 1970. 114p.
A6.5, A35.5, A57.1

Lisa A. Richette (criminal lawyer), Robert I. Townsend (house counsel), Peter Costigan (family lawyer), Harold Baer (corporation lawyer), Helen Johnson (Assistant DA), L.S. Melville (poverty lawyer).

1885

ASHMAN, ALLEN. The new private practice; a study of Piper and Marbury's neighborhood law office. Chicago, National Legal Aid and Defender Assn, 1972. 112p.
A24.5

1886

AUERBACH, JEROLD S. Unequal justice: lawyers and social change in modern America. N.Y., Oxford Univ. Press, 1976. 395p.
A1, A2.5, A35.5, A43.5, A57.1

"...Auerbach's Benthamite attack has a cogency built on careful scholarship not impaired by fanaticism ... It is doubtful if Auerbach fairly balances such examples of the courage of the bar against its cowardly failures. He treats presidents of bar associations as though lawyers regarded them more seriously than doctors regard presidents of medical associations. ...this book will have made an enduring contribution to the sociology of American law. The author will be admired for his vigor, clarity, and shrewd observations." Charles E.Wyzanski, Jr., Harvard Law Rev. 90:283 (1976).

1887

Balancing the scales of justice; financing public interest law in America. Washington, D.C., Council for Public Interest Law, 1976. 444p. [various paging]
A6.5

1888

BALDWIN, SIMEON E. The young man and the law. N.Y., Macmillan [c1920.] 1924. 160p. * +
A35, A46

Sound advice from a distinguished judge and ex-governor on the opportunities which the practice of law offers and the standards to be maintained. See Harvard Law Rev. 58:600 (1945).

1889

BLACK, CHARLES L. The occasions of justice; essays mostly on law. N.Y., Macmillan, 1963. 213p.
A31.7

"A collection of legal articles would have placed him in the very select company of such law professors as Walter Wheeler Cook and Brainerd Currie, of Karl Llewellyn and Felix Cohen, of Eugene Rostow and Herbert Wechsler. The company is even more select ... For then one is in the Valhalla that includes Oliver Wendell Holmes, Learned Hand, Felix Frankfurter, and Earl Warren." Philip B. Kurland, Univ. of Chicago Law Rev. 32:386 (1965). See also the author's Decision according to law (1981) reviewed by Russell L. Caplan in Michigan Law Rev. 80:656 (1982).

1890

BLACK, JONATHAN, et al. Radical lawyers, their role in the movement and in the courts. N.Y., Avon Books, 1971. 320p.
A31.7

"... in this collection, the not so subtle faults in the American system of justice are revealed for what they are - fatal flaws which often render its product a contradiction and a tool of repression. [discusses military court martials, friendly civil liberties lawyers, is there radical law, the law commune]." Marjorie H. Borders, Howard Law Jl 17:725 (1973).

1891

BLAUSTEIN, ALBERT P. The American lawyer; a summary of the Survey of the Legal Profession, [with] Charles O. Porter [and] Charles T. Duncan ...[Chicago] Univ. of Chicago Press [1954.] 360p.
A6, A9, A20, A24, A39, A41, A49, A59, A64, A67, A72 * +

This summarizes the findings of the Survey of the Legal Profession and so contains a good description of what lawyers do and the financial, social and political opportunities in the legal profession. [A59].

1892

BLOOM, MURRAY TEIGH. The trouble with lawyers. N.Y., Simon and Schuster, 1968. 351p.
A57.1

"... neither systematic nor scientific. ...his thesis that lawyers are overpaid, underworked, prone to greed, and highly motivated only when the sanctity and financial security of the legal profession is under attack ...Particular attention is given to divorce cases ... attacks the contingent fee system ... The communication gap between the profession and the public continues. Duquesne Law Rev. 8:204 (1969-70). Mr. Bloom also edited Lawyers, clients and ethics. [A38.5].

1893

BLOOMFIELD, MAXWELL. American lawyers in a changing society,1776-1876. Cambridge, Harvard Univ. Press, 1976. 397p.
A43.5, A57.1

"Not until Morton J. Horwitz illuminated the ideological conservatism of American legal historiography could any sense be made of the disparity between the rise of law and the decline of lawyers. ...The Whiggish bias of the 19th century legal history has now been dealt a fatal blow. ...biographical and thematic essays ... include ... [Peter Van Schaack, William Sampson, and John Mercer; antilawyer sentiment, upgrading the professional image]. Jerold S. Auerbach, Yale Law Jl 85:855 (1976).

1894

BOK, SISSELA. Lying; moral choice in public and private life. N.Y., Pantheon, 1978. 326p.
A2.5

"Bok applies her principles to several widely acknowledged patterns of deception...the attorney-client privilege. She begins with Monroe Freedman's argument that a lawyer has a professional responsibility to build upon his client's testimony in arguing before a court, even when he has strong grounds to think the testimony perjurious." Michigan Law Rev. 77:539 (1979). See also her _Secrets; on the ethics of concealment and revelation_ (1982).

1895

BOLLES, RICHARD N. What color is your parachute? A practical manual for job hunters and careeer-changers. Berkeley, Ten Speed Press, [annual]
A6.5, A57.1

1896

BROWN, ESTHER L. Lawyers and the promotion of justice. ... N.Y., Russell Sage Foundation, 1938. 302p. +
A45

The author is primarily a social scientist, and as such, she surveys the legal profession in its place in the social order. She determines the extent to which lawyers serve society and what lawyers are doing to increase their efficacy in the social order. Brought out too is the evolution of the legal profession in the U.S., legal education and the demand for lawyers. See N.Y.U. Law Q. Rev. 17:319 (1940).

1897

____. Lawyers, law schools and the public service. N.Y., Russell Sage Foundation, 1948. 258p. * +
A8, A30

Emphasized here is the important role played by lawyers in official and legislative positions, the various kinds of legal service and a consideration of legal teaching and curriculum.

1898

BURGER, WARREN. A sick profession? Tulsa Law Jl 5:1 (1968).

A plea for more practical training for law students, particularly, a third year in conjunction with a trial bar.

1899

CARLIN, JEROME E. Lawyers on their own. New Brunswick, Rutgers Univ. Press, 1962. 234p.
A6.5, A43.5

A 1957 statistical study of 84 Chicago lawyers engaged in private practice as individual practitioners. Critisized as to small a sample but valuable for the implications of the study. See Maruice Frey, Buffalo Law Rev. 13:293 (1964).

1900

CHEATHAM, ELLIOTT E. Cases and materials on the legal profession. 2d ed. Brooklyn, Foundation Press, 1955. 585p. +
A6, A12, A23

This book by a distinguished professor of law, is planned for a course on the legal profession. However, it is full of interesting, informative, and readable material on law practice, legal ethics and the problems and the opportunities of the profession. The materials do not presuppose any substantial knowledge of law, and prospective students will find here an excellent background for law study. [A12]. See also Maynard E. Pirsig and Kenneth F. Kirwin, Cases and materials on professional responsibility (3d ed. 1976) for the new direction given to this topic; also Murray L. Schwartz, Lawyers and the legal profession, cases and materials (1979); and Thomas D. Morgan and Ronald D. Rotunda, Problems and materials on professional responsibility (2d ed. 1981).

1901

____. A lawyer when needed. N.Y., Columbia Univ. Press, 1963. 128p.
A31.7

"Five situations are considered 'in which renewed efforts are essential to meet the need for counsel'-those of the hated, the poor, the middle classes, clients needing specialized services, and the public interest." John De J. Pemberton, Jr., Missouri Law Rev. 29:254 (1964).

1902

CHESTNUT, WILLIAM C. A federal judge sums up. [Baltimore., 1947.] 274p. +
A49

The author endeavors to present a realistic account of the day-to-day work of a federal trial court. See also Frank M. Coffin, The ways of a judge; reflections from the Federal Appellate bench (1980).

1903

CHROUST, ANTON-HERMAN. The rise of the legal profession in America. Norman, Univ. of Oklahoma Press, 1965. 2 vols.
A57.1, A57.7

"'[A] narrative history of the American legal profession from its earliest colonial beginnings to the middle of the nineteenth century.' His objective is the instruction of students, 'perhaps...the entertainment of practicing lawyers,'..." Geoffrey C. Hazard, Jr. U.C.L.A. Law Rev. 13:(1965-66).

1904

CLARK, CHRISTINE P. Minority opportunity in law for Blacks, Puerto Ricans, and Chicanos. N.Y., Law Journal Press, 1974. 262p.
A6.5, A57.1

See also Marion S. Goldman, A portrait of the black attorney in Chicago (1972) [A57.1].

1905

COHEN, JULIUS H. The law; business or profession? N.Y., N.Y., Banks, 1916. 415p.
A45

Indicates the close interrelation of business and law, and the implications of business encroaching on the domain of law. An account of the underlying principles and limitations of the practice of law. See Marquette L. Rev. 9:58 (1924).

1906

COOPER, FRANK E. Living the law. Indianapolis, Bobbs-Merrill, 1958. 184p.
A6.5, A43.5

Chapters on the facts, the issue, statutes, administrative procedures, legal planning, negotiation, art of advocacy, drafting, legal writing. The book is designed to be read the summer before law school and has much to recommend it even after twenty-five years.

Mr. Cooper is also the author of Effective legal writing (1953) which emphasizes drafting of opinion letters, briefs, pleading, wills, statutes, etc.

1907

COUNTRYMAN, VERN, TED FINMAN and THEODORE SCHNEYER. The lawyer in modern society. 2d ed. Boston, Little, Brown, 1976. 979p.
A6.5

Sections on: the practitioner, the profession, lawyers and social problems, professional qualifications. Cases, excerpts, quotations covering corporate counsel, malpractice, fees, adversary system, negotiations, advertising, legal education, discipline, etc.

1908

CURTIS, CHARLES P. It's your law. Cambridge, Harv. Univ. Press, 1954. 178p. +
A51, A64, A67

In this collection of four essays, Curtis concerns himself with the legal profession—its duties, its responsibilities, its ethics, its functions when it acts to represent clients in court, to draft legal instruments, to hear and decide cases as a court of first instance and on appeal. His views are pungent, lively and sometimes highly controversial. See N.Y.U.Law Rev. 30:512 (1955).

1909

DORSEN, NORMAN and LEON FRIEDMAN. Disorder in the court, Report of the Association of the Bar of the City of New York. Special Committee on Courtroom Conduct. N.Y., Pantheon Books, 1973. 432p.
A57.1

"...why courtroom disruption occurs and what should be done about it ... thorough cataloging of types of misconduct ... special attention to [Nazi sedition trial, Communist conspiracy case, Chicago conspiracy trial, New York Black Panther case]." Allen Zetterberg, Columbia Human Rights Law Rev. 6:190 (1974).

1910

DRINKER, HENRY S. Legal ethics. N.Y., Columbia Univ. Press, 1953. 448p. +
A20, A28, A39, A49

Part I covers the organization of the Bar and of disciplinary proceedings. Part II. The duties and obligations of lawyers. Set forth are general principles with examples of their application. The book has brought together and crystallized the labors of the Committee on Professional Ethics and Grievances of the American Bar Association. For a current book on this topic, see Raymond L. Wise, Legal ethics (2d ed. 1970).

1911

EDWARDS, HARRY T. and JAMES J. WHITE. The lawyer as negotiator. St. Paul, West, 1977. 479p.
A25.5

Preventive law, as expounded by Professor Louis M. Brown, stresses the non adversarial settlement of disputes. This book is one of many that has become part of the law school curriculum. See also Roger Fisher and

William Ury, Getting to yes; negotiating agreements without giving in (1981, 1983). [See also No. 1985]. Also, Howard Raiffa, The art and science of negotiation (1983).

1912

FISHMAN, JAMES J. and ANTHONY S. KAUFMANN. Practicing law in New York City. N.Y., Council of New York Law Associates, 1975. 195p.
A6.5

Articles on being an associate, Wall Street lawyer, etc.; and essays on specialities such as corporate law, international law, labor law, patent law, tax law; also covers private and public practice, minorities, pro bono practice, interviewing, etc.

1913

FREEDMAN, MONROE H. Lawyers' ethics in an adversary system. Indianapolis, Bobbs-Merrill, 1975. 270p.
A43.5, A57.1

"The task is to resolve the 'perjury trilemma' - the conflict among the obligations of a lawyer to learn all relevant facts known to his client, to hold his client's disclosures in strictest confidence, and to be candid with the court ... Dean Freedman confronts the legal profession, the American Bar Association, and the Code of Professional Responsibility." James F. Neal, Vanderbilt Law Rev. 29:528 (1976).

1914

GINGER, ANN FAGAN. The relevant lawyers. N.Y., Simon and Schuster, 1972. 447p.
A6.5, A43.5, A57.1

"...anecdotes, and sad tales gathered over years on the front lines of some of the most bitter and spectacular legal battles in the ongoing conflict between the establishment and revolutionaries." William Merrill, Hastings Law Jl 25:1289 (1974).

1915

GIRTH, MARJORIE. Poor people's lawyers. N.Y., Exposition Press, 1976. 130p.
A43.5

The author points out the deficiencies in our efforts to deliver legal services to the poor.

1916

GOULDEN, JOSEPH C. The superlawyers; the small and powerful world of the great Washington law firms. N.Y., Weybright and Talley, 1972. 408p.
A25.5, A71.5

"Three of the book's ten chapters focus specifically on three of Washington's leading law firms - Covington and Burling, Arnold and Porter, Mudge, Rose, Guthrie and Alexander. [use of interviews, Clark Clifford, Tom Corcoran, Lloyd Cutler, lawyer and Capitol Hill, lawyer-lobbyist, lawyer-legislator]. Francis X. Beytagh, Notre Dame Lawyer 48:1006 (1973). Mr. Goulden also wrote The Million Dollar Lawyers (N..Y., Putnam, 1978) [A57.1] about divorce and personal injury lawyers, legal research services, etc. See Bernard M. Ortwein, Suffolk Univ. Law Rev. 13:225 (1979).

1917

GREEN, MARK J. The other government, the unseen power of Washington lawyers. N.Y., Viking Press, 1975. 318p.
A38.5, A57.1

"...about the power Washington lawyers wield over the government of the United States ... do ethical principles require a lawyer to temper zeal for his client's interest with concern for the public good? ... do lawyers practicing in the national capital have any special responsibilities to the public interest?" Daniel D. Polsby, Michigan Law Rev. 74:148 (1975). See also Bruce Wasserstein and Mark J. Green, eds, With justice for some; an indictment of the law by young advocates (1970).

1918

HANDLER, JOEL F. The lawyer and his community, the practicing bar in a middle-sized city. Madison, Univ. of Wisconsin Press, 1967. 224p.
A57.1

See also Burton A. Weisbrod, Joel F. Handler and Neil K. Kamesar, Public interest law; an economic and institutional analysis (1978).

1919

HAZARD, GEOFFREY C. JR., ed. Law in a changing America. Englewood Cliffs, Prentice-Hall, 1968. 207p.
A27.5, A57.7

"Each essay concerns some aspect of the way the legal profession is trained and functions. None are particularly complimentary to the bar. But self-serving commendations seldom bring about serious introspection." Neil A. Jackson, American Univ. Law Rev. 18:475 (1969). See also the author's Ethics in the practice of law (1978). [A2.5]

1920

HOFFMAN, PAUL. Lions in the street; the inside story of the great Wall Street law firms. N.Y., Saturday Review Press, 1973. 244p.
A6.5, A25.5, A35.5, A43.5, A57.1

"...a gossipy collection of anecdotes interspersed with data available in Martindale Hubbell." Richard W. Tomeo, Connecticut Bar Jl 48:193 (1974). See also this author's Tiger in the court (1973) about United States Attorney Herbert J. Stern; also 'What the hell is justice'; the life and times of a criminal lawyer (1974) about Jack Evsevoff; also Courthouse (1979) about the New York City criminal courts. [A57.1]. For a stimulating and balanced view, see James B. Stewart, The partners; inside America's most powerful law firms (1983).

1921

HOLLANDER, BARNETT. The English bar; a priesthood: the tribute of an American lawyer. London, Bowes & Bowes, 1965, 1964. 70p.
A57.1

Provides a great deal of factual information on what it is to practice law in England.

1922

HORSKY, CHARLES A. The Washington lawyer; a series of lectures ... Boston, Little, Brown, 1952. 179p. +
A28, A64

An engaging volume describing the activities of attorneys whose "function, broadly is that of principal interpreter between government and private person, explaining to each the need, desires and demands of the others. His corollary function is that of seeking to adjust the conflicts that inevitably arise." Activities in connection with legislation or lobbying, and activities with administrative agencies are discussed. See Geo. Law Jl 41:453 (1953).

1923

JACKSON, ROBERT H. The call for a liberal bar. In Nat. Law Guild Q. 1:88 (1938). A52 +

"Made a profound and permanent inpression on me when I was a law student." Prof. Wm. P. Murphy, Univ. of Miss.

[1924 saved]

1925

JAMES, MARLISE. The people's lawyers. N.Y., Holt, Rinehart & Winston, 1973. 368p.
A57.1

Roger Baldwin, Leonard Boudin, Mel Wulf, Anthony Amsterdam, C.B.King, Charles Garry, D'Army Bailey, Jerome Cohen. Covers civil rights, poverty lawyers, Indian litigation, etc.

1926

JOHNSTONE, QUINTON and DAN HOBSON. Lawyers and their work, an analysis of the legal profession in the United States and England. Indianapolis, Bobbs-Merrill, 1967.
A38.5, A57.1

An interesting comparison of English and American legal systems. Also covers title insurance, specialization, standardization, legal services, and bar admission.

1927

KIRK, HARRY. Portrait of a profession; a history of the solicitor's profession, 1100 to the present day. London, Oyez, 1976. 218p.
A43.5

1928

KUTNER, LUIS. I, the lawyer. N.Y., Dodd, Mead, 1966.
A57.1

1929

LASSERS, WILLARD J. Scapegoat justice: Lloyd Miller and thefailure of the American legal system. Bloomington, Indiana Univ. Press, 1973. 234p.
A57.1

1930

LEONARD, WALTER J. Black lawyers. Senna and Shih, 1977.
A35.5, A57.1

See also Robert Spearman et al, A step toward equal

justice: programs to increase black lawyers in the South (1974); also George Lynn Cross, Blacks in white colleges (1975) [A57.1].

1931

LIEBERMAN, JETHRO K. Crisis at the bar; lawyers' unethical ethics and what to do about it. N.Y., W.W.Norton & Co., 1978. 247p.
A29.5

"...Lieberman's anecdotal, colorful style encourages emotional rather than thoughtful responses." Peter G. Glenn, Texas Law Rev. 57:307 (1979). Mr. Lieberman also wrote The litigious society (1981).

1932

LOVE, ALBERT and JAMES SAXON CHILDERS, eds. Listen to leaders in law. N.Y., Holt, Rinehart and Winston, 1963. 332p.
A57.1, A57.7

Felix Frankfurter, Erwin Griswold, Dillon Anderson, John V. Hunter III, Edward Bennett Williams, Paul Carrington, Philip C. Jessup, Arthur J. Goldberg, Edward S. Silver, Whitney North Seymour, Peter Woodbury, John K. Carlock, Florence M. Kelley, Walter V. Schaefer, Harrison Tweed, Herman Phleger. See E.J.Dimock, A.B.A.Jl 49:679 (1963).

1933

MCCARTY, DWIGHT G. Law office management. N.Y., Prentice Hall, 1955. 525p. +
A62

First published in 1926, this is a working manual for businesslike office management. McCarty tells you how to choose the location of your law office, how to overcome objections of a client to your bill, how to do research for a brief, interview clients, write effective letters, and how to economize in the office. For a current volume in this area see Frank Arentowicz, Jr. and Ward Bower, Law office automation and technology (looseleaf 1981).

1934

MACKINNON, F.B. Contingent fees for legal services. Aldine Publishing Co., 1964. 232p.
A25.5

1935

MARKS, F. RAYMOND, KIRK LESWING, AND BARBARA A. FORTINSKY. The lawyer, the public, and professional responsibility. Chicago, American Bar Foundation, 1972. 305p.
A29.5

The results of interviews with lawyers as to the efficacy of public interest law firms, pro bono departments and other efforts to serve the non corporate client.

1936

MELLINKOFF, DAVID. The conscience of a lawyer. St. Paul, West, 1973. 304p.
A25.5, A43.5

Preface: ...a celebrated Victorian whodunit, in which you have the details of the murder, discovery, arrest, a man on trial for his life, examination and cross-examination, speeches to the jury; verdict.[Courvoisier's case - the limits of a lawyer's obligation to his client].

1937

MEYER, MARTIN. The lawyers. N.Y., Harper & Row, 1967. 586p.
A2.5, A6.5, A27.5, A35.5, A36, A38.5, A43.5, A49, A53, A57.1, A57.7, A71.5

"Mr. Mayer has set out to update ancient and bitter complaints against the lawyers; they are venal, rapacious, corrupt, faithless, ignorant, trouble-making, fee-splitting hypocrites. He has his heroes, notably Chief Justice Warren who must blush at finding himself heralded as a sort of demi-god walking earth." David Mellinkoff, U.C.L.A. Law Rev. 15:1075 (1968). And see A.P. Herbert, Uncommon law ... (1977), Introduction, for the perils of not checking the substance of a citation.

1938

MILLER, CLAUDE R. Practice of law ...Chicago, Callaghan, 1946. 300p. * +
A26, A28, A43

Sets out a comprehensive picture of the kind of professional life that lawyers lead in administrative, corporation and private practice. Covers location of practice, office management, securing business. Two introductory chapters investigate the background of law and study and teaching methods. [A43].

1939

NADER, RALPH and MARK GREEN, eds. Verdicts on lawyers. N.Y., Crowell, 1976. 341p. A43.5, A57.1

"One theme that pervades the book is the duty of the [legal] profession to provide legal services for the public." Howard W. Brill, Arkansas Law Rev. 30:382 (1976).

1940

NATIONAL ASSOCIATION FOR LAW PLACEMENT. Class of ____ employment report [annual]
A6.5

1941

PHILLIPS, ORIE L. Conduct of judges and lawyers; a study of professional ethics, discipline, and disbarment, [with] Philbrick McCoy. Los Angeles, Calif. Published for the Survey of the Legal Profession by Parker, 1952 [i.e., 1953.] 247p. +
A39

Attempts to consider the ethical problems incident to the functions of the advocate and the magistrate. See Columbia Law Rev. 54:147 (1954).

1942

POWELL, ARTHUR G. I can go home again. Chapel Hill, Univ. of N.C. Press, 1943. 301p. * +
A35, A44, A59

A lively story of a country lawyer's life. See Justice Jacksons review in A.B.A.J1 30:136 (1944) [A44].

1943

REDDEN, KENNETH R. Career planning in the law. Indianapolis, Bobbs-Merrill [1951.] 194p. * +
A1, A8, A14, A19, A20, A27, A28, A39, A41, A43, A49, A56, A63, A68, A72

A preview of opportunities in the field of law with practical guidance toward planning a career. [A39] A description is given of the opportunities for lawyers in government service as well as private practice, business and publishing.

1944

____. So you want to be a lawyer! A vocational guidance manual. Indianapolis, Bobbs-Merrill [1951.] 125p. * +
A1, A2, A8, A14, A19, A20, A27, A28, A33, A39, A40, A41, A43, A44, A49, A54, A56, A59, A63, A67, A68, A72

This is designed to assist a student to determine whether to study law. Information concerning what lawyers do, their income, and their education is set forth. [A59]

Also outlines the personal requirements necessary for the profession. This is now dated. Consult more recent books listed in this section.

1945

REDLICH, NORMAN. Professional responsibility; a problem approach. 2d ed. Boston, Little, Brown, 1983. 267p.
A29.5

Each problem is related to the Code of Professional Responsibility or to the Model Rules of Professional Conduct. An intellectually stimulating approach to teaching professional responsibility.

1946

ROBINSON, EDWARD S. Law and the lawyers. N.Y., Macmillan, 1935. 348p. +
A11

Sets forth the reactions of a professional psychologist to some of the underlying problems involved in the ordering of human affairs through law. Law and thinking about law must be drastically modified to take account of the teaching of modern science and especially the teachings of psychology. See Harvard Law Rev. 49:666 (1936).

1947

ROSENTHAL, DOUGLAS E. Lawyer and client: who's in charge? N.Y., Russell Sage Foundation, 1974. 228p.
A57.1

A case study of the lawyer-client relationship in the making of personal injury claims with particular emphasis on the need for a participatory role of the client so that he will have more control over his fate.

1948

ROWE, CLAUDE W. How and where lawyers get practice ...Durham, N.C., Judiciary Pub. Co. [1955.] 212p. +
A19

Answers of 780 lawyers to the question "How and where do lawyers get practice?" Also contains the results of discussion and conference with 1500 lawyers, law school deans, judges, district attorneys, senators, congressmen, governors, and other officials. See also Edward J. Reisner, How many lawyers can dance on the head of a pin? The supply and demand for lawyers, Wisconsin Bar Bulletin 51:15 (May 1978) [A6.5].

1949

SHAFFER, THOMAS L. and ROBERT S. REDMOUNT. Lawyers, law students, and people. Colorado Springs, Shepards, 1977. 252p.
A6.5, A71.8

A summary of statistical findings on the backgrounds of law students; their attitudes, skills, and problems; sex and age, classroom experience; law school climate. Brief summary of legal education in general, verbatim classroom discussion, etc.

1950

SCHWARTZ, BERNARD, ed. American law; the third century. South Hackensack, N.Y.U. School of Law, by F.B.Rothman, 1976. 454p.
A31.7

"The participants fit into two groups: first, lawyers, law professors and judges who had been asked to discuss various topics with emphasis on the legal problems and developments of the next century ... and secondly, non-lawyers who discussed the law from the viewpoint of their particular areas of expertise." H.J.Bourguignon, American Jl of Legal History 22:328 (1978).

1951

SCHWARTZ, MURRAY L., ed. Law and the American future. Englewood Cliffs, Prentice-Hall, 1976. 212p.
A6.5, A38.5, A43.5

Background papers for the American Assembly on Law and a Changing Society II, which met at Stanford University Law School, June 26-9, 1975.

1952

SELECTED READINGS ON THE LEGAL PROFESSION. St.Paul, West, 1962. 565p.
A29.5

"...a well integrated body of material, carefully selected, wisely edited, and arranged in a logical and interesting manner. ...a remarkable collection of writings describing the legal profession, the various tasks and services which lawyers perform, and the many difficult problems of a moral and ethical nature which are indigenous to the practice of law." Milton D. Green,

Temple Law Q. 37:365 (1964). "Assembled under the auspices of a committee of the Association of American Law Schools."

1953

SMIGEL, ERWIN O. The Wall Street lawyer. N.Y., Free Press, 1964. 369p.
A6.5, A36, A38.5, A57.1

"...a sociological collection of facts, statistics, and other data about large law firms ... The recurrent theme ... is that the large law firm is a bureaucracy ... The author seems to miss the spirit, camaraderie and excitement of team play." Arthur H. Dean, California Law Rev. 52:1062 (1964).

1954

STRONG, KLINE D. and ARBEN O. CLARK. Law office management. St.Paul, West, 1974. 422p.
A25.5

1955

STRYKER, LLOYD P. The art of advocacy; a plea for the renaissance of the trial lawyer. N.Y., Simon & Schuster, 1954. 306p. +
A15, A27, A47, A49, A58, A64

A plea for recognition and rejuvenation of the art of advocacy by a late great advocate. Part I, "The Trial," carries the lawyer from his first contact with his client through the actual trial of the action, unveiling to the uninitiated the mysteries, demands and challenges incident to the trial of any cause. See N.Y.U. Law Rev. 29:1309 (1954).

1956

TRACY, JOHN E. The successful practice of law. N.Y., Prentice-Hall, 1947. 470p. +
A1, A10, A12, A14, A19, A23, A27, A29, A30, A40, A43, A45, A49, A55, A56, A62, A63, A65, A68, A71

A practical guide for the young lawyer entering practice. Suggestions are given on such topics as securing clients, fees, drafting instruments, trial techniques and problems of evidence. Presents a good picture of the day-to-day business of practising law. [A43].

1957

UNITED STATES. Bureau of Labor Statistics. Occupational outlook handbook. Wash., D.C., GPO, 1982-83. 484p.
A6.5

1958

UTLEY, FRANCES. Where do I go from here? A career planning manual for lawyers. Chicago, American Bar Association, 1973. 142p.
A6.5

1959

VANDERBILT, ARTHUR T. Forensic persuasion. The 1950 John Randolph Tucker Memorial Lectures delivered at Washington and Lee Univ., Lexington, Va., Journalism Laboratory Press of Wash. and Lee Univ. 1950. 58p. +
A19

Dean Williams of Washington and Lee states in the Preface that this "Contains a wealth of valuable information, suggestions, and advice which will be useful and interesting not only to the law student and recent graduate, but also to the seasoned lawyer." Contents: The six factors in the work of the advocate, the substance and style of arguing an appeal as well as mannerisms, gesturesand voice - opening a case, summation and motions -training for advocacy.

1960

WARKOV, SEYMOUR and JOSEPH ZELAN. Lawyers in the making. Chicago, Aldine, 1965. 180p.
A43.5, A57.1

A statistical study of college graduates to determine the factors that influenced their choice of a career field.

1961

WEYRAUCH, WALTER O. The personality of lawyers; a comparative study of subjective factors in law. Based on interviews with German lawyers. New Haven, Yale Univ. Press, 1964. 316p.
A24.5

1962

WIENER, FREDERICK B. Effective appellate advocacy; how to brief and argue a case on appeal, including examples of winning briefs and oral arguments. N.Y., Prentice-Hall, 1950. 591p. +
A15, A49

An altogether admirable book in which the author draws on his many years of experience in arguing appeals before the U.S. Supreme Court to give a lively and interesting account of appellate advocacy. Recommended for law students preparing moot court work. See N.Y.U. Law Rev. 25:933 (1950). See also his Briefing and arguing Federal appeals ...(1967).

1963

WILKIN, ROBERT N. The spirit of the legal profession. New Haven, Pub. for the College of Law of the Ohio State Univ. by Yale Univ. Press, 1938. 178p. +
A39, A40, A45

A pleasantly phrased exposition of the legal profession's traditional attitude toward the legal profession from the Roman Republic to the present. See Columbia Law Rev. 39:901 (1939).

1964

ZEHNLE, RICHARD H. Specialization in the legal profession. Chicago, American Bar Foundation, 1975. 48p.
A57.1

PREJUDICE

1975

ALLPORT, GORDON W. The nature of prejudice. Cambridge, Mass., Addison-Wesley Pub. Co., 1954. 537p. * +
A8

A survey of group prejudices based on ten years of research. Emphasis is placed on the social, legal and economic aspects of the problem and the psychological reasons of hatred and conflict.

PREVENTIVE LAW

1985

BROWN, LOUIS M. and EDWARD A. DAUER. Planning by lawyers; materials on a nonadversarial legal process. Mineola, Foundation Press, 1978. 942p.
A29.5

"His principle has been that there is a world of law that is never reached by courts and legislatures, or is reached only in mediated, indirect and refracted ways...methods and principles in law office practice..." Thomas L. Shaffer, Southern California Law Rev. 51:761 (1978). See also Jerold S. Auerbach, Justice without law? (1983). [See also No. 1911]. See the Preventive Law Reporter, a bimonthly publication, that stresses the nonadversary approach to law.

PROBLEM SOLVING
SEE CREATIVE THINKING

PROCEDURE
See also CIVIL PROCEDURE

2000

KARLEN, DELMAR. Primer of procedure. Madison, Wis., Campus Publ Co., 1950. 525p. +
A19, A71

A real "primer" which provides the beginning law student in procedure a working tool that will answer thousands of questions that go unanswered in the more advanced and specialized procedure books on the assumption that the point is so simple it is not worthy of treatment. They are answered with clarity, clearness and comprehension. See A.B.A.Jl 37:280 (1951).

2001

MILLAR, ROBERT W. Civil procedure of the trial court in historical perspective. N.Y., Published by the Law Center of N.Y.U., for the National Conference of Judicial Councils, 1952. 534p. +
A56

A general account of the evolution of court procedure from Anglo-Saxon times to the present, in which not only the history but the present status of procedure from summons to execution in the state, federal and English courts is clearly presented.

2002

NEW YORK UNIVERSITY, SCHOOL OF LAW. David Dudley Field; centenary essays celebrating one hundred years of legal reform, edited by Alison Reppy, with an introd. by Russell D. Niles. N.Y., N.Y.U. School of Law, 1949. 400p. +
A18, A19, A43, A56

Lectures in honor of "the father of American legal reform" summarizing codification and procedural reform during the past century. [See note for No. 1661].

PROOF

SEE EVIDENCE

PSYCHOLOGY AND LAW

2010

CHARKIN, SAMUEL. The mind stealers: psychosurgery and mind control. Boston, Houghton Mifflin, 1978. 228p.
A57.1

The predilections of Orwell's Nineteen Eighty-Four are suggested by research into the mysteries of the brain.

2011

MCCARTY, DWIGHT G. Psychology and the law. Englewood Cliffs, Prentice-Hall, 1960. 463p.
A31.7

"This book deals with psychology as it relates to law and the work of the lawyer. ...Many chapters of this book are full of trial hints, practice suggestions, and ideas for the lawyer which are worth careful consideration. They are not psychology in the technical sense, but they have a lot of common sense. ...Whatever the ideas may be called, they are useful and presented in a style that will intrigue many readers." Mason Ladd, Iowa Law Rev. 48:220 (1962).

2012

MARSHALL, JAMES. Law and psychology in conflict. Indianapolis, Bobbs-Merrill, 1966. 119p. 2d ed. 1980. 173p.
A31.7

Mr. Marshall suggests that "the legal profession [is] unwilling to accept the evidence offered by contemporary physical and social sciences that the fact-finding machinery of modern judicial procedure is extremely inaccurate. ...Mr. Marshall has reaffirmed that law and psychology are in conflict; the question today is how may we best approach a conciliation." Joseph G. Cook, Tennessee Law Rev. 34:722 (1967).

2013

TAPP, JUNE LOUIN and **FELICE J. LEVING**, eds. Law, justice, and the individual in society; psychological and legal issues. N.Y., Holt, Rinehart and Winston, 1977. 446p.
A31.7

"...(1) law as a socializing agency, (2) conceptions of justice as a matter of cognitive social development, (3) how people come to be socialized to perceive and behave in terms of legal systems, and (4) decision-making in legal contexts." Contributors: Johanneas Andenaes, Harold Berman, James Davis, Paul Freund, Lawrence Friedman, Lon Fuller, Sanford Kadish, Harry Kalven, Lawrence Kohlberg, Stuart Macaulay, Paul Meehl, Soia Mentschikoff, Ross Parke, Milton Rokeach, David O. Sears, Elaine Walster, Phillip Zimbardo, Franklin Zimring, and June Tapp. Michael J. Saks, Michigan Law Rev. 77:892 (1979).

PUBLIC OPINION

2025

DICEY, ALBERT V. Lectures on the relation between law and public opinion in England during the nineteenth century. 2d ed. London, Macmillan, 1930. 506p. * +
A8, A30

Holdsworth considers this book a work of genius, and a model for legal historians. Dicey takes three great currents of opinion - the Old Toryism (1800-1830), Benthamism or Individualism (1825-1870) and Collectivism

(1860-1900) - and shows how they have influenced the course of legislation during the nineteenth century. Pound adds that it is an economic-political interpretation in terms of public opinion. Also in paperback (1962). See also the author's Law of the Constitution in England in the 20th century (1959). [A74] Also, Richard A. Cosgrove, The rule of law: Albert Venn Dicey, Victorian jurist (1980). See also Walter Lippman, Public Opinion (1922).

2026

MacDOUGALL, CURTIS S. Understanding public opinion. N.Y., Prentice-Hall, 1952. 698p. * +
A8

MacDougall states that "public opinion is the expression on a controversial point within an interest group" and then bases his discussion on this definition - its major principles, relation to culture and media. See Christian Century 69:561.

READING and COMPREHENSION

Lawyers must have the skill of comprehension which involves concentration and effective recollection in reading and listening, perception of meaning conveyed by verbal symbols. [A63].

Read the following for this purpose:

2035

ADLER, MORTIMER. How to read a book; the art of getting a liberal education. N.Y., Simon & Schuster [c1940.] 398p. +
A43, A49

2036

CENTER, STELLA S. The art of book reading. N.Y., Scribner, 1952. 208p. * +
A63

2037

EMSLEY, BERT. Speaking and listening, [with] F. E. Jones [and] W. M. Timmons. N.Y., American Book Co., 1943. 138p. * +
A63

2038

WRENN, C. G. How to read rapidly and well, a manual of silent reading, [with] Luella Cole. Stanford, Stanford Univ. Press, 1935. 15p. * + A63

REAL PROPERTY

2050

BABCOCK, RICHARD. The zoning game; municipal practices and policies. Madison, Univ. of Wisconsin Press, 1966. 202p.
A53

This is one of many books in this burgeoning field. The subtle political and social effects of zoning are only hinted at in the decisions that reach Federal and state courts.

2051

GLENDON, MARY ANN. The new family and the new property. Toronto, Butterworths, 1981. 269p.
A29.5

Property law is no longer a simple recitation of the Rule in Shelley's Case as succintly laid out in Cornelius J. Moynihan's _Introduction to the law of real property_ (1962) or W. Barton Leach's Perpetutities in a nutshell, Harvard Law Rev. 51:638 (1938) reprinted with additions in Leach, _Cases and text on the law of wills_ (2d ed. 1960). It's further implications can be seen in this important book reviewed by Joan H. Hollinger, Michigan Law Rev. 81:1065 (1983).

2052

HAAR, CHARLES M. and LANCE LIEBMAN. Property and law. Boston, Little, Brown, 1977. 1144p.
A29.5

This property casebook "is attractively designed, readable, and dotted with photographs and maps which the student eye can rest upon and the student mind can ponder ...The book is divided into six parts: private property, estates and the landlord-tenant estate, controlling the future, land in commerce, shared use, and public property." Michigan Law Rev. 77:939 (1979).

2053

POLLOCK, SIR FREDERICK. Land laws. 3d ed., London, Macmillan, 1896. 233p. * +
A35

Pollock has a faculty for investing the driest of matters with interest. A student could not desire a more agreeable introduction to the technical treatises on the law of real property. See Harvard Law Rev. 9:552 (1896).

RHETORIC

See also FORENSIC ENGLISH; LANGUAGE

Language is the lawyer's working tool. The lawyer must obtain skill in expression: adequate vocabulary, familiarity with modern usage, grammatical correctness, organized presentation, conciseness and clarity of statement in writing and speaking. [A63].

Read the following for this purpose:

2060

BENDER, JAMES F. How to talk well. N.Y., McGraw Hill [1949.] 262p. * +
A63

2061

CICERO, MARCUS TULLIUS. De oratore. (In many editions.) +
A47

See note for No. 2065.

2062

FEARNSIDE, W. WARD AND WILLIAM B. HOLTNER. Fallacy; the counterfeit of argument. Englewood Cliffs, Prentice-Hall, 1959. 218p.
A49

2063

FLESCH, RUDOLF F. The art of plain talk ...foreword by Lymon Bryson ...N.Y., Harper & Bros. [1946.] 210p. * +
A28

Gives a formula for effective speaking and writing. [See also No. 1455].

2064

HAZLITT, HENRY. Thinking as a science. Los Angeles, Nash Publishing Co., 1969. 162p.; N.Y., Dutton, 1915. 251p.
A49

2065

QUINTILIANUS, MARCUS. Institutes of oratory; or education of an orator. (In many editions). +
A47

This great work and Cicero's well-known dialogue de Oratore (See No. 2061) are amazing repositories of information and suggestion on the art of pleading ...It is remarkable to find how fully alive were these ancient experts to all the refinements of advocacy. See Lord Macmillan, Law and other things (1937, 1971) p.207.

ROMAN LAW
SEE ALSO ANCIENT AND PRIMITIVE LAW

2075

BUCKLAND, W.W. and **ARNOLD D. MCNAIR.** Roman law and common law. 2d ed. by F.H. Lawson. N.Y., Cambridge Univ. Press, 1952. 439p.
A24.5

"[Jolowicz's Historical Introduction to the Study of Roman Law and the Buckland book] are not merely reprints lightly revised after some two decades, but contain a great many instructive and illuminating additions in which either the scientific progress of the intervening years is taken into consideration (as in the case of Jolowicz) or valuable supplements are offered to complete the picture previously given (as in the case of Lawson)." Adolf Berger, Columbia Law Rev. 53:758 (1953).

2076

JOLOWICZ, HERBERT F. Historical introduction to the study of Roman law ...Cambridge, [Eng.] Univ. Press, 1939. 549p. 3d ed. with Barry Nicholas. 1972. 528p. * +
A7, A8

An excellent and well written historical introduction to Roman law development.

2077

____. Roman foundations of modern law. N.Y., Oxford Univ. Press, 1957. 217p.; Greenwood Press, 1978.
A24.5

The author states: [This book] will attempt, with a minimum of legal history, to set out the outline of what appears in the Corpus Juris and then the highest common factor of the deductions which European lawyers have made from the text, together with some of the main variations." See W.A.J. Watson, Harvard Law Rev. 71:1181 (1958).

2078

WOLFF, HANS J. Roman law, an historical introduction. Norman, Univ. of Oklahoma Press [1951.] 260p. * +
A16

This was recommended by Dean Hebert of Louisiana State for the purpose of providing a more balanced selection in the list and to give some indication of the Roman legal culture which is not elsewhere referred to in the list.

SCIENCE

2085

DARWIN, CHARLES. Origin of species by means of natural selection; or the preservation of favored races in the struggle for life. (First published in 1859, now available in many editions).+ A19

This was an original presentation, and has had such far-reaching influence that the period after its publication was known as the Darwinian era in biology. His theory that man was a product of the organic realm alone created disbelief in many established religious precepts. Darwinian concepts have been transferred from the biological to the ethical, political, economic and sociological fields. See Encyc. Soc. Sci.

2086

WHITEHEAD, ALFRED N. Science and the modern world. N.Y., Macmillan, 1926. 296p. + A59

A study of some aspects of Western culture during the past three centuries, insofar as they have been influenced by the development of science. Professor Whitehead, a distinguished mathematical philosopher, analyzes the reactions of science in forming the background of thought of successive generations, studying in particular the influences at work in the 17th, 18th and 19th centuries. See Book Rev. Dig. 1926. [See also annotation to No. 911].

SECURITIES

2095

KRIPKE, HOMER. The SEC and corporate disclosure; regulation in search of a purpose. N.Y., Harcourt, Brace, Jovanovich, 1979. 334p. A31.7

"It is not necessary to agree with every facet of Kripke's admirably literate argument in order to share his disaffection with a policy of administration of the federal securities laws. Enforcing ever more detailed historical disclosure with respect to each registered company seems, after almost a half-century, to have come to be considered a sort of end in itself." Patrick A. McGraw, Univ. of Toledo Law Rev. 11:705 (1980). No mention of securities would be complete without including Louis Loss. See his Fundamentals of securities regulation (1983). See also Joel Seligman, The transformation of Wall

Street, a history of the SEC and modern corporate finance (1982).

SEMANTICS

See FORENSIC ENGLISH

SEX and THE LAW

2100

PLOSCOWE, MORRIS. Sex and the law. N.Y., Prentice-Hall [1951.] 310p. +
A10

A diagnosis of the legal problems involved by a former magistrate and law teacher. Judge Ploscowe analyzes the methods of our courts and legislatures in attempting to solve these problems. He also traces the development of legal and social thinking concerning sex and explains what makes sexual behavior criminal. Sexual mores have changed considerably since this book was written. No successor has been written probably because the scene has not yet lent itself to description.

SOCIOLOGY AND THE LAW

2110

BLACK, DONALD and MAUREEN MILESKI, eds. The social organization of law. N.Y., Seminar Press, 1973. 405p.
A43.5

Essays on natural law, dispute settlement, contracts, legal services, custom, witchcraft, etc. Essays cover United States, Israel, E. Africa, etc. Essayists include W. Chambliss, L. Nader, R. Nisbet.

2111

CAVANAUGH, JAMES J. The lawyer in society. N.Y., Philosophical Library, 1963. 82p.
A43.5

Pithy essays on the lawyer as entrepreneur, social engineer, arbiter, leader, advocate, partisan, judge, observer, in literature and as non-lawyer.

2112

DAVIS, F. JAMES, HENRY H. FOSTER JR, C.RAY JEFFERY and E. EUGENE DAVIS. Society and the law. N.Y., Free Press, 1962. 488p.
A29.5

"Two sociologists, a law professor, and a practicing attorney have collaborated to write a book to persuade the student of sociology that law is relevant to an understanding of society and the student of law that it is always pertinent to look at the social purposes and consequences of a legal rule." See also William M. Evan, ed. Law and sociology; exploratory essays (N.Y., Free Press, 1962) reviewed by Yehezkel Dror, Harvard Law Rev. 77:398 (1963); and Edwin M. Schur, Law and society; a sociological view (N.Y., Random House, 1968) reviewed by Jack P. Gibbs, Law and Society Rev. 3:617 (1969).

2113

FRIEDMAN, LAWRENCE M. The legal system; a social science perspective. Russell Sage, 1975. 338p.
A36, A43.5

See Klaus A. Ziegert's review in Law and Society Rev. 12:151 (1977) in which the following books are reviewed: The Friedman book, Donald Black, The Behavior of Law (1976); Roberto Mangabeira Unger, Law in Modern Society (1976); and Adam Podgorecki, Law and Society (1974). Mr. Friedman (with Stewart Macaulay) edited Law and the Behavioral Sciences 2d ed. (1969) reviewed by Elliott Currie, Yale Law Jl 81:134 (1971). He also wrote Law and Society; an introduction (1977). Also (with Robert V. Percival) The roots of justice (1982).

2114

FRIEDMANN, WOLFGANG. Law in a changing society. N.Y., Columbia Univ. Press, 1972. (also published in London, Stevens, 1959. 503p.).
A25.5, A43.5

Preface: I claim no more than to have dealt with major social phenomena of our time, as a challenge to which we must seek a solution, and which we cannot ignore by pretending that they are not the lawyer's province, but that of the legislator, the politician, the sociologist, or the economist." See also Roscoe Pound, Minnesota Law Rev. 46:117(1961).

SPEECH
See RHETORIC

STUDY OF LAW
See also LEGAL EDUCATION

2124

AKERS, RONALD L. and **RICHARD HAWKINS**, eds. Law and control in society. E.C., Prentice-Hall, 1975. 383p.
A43.5

2125

CANADA, RALPH, et al. Surviving the first year of law school. Dover, MA, Lord Pub. Co., 1978. 160p.
A27.5, A38.5

Hints on getting through law school by some Harvard Law School graduates.

2126

CROSS, ALFRED RUPERT NEALE. Precedent in English law. 3d ed. Oxford, Clarendon Press, 1977. 242p.
A29.5

"[A] valuable book for both law students and laymen wishing to gain a knowledge of case law ... [T]he only systematic and comprehensive study of the English doctrine of precedent to be published and any lawyer will benefit from it. The account is clear and readable so a layman should be able to follow it." J. Levin, Modern Law Rev. 33:105 (1970).

2127

DELANEY, JOHN. How to brief a case: an introduction to legal reasoning. N.Y., John Delaney Publications, 1983. 133p.
A29.5

Explains the techniques of briefing within the framework of first year work. Professor Delaney's mission is to increase student's competence and confidence in the classroom. He is also the author of How to do your best on law school exams (1982).

2128

DOBBYN, JOHN F. So you want to go to law school. Rev. 1st ed. St. Paul, West, 1976. 206p.
A1, A43.5

2129

EHRLICH, THOMAS and GEOFFREY C. HAZARD JR., eds. Going to law school? Readings on a legal career. Boston, Little, Brown, 1975. 246p.
A2.5, A6.5, A27.5, A35.5, A38.5, A57.1

Many of the books in this section reflect the soul searching of the 1950s and 1960s as to the relevance of lawyering. See, particularly, Duncan Kennedy, Legal education and the reproduction of hierarchy; a polemic against the system (1983). One should also read the drafts of the Harvard Law School, Committee on Educational Planning and Development (April 21, 1982) and Harvard President Bok's 1983 Report to the Overseers of Harvard College. See also Professor Hazard's Competing aims of legal education, North Dakota Law Rev. 59:533 (1983).

2130

ELLIOTT, SHELDON D. Opportunities in a law career. N.Y., Educational Books, Div'n of Universal Pub. & Dist. Corp., 1969 Rev. ed. 112p.
A43.5

New edition by Gary A. Munneke. [A6.5] See also Paul Sarnoff, Careers in the legal profession (1970). [A57.1]

2131

EPSTEIN, ELLIOT M., et al. Barron's guide to law school. Woodbury, Barrons' Educational Series, [annual]
A6.5

See also A. Glotzer, Monarch's complete guide to law schools (1982); also S. F. Goldfarb, Inside the law schools (Rev. 3d ed. 1983); also A. Shapiro, etc. Getting into law schools (1979) [A57.1].

2132

FARNSWORTH, E. ALLEN. An introduction to the legal system of the United States. Dobbs Ferry, Oceana, 1963. 184p.; 2d ed., 1983.
A43.5, A57.1

"...based on lectures given ... to foreign students abroad. Sources and Techniques includes an historical introduction and brief essays on legal education, the legal profession, the judicial system, case law, the legislative system, statutes and secondary authority. Much of this...despite exemplary brevity, is written so brilliantly that one is tempted to read it like a work of fiction. ...Organization and Substance, which includes chapters on classification, procedure, private law and public law, is open to easy criticism [as to] whether a description of a legal system...should be attempted in a space of some seventy pages." Albert A. Ehrenzweig, California Law Rev. 51:823 (1962).

2133

FULLER, LON L. Anatomy of the law. N.Y., Praeger, 1968. 122p.
A6.5, A25.5, A27.5, A49, A57.7, A71.5, A74

This book "effectuates its title not by being a complete description of the law's bones and muscles but rather in constituting a brilliant dissection of a few tissues. It is full of the perceptive and sensible observations for which the profession has been indebted to Professor Fuller since his Rosenthal lectures..."
Duquesne Law Rev. 7:(1968-9).

2134

GAVIT, BERNARD C. Introduction to the study of law. Brooklyn, Foundation Press, 1951. 388p. * +
A4, A6, A20, A28, A33, A38, A43, A49, A56, A60, A65, A72

Contains a brief examination of pre-legal and of legal education. It discusses the sourcees and forms of law, legal concepts and classifications, the judicial functions and process, procedure, the court systems, the legal profession and legal ethics. Useful for anyone who desires to know at least a little bit about our legal system. [A43].

2135

GOODHART, ARTHUR L. Determining the ratio decidendi of a case. (In Yale L. J. 40:161-183 (Dec. 1930); also in Vanderbilt, Studying Law, pp.493-525. * +
A19, A41

Law students and lawyers deal with the reports of decided cases. What do these cases mean legally or better still, what did the judge who wrote the opinion intend to say? This article is very helpful in that it sets up rules for finding the principle of a case. But see the critique in the Cross book [No. 2126].

2136

GRILLIOT, HAROLD J. Introduction to law and the legal system. 2d ed. Boston, Houghton Mifflin, 1979. 589p.
A43.5

2137

HAY, PETER. An introduction to United States law. Amsterdam, North-Holland, 1976. 232p.
A43.5

Similar to the Farnsworth book in purpose. [No. 2132].

2138

HOROWITZ, HAROLD and KENNETH KARST. Law, lawyers, and social change. Indianapolis, Bobbs-Merrill, 1969. 531p.

"A law school casebook for a course in what is commonly called 'legal process.' The authors [state] 'Every course in law school is a course in the legal process, reflecting the entire legal system as it comes to bear on a single subject area. Most courses, however, emphasize the development of the legal doctrine that governs their fields, and not the institutional process that produces the doctrine ... Our focus is institutional, not doctrinal ...'" Scott H. Bice, Duke Law Jl 1255 1970:(1970).

2139

HOWARD, CHARLES G. and ROBERT S. SUMMERS. Law, its nature, functions and limits. Englewood Cliffs, Prentice-Hall, 1965. 466p.
A24.5

"One tends to assume that [this book] was intended chiefly for the college undergraduate who may be, but probably is not, planning to attend law school. The broad appeal of the book invites consideration, however, of three other possible audiences: foreign graduate students who need a quick and comprehensive grounding in the American legal system, laymen who seek an understanding of the law apart from any formal course, and first-year law students in the regular curriculum." Texas Law Rev. 44:590 (1966). [See also Nos. 1700-1705].

2140

KINYON, STANLEY VAN E. How to study law and write law examinations ...St. Paul, Minn., West Pub. Co., 1940. 116p. 2d ed. 1951, 2d ed. rev. 1968. * + A43, A54

A brief summary of the objects and technique of law study under the casebook and textbook methods, as well as suggestions for writing law examinations in law school and for admission to the bar. [A54] Professor Kinyon's new edition of this work is called _Introduction to Law Study and Law Examinations in a Nutshell_ (1971). A1, A25.5, A38.5, A57.7, A71.8

2141

LEWIS, ALFRED J. Using law books. Dubuque, Iowa, Kendall/Hunt Pub. Co., 1976. 91p.
A57.7

A quaint step-by-step introduction to law books that, compared to most legal research books, has the advantage of brevity. His Using American law books (1983) is 171p. A more sophisticated approach is Christopher G. Wren and Jill Robinson Wren, The legal research manual; a game plan for legal research and analysis (1983).

2142

LLEWELLYN, KARL N. The bramble bush; on our law and its study. N.Y., Oceana Pub., 1951. 160p. * +
A1, A2, A2.5, A3, A6.5, A7, A8, A11, A12, A13, A14, A19, A20, A23, A24, A25.5, A26, A27, A27.5, A28, A29, A33, A34, A35.5, A36, A38, A39, A40, A41, A43, A43.5, A44, A47, A48, A48.5, A49, A50, A51, (1st year); A54, A55, (1st year); A56, A57, A57.1, A57.7, A60, A63, A66, A67, A68, A71, A71.5, A71.8,A72

A brilliant survey for students and lawyers of what law is and what legal education does and can do to make a person a lawyer. [A12] But see comment of Dean O'Meara of Notre Dame in editor's Preface to the first edition of this Dean's List (reprinted in this edition).

2143

MORGAN, EDMUND M. Introduction to the study of law, [with] Francis X. Dwyer. 2d ed. Chicago, Callaghan, 1948. 357p. * +
A6, A8, A9, A20, A28, A30, A38, A40, A41, A43, A49, A54, A56, A60, A71, A72

A terse summary of the court system, nature and sources of law, forms of action at common law, procedure and pleading; also material on how to read and abstract reported cases and how and where to find the law. [A54].

2144

MORRIS, CLARENCE. How lawyers think. Denver, A.Swallow, 1937, 1962. 144p.
A43.5

A standard work in the field. Mr. Morris has also written The Justification of the Law (1971) which was most favorably reviewed by W.F.Young, Jr. in Univ. of Pennsylvania Law Rev. 121:691 (1973).

2145

O'MEARA, JOSEPH. An introduction to law and how to study it. South Bend, Notre Dame Law School, 1973. 131p.
A2.5

2146

PICKERING, HAROLD G. Preview of law study. San Francisco, Harry B. Lake, 1965. 223p.
A27.5

2147

POST, CHARLES GORDON. An introduction to the law. Englewood Cliffs, Prentice-Hall, 1963. 185p.
A43.5

2148

SMITH, CHESTER H. How to answer law examinations. St. Paul, Minn., West Publishing Co. [1946.] 250p. +
A49

Sets up general principles for answering problem case type of examination which is prevalent in law schools and bar examinations. For more recent material see the Younger article in No. 1581; or, the Delaney book in No. 2127; or for a fictional account of exam-taking, see Nos. 897 and 930.

2149

STONE, FERDINAND F. Handbook of law study. N.Y., Prentice-Hall, 1952. 164p. * +
A1, A4, A14, A19, A20, A22, A23, A24, A27, A28, A31, A32, A33, A34, A39, A40, A41, A43, A49, A54, A56, A57.1, A59, A60, A63, A64, A67, A68, A70, A72

A brief, lively and informative guide for prospective and beginning law students. Written simply but realistically it presents a succinct account of the requirements of the legal profession, the rationale of legal education and the rules of the legal system. [A39] In the first edition of this work, the faculty of the Stanford Law School strongly urged each member of the first year class to read this work. [A28].

2150

STRICKLAND, RENNARD. How to get into law school. Rev. ed. N.Y., Hawthorn Books, 1977. 194p.
A25.5

2151

UNIVERSITY OF CHICAGO LAW SCHOOL. The study and practice of law. Chicago, [the author.] 1949. 56p. * + A43

A consideration of some of the factors involved in the choice of law as a career, among them: job opportunities open to lawyers, qualifications for admission to the bar, earning prospects of lawyers and selection of a law school. Comment is made on careers for lawyers in the international field and in the area of community service. [A43].

2152

VANDERBILT, ARTHUR T., ed. Studying law; selections from the writings of Albert J. Beveridge [and others. 2d ed. N.Y.] N.Y.U. Press, 1955. 753p. * +
A19, A28, A30, A31, A38, A40, A41, A43, A43.5, A47, A54, A56, A57.1, A65, A67, A70, A71.5

A very readable summary of the history of the common law, elements of law, reading of cases and interpretation of statutes, evidence in jury cases, problems of pre-legal education, and finding one's place in the legal profession. [A54].

Judge Vanderbilt suggested that after reading the Introduction and Chapter I, read Chapter III by Professor Smith, which he believed contained the best summary of the elements that go into the making of our modern system of law. Then go on to Chapter II by Zane to be skimmed through rather than memorized. Follow this by Chapter VIII by Wambaugh, the best thing ever written on the use of decisions and statutes. Chapters VI and VII are closely related to Chapter VIII and should be studied just as intently. Chapters X and XI may be read or not, but do not read Chapters IV, V and IX until you are in law school.

2153

WHITE, JAMES B. The study of law as an intellectual activity, Jl of Legal Education 32:1 (1982).
A24.5

"This talk was first given to entering students at the Univ. of Chicago Law School in 1976 and revised in 1977."

2154

WILLIAMS, GLANVILLE L. Learning the law. 11th ed. London, Stevens, 1982. 241p. +
A19, A27.5, A28, A43, A60

Although keyed to the needs of the English law student, this "rather unconventional" little book will solve many of the puzzling problems faced by the beginning law student. Excellent advice is given on what to study. Williams is also good on ascertaining the ratio decidendi of a case, and on precedents. There is also a good section on the literature of the law.

2155

WITKIN, B. E. Analysis of legal problems in law examinations. (In Ballantine's Problems in Law, 3d ed. St. Paul, West Pub. Co., 1949, pp1-39). +
A41

A treatment of the methods of analyzing and answering questions for law school and bar examination purposes.

2156

ZELERMYER, WILLIAM. Legal reasoning; the evolutionary process of law. Englewood Cliffs, Prentice-Hall, 1960. 174p.
A29.5

"...could serve as an introduction to what law school work is all about for those who are contemplating the study of law ... Too many students enter law school with only the vaguest idea of what they are undertaking..." Susan G. Fonner, Indiana Law Jl 36:255 (1961).

SUPREME COURT

See also CONSTITUTIONAL LAW

The United States Supreme Court as an institution. This section focuses more on the institutional role than the Constitutional role of the court. Readers are also referred to the topic "Biography" for readings in this vein.

2165

BAXTER, MAURICE G. Daniel Webster and the Supreme Court. Amherst, Massachusetts Univ. Press, 1966. 265p.
A43.5

2166

BIDDLE, FRANCIS B. Justice Holmes, natural law, and the Supreme Court. N.Y., Macmillan, 1961. 77p.
A43.5

2167

CLAYTON, JAMES E. The making of justice; the Supreme Court in action. N.Y., Dutton, 1964; Cornerstone Library, 1965 (c.1964). 319p. A43.5

2168

COX, ARCHIBALD. The Warren Court, constitutional decision as an instrument of reform. Cambridge, Harvard Univ. Press, 1968. 144p.
A43.5

Mr. Cox has also written _The Role of the Supreme Court in American Government_ (1976) reviewed by Patrick Higginbotham, A.B.A.Jl 62:962 (1976). The essays in this book cover the Watergate tapes, Marbury v. Madison, constitutional adjudication, school desegregation cases, and constitutionalism and politicalization. He has also written _Freedom of expression_ (1981).

2169

DONALDSON, KENNETH. Insanity inside out; the personal story behind the landmark Supreme Court decision. N.Y., Crown, 1976. 338p.
A57.1

2170

EQUAL JUSTICE UNDER LAW; The Supreme Court in American life. Rev. ed. Wash., D.C., Foundation of the Federal Bar Ass'n, 1975. 143p.
A29.5

"This fully illustrated, revised edition provides a treasure of background and information about our nation's highest court. What goes on both onstage and backstage is told. ...The scheme of the book is to describe in readable, nontechnical terms some thirty landmark decisions selected by a hundred-member advisory board." Arthur John Keeffe, A.B.A.Jl 61:1509 (1975).

2171

FRANK, JOHN P. Marble palace; the Supreme Court in American life. N.Y., Knopf, 1958. 302p.
A31.7

The author "has sought to assay the role of the Court in relation to the Congress, to the Executive Department, to the states, and to the individual members of the general populace. [In the 'Practicalities of Power'] the reader is given insights into the ways in which judicial decisions are influenced by the practical necessity of seeking judgments which can be enforced. ...[T]he book is a welcome testimonial to an important, but little-understood, American institution which deserves better treatment than it has usually received." Robert B. McKay, California Law Rev. 47:203 (1959). Mr. Frank's observations on judicial prose are worth the price of the book.

2172

FREUND, PAUL A. The Supreme Court of the United States, its business, purposes and performance. Cleveland, Meridian Books, 1961. 224p.
A27.5, A57.7, A71.5

"...an excellent analysis of the Court's role in our national life, ... also a guidepost in predicting future judicial behavior." William B. Gould, Washington Univ. Law Q. 1962:279.

2173

RODELL, FRED. Nine men. N.Y., Random House, 1955. 322p.

A cursory, curmudgeony, realist survey of the Court and its keepers.

2174

SCHUBERT, GLENDON. The judicial mind; the attitudes and ideologies of Supreme Court Justices. Evanston, Northwestern Univ. Press, 1965. 295p.
A29.5

"...how Supreme Court Justices decide cases. ... Schubert's statement of his theory and presentation of his empirical results occupy the first half of The Judicial Mind. The second half of the book is a breathless uphill spiraling of unscientific conjecture about judicial thinking ..." Douglas Rosenthal, Yale Law Jl 77:1432 (1968). Mr. Schubert subsequently wrote The Judicial Mind Revisited; Psychometric Analysis of Supreme Court Ideology (1974) reviewed by Robert J. Glennon, Jr. in A.B.A.Jl 61:1182 (1975).

2175

SCHWARTZ, BERNARD. Super Chief: Earl Warren and his Supreme Court - a judicial biography. N.Y., N.Y.U. Press, 1983. 853p.
A31.7

Drawing extensively on interviews, diaries, court documents, this book shows the pervasive influence Earl Warren had on the Supreme Court and our country. Professor Schwartz has "chronicled ... a blow-by-blow account of these competing strategies, and some complicating tactics, in the court's business during the fifteen terms that Warren presided over it." Geoffrey Marshall, Times Literary Supp., Oct. 28, 1983, p. 1175. [See also No. 308]. Professor Schwartz (with Stephan Lesher) also published Inside the Warren Court (1983), a shorter and popular version of Super Chief. See also Richard H. Sayler, Barry B. Boyer and Robert E. Gooding, eds., The Warren court; a critical analysis (1969). This book has essays by Anthony Lewis, Robert McKay, Robert L. Carter, Paul Kauper, A. Kenneth Pye, Henry Kalven, Jr., John MacKenzie, Theodore J. St. Antoine, Thomas E. Kauper, William M. Beaney, and Philip B. Kurland. See the review by Alpheus T. Mason, New York Law Forum, 15:986 (1969).

2176

SHOGAN, ROBERT. A question of judgment; the Fortas case and the struggle for the Supreme Court. Indianapolis, Bobbs-Merrill, 1972. 314p.
A31.7

"...an biography of Justice Fortas focusing on the events leading to his resignation from the Supreme Court. ... [a comparison with the circumstances surrounding Justice Black's membership in the Ku Klux Klan] ... Fortas' otherwise successful career is beclouded by the unhappy story ... of superior talent derailed on judicial impropriety." Daniel J. Meador, Univ. of Illinois Law Forum 1973:204.

2177

STRICKLAND, STEPHEN PARKS, ed. Hugo Black and the Supreme Court; a symposium. Indianapolis, Bobbs-Merrill, 1967. 365p.
A24.5

"If I am right in this, it is a reminder that the number of people with the gift of insight into either the Supreme Court or the judicial process is limited [only two of essays offer unusual insights]. ...a timely collection of views about one of the more memorable personalities to have sat on the nation's high bench." A.B.Dick Howard, Virginia Law Rev. 53:1660 (1967).

2178

STRUM, PHILIPPA. The Supreme Court and 'political questions'; a study in judicial evasion. Univ. of Alabama Press, 1974. 188p.
A24.5

"...The author ... appears to advocate unlimited judicial interference with the other branches." Gerald J. Clark, Suffolk Univ. Law Rev. 9:1549 (1975).

2179

TODD, A.L. Justice on trial; the case of Louis D. Brandeis. N.Y., McGraw-Hill, 1964. 275p.
A38.5

"...The story of the Brandeis nomination fight is a fascinating and instructive historical vignette which is retold in the present volume in a clear and perceptive narrative style ... This is a gripping story and it has a happy ending ..." Michael J. Silverberg, Utah Law Rev. 9:837 (1965).

2180

WILKINSON, J. HARVIE III. Serving justice; a Supreme Court clerk's view. N.Y., Charterhouse, 1974. 207p.
A57.1

See also this author's From Brown to Bakke: the Supreme Court and school integration: 1954-1978 (1979) [A57.1]; also John B. Oakley and Robert S. Thompson, Law clerks and the judicial process; perceptions of the qualities and functions of law clerks in American courts (1980). [A20.5]. [See also No. 1290].

2181

WOODWARD, BOB and SCOTT ARMSTRONG. The Brethren; inside the Supreme Court. N.Y., Simon and Schuster, 1979. 467p.
A1, A6.5, A35.5, A43.5

This book occasioned a storm of disapproval for its use of law clerks to reveal the petty displeasures and occasional dyspepsia of United States Supreme Court Justices during a short span of the Burger Court. For a more scholarly assessment, see Blasi, ed., The Burger Court, the counter-revolution that wasn't (1983). Essayists for this volume were Thomas Emerson, Norman Dorsen, Joel Gora, Robert W. Bennett, Yale Kamisar, Robert A. Burt, Paul Brest, Ruth B. Ginsburg, Theodore J. St. Antoine, R.S. Markovits, Vincent Blasi, and Martin Shapiro. This book also has short profiles of the Justices, a chronology of significant cases, and a bibliography.

TAXATION

2200

BLUM, WALTER J. and **HARRY KALVEN, JR.** The uneasy case for progressive taxation. Chicago, Univ. of Chicago Press, 1953. 104p.
A24.5

"... It is a stimulating and highly informative book. ...a carefully documented, closely reasoned, highly readable discussion of one of the most difficult problems of our troubled times. ...that many liberals and conservatives are not different under the skin because they both object to the presentation of arguments against propositions in which they deeply believe." Randolph Paul, Harvard Law Rev. 67:725 (1954).

2201

GALVIN, CHARLES O. and **BORIS BITTKER.** The income tax; how progressive should it be? Wash., D.C., American Enterprise Institute for Public Policy Research, 1969. 184p.
A24.5

"This little book is the script of a Rational Debate Seminar ..." John C. O'Byrne, Northwestern Univ. Law Rev.65:524 (1970). See also Boris I. Bittker, Federal taxation of income, estates and gifts (4v. 1981, 1983 supp.) for a comprehensive analysis of our tax law. Reviewed by Parker C. Fiedler, Texas Law Rev. 61:1379 (1983).

2202

PAUL, RANDOLPH E. Taxation in the United States. Boston, Little, Brown, 1954. 830p.
A24.5

The author "carries forward his work of describing and interpreting the federal tax system. ...Essentially, it tells the story of federal taxation in American history. Here we find the role that our tax system has played in war and peace, in inflation and depression." Stanley S. Surrey, Northwestern Univ. Law Rev. 49:709 (1954).

THINKING

See CREATIVE THINKING

2210

KEETON, ROBERT E. Legal cause in the law of torts. Columbus, Ohio State Univ. Press, 1963. 137p.
A31.7

"This volume culminates the efforts of a thoughtful and earnest scholar to resolve an ancient riddle of torts law: where should the line be drawn in determining the ambit of liability for unintended consequences which were caused in fact by the defendant's conduct? Professor Keeton advances a thesis which, in abbreviation, he labels the Risk Rule ... [which] arises as a corollary of the assumption that fault is the foundation of negligence law." Jl. of Legal Education 17:97 (1964).

2211

SPEISER, STUART M. Lawsuit. N.Y., Horizon Press, 1980. 617p.
A31.7

A defense of the personal injury bar and the contingent fee system by a noted aviation tort litigator. See Michigan Law Rev. 80:980 (1982).

2212

STROBEL, LEE PATRICK. Reckless homicide? Ford's Pinto trial. South Bend, And Books, 1980. 286p.
A31.7

An absorbing book that presents the anatomy of Indiana v. Ford Motor Co. ... [Ford was acquitted but corporations can now be criminally liable for their dangerous instrumentalities] William E. McSweeney, A.B.A.Jl 66:1547 (1980).

2213

WHITE, G. EDWARD. Tort law in America; an intellectual history. N.Y., Oxford Univ. Press, 1980. 283p.
A2.5

I. The intellectual origins of torts in America. II. The impact of legal science on tort law, 1880-1910. III. The impact of realism on tort law, 1910-1945. IV. The 20th century judge as torts theorist: Cardozo. V. William Prosser, consensus thought, and the nature of tort law, 1945-1970. VI. The 20th century judge as torts theorist: Traynor. VII. The 1970s: Neoconceptualism and the future of tort law.

TRADE REGULATION
See also ECONOMICS

2220

BORK, ROBERT H. The antitrust paradox; a policy at war with itself. N.Y., Basic Books, 1978. 462p.
A24.5

"[I]n a biting, often scathing book, he decimates antitrust policy as it has been enforced by the Department of Justice and the Federal Trade Commission and interpreted by the Supreme Court. Building on a series of provocative law review articles that span a quarter of a century, Bork outlines an alternative interpretation of the Sherman and Clayton Acts and proposes a radically different yet simple standard for determining their application to assure consumer welfare. [His theory of antitrust law] can be summarized in a word, efficiency. ... a profound, indeed seminal work ... occasional but serious flaws." Walter Gellhorn, Harvard Law Rev. 92:1377 (1979).

2221

POSNER, RICHARD A. Antitrust law; an economic perspective. Chicago, Univ. of Chicago Press, 1976. 262p.
A24.5

"This compact, lucidly written book by one of our leading antitrust scholars will surely take its place as one of the major antitrust works of recent years, even though its primary conclusion, that all antitrust statutes except section 1 of the Sherman Act be repealed, is totally unrealistic and acknowledged by Posner to be so. ...I believe this is the only book in the anti-trust field I have read from cover to cover in one sitting ... One cannot simply assume that Supreme Court justices are persistently misguided, ignorant, or malevolent, although some portions of this book might create that impression." Thomas E. Kauper, Michigan Law Rev. 75:768 (1977).

THE TRIAL and ITS PRELIMINARIES

2230

BUSCH, FRANCIS X. Law and tactics in jury trials; the art of jury persuasion, tested court procedures. Indianapolis, Bobbs-Merrill Co. [1949.] 1147p. +
A15

A treatment of almost all conceivable legal and procedural problems that confront the active jury trial lawyer.

2231

CORNELIUS, ASHER L. The cross-examination of witnesses; rules, principles and illustrations ... Indianapolis, Bobbs-Merrill [c1929.] 633p. +
A15

Read a small portion at a time of this book for its scope is so wide. The book is replete with suggestions and hints to the lawyer, from the first question to be asked on through the end. Part II gives examples of cross-examination taken from actual trials over a period from 1699 to 1927. See Georgetown Law Jl 20:545 (1959).

2232

CUTLER, AARON S. Successful trial tactics; with a foreword by Jerome Frank. N.Y., Prentice-Hall, 1949. 319p. +
A71

An easily readable book by "a highly intelligent lawyer" with many years of trial experience. Keyed to the training of the neophyte in trial work. Numerous examples and interesting reminiscenses enrich the text.

2233

GOLDSTEIN, IRVING. Trial technique. Chicago, Callaghan, 1935. 790p. +
A15, A55 (for 3rd year students)

A lawyer's guide book for the trial of law suits as they are actually conducted. Considered first-rate as such. See Harvard Law Rev. 49:1387 (1936). A 2d ed. is in three volumes, looseleaf. Fred Lane is the coauthor.

2234

STEUER, AARON. Max D. Steuer, trial lawyer. N.Y., Random House [1950.] 301p. _
A27, A28

This is actually a reprint of parts of the transcripts of five important trials, illustrative of Steuer's great skill in cross-examination.

2235

WELLMAN, FRANCIS L. The art of cross-examination; with the cross examinations of important witnesses in some celebrated cases. 4th ed. Garden City, N.Y., Garden City Pub. Co. [1948.] 479p.* + A15, A21, A37, A40, A46, A49, A71

Books about trials and the exploits of trial lawyers are also entertaining and inspiring. No doubt they help to account for the fact that so many law students hope to become trial lawyers. But whether you have ambitions along this line or not, you will certainly want to read a few books of this kind. There is Stryker's For the Defense (See No. 184); and there is a book that goes back quite a number of years but is still very good reading - Wellman's Cross-Examination. Dean Havighurst.

2236

___. Success in Court ... in collaboration with nine prominent American trial lawyers. N.Y., Macmillan, 1941. 404p. + A49, A71

This book not only educates but is also highly entertaining. Its purpose is to help trial lawyers achieve success in court. One half is written by Wellman who achieved great success himself as an advocate.

TRIALS and CASES

2249

"The historian, the devotee of detective fiction, the student of advocacy, and the novelist in searth of a plot, should not ignore the very full collection of trials that may be found in some libraries. Cases of historical interest are reported at length in the thirty-four volumes of Howell's State Trials, such for example as Coke's virulent prosecution of Sir Walter Raleigh (vol.2, p.1). A selection from these trials was published in three volumes by J. W. Willis-Bund. Other series are the Notable British Trials series, the Famous Trials Series, and the Old Bailey Trials series; all these give a full transcript of the cases, so that each step in the evidence can be studied. The series presently running is called Celebrated Trials ... There is also an inexpensive series of Famous Trials in Penguins, each volume containing condensed accounts of a number of trials." [A74, p.233]. See also John M. Ross, Trials in collections: an index to famous trials throughout the world (1983).

2250

ARLEN, MICHAEL J. An American verdict. N.Y., Doubleday, 1973. 196p.
A43.5

A reporter's view of the Black Panther case. See also Murray Kempton, The Briar Patch; The People of the State of New York v. Lumumba Shakur et al. N.Y., (1973). See also the work of a prosecutor and professor, Peter L. Zimroth, Perversions of justice; the prosecution and acquittal of the Panther 21 (1974) [A43.5].

2251

ATLAY, JAMES B. Famous trials of the century. London, G. Richards, 1899. 393p. * +
A35

Atlay is entertaining and writes well. Some of these trials were quite dramatic, such as The Tichborne Case and The Queen v. Madeline Smith. See also Brandt Aymar and Edward Sagarin, Laws and trials that created history (1974). [A57.1]

2252

BAILEY, F. LEE. The defense never rests. N.Y., Stein & Day, 1971. 262p.
A35.5, A43.5, A72.5

"Courtroom warriors make fascinating subjects for biographies, even if they are self-serving, egotistical tributes to their most memorable cases...a remarkably blunt and fascinating book. In recounting his handling of [Dr. Sam Shepard], the Boston Strangler [Albert DeSalvo], and Dr. Carl Coppolino, Bailey reveals a good deal of himself...He heads a growing list of lawyers and scientists who urge [the] formal acceptance [of lie detectors] by the courts." Also comments on legal education, due process, grand jury, penal reform, and ethics. Charles R. Ashman, Syracuse Law Rev. 23:985 (1972). Mr. Bailey has also written To be a trial lawyer (1982), and a novel, Secrets (1978).

2253

____. For the defense (with John Greenys). N.Y., Atheneum, 1975. 367p.
A43.5

The Medina court martial, Bailey's defense of himself for complicity in fraud with Glenn W. Turner, and other matters.

2254

BEDFORD, SYBILLE. The trial of Dr. Adams. N.Y., Simon and Schuster, 1959. 245p.
A71.5

"...Selecting the most interesting materials in a trial of three weeks duration in such fashion as to present an accurate picture of the entire case, eliminating the repetitions which abound in such a trial, while, at the same time, accurately describing the dramatis personae and their efforts, is no easy effort and Miss Bedford has done it well. ...The issue was simply whether Dr. Adams had intentionally killed Mrs. Morell by medically unjustified overdoses of heroin and morphine ... Miss Bedford's presentation also demonstrates the widely heralded gentility, objectivity, and candor for which the English bench and bar are constantly praised ... a nice job of reporting." John Rogers Carroll, Temple Law Q. 32:467 (1959). See also the author's The faces of justice; a traveller's report (1961); accounts of trials in several foreign countries.

2255

BERRIGAN, DANIEL. Trial of Catonsville Nine. Boston, Beacon Press, 1970. 122p.
A43.5

On May 17, 1968, selective service records were seized by militants led by Father Berrigan. This is an edited record of the trial for willful injury to government property.

[2256 saved]

2257

BOX, MURIEL, ed. Birth control and libel, the trial of Marie Stopes. N.Y., A.S.Barnes, 1967. 392p.
A57.1

The libel action by Ms. Stopes against Dr. Sutherland who castigated her birth control advocacy as an affront and injustice to the ignorant and poor. The House of Lords (sans Ladies) ruled against her.

2258

BUGLIOSI, VINCENT with **CURT GENTRY.** Helter skelter; the true story of the Manson murders. N.Y., W.W.Norton, 1974. 502p.
A29.5

> "Not only were the victims murdered in a macabre and gruesome fashion, but the trial was a record for longevity in American jurisprudence. The jury, itself, was sequestered for more than eight months. ...Mr. Bugliosi gives an insider's view from the discovery of the murders until the trial and conviction of the defendants....[He] skilfully marshals the voluminous and complex evidence in the Manson case and presents it in an orderly and lawyerlike fashion, much as he did before the jury." John C. Spence III, A.B.A.Jl 61:928 (1975).

2259

BURANELLI, VINCENT, ed. The trial of Peter Zenger. N.Y., N.Y.U. Press, 1957. 152p. Greenwood, 1975.
A43.5

> The seditious libel case against Peter Zenger in 1735. His lawyer, Andrew Hamilton, became a hero when he persuaded a jury to ignore the law and acquit his client.

2260

BUSCH, FRANCIS X. Guilty or not guilty? An account of the trials of The Leo Frank Case, The D. C. Stephenson Case, The Samuel Insull Case, The Alger Hiss Case. Indianapolis, Bobbs-Merrill [1952.] 287p. * +
A43, A43.5

> This author's books contain colorful accounts of dramatic criminal trials.[A43].

2261

____. Prisoners at the bar; an account of the trials of The William Haywood Case, The Sacco-Vanzetti Case, The Loeb-Leopold Case, The Bruno Hauptmann Case. Indianapolis, Bobbs-Merril [1952]. 288p. * +
A43, A71.5

2262

____. They escaped the hangman; an account of the trials of The Caleb Powers Case, The Rice-Patrick Case, The Hall-Mills Case and The Hans Haupt Case. Indianapolis, Bobbs-Merril [1953.] 301p. * +
A43

2263

CAPOTE, TRUMAN. In cold blood. N.Y., Random House, 1966. 343p.
A29.5

"...[The Clutter family was brutally murdered by two sadistic young parolees.] There was no motive for the murders and almost no clues. ...Seven weeks thereafter the killers were apprehended, and Capote ... spent hundreds of hours in their company ... My personal opinion is that the book is a masterpiece ... the book portends a graphic example of the necessity of confessions for effective law enforcement." Michael J. McArdle, De Paul Law Rev. 16:274 (1966).

2264

CARTER, DAN T. Scottsboro; a tragedy of the American South. Baton Rouge, Louisiana State Univ. Press, 1969. 431p.
A43.5

"As Carter irrefutably shows, at no time during the legal proceedings did the state present any evidence which could convince a reasonable man that any of the nine accused were guilty of rape." William Henry Leary Yale Law Jl 79:338 (1979).

2265

CHAMBERS, WHITTAKER. Witness. N.Y., Random House, 1952. 808p.
A29.5

"Seldom does as much burning emotion surround a public issue as was ladled out by partisans over the Hiss-Chambers case. ...Because speculation continues, one examines with interest the book Witness, in which [the author] gives his version of the epic in which he was an enigmatic participant." James J.G.Miller and Jessie L. Miller, Univ. of Chicago Law Rev. 20:598 (1952-3). See also An interview with Alger Hiss, The Advocate (Suffolk Univ. Law School) 10:2 (Fall 1978). [See also No. 2282].

2266

CONNERY, DONALD S. Guilty until proven innocent. N.Y., Putnam, 1977. 377p.
A57.1

The Peter Reilly case; the heart breaking saga of a young man sentenced to prison for a murder he did not commit.

2267

DICKLER, GERALD. Man on trial. N.Y., Doubleday, 1962. 451p.
A43.5

"Socrates, Jesus, Joan of Arc, Galileo, Charles I, Salem Witchcraft trials, Andrew Johnson, Dreyfus case, Scopes trial, Reichstag fire trial, Moscow trials, Nuremberg trials, Oppenheimer hearing ... Each trial is discussed in light of its own social and historical setting." Jan D. Myster, North Dakota Law Rev. 39:265 (1963).

2268

DREYFUS, ALFRED, def. Captain Dreyfus, [by] Nicholas Halasz. N.Y., Simon & Schuster, 1955. 274p. * +
A22, A43.5

An excellent evaluation of the famous cause-celebre that stirred France and the world so vehemently before World War I. For a recent book, see Robert L. Hoffman, More than a trial (1980).

2269

EHRMANN, HERBERT B. The case that will not die. Commonwealth v. Sacco and Vanzetti. Boston, Little, Brown, 1969.
A35.5

See No. 2273.

2270

EPSTEIN, JASON. The great conspiracy trial. London, Faber & Faber, 1972. 433p
A29.5.

"In September 1969 began the six months long trial of eight men for conspiracy to incite riot in Chicago ... Mr. Epstein provides useful information about the background to the trial and about the origins of the law relating to conspiracy." Law Q. Rev. 88:580 (1972).

2271

FAULK, JOHN HENRY. Fear on trial. N.Y., Simon and Schuster, 1964. 398p. A53

"...something more than a layman's dramatic version of his own successful libel suit against a group of men who conspired to destroy his career as a radio and television entertainer. It is also a triumphant exposure of a recurring, ugly tendency toward political lynching that is found in American history." Arnold Forster, N.Y.U. Law Rev. 40:393 (1965).

2272

FEHRENBACHER, DON E. The Dred Scott case; its significance in American law and politics. N.Y., Oxford Univ. Press, 1978. 741p.
A43.5

"[A book] eminently worthy of the Pulitzer Prize that it has received. ...Part II examines the case itself. It describes the personalities involved, Dred Scott's unsuccessful attempts in Missouri's state and federal courts to free himself from bondage, and the grounds for decision shared by a majority of the Supreme Court when it rejected Scott's claim for freedom." Gary J. Simon, Stanford Law Rev. 32:979 (1980).

2273

FEUERLICHT, ROBERTA STRAUSS. Justice crucified; the story of Sacco and Vanzetti. N.Y., McGraw-Hill, 1977. 480p.
A43.5

"By setting forth the many instances in which the state unjustifiably disregarded evidence exculpating Sacco and Vanzetti, the author ridicules the judicial system that condemned them to death. ...She reviews the trial evidence and concludes quite properly that the defendants were not proved guilty beyond a reasonable doubt." Harvard Law Rev. 92:781 (1979). For a book that believes that Sacco was guilty, see Francis Russell, Tragedy in Dedham (N.Y., McGraw-Hill, 1962) reviewed unfavorably by Michael A. Musmanno, Univ. of Kansas Law Rev. 11:481 (1963).

2274

FLEMING, ALICE. Trials that made headlines. N.Y., St. Martin's Press, 1974. 146p.
A57.1

Boston Massacre, Peter Zenger, Amistad case, John Brown, impeachment of Andrew Johnson, Haymarket bomb trial, Triangle fire trial, Scopes trial, Sweet trial, and the Nurenberg trial.

2275

FOX, SANFORD J. Science and justice; the Massachusetts Witchcraft Trials. Baltimore, Johns Hopkins Press, 1968. 116p.
A29.5

"[A] major work of historical scholarship on an aspect of the [trials] which hitherto has not been explored in depth: the relationship of law and science." Ferald Abraham, Villanova Law Rev. 14:779 (1969).

2276

GAINES, MYRA CLARK. The famous case of Myra Clark Gaines, [by] Nolan B. Harmon. Baton Rouge, Louisiana State Univ. Press, 1946. 481p. A7, A43.5

An able account of the litigation over Clark's estate. Clark was a merchant prince in New Orleans during the Spanish, French and early territorial rule. The case came before the Supreme Court of the U.S. on thirteen different occasions between 1839 and 1891.

2277

____. New Orleans woman, a biographical novel of Myra Clark Gaines, by Harnett T. Kane. Garden City, N.Y., Doubleday, 1946. 344p. * +
A8

See Note for No. 2276.

2278

GERTZ, ELMER. Handful of clients. Chicago, Follet, 1965. 366p.
A29.5

"Elmer Gertz, a Chicago lawyer, is the author of the latest in a trend of lawyers with literary aspirations to divulge, in book form, their public trials and the not-so-public extrajudicial, lives of their clients. ... [Nathan Leopold, Otto Eisenschiml, Henry Miller and his book the Tropic of Cancer, and criminal trial of three Chicago detectives on narcotic detail.] Richard J. Friedman, De Paul Law Rev. 15:523 (1966).

2279

GINGER, RAY. Six days or forever? Tennessee vs. John Thomas Scopes. Boston, Beacon Press, 1958. 249p.
A57.1

"[The author] achieves significant success in his objectives of getting the facts straight and viewing the Scopes case in broad context. ...He brings to life ...the famous "Monkey Trial,"...Victor M. Goirdon, Connecticut Bar Jl 32:174 (1958).

2280

HASTINGS, PATRICK. Cases in court. London, Heinemann, 1953. 342p.
A29.5

"[The author] has participated in some of the most celebrated cases which have reached the English courts. ... Included are cases of libel and slander, conspiracy and fraud, theft and murder, involving persons from all classes of English society, from royalty to postal clerks." William D. Neary, Texas Law Rev. 32:898 (1954).

2281

HAYWARD, WILLIAM D. On trial.

A72.5

See also George Harrison, The IWW trial (1969). Also Roughneck, the life and times of Big Bill Haywood by Peter Carlson (1983).

A72.5

2282

HISS, ALGER. In the court of public opinion. N.Y., Knopf, 1956. 424p.

A29.5

"Review after recent review of [this book] - some of them fairly friendly - has stressed the omni-absent omissions, the lawyerlike ignoring or brushing off of opponents' points, the unlawyerlike conjecturings about stuff that is tough to explain away. ... Another gap left unfilled is the real relationship between Hiss and Whittaker Chambers." Fred Rodell, Texas Law Rev. 35:882 (1957). For a pro Hiss interpretation, see Earl Jowitt, The Strange Case of Alger Hiss (1953) reviewed by John D. Calhoun in Stanford Law Rev. 6:190 (1953). In agreement with the verdict in the Hiss case is Alan Weinstein, Perjury; the Hiss-Chambers case (1978),[A72.5] reviewed (along with the Sacco-Vanzetti and Rosenberg cases) by Terry A. Cooney, Michigan Law Rev. 77:834 (1979).

2283

HOLT, DONALD. The justice machine; the people vs. Donald Payne. N.Y., Ballantine Books, 1972. 217p.

A57.1

"... seeks to do for Donald Payne what Capote did for his two 'heroes' [See No. 2263] ...seeks to elevate a single, tawdry case into a wholesale attack on a system of justice. ... it is not true that all prosecutors and all defense attorneys are like the persons mentioned in this book or that all defendants act or react like Donald Payne. James B. Krasnoo, Boston Univ. Law Rev. 53:249 (1973).

2284

HYDE, H. MONTGOMERY, ed. The three trials of Oscar Wilde. N.Y., Univ. Books, 1956. 384p.

A29.5

"Lawyers can derive satisfaction from the Wilde case because he was tried fairly and impartially. ...What caused Wilde's final destruction was not the lawyers, but the social reformers ... and his faithless friends." Richard F. Wolfson, Univ. of Chicago Law Rev. 23:743 (1956). See also the author"s Oscar Wilde; the Aftermath (1963).

2285

JACKSON, ROBERT H. The Nurnberg Case, as presented by Robert H. Jackson, Chief of Counsel for the U.S., together with other documents. N.Y., Knopf, 1947. 268p. * +
A8

Presents in brief, highly readable form the views of this country on the case against the Nazi war criminals and the probable shape of future international justice. See Columbia Law Rev. 47:515 (1947).

2286

JAWORSKI, LEON. The right and the power; the prosecution of Watergate. Houston, Gulf Publishing Co., 1976. 292p.
A25.5

"...a dry, naive, and banal recitation of the daily events that befell Leon Jaworski during his tenure as the Watergate Special Prosecutor ... The major flaw lies in the overstatements and gross generalizations in his conclusions." Marc Lackritz, American Univ. Law Rev. 26:770 (1977). A more scholarly book on the Watergate affair is Philip B. Kurland, Watergate and the Constitution (1978) reviewed by Rex E. Lee, Brigham Young Univ. Law Rev. 1978:779 (1978). The literature on the Watergate trials is too voluminous to list. A cursory glance in the card catalog of a library will reveal many titles.

2287

KUNSTLER, WILLIAM M. The case for courage. N.Y., William Morrow, 1962. 399p.
A38.5, A43.5, A71.5

Cases of lawyers representing unpopular causes. Andrew Hamilton for John Peter Zenger, Joseph Welch and the Army-McCarthy hearings, Homer S. Cummings for Harold F. Israel, Harold R. Medina for Nazi collaborators, Anthony Cramer; Clarence Darrow for Eugene v. Debs, Reverdy Johnson for Mary Surratt. See Alan V. Kurland, Conn. Bar Jl 37:176 (1963).

2288

____. Deep in my heart. N.Y., William Morrow, 1966. 384p.
A43.5

"The nightmarish frustration he encountered as a civil

rights lawyer in the South." Saturday Review 49:40 (March 12, 1966).

2289

____. First degree. Dobbs Ferry, Oceana, 1960. 239p.
A43.5

Other Kunstler titles are _...and justice for all_ (1963), _The minister and the choir singer, the Hall-Mills murder case_ (1964).

2290

LEWIS, ANTHONY. Gideon's trumpet. N.Y., Random House, 1964. 262p.
A2.5, A6.5, A27.5, A35.5, A38.5, A43.5, A47, A49, A53, A57.1, A57.7, A71.5, A72.5

"Mr. Lewis (a non-lawyer) demonstrates that he is indeed learned in the law, and that he has an understanding of the work of the Supreme Court, and of the process of constitutional adjudication, far superior to that of most lawyers. ...The principal reaction a lawyer will have on reading this book ... is pride in being a citizen of a country where an uneducated prisoner can take on a sovereign state before the highest tribunal in the land, and emerge victorious." Charles Alan Wright, Texas Law Rev. 42:935 (1964).

2291

LUSTGARTEN, EDGAR M. Defender's triumph. N.Y., Scribners, 1951. 239p. +
A28, A74

A narrative account of four famous English murder trials (Adelaide Bartlett, Robert Wood, Elvira Barney, and Tony Manani.) of the late 19th and early 20th centuries; from the viewpoint of the defendant's attorneys - all outstanding advocates. See also his _Verdict in dispute_ (1950). This volume contains the following trials: Florence Maybrick, Steinie Morrison, Norman Thorne, Edith Thompson, William H. Wallace, and Lizzie Borden. Also _The woman in the case_ (1955). This volume contains: Alma Rattenbury, Helen Lambie, Harriet Staunton, Madeline Smith. Also _The murder and the trial_ (1960). This volume contains Edith Thompson, Steinie Morrison, William Herbert Wallace, Norman Thorne, Lizzie Borden, the brothers Staunton, Barney Blitz, Adelaide Bartlett, Robert Wood, Elvira Barney, Tony Mancini, Jones & Hulten. Also _The Business of murder_ (1968). This volume contains John G. Hiahg, Neville G.C. Heath, Irma Grese, Henri D Manuel, John R.H. Christie. Also _The illustrated story of crime_

(1976) with chapters on gangsters, city cases, political murders, kidnapping, insanity, sex, and unsolved cases.

2292

MACDONELL, SIR JOHN. Historical trials ... edited by R. W. Lee ...Oxford, Clarendon, 1927. 234p. +
A62

In order to give a comparative view of legal procedure in various countries the author describes with some detail certain classic trials illustrative of the chief systems of procedure, such as trials of Socrates, Joan of Arc, Galileo, Servetus, Sir Walter Raleigh and Scotch and German trials for witchcraft.

2293

MARTIN, CHARLES H. The Angelo Herndon case and Southern justice. Baton Rouge, Louisiana State Univ. Press, 1976. 234p.
A43.5

2294

MITFORD, JESSICA. The trial of Dr. Spock. N.Y., Knopf, 1969. 272p.
A35.5, A43.5

An account of the trial of Dr. Spock and his coconspirators that grew out of antiwar protests.

2295

NIZER, LOUIS. The implosion conspiracy. N.Y., Doubleday, 1973. 495p. A43.5

"...not only a painstakingly thorough analysis of the trial of the Rosenberg espionage case and its aftermath, but at the same time succeeds in being both a defense of the American system of criminal justice and a practical primer for the student interested in pursuing trial law." Spero, Cleveland State Law Rev. 22:388 (1973). For a book that claims that the Rosenbergs were framed, see Walter and Miriam Schneir, Invitation to an Inquest (1965) critically reviewed by Robert Pitofsky, Columbia Law Rev. 66:608 (1966). For what has been characterized as a balanced reappraisal, see Ronald Radosh and Joyce Milton, The Rosenberg file, a search for the truth (1983). This book was reviewed by Alan M. Dershowitz in the N.Y. Times Book Review, Aug. 14, 1983, p.1. Also, The Book of Daniel (1971) by E.L. Doctorow is a fictional recreation of this trial, from which the moveie, Daniel, was filmed. See Janet Maslin, N.Y. Times, Sept. 4, 1983, p.H11.

2296

____. The jury returns. N.Y., Doubleday, 1966. 438p.
A35.5

"...a good collection of interesting cases well-told." George J. Glendening, De Paul Law Rev. 16:535 (1967). The book covers the Paul Crump murder trial, divorce, Fruehauf bribery case, John Henry Faulk's libel case.

2297

____. My life in court. N.Y., Doubleday, 1961. 524p.
A43.5, A71.5, A72.5

"...the book consists of detailed accounts of litigation which the author has conducted. The cases are organized under six main headings or chapters: defamation [Quentin Reynolds v. Westbrook Pegler], domestic relations [Eleanor Holm v Billy Rose; Dooly Astor v. John Astor], copyright [plagiarizing of Rum and Coca-Cola song], tort [malpractice trial and a railroad death case], and corporations [proxy battle between Loew and MGM], [also Foerster v. Ridder, the issue of Nazism in America]. ...the starting practitioner needs to read it, and the experienced practitioner will surely relish it." Curtis Wright,Jr., Temple Law Q. 362 (1962).

2298

____. Reflections without mirrors. N.Y., Doubleday, 1978. 448p.
A57.1

"We are treated to fascinating and intimate details of his representation of author Jacqueline Susanne, Ohio Governor James A. Rhodes, the original group of astronauts, columnist Igor Cassini, and millionaire Armand Hammer." James H. Manhan, A.B.A.Jl 64:1408 (1978).

2299

O'DONNELL, BERNARD. The Old Bailey and its trials. London, Clerke & Cockeran [1950.] 226p. * + A43

The story of this famous English criminal court together with descriptions of the outstanding dramas which have been played out within its walls over the centuries. [A43].

2300

PECK, DAVID W. Decision at law. N.Y., Dodd, Mead & Co., 1961. 303p. A27.5, A57.1, A57.7

"[the author] gives the uninitiated an insight into the legal process in action by following the development of the law through leading cases. The cases chosen begin before the cradle with pre-natal injuries. Continuing with a variety of the vicissitudes of life, they go on beyond the grave with estate taxes, life insurance, and circumstantial evidence on who killed whom." Elliott E. Cheatham, Vanderbilt Law Rev. 15:1042 (1962). See also The Greer case [No. 901].

[No. 2301 saved]

2302

PHILLIPS, STEVEN. No heroes, no villains; the story of a murder trial. N.Y., Random House, 1977. 243p.
A57.1

2303

ROLPH, C.H., ed. The trial of Lady Chatterly. Baltimore, Penguin Books, 1961. 250p.
A74

"...The transcript of the trial in England ... editorial asides are heavily weighted in favor of the defendant...It is a valuable addition to the legal literature on censorship and a fitting monument to a great case." Abe Karsh, Yale Law Jl 71:1351 (1962).

2304

RUBENSTEIN, RICHARD E., ed. Great courtroom battles. Chicago, Playboy Press distributed by Simon and Schuster, 1973. 305p.
A57.1

Lizzie Borden, torso murder, poison vaccine, Fanny Hill, Al Capone tax case, Alger Hiss, R.L. Tijerino, Billy Mitchell, Adolf Eichmann, Lt. Calley as told by masters of the genre.

2305

RUNYON, DAMON. Trials and other tribulations. Phila., Lippincott [1947.] 285p. * +
A8, A39, A43

A collection of the better newspaper stories of sensational trials as reported by Runyon, the master reporter and story teller. [A43]. Henry Judd Gray, Frances Stevens Hall, Ruth Snyder, and Henry and William Stevens.

2306

ST.JOHNS, ADELA ROGERS. Final verdict. N.Y., Doubleday, 1962. 512p.
A43.5, A71.5

The courtroom life of Earl Rogers as told by his daughter, including his defense of Clarence Darrow for attempted bribery of a juror.

2307

SMITH, A. ROBERT and JAMES V. GILES. An American rape; a true account of the Giles-Johnson case. Wash.,D.C., New Republic Book Co., 1975. 307p.
A43.5

A controversial trial involving the alleged rape of a white girl by three blacks. In recounting the case, involving the suppression of evidence by the state and the adverserial system, the author critisizes our system of justice.

2308

SULLIVAN, ROBERT. The disappearance of Dr. Parkman. Boston, Little, Brown, 1971. 241p
A29.5.

The cast of characters: John White Webster, a professor at the Harvard Medical School, accused of murder. Dr. Parkman, the victim, a Beacon Hill resident, and a creditor of Webster. Lemuel Shaw, the judge who presided over the murder trial, and whose charge on circumstantial evidence is still cited. "[the author] presents an indictment of the prosecutors, defenders, and judges of John White Webster." American Jl of Legal History 16:373 (1972).

2309

TIMOTHY, MARY. Jury woman; the story of the trial of Angela Davis. Palo Alto, Emth Press, 1974. 307p.
A43.5

2310

WEST, REBECCA, pseud. The meaning of treason. N.Y., Viking, 1947. 307p. * +
A43

A brilliant report of the English treason trials after World War II. Here is a drama of great events, reflected by the disastrous evolution of petty personalities. [A43] This volume was revised and enlarged as The New Meaning of Treason (1964). [A43.5].

2311

WESTIN, ALAN F. and BARRY MAHONEY. The trial of Martin Luther King. N.Y., Crowell, 1974. 342p.
A57.1

The arrest of Reverend King in Birmingham, Alabama on April 12, 1963 and the resulting trial and impact this case had on the protest movement.

2312

WILLIAMS, EDWARD BENNETT. One man's freedom. N.Y., Atheneum, 1962. 325p.
A43.5, A71.5

Chapters on guilt by client, trial by Congress (Icardi), defense of Senator McCarthy, fair congressional investigations, eavesdropping, wiretapping (Costello), right to remain silent, arrest procedures, discovery, cross-examination, Adam Clayton Powell case, TV in court, death penalty, insanity, censorship, and defending a Russian. See also Robert Pack, Edward Bennett Williams for the defense (1983).

WOMEN

2325

BROWNMILLER, SUSAN. Against our will; men, women and rape. N.Y., Simon and Schuster, 1975. 472p.
A29.5

"...all women have been and continue to be affected by the 'threat, use and cultural acceptance of sexual force.'...In the author's view, slavery, private property, and hierarchy are predicated on this original female submission....She describes how the criminal justice system uses evidentiary standards of consent, resistance, chastity, and corroboration to inculpate the rape victim rather than the rapist. ...willingness to sacrifice first amendment protection of freedom of speech in order to censor pornographic materials." Diane Slaikeu, American Jl Criminal Law (1975).

2326

DE CROW, KAREN. Sexist justice. N.Y., Random House, 1974. 329p.
A43.5

How the law discriminates against women in matters of money, employment, credit, estate law, marriage, crimes, abortion, names and education. See also Nancy E. McGlen and Karen O'Connor, Women's rights; the struggle for equality in the nineteenth and twentieth centuries (1983).

2327

DU BOIS, ELLEN C. Feminism and suffrage; the emergence of an independent women's movement in America, 1848-1869. Ithaca, Cornell Univ. Press, 1978. 220p.
A72.5

The author argues that woman suffragism ranks alongside the black liberation and labor movements as one of the major democratic reform efforts in American history. This book depicts the trials and struggles of the women who started the movement for sexual equality.

2328

EPSTEIN, CYNTHIA F. Women in law. N.Y., Basic Books, 1981. 438p.
A38.5

From "ladies days" at law school to male chauvinist practices on Wall Street firms. A sociological study of how women in law are effected by and effect our society.

2329

GILLIGAN, CAROL. In a different voice; psychological theory and women's development. Cambridge, Harvard Univ. Press, 1982. 184p.
A29.5

2330

KANOWITZ, LEO. Women and the law; the unfinished revolution. Albuquerque, Univ. of New Mexico Press, 1968. 312p.
A6.5

Statutes and court decisions that establish differences in treatment between sexes. The application of the Civil Rights Act of 1964 and the Equal Pay Act of 1963 to address these problems. See Sylvia E. Kelman, Rutgers Law Rev. 24:183 (1969).

AUTHOR INDEX
TO DEANS' SELECTIONS AND ANNOTATIONS

NOTE: This is an index to the numbered items.

DEANS' LIST OF RECOMMENDED READING FOR PRELAW AND LAW STUDENTS

AUTHOR INDEX
TO DEANS' SELECTIONS AND ANNOTATIONS

NOTE: This is an author index both to the numbered items and to the annotations in the text. For a subject listing, see the table of contents.

-L-

-W-

-Z-

INDEX TO TABLE OF CASES, CAUSES CELEBRES AND FICTITIOUS CASES